New Canadian Readings

CANADIAN
FOREIGN POLICY

HISTORICAL READINGS

Edited by
J.L. Granatstein

Copp Clark Pitman Ltd.
Toronto

ISBN 0-7730-4600-3

Canadian Cataloguing in Publication Data

Main entry under title:
Canadian foreign policy
(New Canadian readings)
Bibliography: p.
ISBN 0-7730-4600-3

1. Canada — Foreign relations — 1867-   —
Addresses, essays, lectures. *I. Granatstein, J. L.,
1939-   II. Series.

FC242.C35 1986   327.71   C86-093464-0
F1029.C35 1986

Editing: Barbara Tessman
Design: Kathy Cloutier
Typesetting: Compeer Typographic Services
Printing and Binding: Webcom Ltd.

Copp Clark Pitman Ltd.
495 Wellington Street West
Toronto, Ontario
M5V 1E9

Printed and bound in Canada

FOREWORD

New Canadian Readings is an on-going series of inexpensive books intended to bring some of the best recent work by this country's scholars to the attention of students of Canada. Each volume consists of ten or more articles or book sections, carefully selected to present a fully-formed thesis about some critical aspect of Canadian development. Where useful, public documents or even private letters and statistical materials may be used as well to convey a different and fresh perspective.

The authors of the readings selected for inclusion in this volume (and all the others in the series) are all first-rank scholars, those who are doing the hard research that is rapidly changing our understanding of this country. Quite deliberately, the references for each selection have been retained, thus making additional research as easy as possible.

Like the authors of the individual articles, the editors of each volume are also scholars of note, completely up-to-date in their areas of specialization and, as the introductions demonstrate, fully aware of the changing nature of the debates within their professions and genres of research. The list of additional readings provided by the editor of each volume will steer readers to materials that could not be included because of space limitations.

This series will continue into the foreseeable future, and the General Editor is pleased to invite suggestions for additional topics.

J.L. Granatstein

CONTENTS

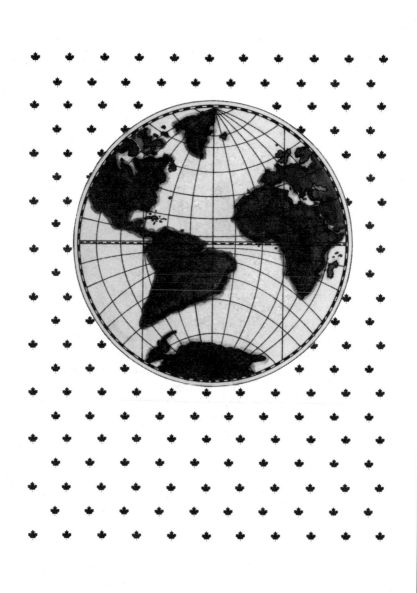

INTRODUCTION

"Colony to nation". That was how an earlier generation of politicians and historians viewed Canada's progression from a colony of Britain and a Dominion to a proud, autonomous status. Many critics demurred. A more apt phrase, they suggested, was "colony to nation to colony," a pointed reference to the way the country had passed from being a colony of the British Empire to a vassal of the United States, with only a brief, and perhaps illusory, period of independence. The truth, as usual, is both less simple and less clear, and this collection of readings on the history of Canadian foreign policy hopes to illustrate both the development and the complexity of the question.

From Confederation in 1867 to 1909 when the Department of External Affairs was established (and for some years after that), Great Britain had responsibility for handling Canadian relations with the world. The prime minister talked to the governor general, always a Briton, and His Excellency communicated with the Colonial Office in London. Eventually Whitehall would rouse itself from its habitual torpor about Dominion questions and seek to resolve — or to shelve — the Canadian concerns. This was not a very satisfactory way to handle Canada's manifold relations with the United States, for example, and too often, or so Canadians believed very strongly, the British were all too prepared to sacrifice Canadian concerns for the sake of Anglo-American amity. That had happened during the negotiations to resolve claims arising from the American Civil War; it had happened again during the arbitration of the Alaska boundary dispute. The logic was clear to nationalistic Canadians: Canada had to get control over its own foreign relations.

The establishment of a Department of External Affairs was only a first step. Someone had to keep track of the treaties and telegrams; someone had to develop the expertise necessary to deal with the professional diplomats of the Powers. But the first officers of the Department were few in number, limited in their mandate, and kept firmly under the control of the prime minister.

The Great War began to alter matters. Canada raised and sent overseas a huge army. That demanded a greater presence in London and Paris. The size of the army and the duration of the war eventually led the government of Sir Robert Borden to press first for more information, and then for a greater say in planning the war and for the peace. The Imperial War Cabinet and Conference were the result and so were promises that after the war the Dominions would have both greater autonomy and some vague role in making the foreign policy of a unified Empire. The war's outcome also saw the victorious Allies create the League of Nations with Canada having a place of its own. That too was a badge of nationhood.

In the interwar years, the course of Canadian development changed. Mackenzie King was a nationalist, someone who believed that Canada was a North American nation under the Crown. To King, the idea that there could ever be a centralized British Empire foreign policy was a chimera. Inevitably the British with their world-wide interests would cause difficulties for Canada. What would happen, for example, if Britain was allied to a nation that got into war with the United States? The consequences for Canada were too terrible to contemplate, and that example was not far-fetched at all. Only with strenuous efforts (significantly from the Conservative Prime Minister Arthur Meighen) had Britain been persuaded not to renew its alliance with Japan in 1921, a country with interests in the Pacific that clashed head-on with those of the Americans. Moreover, the British tended to take Dominion support for granted, something that had become all too clear during the Chanak crisis of 1922 when King learned from the press that Canada was being asked to provide troops for a politically-inspired Dardanelles expedition. King's instinctive answer was "Parliament will decide," a phrase that offered only delay to London and one that became a watchword of his policy.

King's reasons for caution also had their domestic basis, of course. The war had divided French and English Canadians, and conscription for Britain's wars had become a shibboleth in Quebec. Liberal support came from Quebec, obviously, and King knew that the best way to prevent another conscription crisis from taking place was to keep Canada at peace. There was also substantial isolationist sentiment in English Canada — thousands of families had suffered because of the war in Europe — and there could be no doubt that, except for imperialist diehards in places like Toronto, King had the people's support.

He soon had some help from the Department of External Affairs. The Prime Minister recruited a Queen's University political scientist named Oscar Douglas Skelton to come to Ottawa, and Skelton, a good Liberal who had written the best biography of Laurier, became the true creator of Canada's foreign service. He had the contacts in the universities and the reputation that could attract able people to Ottawa, and he also had the right views, in King's opinion, with which to inculcate them. Canada had to move slowly to independence, King and Skelton believed, winning the right to sign treaties on its own, winning changes in the role of the governor general, and eventually securing a formal statement of its right to act on its own in foreign policy. The Statute of Westminster of 1931 made that clear.

But what was to be done with independence? As it turned out, not much. The government expanded its foreign missions very slowly, and without information independent policy was impossible. More important, Mackenzie King might have been a nationalist but he remained a monarchist and an imperialist too. He could negotiate trade arrangements with Washington and occasionally talk toughly to London, but he would not do what Skelton wished and keep Canada out of war in 1939. The great majority of English Canadians wanted to go to war, and King did too, telling himself that Hitler was evil (which was certain) and that Britain was acting to defend right and honour (which in the circumstances of post-Munich 1939 was arguably less clear).

Again war altered everything. The country's massive effort gave it power; its able diplomats, recruited and trained by Skelton, gave it a voice. Gradually the country asserted itself, demanding a share in the Great Power decisions that affected Canada and even asserting in the functional principle a rationale for Canadian claims. The country also played a major role in working out the post-war trading world and in creating the United Nations. The isolationism that had characterized the interwar years was gone forever, or so it seemed.

Certainly the post-1945 era made that seem clear. Canada served with distinction at the UN, and when the world organization proved a weak reed to check the advance of Soviet Communism, Canada and its diplomats played a crucial role in creating the North Atlantic Treaty. Canada even sent troops to Europe in peacetime, as well as to share in the United Nations "police action" in Korea and a variety of peacekeeping operations around the world. It was the "golden age" of Canadian diplomacy, and the capstone on the era came when Lester Pearson, the Secretary of State for External Affairs, won the Nobel Peace Prize for his efforts in helping the British and French escape the consequences of their assault with the Israelis against Egypt in 1956.

But golden ages must end, and when John Diefenbaker became prime minister in 1957 the era was already over. The war-ravaged countries of Europe and Asia had recovered by then and Canada's unaccustomed power was returning to its more-usual status. We were a middle power, and not the richest or strongest of those less-than-Great Powers either. Even so, Diefenbaker made matters worse. There was initially a pro-British inclination, a feeling that Canada's trade could be switched from the U.S. to the U.K. It couldn't. There was a desire to tweak the eagle's tailfeathers, again something that could not succeed for long, and certainly not where the defence of the continent was involved. Diefenbaker's dithering on nuclear weapons roused Washington's ire and eventually brought down the Tory government in 1963.

That was not a mistake the Liberals would make. They were willing to tweak tailfeathers, but not on vital questions. Pearson could complain about the Americans' Vietnam adventure in public and in private, but he was still willing to act as an intermediary between Hanoi and Washington, conveying President Johnson's tough messages. His successor, Pierre Trudeau, could reduce the Canadian Forces in strength and, after 1980, create nationalistic oil policies or even dabble at efforts to control foreign investment. Those were important questions and they troubled the Americans, but they were not so important that the United States would want to send in the Marines.

But the United States was the major player in Canada and around the world. And when the Conservative Mulroney government came to power in 1984, one of its main priorities was to restore good relations with the Great Power to the south. The National Energy Program was dismantled and the Foreign Investment Review Agency, its name and mandate altered to Investment Canada, now sought foreign investment. The armed forces were strengthened and more troops sent to Europe. And most important, the push was on to try to reach a general trade agreement with the United States. Free trade had destroyed the Liberals in

1911 and brought Robert Borden to power. By 1985, Borden's successors were pressing the case for reciprocity, and that noise offstage was made by Borden's bones spinning in their grave.

Colony to nation? Of course. Colony to nation to colony? That too. Canada was an independent state — in certain spheres. It could set its own policies — in some areas. But the inescapable reality was that in the nuclear world Canada could not act on its own in the critical areas of war and peace or global economics. This book's purpose is to help Canadians realize how we got to our present pass.

SECTION 1
GOVERNMENT POLICY

This first section contains key government statements on foreign policy extending over more than sixty years. It opens with Mackenzie King's comments before a session of the Imperial Conference in London in 1923. The prime minister had been furious when the British government the year before had tried to hustle Canada into pledging military support for a foredoomed venture in the Dardanelles, and King had vowed that there would be no more Chanak-style crises. His statement to the British and Dominion prime ministers, a statement that had been largely prepared by Oscar Douglas Skelton of Queen's University, who would soon become King's closest adviser, set out his conception of a proper foreign policy for Canada. Mackenzie King largely followed his own precepts through the interwar years and carefully steered his country away from the shoals of imperial entanglements.

But the coming of the Second World War forced new responsibilities and new roles on Canada. In 1943, King addressed Parliament with one of his first general foreign policy statements of the war and laid out the doctrine of the functional principle. No longer was Canada to be satisfied with a colony's role: now in those areas (such as food or mineral production or civil aviation) where Canada had the capacity and power to play a major role, King gave notice that it intended to do so. The age of isolationism was over. This was even clearer after the war when Louis St. Laurent, the Secretary of State for External Affairs (and the first minister other than a prime minister to hold this post), enunciated the guiding principles of postwar Canadian foreign policy. Deceptively simple and clear, those foundation stones have largely remained unaltered.

But policy has changed. In the mid-1960s after Canadian-American relations had reached their nadir during the Diefenbaker years, the Pearson government and the Johnson administration assigned two senior diplomats, Arnold Heeney and Livingston Merchant, to attempt to draw up principles that should govern the relations between the two countries. The result was hailed by the White House, which believed that there would be no more public Canadian grumbles about the Vietnam War, and condemned by commentators in Canada who read the report's praise for "quiet diplomacy" as being unsubtle instructions to Canada to keep quiet on U.S. policy.

Five years later, the new Trudeau administration issued its own foreign policy white paper, this time in the form of six brightly coloured booklets. The message here was that the age of the Pearsonian "helpful fixer" was over; henceforth, Canada was to be more inward looking, more concerned with economic growth than with playing at peacekeeping around the world. Much the same message was stated all the more clearly in the Mulroney government's foreign policy paper of 1985. *Competitiveness and Security*, the title, expressed the priorities exactly, and the paper's emphasis on the need for increased trade as a creator of jobs and for a comprehensive trade agreement with the United States clearly set out the new Conservative government's priorities.

MACKENZIE KING AT THE IMPERIAL CONFERENCE, 1923†

Appreciation of Lord Curzon's Statement

MR.MACKENZIE KING: The survey of activities and problems which have engaged the attention of the Foreign Office during the past two years, as given by the Foreign Secretary on Friday, was deeply impressive, in the range, the intricacy, the delicacy of the issues, and the ceaseless shifting of the panorama, in the strong evidence afforded of the desire of the British Government to act as a moderating force, and in the skill and knowledge and imperturbable temper displayed in the conduct of these affairs.

Review of Canadian External Affairs

Before proceeding to make any observations on the great issues raised by the Foreign Secretary's statement, I may be expected to give a brief review of some of the external affairs of primary concern to Canada which have developed since the last meeting of this Conference. Our direct international relations are preponderatingly, though not wholly, with a single country. The issues in this connection are not unlike those which arise among European States, and which often prove very difficult to solve. If ours have not proved insoluble, it is due mainly to the fact that in the settlement of differences between the United States and Canada we have the inestimable advantage of speaking (for the most part) the same language, and that not merely in the linguistic sense, for we have, in larger measure than is the case of Continental Europe, the same values, the same standards, in part the same traditions. And we are fortunate again as compared with the peoples of Continental Europe in having less history and more geography, fewer traditions of ancient wrongs to redress, larger space and elbow room for our expansion.

Relations with United States

The United States is not, as the Foreign Secretary has very rightly implied, always easy to deal with. The great diversity of occupation and cultural background in that vast area, the frequent lack of coordination among the branches of its Government, the power of unscrupulous politicians and newspapers to create a sudden stampede, must all be taken into account. But as far, at least, as Canada is concerned we have found the United States of late years an increasingly friendly and dependable neighbour. It has been our aim, the aim of all Governments, irrespective of party, in the last quarter-century, to maintain and develop this good feeling. That does not mean that we are prepared to sacrifice vital interests

†Mackenzie King Papers, Public Archives of Canada.

on the altar of American friendship, that is not the way to deal with our United States friends. But neither do we believe in a policy of pinpricks such as perhaps characterised relations during the previous quarter-century. We have our differences, we thresh them out, and usually a solution develops. It is our firm belief that there is no contribution that Canada can make to the fair and peaceful settlement of international affairs, no way in which she can so strengthen the Empire of which she is a part, as by so handling our relations with the United States as to build up an enduring fund of goodwill, and work for that common understanding among the English-speaking peoples which is the chief hope of the world. That is our primary task; the task assigned to us in the division of Imperial labour, by our proximity, our constant intercourse, our knowledge of their idiosyncrasies. I think it will long remain our primary task.

International Joint Commission

Perhaps of first importance in the field of Canada's external affairs is the International Joint Commission. This body is unique, I believe, in its range and composition, and not without significance for wider fields. It was devised to meet a very difficult situation. In the three thousand miles and more of common boundary between the United States and Canada, constant disputes were arising, particularly as to boundary waters, navigation rights, water power rights, irrigation rights, and so on. Many of these problems contained possibilities of serious trouble; with thousands of farmers in irrigated areas on each side of the boundary dependent for their prosperity on the development or diversion of a given river basin, or with corporations with capital running into tens of millions jockeying for water power development rights, international incidents might at any moment occur. Accordingly, some fourteen years ago, provision was made for the establishment of an International Joint Commission, consisting of three members appointed by the President of the United States, and three appointed by His Majesty on the recommendation of the Governor-General-in-Council, or Cabinet, of the Dominion of Canada. Upon this Commission is conferred authority to enquire into and decide upon any operations as to use, obstruction or diversion of boundary waters which would affect interests on both sides; a majority of the Commission has power to render a decision binding on the Governments and private interests affected; if it is evenly divided, a report is made to the two Governments, which will then endeavour to reach a solution. It is interesting to note that in the many cases which have come before the Commission there has been absolute unanimity of finding in every instance but one — that is out of about twenty cases, I think — and in that instance the difference of opinion was as to jurisdiction rather than as to the merits of the case. This remarkable result is in large part due to the permanent character of the Commission; its members come to know one another well, and realise that a principle which may tell against their country to-day may tell for it in another case next year. The Commission is not narrowly legal in its procedure. Any private citizen of either country may bring his case directly before it, without the intervention of the Government, a procedure which lessens political tension and permits the emergence of several different points of view on the same side of the boundary.

A reference to the map will show the wide range of cases covered. I thought it would be possibly of interest to the members of the Conference present to glance at leisure at the number of cases that have come before that Joint Commission, as illustrated by a map that I should like to have placed on the record. It shows how considerable is the number and variety of the subjects with which this Commission has to deal. Time will not permit detailed reference to the many intricate questions of navigation and power and irrigation rights, each of which might otherwise have provided a distinct diplomatic incident. . . .

But the powers of the International Joint Commission are not limited to boundary water questions. It is provided further that any questions or matters of difference whatever "involving the rights, obligations or interests of the United States or Canada, either in relation to each other, or to their respective inhabitants," may be referred for decision to the Commission by the consent of the two parties, any such action being taken on the advice and consent of the United States Senate, on the one hand, and of the Canadian Governor-General-in-Council, on the other; a majority of the Commission shall have power to render a decision upon any matter so referred. Thus far the necessity has not arisen for referring any such general issue to the Commission, but the existence of this machinery to meet any sudden emergency is a very valuable safeguard. . . .

In this connection, a personal incident of much interest was the visit to British Columbia of the late President, Mr. Harding, in the course of his Western tour. His extremely cordial and sympathetic addresses produced an impression which was deepened by the sudden illness and death which followed a few days later. I should like to quote the concluding paragraphs of a speech made by the then President in Vancouver:

> It is the public will, not force, that makes for enduring peace, and is it not a gratifying circumstance that it has fallen to the lot of us of North America, in living amicably for more than a century under different flags, to present this most striking example produced, of the basic fact that peace can always be kept, whatever be the grounds of controversy, between peoples who wish to keep it.
>
> What an object-lesson of peace is shown to-day by our countries to all the world. Only a scrap of paper, recording hardly more than a simple understanding, safeguards lives and properties on the Great Lakes, and only humble mile-posts mark the inviolable boundary line for thousands of miles through farm and forest.
>
> Our protection is in our fraternity; our armour is our faith, and the tie that binds more firmly year by year is an ever-increasing acquaintance and comradeship through interchange of citizens. The compact is not of perishable parchment, but of fair and honourable dealings, which God grant shall continue for all time.

Goodwill Between Canada and United States

I place these on record largely because I think they help to illustrate the new-world point of view that is in very striking contrast to the old-world attitude of the past, if not of the present, that force is always essential in the preservation of peace. The emphasis the President has placed upon the will to peace, that peace can always be kept, whatever the grounds of controversy may be, between peoples who wish to keep it, is a fact to which we on the North American continent are inclined to give a great deal of attention. We believe that by frequent intercourse between the public men of both countries, by the constant interchange there is between the populations of the two countries, we are developing a common attitude towards each other in the matter of solving our differences by machinery arranged for purposes of conciliation and arbitration, and that in that way we are perhaps rendering the greatest service that it is possible for us to render as a part of the British Empire in maintaining the friendly relations so essential between the United States and the British Empire. A fund of goodwill is being built up, and to appreciate its real value one has to consider what is gained by the elimination of the enormous cost and waste involved in competitive arming, which would be the other alternative. If we started on a policy in America which meant that we were looking to force for the solution of our difficulties with the United States, and began to fortify our boundaries from the Atlantic to the Pacific, I am afraid we should not have public funds left for any other purpose. Neither America nor ourselves is put to any material expense in the matter of international frontier cost for armed purposes. . . .

Canadian Representation at Washington

During Sir Robert Borden's term of office, an agreement was reached between the British, Canadian and United States Governments for the appointment of a Canadian representative at Washington. No appointment was made during Sir Robert's term of office or that of his successor, Mr. Meighen, and no appointment has thus far been made by the present Government. We shall probably suggest some revision of the original agreement, particularly in the way of omitting the provision that in the absence of the British Ambassador the Canadian Minister should take charge of the Embassy. I might add that I recently spoke with General Sir Arthur Currie about the possibility of the Government securing him for the post of Canadian Minister at Washington. He has informed me that personal and financial factors would prevent his acceptance should the position be formally offered to him. The matter stands in that way at the present time. . . .

Halibut Treaty

The threatened depletion of the halibut fisheries on the [Pacific] coast has been met, on the initiative of the United States by an agreement between the two Governments concerned. The agreement provides for the establishment of a closed season during the winter spawning season — November to February — and, the establishment of a joint scientific Board to study the life history of the halibut and make further recommendations as may be required for its preservation. The treaty was signed on the 2nd March, by Plenipotentiaries representing the parties, Mr. Hughes for the United States, and Mr. Lapointe, Minister of Marine and Fisheries, to whom at our request, conveyed through the British Government, Full Powers had been issued by His Majesty. The treaty was then laid before the United States Senate, which was to come to the end of its statutory term on the 4th of March, and approved by that body. At the last moment, on the suggestion of a Senator from Washington, and in pursuance of the custom which is oddly termed "senatorial courtesy," a reservation was added providing that "none of the nationals and inhabitants and vessels of any other part of Great Britain shall engage in halibut fishing contrary to any of the provisions of this treaty." While, as a matter of fact, no other British nationals have taken part in these fisheries, or are likely to do so, Canada did not desire to undertake on their behalf that they should so act. The Canadian Government was, therefore, unwilling to accept this reservation. The Parliament of Canada has given its approval to the treaty apart from the reservation and has passed an Act, to come into effect by Proclamation, forbidding all persons to fish for halibut in our territorial waters during the closed season, forbidding Canadian nationals to fish in prohibited waters beyond the territorial limit, and barring the use of our ports by any persons as a fishing base during the closed season, which under the conditions existing there will effectively bar any operations. Since we arrived in London, information has been received through the British Embassy that the Under-Secretary of State of the United States has stated confidentially that the President had agreed, as we anticipated, to reintroduce the Halibut Treaty as originally signed, without Senator Jones' reservation, and that the presumption was that it would pass. In the meantime, the beginning of the closed season will be postponed until next year.

We are setting apart, I think, a special time for the discussion of treaties, and perhaps I should not go further into the Halibut Treaty matter at this moment; perhaps, however, it might clear up a misconception in the minds of some of the members present as to the significance of our action in negotiating an agreement with the United States over the conservation of halibut, were I to point out at once the real character of the subject matter of the treaty. It relates entirely to the conservation of the halibut in the Pacific Coast waters of the United States and Canada. It is as much to our interest as to the interest of the United States, as much to their interest as ours, that we should try to conserve the halibut, and the most effective way is to bring about an agreement between the two of us that neither of us will permit fishing from our ports in those waters during a certain closed season. I have seen the question asked, what will be done if the United States does not carry this out: whom will Canada look to to see that the treaty is enforced? A question of this kind reveals a lack of appreciation of the subject-matter and the purpose. Of course, if the United States do not carry out their part we will not carry out ours, and vice versa; both of us will be losers; we shall lose some of our fish, a valuable resource; the whole Empire will lose to that extent, inasmuch as some of its resources will be depleted in part, but the factor that would compel enforcement of that treaty is the one referred to by the President — the obvious mutual interest of the two countries to see that it is carried out. Let me make this also clear, that by no conceivable construction could it be shown that any other part of the British Empire would be affected in any adverse way by our action. Australia, New Zealand, South Africa, Newfoundland — no part of the British Dominions could be other than helped by the agreement we have made. Their rights are in no way affected; the rights of the British Isles, the citizens of the British Isles, are in no way affected. I might further point out this, that, had we wished so to do, we could have referred — and I speak of this more particularly in connection with the signing of the treaty — we could have referred the whole subject-matter of this treaty to the Joint Commission to which I have just made reference, and asked its members to deal with it. Had they dealt with it under the powers which have been given to them, three of the citizens of the United States and three of the citizens of Canada — or rather the chairman on each side — could have signed that agreement and it would have had the same force as the signatures of the Ministers which are on it at the present time. In other words, two gentlemen, neither of whom has any powers other than those they derive from the Governments themselves, could have done all that has been done by a Canadian Minister and an American Minister in signing the treaty. It is perhaps as well to mention those points at once, as apparently, judging from what I have seen in the press of comments from different parts, there appears to be a fear that we in Canada have sought in some way to invade the rights of other parts of the British Empire. . . .

Position of Canada

I mention these facts simply to illustrate what I am going to speak of, perhaps more particularly near the end of this review, why in Canada we feel very strongly that in these matters of international relations we must to some extent have a foreign policy of our own, if I may use that expression in this connection — not a policy necessarily distinct from the policy of the British Empire — rather, I should perhaps say, we feel that we cannot confine our rights of self-government to matters of a purely domestic character, but that any questions which we have with our neighbours, or with others, which are matters of immediate and direct concern to each of us, we must have freedom in negotiating and settling. May I say at once that I do not wish to imply that we have thus far experienced any handicap or restriction from the British Government in any particular in this matter? . . .

Inter-relations of Canada and United States

In completing this hasty review of our relations with the United States, I might refer to the very true observation which Lord Curzon made on Friday as to the power of the West in United States politics. The same thing is observable and increasingly true in Canada; the prairie provinces are coming to hold the balance of power. They are largely influenced by the same factors which influence the Western States. In fact our neighbourhood to the United States is a factor which comes into nearly every equation of ours. It has a direct bearing on the question of our policy towards Europe. There is no question that, if the United States persists in its policy of isolation, and if we were to go to the other extreme of assuming daily responsibility for settling the affairs of Europe, the result would be a distinct growth of Continental sentiment which would have grave danger for the Empire and afford a renewed stimulus to emigration to the United States. That is a consideration which may be overruled. If a great and clear call of duty comes, Canada will respond, whether or no the United States responds, as she did in 1914, but it is a most important consideration against intervention in lesser issues.

True Basis for Foreign Relations of Empire

May I say, Prime Minister, that, in what I am now going to take up, I feel the great wisdom of what Lord Curzon said at the outset, as to the importance of the truth in all matters which we are here to discuss. It would be very pleasant and easy for me to say that Canada would do this or would do that as occasion arises, but ill-considered statements will not help in what we here are all most concerned about, namely, laying the basis of the British Empire in an enduring fashion and furthering the development of its strength. Whatever I have to say will have that end primarily in view. I think we should differ, some of us who have discussed these questions in our own countries, as to how our objects can best be effected, but I will give to this gathering what my colleagues and myself believe to be the basis on which foreign relations can be most satisfactorily worked out. . . .

Relations of Various Parts of Empire in Foreign Policy

From this brief survey of some of the external affairs which have occupied the attention of the Canadian Government during the past two years, I may now pass to some general considerations as to the relations of the different parts of the Empire on questions of foreign policy. I have thought it well to bring this matter up at once, because it arises out of the remarks of the Foreign Secretary on Friday, and, if we are going to discuss any further phases of it, it will perhaps present our point of view. The question is involved in the Foreign Secretary's opening remark as to our coming here to assist in carrying on "the foreign policy which is not that of these islands alone, but that of the Empire," but it has been raised many times and in more specific fashion.

Public opinion in Canada was surprised some time ago by a statement of the late Prime Minister, Mr. D. Lloyd George, in the House of Commons in December 1921 to the effect that the position of the Dominions in reference to foreign affairs had been revolutionised since 1917, that the Dominions had been given equal rights with Great Britain in the control of the foreign policy of the Empire, that the instrument of this policy was, and must remain, the British Foreign Office, and that the advantage to Britain was that such joint control involved joint responsibility.

If any such sweeping and general agreement as Mr. Lloyd George assumes had been made, implying, if it means anything, that all the foreign affairs of the whole Empire are to be carried on through a single channel, the people of Canada have no knowledge of it. This arrangement has never been sanctioned by our Parliament. It may be sufficient to quote a comment made by Sir Clifford Sifton, who, it may be recalled, organised the campaign against the Laurier Government on Reciprocity in 1911, and the campaign for conscription in 1917:

This statement is rather startling after Sir John Macdonald and Sir Charles Tupper, Sir Wilfrid Laurier and Sir Robert Borden for fifty years have asserted the right of Canada to have no military or financial responsibility for a war, unless her Parliament voluntarily takes on that responsibility. We now find the Prime Minister of Great Britain making the statement that we have entered into an arrangement by which we assume responsibility for the wars of Great Britain all over the world in return for being consulted. . . . Premiers drift into London . . . no one very sure what is decided . . . and the Dominions become jointly responsible for everything the British Foreign Office does in every part of the world.

I consider it an entirely impossible arrangement. I think it a complete abandonment of the theory of Dominion autonomy as it has developed for fifty years. The people of Canada have never agreed to any such arrangement, and in my judgment they never will. I think the people of Canada will demand that responsibility for engaging in any war or contributing to it shall rest exclusively with the Parliament of Canada.

GENERAL SMUTS: Who are you quoting from?

MR. MACKENZIE KING: From Sir Clifford Sifton, formerly a member of the Government of Canada. Sir Clifford has been giving a number of public addresses in Canada, and these statements seem more precisely than any other I have yet read to present the point of view of our country, as I understand Canadian opinion, on the question of foreign policy.

LORD CURZON: I suppose he spoke without official authority, did he, though he is an influential and powerful person?

MR. MACKENZIE KING: That is quite right, Lord Curzon. I am merely quoting his speech as an illustration of a view widely held. Speaking after conference with my colleagues in the Cabinet, we would feel that those statements substantially express the Canadian Government's view.

Implications of Phrase "Foreign Policy of the British Empire"

May I take a few minutes to examine briefly the implications of both halves of a phrase frequently used, "the foreign policy of the British Empire"? As to foreign policy (the sum of those dealings or relationships or policies which the Government of one country carries on in connection with other countries), a few observations may be hazarded. May I say that I speak with very great deference? My reason for presenting these views is that there may be no mistake in appreciating our particular position. If we are wrong in that position, I hope, as the result of the Conference here, we will see our mistake. On the other hand, it may be that in using phrases such as "foreign policy" there are different things in the minds of each of us. As I have tried to make clear, we have, the moment we go beyond our own boundary, to deal with a neighbour next door to us, and so we must have a foreign policy. We must meet him either with a smile or with a frown in the relations we are going to have. Take the whole question of International Agreements between the two Governments, such as the work of the International Joint Commission — that is an expression of our foreign policy. It is true it is a part of the foreign policy of the British Empire, as it is acquiesced in by the others. In one sense we are prepared to agree that the policy of Great Britain is the policy of the British Empire, but what we want to know is how far the obligations arising out of that policy are material and how far they extend in reference to ourselves.

Foreign policy, I take it, is in a large measure an extension of domestic policy. It depends upon the balance of social and political forces, upon the industrial organisation, upon the racial aspirations, upon the whole background of the people's life. As an illustration I may refer to a matter briefly touched upon by the Foreign Secretary on Friday — the attitude of the United States as to the seizure of liquor on ships in territorial waters or hovering outside the presently recognised territorial limit. This attitude arose out of the policy of prohibition adopted as a domestic policy without any thought of the international complications which it might involve later. So, in the same matters, with ourselves; some provinces in Canada have adopted prohibition, some have rejected it. It makes a great deal of difference in our relations with the United States what the precise policy of each province is upon this matter. Again, foreign affairs nowadays have to do very largely with economic questions — trade, tariff, coal or oil or railway concessions, international debts, immigration, fishery or power or navigation rights in boundary waters, &c.

They are largely neighbours' disputes, naturally arising most frequently with the countries which have most intercourse with it.

The question whether a certain matter in dispute will lead to war is frequently not so much a question of the character of the specific issues as of the spirit and traditions and supposed general interests of the countries concerned.

The British Empire, again, is not a single community, homogeneous, concentrated, with uniform neighbours, problems, needs. It is a league of peoples plus an Empire; it covers all the Seven Seas; it includes communities of every conceivable stage of civilisation, every variety of resources, every range of neighbours, every combination of problems and interests. The more advanced of these communities have developed rapidly in numbers and trade and international intercourse; they have developed relations with other countries varying with their situation; they have developed distinct problems in external as well as in home affairs, a distinct national consciousness, distinct Parliaments and Governments to control their affairs. Some problems are distinct and primarily concern only one or a group of these Empire States; some are of common interest or common menace, and concern the whole Empire and it alone, some are of still wider implications and concern all or a great region of the world, whether organised in permanent Leagues of Nations or in temporary conferences, or not organised at all.

Given then these conditions — given wide scattered communities within the British Empire growing steadily in numbers, in intercourse with the world, and in the habit of self-government; given the growth of problems and difficulties especially with neighbouring countries; given the diversity of conditions and of interest and of knowledge which makes these problems in many cases distinct in each country — it is inevitable that each of these communities should seek to control those foreign affairs which concern it primarily.

This is obviously true, and has long been true of the United Kingdom. Its foreign affairs have been of such overshadowing importance — it is on the verge of a crowded and troublesome and uneasy continent, it is the greatest trading nation in history, it has dependencies, protectorates, coaling-stations, in every quarter of the globe — that they have in the past been practically identical with the foreign affairs of the whole British Empire, and are still, and must long remain, immensely more important and complicated than the distinctive foreign affairs of any other part of the Empire.

It is increasingly true also of the Dominions. In this field Canada has naturally been most active, as the oldest federation and as the community which, next to the United Kingdom, is in most intimate and constant intercourse with powerful neighbours, pre-eminently with one great neighbour. It is unnecessary to review the process by which Canada has steadily widened the range of foreign affairs with which she deals through her own Parliament and Government; trade, tariffs, immigration, boundary disputes as to power, navigation or fisheries and other questions which half a century ago were considered beyond her jurisdiction, are now unquestionably matters for her own decision, as my opening observations concretely indicated.

Clearly, then, as regards this wide and growing range of foreign affairs, the Dominions, or some of them, now possess control, and determine the policy to be followed.

Right of each Part of Empire to Control its own Affairs

It is not possible that this evolution which has proceeded steadily and with increasing acceptance for more than two generations should now be reversed, that Great Britain or Canada should decide Australia's trade policy or that South Africa should determine whether Canada shall join with the United States in the development of the proposed St. Lawrence waterway. Self-government means the right of each part of the Empire to control its own affairs, whether those affairs are domestic or foreign, or both. That is the principle on which this Empire has been maintained, that is its unique and distinctive contribution to the world, that is the principle which has been tested in fire in late years and not found wanting. I can hardly think that anyone would now propose that it be abandoned. I repeat, Canada has perhaps been more active than other of the newer parts of the Empire in assuming direction of such foreign affairs as distinctly affect her own interests. This is an outcome partly of our longer history, but much more of geography; the outcome of the fact that for 3,000 miles we lie side by side with a great foreign country which is yet of English speech, and with which our people have constant and unending business and social intercourse. Possibly, if we were in the position of some of the other Dominions, we would regard the question somewhat differently; possibly, if they were in our position, they would take the stand that we do. We are not asking that these differences be overlooked, or that the same policy be adopted by Dominions which differ in their circumstances.

I may say that, listening to the discussion of the questions that come up here, I have been more and more impressed with the part that geographical situation plays in determining the point of view in many of these matters. When I heard General Smuts the other day refer to matters that concern him in Africa and Egypt, and when I thought of the route that he and his colleagues have had to take in coming from Africa to Britain, I could see that many questions might arise in the area between London and South Africa which for him could not be satisfactorily solved without considering many aspects of British foreign relations with countries between here and there; and, similarly, perhaps in a more far-reaching manner in the case of Mr. Massey and Mr. Bruce in coming from Australasia. This aspect of means of personal and trade communication between Britain and Australia or New Zealand, and the consequences arising out of it, brings to the fore the whole question of their possible desire to express views about British foreign policy as it relates to any of those countries which they must pass in a way which does not come up at all so far as Canada is concerned. That has to be considered, because, after all, the people themselves are the ones who are doing the thinking on these questions, and it is not sufficient that those of us who have the privilege of attending this Conference should have views as individuals. We should, in all we express, indicate the views of the people we represent; they are the most concerned about the matters of which we are speaking. It would be simply ludicrous for me to say, for example, that the people of Canada have, as a whole, given any thought to some of the matters which are perhaps of vital concern to General Smuts — they have not. It is in the nature of things that they could not, neither could General Smuts, nor Mr. Massey, nor Mr. Bruce, in such a matter as the development of the Chicago Canal or the level of our Great Lakes express opinions representative of the views of their people who would be likely to be interested in such matters.

If it is not possible or desirable that Great Britain or other Dominions should control those foreign affairs which are distinctly of primary concern to one Dominion, so it is equally impossible and undesirable for the Dominions to seek to control those foreign affairs which primarily affect Great Britain. Her geographical situation, her foreign trade, the enterprise of her investors, create many relations, interests, problems which are primarily her concern and which have intimate connection with her domestic problems. As to those affairs, the Dominions have not the knowledge, the direct interest, the responsibility, which would warrant their seeking control. Great Britain also is entitled to claim self-government.

Need for Consultation on Fundamental Issues

Each part of the Empire, then, has its own sphere. But at certain points the arcs cut, the interests become common. There are issues which are of fundamental concern to all parts of the Empire; and with these all parts of the Empire must deal; the Governments of the Empire must confer; the Parliaments of the Empire, if need be, must decide.

It is true that there is no clear cut and enduring line of demarcation between these fields, between those foreign affairs which are of primary concern to one part of the Empire and those which are of joint concern. No foreign question affecting one part of the Empire is without its influence on other parts, however small and indirect that influence may be, but it is equally true that no domestic affair of one part of the Empire, no foreign problem of any foreign country, is without some bearing on the fortunes of the rest of the Empire and the world. It is a question of degree. Again, issues which were primarily of concern to one part may grow to vast proportions and afford a menace or an opportunity that has substantial concern for all parts; if so, it can then be dealt with by all concerned. In drawing the lines there will inevitably be difficulties, but goodwill and common sense and experience will settle these as they have in the past.

Again, were it considered desirable to establish a unified foreign policy on all issues, it would not be practicable.

No scheme has been worked out, no scheme, I venture to say, can be worked out, by which each part of the Empire can be not only informed but consulted as to all the relations of every other part of the Empire with foreign countries, and a really joint policy worked out. The range is too vast, the situation too kaleidoscopic, the interests too diverse, the preoccupation of each Government with its own affairs or its own existence too absorbing, to make this possible. We must face facts. It is possible to consult on matters of overwhelming and enduring common interests; it is not possible to consult on the great range of matters of individual and shifting concern.

Concern of Parliaments and Peoples in Foreign Policy

A further questionable feature of the Empire one-foreign-policy theory is that it ignores the necessity for associating the Parliaments and peoples in the decision of foreign policy. Granted that a measure of secrecy is essential in the course of negotiations, granted that the conduct of affairs must rest largely with an experienced and specialised executive department, still it is true that it is not desirable for any Dominion or for the Empire that vital issues of foreign policy should be determined decisively in a small executive or Conference group. The problem of foreign policy is not settled when provision is made for bringing Prime Ministers together. Each Prime Minister must on important issues secure the backing of his Parliament and his people.

May I say, Prime Minister, the reason I have spoken as I have here to-day is primarily the one I have already referred to, the desire to face the truth regardless of how it may affect the feelings of any of us, and also in part because I feel that if we are to render any service to each other we must let each other know very frankly what we can do and what we cannot do; what we may expect and what we have no right or reason to expect. There are many things right in principle which are not possible in practice. I was struck in looking over the 1921 Conference report by a remark made by Lord Curzon in regard to what had been the view taken in England as to what should be done with the Kaiser and certain of the German war criminals. It was right in principle that they should be tried, and I think Lord Curzon mentioned that, but he also stated that where a short-sighted attitude had been taken, and where the Government was in the wrong, was in assuming that it could be done. If there is one thing above another which must have impressed all of us it is the deplorable condition in which ex-President

Wilson has brought himself and his country in view of the part he took at the Versailles Conference. President Wilson went in there with high ideals, believing in certain principles which he thought were right; he did his utmost to have certain views accepted, and he had them accepted, but he left out of account one factor of vital concern, namely, the extent to which the people of the United States were behind him. I do not wish to come to the Conference and say to the gentlemen gathered round this table, "Yes, Canada will do this and Canada believes that," unless I am sure that I can say the same thing in Canada on my return and get the same amount of applause there as I do here. That is the sole reason I have for dwelling at such length on this question of foreign policy. We must speak here in regard to the extent to which we are going to be able, through our Parliaments and by our appeal to the people, to make good every single undertaking we give and every implication for which we are responsible.

Recent International Conferences

I must say just a word about International Conferences. When we came into office the Conference on the Limitation of Armaments was being held at Washington. Sir Robert Borden was representing Canada. His report was made to the Government, and later I would like to draw the attention of the members of this Conference to two or three of its pages, more particularly where Sir Robert Borden sets forth his views on the matter of treaties. It is a point of view I think we all hold in common.

At Genoa and at The Hague we were represented. We had been invited to be present at these Conferences and, considering their nature, we felt it would perhaps be not only of interest and benefit to ourselves, but also to others if we were represented there. At Lausanne we were not represented; we were not invited. We took and we take no exception to not being invited. We felt that the matters that were being discussed there were not of the same immediate and direct interest to ourselves as they were to those who were represented at the Conference and we have no exception to take to the course that was adopted. . . .

Canadian Conception of Imperial Relations

It is sometimes asserted that Canada or the Canadian Government has latterly put forward new principles of imperial relationship, and claimed special privileges in status. That is not the case. Canada is not putting forward any new principles, though, naturally, every new year and every new problem may make it necessary to apply the old principles in somewhat new fashion or in a wider range. Canada stands on the old principle of responsible democracy. She still believes in democracy, in representative democracy, in the rule of the people through, in large part, their representatives in Parliament. She still believes in responsible government, self-government, the right of each part of the Empire, as it attains a fitting degree of strength and capacity and experience, to undertake the control of its own affairs. For seventy years our most honoured leaders have done what they could to develop the basic principle of responsible government, and to apply it in steadily increasing measure to the whole range of domestic and foreign affairs. That principle, which Canadians are proud to remember was, in notable measure, pioneered and developed by their leaders in the past, has proved itself beyond dispute in the testing times of these later years.

Canada desires no special privilege. We believe that the decision of Great Britain on any important public issue, domestic or foreign, should be made by the people of Britain, their representatives in Parliament, and the Government responsible to that Parliament. So the decision of Canada on any important issue, domestic or foreign, we believe should be made by the people of Canada, their representatives in Parliament, and the Government responsible to that Parliament. Some of these questions will be of direct concern to more than one part of the Empire, and in that case consultation, in formal conferences, like that of to-day, or in more informal discussion, is necessary to give the Government and Parliament and people of each country an understanding of the needs and point of view of the others, so that their decision can be made in the light of this knowledge and the sympathy that is born of knowledge.

I hope I have made it clear that in speaking for Canada as to what we feel should be the extent and scope of our rights in matters of government, whether they pertain to domestic or foreign affairs, I have had wholly in mind only the point of view of how to help to make the relations between all parts of the Empire of a character that will tend towards permanency of relations and the successful working out of a wise development in matters pertaining to foreign policy. Also, I hope I have made it clear that, while we do feel strongly that there are some matters which more immediately affect us than they do other parts of the Empire and over which we desire an immediate and direct control, nevertheless, we are equally appreciative of the fact that there are great common interests in which all of us have an equal concern and are equally ready to share. . . .

MACKENZIE KING ON THE FUNCTIONAL PRINCIPLE, 1943†

RIGHT HON. W.L. MACKENZIE KING (SECRETARY OF STATE FOR EXTERNAL AFFAIRS): The leader of the opposition (Mr. Graydon) and other members of the house have asked me if I would make, when it came to a discussion of the estimates of the Department of External Affairs, a somewhat fuller statement on the war situation than it was possible to make earlier in the session. Hon. members also at different times have requested that in dealing with the estimates of external affairs I should take up particular subjects which they have specified. I have thought that it would facilitate the discussions in committee were I to anticipate as far as possible the information with which hon. members would wish to be supplied. . . .

I shall now come to speak of the united nations organization and planning.

The supreme direction of the war, the coordination of the war effort of the united nations, and the planning of certain aspects of the post-war period and the peace, are all matters which are engaging the attention of appropriate boards or committees representing the united nations.

The united nations have no formal organization. In the prosecution of the war they act together by constant consultation through the usual channels between governments. These channels are supplemented by a series of international advisory bodies which have been set up to facilitate rapid agreement and speedy execution of joint plans. Canada now has very extensive machinery for consultation with the other united nations. Through the Canadian high commissioners in all the countries of the British commonwealth, through the Canadian ministers in the United States, the Soviet Union, China, and diplomatic relations with other allied governments, and through the high commissioners and ministers of the united nations represented in Ottawa, we have the equipment for constant day to day consultation regarding the conduct of the war and the framing of the peace. In addition we have the continually improving methods of consultation and cooperation by direct exchange of cables between governments.

These channels of communication have been supplemented, especially in London and in Washington, by enlarging staffs and by establishing missions representing particular Canadian departments and services, such as the joint staff mission in Washington, the representation of the Department of Munitions and Supply in both capitals, and the offices abroad of the war-time information board. There has been a similar growth of specialized representation in Ottawa, particularly in the case of the United Kingdom and the United States. On the military side, I need scarcely refer to the work performed in England by General McNaughton and by the overseas headquarters of the three armed services.

Before the United States entered the war we had supplemented our methods for considering problems of common interest by the creation of a series of joint advisory bodies dealing with the defence of North America, with raw materials,

†Canada, House of Commons, *Debates*, 9 July 1943, 4555–58, 4561.

with economic coordination, and with war production. To these a joint committee on agriculture has recently been added. These committees and bodies supplement but do not replace the normal methods of consultation.

Shortly after Pearl Harbor, in order to secure more rapid cooperation between the war efforts of the United States and the United Kingdom, a group of combined agencies was established. These agencies are:

1. The combined chiefs of staff, meeting continuously in Washington, composed of the United States chiefs of staff and representatives of the British chiefs of staff;

2. The munitions assignments boards, meeting in Washington and in London, to allocate finished war materials on strategic grounds as they become ready for delivery;

3. The shipping adjustment boards, also meeting in Washington and in London, to regulate the pools of shipping controlled by the United States and the United Kingdom; and

4. The combined raw materials board, meeting in Washington, charged with the duty of planning the most effective use of raw materials. There were later added two further boards, both meeting in Washington;

5. The combined food board; and

6. The combined production resources board.

With one exception these bodies are composed of representatives only of the United States and the United Kingdom and their chief duty is to make recommendations to these two governments in the light of the joint study of the problems before them. They are war bodies formed for special purposes to facilitate the rapid taking of decisions on matters vital to the conduct of the war.

It is essential that the high strategy of the war should be discussed by a small group in conditions of the most absolute secrecy. To avoid giving aid to our enemies, a degree of secrecy, which would be intolerable in times of peace, must surround the taking of decisions, not only on strategy but on almost every aspect of war direction. The recommendations of the combined boards frequently concern governments other than the United States and the United Kingdom. When Canadian action is required to give effect to their recommendations, these recommendations are referred to Canada for approval. The government has sought, with a considerable measure of success, to ensure that in framing their recommendations the combined boards should give the fullest consideration to the position and resources of Canada.

A Canadian joint staff mission has offices in the building which houses the combined chiefs of staff, and it is represented at discussions of direct concern to Canada. We have developed special methods of liaison with each of the combined boards. In the case of the combined food board, for example, a representative of the Canadian government participates as a full member on all the commodity subcommittees.

On one board, the combined production and resources board, Canada is represented by a full member. The Minister of Munitions and Supply (Mr. Howe) is a member of this board. The board, by the way, as hon. members are aware, is meeting in Ottawa this morning.

I have outlined the chief agencies that have been established for the direction of the war effort. The government hopes that it will be found possible to have a broader basis given to some of these bodies.

Turning now to the planning of the settlement, I have said on previous occasions in this house that informal and exploratory discussions about international aspects of the settlement were constantly taking place, and that Canadian experts and officials were participating in these discussions. On matters as complex as methods for stabilizing currencies, it is obvious that there must be many preliminary talks between experts from many countries before plans can be framed for the consideration of governments. Canadian officials have participated in such talks in London and in Washington. These meetings are supplemented by the constant exchange of information through the usual inter-governmental channels. As the end of the war comes closer, such meetings will grow in number. As plans are framed, they are likely to become the subject of more formal conferences at which most, if not all, of the united nations will be represented.

The first of such conferences — the united nations conference on food and agriculture — has already been held at Hot Springs, Virginia. Hon. members will recall that on June 14, in tabling the final act of this conference, I made a statement on the general work of the conference and the programme for future action. A further united nations conference to consider the international organization of relief in the immediate post-war period will be held later in the present year.

Other meetings will follow as the preliminary discussions complete the preparatory work on each major subject for international agreement. I cannot yet indicate exactly what these subjects will be. Doubtless among them will be included the distressing and baffling problem of refugees, which has lately been discussed at a meeting in Bermuda between representatives of the United States and the United Kingdom. I shall speak of this problem in a moment.

It is too early for me to attempt even a shadowy outline of the form of the international settlement, political and economic, which may follow the ending of hostilities. It may be useful, however, to say a word about one of its aspects. The strong bonds which have linked the united nations into a working model of cooperation must be strengthened and developed for even greater use in the years of peace. It is perhaps an axiom of war that during actual hostilities methods must be improvised, secrecy must be observed, attention must be concentrated on victory. The time is approaching, however, when even before victory is won the concept of the united nations will have to be embodied in some form of international organization. On the one hand, authority in international affairs must not be concentrated exclusively in the largest powers. On the other, authority cannot be divided equally among all the thirty or more sovereign states that comprise the united nations, or all effective authority will disappear. A number of new international institutions are likely to be set up as a result of the war. In the view of the government, effective representations on these bodies should neither be restricted to the largest states nor necessarily extended to all states. Representation should be determined on a functional basis which will admit to full membership those countries, large or small, which have the greatest contribution to make to the particular object in question. In the world there are over sixty sovereign states. If they all have a nominally equal voice in international decisions, no effective decisions are likely to be taken. Some compromise must be found between the theoretical equality of states and the practical necessity of limiting representation on international bodies to a workable number. That compromise can be discovered, especially in economic matters, by the adoption of the functional principle of representation. That principle, in turn, is likely to find many new expressions in the gigantic task of liberation, restoration and reconstruction. . . .

Since the outbreak of war Canada's diplomatic representation has been greatly extended. In September, 1939, Canada had, in addition to the long-established office of the High Commissioner in London, legations in the United States, France, Japan, and in Belgium and the Netherlands, as well as the office of the permanent delegate to the League of Nations. Since that time the legations in Paris, Tokyo, Brussels and the Hague and the office in Geneva have been closed. But in the interval, fourteen new offices abroad have been established. Of these, five represent the appointment of high commissioners within the British commonwealth, to Australia, New Zealand, South Africa, Ireland and Newfoundland. Five are of new legations, to U.S.S.R. and China, and in South America to Brazil, Argentine and Chile. In addition, one minister has been accredited to seven of the allied governments established during the war in London: Belgium, the Netherlands, Poland, Norway, Yugoslavia, Greece and Czechoslovakia. All of the countries I have mentioned are represented in Ottawa by ministers, high commissioners or accredited representatives as the case may be.

Consular officers of Canada are serving in Greenland, and in St. Pierre and Miquelon. Most recently, with the appointment of a consul-general to New York, the first separate consular establishment in the United States has been opened.

The supervisory commission of the League of Nations still meets, though not at Geneva, and there is a Canadian representative on this continuing body. An important part of the league, the International Labour Organization, has, since 1940, had its headquarters at Montreal.

All of these formal relationships speak of the developing importance of Canada in the world community. The fortunes of war — or perhaps something more than the fortunes — have brought to Canada valiant men and women of many nations: sovereigns, prime ministers, foreign ministers and officers of state; chiefs of staff and ranking officers of armies, navies and air forces of many lands.

The stature of nationhood which Canada has reached — I mean the position of Canada as a world power — has been reached, not on material grounds alone, though Canada's contributions to mutual aid have been impressive by any standard. Neither does it owe its emergence to political considerations. It has arisen, I believe, from our recognition of the needs of humanity. Our conception of nationhood rejects, as it must always reject, any attachment to ideas which are non-democratic, or to usages which would constitute the negation of free institutions and the untrammelled expression of the free souls of free men. It is something which speaks not simply for to-day, or next month, or the year after next, but for all the future of Canada. . . .

St. Laurent on the Principles of Canadian Policy, 1947†

. . . I propose to make this lecture an enquiry into the foundations of Canadian policy in world affairs. . . . We in Canada, of English and French origin, have embarked on the joint task of building a nation. One aspect of our common enterprise is our external relations. The subject is one of special interest to me because of my present responsibilities in the Government. The founder of this lectureship has said — "If we discover and dwell upon what binds us together, we shall accept our differences as the members of a true family accept their differences without losing sight for a moment of the things which hold them together in a vital unity". It is in keeping with this spirit that I propose to discuss the background of our external policy.

A policy of world affairs, to be truly effective, must have its foundations laid upon general principles which have been tested in the life of the nation and which have secured the broad support of large groups of the population. It is true that differences of opinion about foreign policy must continually be reviewed in discussion and debate inside and outside of Parliament. Such discussions, however, can result in constructive conclusions only if they take place against the background of a large measure of agreement on fundamentals.

It may be objected that we are not old enough as a nation to have worked out such agreed principles. But let us not forget that much which forms the basis of our agreement in that respect is the result of circumstances over which we have had little if any control. The century old struggles between France and England, their rivalry in the New World, the Battle of the Plains of Abraham, the Treaty of Paris of 1763, the revolt of the Thirteen Colonies, the wave of more liberal thinking unleashed by the French Revolution, the geography, the climate, the kind of natural resources of our country all tended to create conditions for our ancestors and tend to create conditions for our own generation which lead to almost inevitable results. They have forced French-speaking and English-speaking men and women to live side by side as members of the same community. They have inspired them to work together to obtain an ever increasing measure of self-government; they have tempered the resistance of the metropolitan government to this healthy development; they have made natural and easy the creation of an economy productive of large surpluses of certain kinds of commodities and lacking in certain other kinds and thus dependent in an extraordinary degree upon exchange and trade to get some benefit out of the surpluses and to secure the commodities not available from our own production.

We are now within close range of two significant anniversaries in the life of this nation. It is almost exactly a century since the decision was taken that the

†"The Foundation of Canadian Policy in World Affairs." An address by Right Hon. Louis S. St. Laurent, Secretary of State for External Affairs, Inaugurating the Gray Foundation Lectureship at Toronto University, January 13, 1947. Department of External Affairs, *Statements and Speeches*, no. 47/2, 13 January 1947, 3–11.

affairs of this part of the world should be conducted upon the principles of responsible government. For a hundred years, therefore, French speaking and English speaking people living in the valley of the St. Lawrence River and the Great Lakes, together with their fellow countrymen elsewhere across this continent have been engaged upon the experiment of building, on their own responsibility and under their own direction, a modern nation. It is, as it had to be, a nation constructed on the foundation of two cultures and two languages. A century ago the Canadian people in winning responsible government staked their future on the political principles which had been defined in Lord Durham's famous report. They staked their future equally on a denial of Durham's assertion that the country could not survive with two cultures. They said that this could be a free country, notwithstanding that it had also to be a country with both English and French culture. For a hundred years now they have been shown to be right.

The second anniversary of which I would remind you is that of "Confederation" eighty years ago. It was then that the challenge was accepted to build into a single state the scattered communities which stretched across the northern half of this continent. We have therefore been working together on this task of nation building for some considerable time. It is not too soon to look back and determine what principles have had to be and have become generally acceptable throughout this country in the conduct of our relations abroad. When we have defined these principles, we may examine the manner in which we have habitually embodied them in our relations with other states where our associations are especially close. We may also consider them with respect to the international organizations of which we are or have been members.

The Basic Principles

National Unity

The first general principle upon which I think we are agreed is that our external policies shall not destroy our unity. No policy can be regarded as wise which divides the people whose effort and resources must put it into effect. This consideration applies not only to the two main cultural groups in our country. It applies equally to sectionalism of any kind. We dare not fashion a policy which is based on the particular interests of any economic group, of any class or of any section in this country. We must be on guard especially against the claims of extravagant regionalism no matter where they have their origin. Our history has shown this to be a consideration in our external policy of which we, more even than others, must be perpetually conscious. The role of this country in world affairs will prosper only as we maintain this principle, for a disunited Canada will be a powerless one.

Political Liberty

Second amongst the ideas which shape our external policy I will place the conception of political liberty. This is an inheritance from both our French and

English background, and through these parent States it has come to us from the whole rich culture of western Europe. It is a patrimony which we ourselves have enlarged by working out on our own soil the transition from colony to free community. These are days in which the vocabulary of political thought has been so debased that there are many familiar coins that one hesitates to lay on the counter. I make no apology, however, for speaking to a Canadian audience of political liberty because I know that this phrase has content for us. I know, also, that we are all conscious of the danger to our own political institutions when freedom is attacked in other parts of the world. In the complex series of events which twice in a generation has led us into war, we have been profoundly influenced in our decisions by the peril which threatened the democracies of western Europe. From our joint political inheritance, as well as from our common experience, we have come as a people to distrust and dislike governments which rule by force and which suppress free comment on their activities. We know that stability is lacking where consent is absent. We believe that the greatest safeguard against the aggressive policies of any government is the freely expressed judgment of its own people. This does not mean that we have ever sought to interfere in the affairs of others, or to meddle in situations which were obviously outside our interest or beyond our control. It does mean, however, that we have consistently sought and found our friends amongst those of like political traditions. It means equally that we have realized that a threat to the liberty of western Europe, where our political ideas were nurtured, was a threat to our own way of life. This realization has perhaps not been comprehended or expressed by every group and every individual in the country with as much clarity and coherence as, looking back on the events, we should like. I have no doubt, however, that for the young men of our Universities who fought in this war, it was a part of our national inheritance which they well understood.

The Rule of Law in National and International Affairs

In the third place respect for the rule of law has become an integral part of our external as of our domestic policy. The supremacy of law in our own political system is so familiar that we are in constant danger of taking it for granted. We know, however, that historically the development of this principle is a necessary antecedent to self-government. The first great victory on the road to freedom was the establishment in early modern times of the principle that both governments and peoples were subject to the impartial administration of the courts. Only then could the further step be taken by which the people gave their consent to the laws by which they were governed.

Within the past decade we have been reminded by the hideous example of the fascist states of the evil which befalls a nation when the government sets itself above the law. Beneath the spurious efficiency of such a state, we have perceived the helpless plight of individuals who have been deprived of the primary right of an impartial administration of the law.

We have seen also the chaos which is brought to world affairs when lawlessness is practised in the field of international relations. The development of an international code of law is still in its early stages. The past decade has done much to delay and distort this growth. I feel sure, however, that we in this country are agreed that the freedom of nations depends upon the rule of law amongst states. We have shown this concretely in our willingness to accept the decisions of international tribunals, courts of arbitration and other bodies of a judicial nature, in which we have participated. There can be no doubt that the Canadian people unanimously support this principle.

The Values of a Christian Civilization

No foreign policy is consistent nor coherent over a period of years unless it is based upon some conception of human values. I know that we live in an age when it is fashionable to speak in terms only of hard realism in the conduct of international affairs. I realize also that at best the practice of any policy is a poor approximation of ideals upon which it may be based. I am sure, however, that in our national life we are continually influenced by the conceptions of good and evil which emerged from Hebrew and Greek civilization and which have been transformed and transmitted through the Christian traditions of the Western World. These are values which lay emphasis on the importance of the individual, on the place of moral principles in the conduct of human relations, on standards of judgment which transcend mere material well-being. They have ever influenced our national life as we have built a modern state from East to West across this continent. I am equally convinced that on the basis of this common experience we shall discern the same values in world affairs, and that we shall seek to protect and nurture them.

The Acceptance of International Responsibility in Keeping with our Conception of our Role in World Affairs

There is a fifth basic principle which I should like also to mention before considering the background of our relations with particular countries. That is willingness to accept international responsibilities. I know that there are many in this country who feel that in the past we have played too small a part in the development of international political organizations. The growth in this country of a sense of political responsibility on an international scale has perhaps been less rapid than some of us would like. It has nevertheless been a perceptible growth; and again and again on the major questions of participation in international organization, both in peace and war, we have taken our decision to be present. If there is one conclusion that our common experience has led us to accept, it is that security for this country lies in the development of a firm structure of international organization.

I have been speaking of certain general principles which I think underlie the conduct of our external policy. These are principles which have been defined and articulated in the practice of relations with other countries over many decades. In this application of our principles, too, we have reached certain general conclusions on which we are all agreed, and which serve as a guide to policy.

The Practical Application

The Commonwealth which we Ourselves have Fashioned for Achieving the Ends we Desire in World Affairs

We have never attempted to define in precise terms our relations with the Commonwealth. They are nevertheless a basic consideration in the external policy of this country. In discussing them I will recall two aspects of this relationship concerning which I am sure there will be no disagreement. In the first place the Commonwealth is a form of political association which is unique. There has never been anything like it before in history. There is no parallel to it in the contemporary world. It is the only case on record of a Colonial Empire being transformed to an association of free nations by experiment, by compromise, by political evolution. I have no doubt that, whatever its future, it will be regarded by the historians of another age as one of the great constructive political achievements of our time. The other fact that I would call to your mind is that the Commonwealth is in a very real sense an achievement in which Canadians can take special pride. We Canadians, perhaps more than any other of its members, have contributed to its development. We have regarded it as an instrument which, in co-operation with like-minded people, we could use for our common purposes. It has, therefore, the vitality of a living, functioning organism which has been and which can continue to be used for good, according to the wisdom and foresight of our policies.

It is now only twenty years since the term "Commonwealth" came into popular use as a result of the Declaration which was adopted by the Conference of 1926. Even in that short period the meaning of the word has changed. There are already important differences between the Commonwealth of today and that described in Lord Balfour's famous statement. Even while this change was taking place, however, there has been a further compelling demonstration of the fact that we are members in an association of free nations, capable of common action in an emergency, greater and more striking than that of any formal military or diplomatic alliance that the world has ever known.

Even though they are not precisely defined, the principles on which we act in regard to the Commonwealth may be clearly discerned. We seek to preserve it as an instrument through which we, with others who share our objectives, can co-operate for our common good in peace as in war. On the other hand, we should continue to resist, as in the past, efforts to reduce to formal terms or specific commitments this association which has demonstrated its vitality through the common understanding upon which it is based. We should likewise oppose developments in our Commonwealth relations which might be inconsistent with our desire to participate fully in the task of building an effective international organization on a wider scale.

Within the Commonwealth, our relations with the United Kingdom have, of course, a very special value and significance. We shall not forget in our history the imaginative collaboration of British and Canadian leaders who, a century ago, laid the political foundations for the modern Commonwealth. Nor can we fail to be influenced by the fact that our political institutions are those of the British Isles, and that we now share with other parliamentary democracies the responsibility for preserving and developing this system. We shall not forget either the peril in which we shared, together with other Commonwealth countries, but especially with the United Kingdom during the dark days of 1940. This was an episode which threw in dramatic relief the measure to which we have common interests and the degree to which we are alike concerned in the establishment of a world order based on principles of freedom.

The United States — the Settlement of International Affairs by Negotiation and Compromise

It is not customary in this country for us to think in terms of having a policy in regard to the United States. Like farmers whose lands have a common concession line, we think of ourselves as settling, from day to day, questions that arise between us, without dignifying the process by the word "policy." We have travelled so much of the road together in close agreement that by comparison the occasions on which our paths may have diverged seem insignificant.

There has, however, been more to our relations with the United States than mere empirical neighbourliness. For the century during which we have been building this nation, we have kept company with an adjoining state vastly more powerful, more self-confident, more wealthy than we. It is a state with purposes and ambitions parallel to ours. One by one, the major areas of disagreement have been reduced. Our common border has long since been defined to our mutual satisfaction. The people of this country have taken a final decision to remain outside the United States. There is no longer any body of opinion in this country which looks towards annexation. The people of the United States on their part, have come to a parallel conclusion that they will not extend their boundaries beyond their present limits on this continent. On both sides the fact has been accepted that there shall be a free land and independent federation in the northern part of this continent. None of this has been achieved, however, without reflection and forethought, nor will it be maintained without constant watchfulness. I do not say this because I think there is the slightest intention on either side to move away from the present happy state of our relations. I say it merely because even the simplest relationship between human beings requires the constructive action of both parties. The relationship between a great and powerful nation and its smaller neighbour, at best, is far from simple. It calls for constant and imaginative attention on both sides.

Defined more precisely, our policy in regard to the United States has come with the passage of years to have two main characteristics. On the one hand, we have sought by negotiation, by arbitration, by compromise, to settle upon the basis of mutual satisfaction the problems that have arisen between us. As I suggested a moment ago, this has been far more than the unimaginative clearing away of parochial questions. It has succeeded precisely because it is based on the determination of both nations to conduct their affairs, as a matter of policy, on this basis. The other aspect of our relations with the United States which I shall emphasize is our readiness to accept our responsibility as a North American nation in enterprises which are for the welfare of this continent. In support of this assertion, there is a long and creditable record of joint activity. In making it, however, I must add that it has never been the opinion of any considerable number of people in Canada that this continent could live unto itself. We have seen our own interests in the wider context of the western world. We have realized also that regionalism of any kind would not provide the answer to problems of world security. But we know that peoples who live side by side on the same continent cannot disregard each other's interests, and we have always been willing to consider the possibility of common action for constructive ends.

France — a Tradition of Common Interests

With France also our relations rest upon principles that have emerged clearly from our history. We have never forgotten that France is one of the fountainheads of our cultural life. We realize that she forms an integral part of the framework of our international life. We have so much in common that, despite the differences between the French political system and our own, we cannot doubt for a moment that our objects in world affairs are similar. We in this country have always believed in the greatness of France, even at times when her future seemed most obscure. During the war, we were confident that France herself would play a major role in her own liberation. We gave our support to those leaders of the French people whom the French themselves were prepared to follow. We are aware of the heavy burden which invasion twice in a generation has laid upon France. We shall support her recovery not merely out of sympathy, but because we know that her integrity is a matter of great consequence to us.

The Support of Constructive International Organization

I shall not endeavour to discuss in detail the question of our relationship with other states. Rather, I shall turn now to our attitude towards international organizations. As I suggested when I was discussing the general principles which underlie our policy, we have been ready to take our part in constructive international action. We have, of course, been forced to keep in mind the limitations upon the influence of any secondary power. No society of nations can prosper if it does not have the support of those who hold the major share of the world's military and economic power. There is little point in a country of our stature recommending international action, if those who must carry the major burden of whatever action is taken are not in sympathy. We know, however, that the development of international organizations on a broad scale is of the very greatest importance to us, and we have been willing to play our role when it was apparent that significant and effective action was contemplated.

We have already given good evidence of this willingness by the record of our international activities since the war. We sent a strong delegation to the Conference at San Francisco, and I had every reason to be gratified with the delegations which accompanied me to the first part of the General Assembly in London and second part in New York. We were elected to membership on the Economic and Social Council, and have tried to show by the attention we have paid to that body the measure of importance we attached to its creation. We have taken part in the formation of the World Bank and Fund, of the Provisional International Civil Aviation Organization, of the World Health Organization, of UNESCO, of the International Refugee Organization, of the Food and Agriculture Organization and of the projected International Trade Organization. We have continued to support the International Labour Organization, as we did before the war. We have played a prominent part in the work of the Atomic Energy Commission and of the Peace Conference in Paris. This list is not exhaustive, but it indicates the measure of our activity. We have not found it easy to provide delegates and advisers for all the conferences which the task of creating a new structure of world organizations has required. I think, however, that we may take pride in the work of our representatives, and that if you had observed them at any of these gatherings, you would have seen them doing competent energetic and constructive work. I think you would find, also, that they had regularly won the respect and confidence of their colleagues from other countries.

In economic as well as political affairs we have put our shoulder to the wheel of post-war reconstruction. Our contribution to UNRRA was more than 150 million dollars, and Canadian food and equipment have been shipped into devastated areas all over the world. We supplied goods freely to our allies during the war under Mutual Aid Legislation, and we have since provided export credits on a vast scale to help in rebuilding the economic life of Europe and of China. We have done this as a matter of policy, because we believe that the economic reconstruction of the world must go hand in hand with the political reconstruction. We are aware, too, that economic revival is a matter of great importance to us. We are dependent on markets abroad for the large quantities of staple products we produce and cannot consume, and we are dependent on supplies from abroad of commodities which are essential to our well-being. It seems to me axiomatic, therefore, that we should give our support to every international organization which contributes to the economic and political stability of the world.

The Development of an Effective Diplomatic Service

Seen in the light of these historic developments, the recent expansion of the diplomatic service of this country is a natural development. We are preparing ourselves to fulfil the growing responsibilities in world affairs which we have accepted as a modern state. We wish the Commonwealth to be an effective instrument of co-operation, and we have, therefore, appointed High Commissioners in the capitals of every Commonwealth country. I am glad to say that within recent weeks this process has been completed with the appointment of a High Commissioner to India. I earnestly hope that through his mission there and through the High Commissioner for India in Canada, who will soon be appointed, we may experience the same informal and helpful co-operation which has been characteristic of our relations with the Commonwealth countries.

We have also multiplied rapidly our diplomatic representation in foreign countries. Before very long, we shall have provided ourselves with diplomatic representation in the capitals of every major country in the world. We have not taken this step merely through a desire to follow a conventional practice, or to advertise ourselves abroad. We have done so because our geography, our climate, our natural resources have so conditioned our economy that the continued prosperity and well-being of our own people can best be served by the prosperity and well-being of the whole world. We have thus a useful part to play in world affairs, useful to ourselves through being useful to others, and to play that part we must have our own spokesmen amongst our neighbours.

It is not only in our foreign service that this expansion is taking place. We are trying also to construct a Department in Ottawa which will build upon the activities of our representatives abroad. Our own national interests compel us to take a creditable part in the international conferences which are now determining the nature of the post-war world. We are, therefore, constructing a service which can provide strong and well informed advisers for the delegations which we must send to these gatherings. This is no easy task. It will, of course, make demands upon our financial resources. I am strengthened, however, in my determination to recommend the continuation of this policy because it is no transitory experiment. It is the natural result of a long historic process, and I feel that it will be supported by all sections of our people. And that is as it should be. Canadian policy in its external relations should not be allowed to become a matter of party political controversy at home. Of course the government in office must take full responsibility for each one of its actions as well as in Canada's external relations as in the conduct of purely domestic Canadian affairs. But in its external relations the Government in office should ever strive to speak and to act on behalf of the whole of Canada and in such manner as to have the support of all the Canadian peoples regardless of party affiliations at home.

Conclusion

A few moments ago I said that we must play a role in world affairs in keeping with the ideals and sacrifices of the young men of this University, and of this country who went to war. However great or small that role may be, we must play it creditably. We must act with maturity and consistency, and with a sense of responsibility. For this reason I return in conclusion to the point at which I began. We must act as a united people. By that I mean a people who, through reflection and discussion, have arrived at a common understanding of our interests and our purposes. . . .

A former High Commissioner for the United Kingdom in Canada, Mr. Malcolm MacDonald, speaking to a Canadian audience before his departure, referred to Canada as "a unity, a harmony, a nation — a people with national sentiment pursuing national aims." He added these words; "there is a sanity, a wisdom, a true statesmanship about the Canadian outlook and policy in international affairs which is uncommon."

These are words of great praise. In repeating them to you may I add a comment about them which I have made previously: "May Canada never be less deserving of them than she has been during these few recent troubled years."

THE HEENEY-MERCHANT REPORT, 1965†

The Character of the Relationship

. . .

8. The feasibility of working out acceptable principles to govern or guide the behavior of our two countries in their dealings with one another must depend upon the possibility of agreeing on the principal facts. In other words, there must be, on both sides of the border, a common appreciation of at least the main features of the relationship.

9. It is trite to refer to relations between Canada and the United States as "unique." Nevertheless, this is the principal fact. There are elements in our situation which are not to be found in that of any other pair of independent countries in the world. Furthermore, the impact of the relationship, though unequal in its incidence on the two sides of the boundary, extends into virtually every aspect of the national life of each. This, we believe, will be increasingly so as the years go by.

Mutual Involvement

10. The volume and variety of mutual involvement of the two countries and their peoples are without parallel. Perhaps first in importance is the vast network of personal and family connections, the effect of which is incalculable but certainly great. There can be few Canadians who do not acknowledge some close American relative by blood or marriage, while the number of Americans resident in the Canadian society is substantial. The density of travel between our countries testifies to their interest in each other. Last year a total of more than 16 million Americans and Canadians headed north or south for work or play, with little formality or inconvenience. They have both taken good advantage of the open border.

11. There is a myriad of other close links between Canada and the United States. In religion, in all the professions, in business, in labor, in education and in the arts, the pattern of organization and exchange straddles the boundary. As one perceptive official recently put it: "From businessmen to Boy Scouts, women's clubs to engineers, and scientists to little league hockey teams, Canadian and American counterparts find fraternal interests and often organizational affiliation in a magnitude defying description. Meetings, conventions, cross-border visits, and mail, telegraphic and telephone contacts have combined in a pattern of North American neighborhood so common-place that we rarely give it special thought." Within such groups the habit as well as the means of communication between our two peoples is strong and growing stronger daily.

12. We have cooperated naturally and easily in measures for the conservation of wildlife. Wild animals, fish and birds recognize no boundary drawn by men. Similarly we have worked together in the preservation of adjacent wilderness areas and contiguous public parks.

†Department of External Affairs, *Canada and the United States: Principles for Partnership* (Ottawa: 28 June 1965): 2–14.

13. Competent American and Canadian authorities have cooperated in a number of mutually advantageous local interchanges of electric power and for the movement of oil and natural gas across the border.

14. A significant proportion of trade between our two countries moves free from tariffs or other restrictions and efforts are on foot for further improvement. Subject to the required legislative approval, trade by manufacturers of automobiles and new auto parts is to be free of duty in both countries under a special agreement concluded earlier this year between the two governments.

15. Much has been said and written about aspects of the cultural involvement of the two countries. In this area the preponderance of the United States is most notable. The stream of television and radio programs and of publications from hundreds of private sources in the United States encounters no natural barriers in its northward surge, except in French Canada. In larger measure than any other people, Canadians share with Americans the mixed and massive output of the United States.

16. In commerce and finance the situation is well known. Canadians and Americans remind themselves constantly that they are each other's best customers, that the trade crossing the border is the largest between any two countries in the world. Of recent years they have become especially conscious of the importance of their financial relations. Americans are deeply involved in the strength and prosperity of the Canadian economy by reason of the magnitude and variety of their investments as well as the absorptive capacity of the Canadian market. The stability of the Canadian dollar is of importance to the United States. As recently as 1962 when the Canadian dollar was under serious pressure, the financial authorities of the United States promptly rallied — with others — to its support. On the other hand, the cooperation of Canadian financial institutions and the continuing Canadian deficit in bilateral transactions has contributed materially to lessening the balance of payments problem of the United States. Moreover, the importance of the United States dollar as a world currency is accepted in Canada. Access to the United States capital market has been of major importance to the Canadian economy and private United States investment continues to play a significant role in the rate of Canadian growth. The existence of conditions which attract foreign capital is of course an element in its availability. It should also be noted that private Canadian funds flow southward for investment in substantial volume. On a per capita basis — though not of course overall — Canadian investment in the United States exceeds the American investment in Canadian business. The financial and commercial stakes of each country in the other are high.

17. In recent years the revolution of modern technology, the consequent acceleration in the tendency toward specialization and the "internationalization" of business, with technical "know how" accompanying capital investment, have been striking features of the world economic scene. They have been especially apparent in United States-Canada relations where their effects continue to multiply and extend the interdependence of the two economies.

18. The changing technology of war may diminish the significance of geography but, for the years immediately ahead, Canada will remain of great importance to United States' defense while the United States is essential to the defense

of Canada. The considerations which, since World War II, led increasingly to the integration of continental air defense still obtain. The logic of our military partnership has been extended effectively into the fields of production and supply. The network of joint arrangements between the two governments and their military services is striking evidence of the degree to which the two countries are involved with one another in the ultimate and fundamental business of national security.

Wherein Our Countries Differ

19. Canada and the United States are — in Churchill's phrase — "mixed up together" more than any other two countries on earth so that the similarities in our "ways of life" often lead observers to erroneous conclusions. For there are important differences. Both understanding and acceptance of this fact are essential to the successful working of the partnership. Many of these differences have their roots in history.

20. First and foremost in this context, the United States is a unicultural society, while Canada, founded upon the partnership of two races, is discovering anew in its bicultural composition a distinguishing national quality of growing vigor and significance. We believe that this distinction is likely to have increasing importance in the development of relations between the two countries. An example of its relevance in the cultural area is one response of Canadians to the northward stream of the products of contemporary American mass media, a recent comment on which was that "the danger from the United States to English-speaking Canada is that of cultural absorption, while for French Canada it is cultural destruction."

21. The political traditions and institutions of the United States are a strong element in the national character which profoundly affect American attitudes. The same is true of Canada and Canadians. We have already alluded to the importance of French Canada in this connection. We have also been impressed, in our own experience, by the misunderstandings which can develop from institutional differences, for example, the congressional system on the one hand and the parliamentary on the other. The division of powers is a concept natural to every American but it is often difficult for Canadians, raised in the tradition of parliamentary government, to appreciate its practical consequences.

22. Until recent years Canadians and Americans have had a somewhat different view of the outside world. Since World War II, the United States has taken over the immense and necessary burden of leadership and protection of the free nations. The Canadian connection with Europe has always been a main influence in the development of Canada's national attitudes. But it is only in recent years that Canada has become deeply involved in the wider international context and then, with different capabilities and responsibilities, not as a military power of the first rank but as one of the leaders in world trade, highly developed economically, and respected in world councils, with a demonstrated willingness to assume varied obligations around the globe.

23. In world affairs — as in the bilateral relationship — the most conspicuous difference between the United States and Canada is the disparity between the

two countries in power and the responsibility that goes with it. Since World War II, while Canada has emerged as a country of importance and influence, in the same period the United States has become the most powerful nation on earth.

24. The disparity is striking, whatever the area or terms of comparison — manpower, military or economic capabilities, what you will. By every material test other than geographic extent, and possibily undeveloped resources, the United States is immensely stronger than her northern neighbor. There is no satisfactory factor or combination of factors — ten to one in population, fourteen to one in Gross National Product — by which this inequality can be measured realistically. Degree in most areas of comparison becomes kind; the contrast more significant than the figures.

25. The consequences of this disparity are among the most difficult features in the relations between our two governments and peoples.

Problems Arising From the Relationship

26. The direct and inevitable result of the great and growing volume and variety of mutual involvement is the multiplication of actual and potential points of friction. It is our impression, however, that, considering the extent and frequency of contact between our governments and peoples, the actual conflicts are remarkably few. For the most part, our two governments seem able to settle their differences much as conflicts of interest are resolved within our own two countries. Nevertheless, because ours are independent countries and separate peoples whose attitudes and interests do not always coincide, there are, and will continue to be, problems between them. Mutually acceptable solutions or accommodations to these problems require, on both sides, wider and deeper understanding of their origins.

27. Over the course of the history of the two countries, there have been times of emotional outburst which have clouded relations between the two governments and peoples. We do not accept the theory that such phenomena are endemic or inevitable. Nevertheless, it is true that Canada owes its national existence largely to the determined, negative response of Canadians to the challenge inherent in the size and power of the United States. The once real Canadian fear of military aggression from the south has long since passed. Current Canadian anxieties do not arise from warlike pressures, and release from them is not to be found in simple heroic measures.

28. The current concern in Canada — determined as ever upon its independent North American future — has its roots in history, in its struggle to achieve its own destiny, and in the disparity of size and power. The present preoccupations of Canadians, however, relate primarily to social and economic developments of more recent date — the massive influence of American cultural expression upon Canadian life, the extent of American ownership of Canadian industry and resources, and the prevailing attractions south of the border for Canadian scientists, engineers and professional men and women. Such present phenomena must be seen by Americans as well as Canadians within the context of history and national aspirations. If in their dealings, public and private, there is to be the mutual

confidence that both desire and need, there must be conscious effort on both sides to appreciate the historical as well as the current factors which tend to divide them.

29. The mutual involvement of the two countries and peoples has also complicated, on both sides, the problems arising from the disparity in power. In most — though not all — of their bilateral affairs the capacity of the United States to benefit or harm Canadian interests is greater than that of Canada to affect the prosperity and security of the United States. Canadians are more conscious than Americans of this element in their dealings with the United States. On the other hand, the United States, preoccupied with the responsibilities of world power, may sometimes be inhibited in its bilateral dealings by considerations which do not operate directly on Canadian attitudes. Here restraint is required of both sides.

30. Canadians sometimes feel that, because they are so close, so "American," there is a disposition on the part of the United States to expect more of Canada than of other allies — as in setting other countries a good example — reflecting a tendency to apply to Canada a kind of "double standard" of international conduct. The result is sometimes to tempt Canadians into demonstrating their independence by adopting positions divergent from those of the United States. In a quite different sense, Americans are inclined sometimes to suspect the application of a "double standard" on the part of Canada when, for example, in an international negotiation, the United States is urged to be "reasonable," to make unilateral concessions to break a logjam which has been created by the intransigence of others. For Canadians cannot but be disturbingly aware that, despite their underlying confidence in the basic motives of the United States, Canada could be involved inevitably in the consequences of United States' decisions in circumstances over which Canadians had little influence or control. Such tendencies, on each side, arising from mutual involvement, inequality and the facts of international life, should be recognized but not exaggerated.

The Conclusions to be Drawn

31. We take as basic fact the will on both sides of the border to live together in peace and prosperity and to that end to work together. Given that fact, we believe that certain general conclusions can be drawn from the present situation and experience in the past.

32. In the first place, we are convinced that the nature and extent of the relationship between our two countries is such as to require, in the interests of both, something more than the normal arrangement for the conduct of their affairs with one another. The reasons which lead us inexorably to this conclusion have been touched on in the two preceding sections. We will have more to say later as to the kind of arrangements these should be. Meantime, we wish to emphasize our conviction that the strength of the friendship and the value of the partnership — of great and increasing significance to both countries — depend not only upon mutual understanding and respect, but upon the ability and determination on both sides to find solutions or accommodations to the problems which inevitably arise from an intimate and involved relationship.

33. The majority of the issues which reach the government level are, in fact, resolved in a fashion at least reasonably satisfactory to both sides. The evidence we have studied in the course of the present exercise confirms this conclusion. Indeed, the marvel is that, with such varied questions arising literally every day, so many are resolved without the need for consideration at a high level of government. Considering the volume, the number of problems which have to receive top treatment is not large. But those which do emerge are often very difficult and delicate, not only intrinsically but in terms of national attitudes. The intimacy, breadth and depth of the relationship make it certain that there will always be problems between our two countries, large as well as small. And, as they are resolved, new ones will replace them. This is a condition of continental cohabitation.

34. Many of the problems which have been satisfactorily solved in the past are by their nature likely to recur. Those associated with wheat marketing, labor relations and defense production are examples. In this connection, it should be noted that prosperity acts as a lubricant. By the same token, hard times can exacerbate difficulties.

35. In every case that we have examined where difficulties have developed, and ultimately been satisfactorily resolved or accommodated, full and timely consultation has been an essential element in its disposition. Similarly, the absence of prior consultation or the fact that such consultation as did take place was regarded as insufficient, has been a feature of many cases where an impasse has occurred and no acceptable compromise has been reached.

36. It should be frankly recognized that, in the future as in the past, there are bound to arise cases of genuine conflict of national interest which by their nature are, at the time at least, incapable of mutually acceptable solutions. In such matters there may indeed be no immediate alternative to an agreement to disagree. On the other hand, it may be that, within a larger framework of national interests, some solution can be worked out. For it is important that individual issues should not be insulated from one another within the wide range of our relationship.

37. We have noted a surprising number of areas in which our governments have adopted a common approach to our common advantage. Their recital is both impressive and reassuring. We are of the opinion that there are further promising possibilities which could and should be jointly explored with a view to the extension of this mutually advantageous partnership.

The Importance of Consultation

38. Given the long experience of our two countries in dealing with one another and the virtual certainty that their interdependence will grow rather than be washed away by inward-looking and protectionist policies, we believe it is feasible to identify certain principles of conduct which would reduce the possibilities of divergencies in economic and other policies of interest to each other.

39. We are convinced that the cornerstone of a healthy relationship between our two countries is timely and sufficient consultation in candor and good faith at whatever level or levels of government are appropriate to the nature and importance of the subject. To consult in this fashion, however, cannot be taken to

imply that agreement must always result. The purpose rather is that each be enabled to hear and weigh the other's views. The outcome will depend upon the circumstances of the case and, ultimately, upon the judgment by each of its national interest.

40. Effective consultation depends far less on machinery and procedure than on the will to consult. This applies at all levels. In fact the kind of consultation which the breadth and intimacy of the relationship demands should develop into ineradicable habit in the two capitals.

41. While manner must give place to substance, it may be well to glance at existing machinery for consultation before expressing further views on this topic.

Machinery for Consultation

42. Especially since the days of Prime Minister Mackenzie King and President Franklin Roosevelt, certain major problems have been the subject of informal interchanges between the two heads of government. It is assumed that this useful personal relationship will be maintained in the future. In some circumstances, there is literally no substitute for it.

43. Our respective Embassies, dealing in each case principally with the department charged with responsibility for foreign affairs, but also with other departments, are the normal and official means of communication between the two governments. It is their function to conduct a continuing exchange of views and information over the whole range of the relationship.

44. There is a responsibility on each side to ensure, within its governmental apparatus, a high degree of interdepartmental coordination and discipline. Otherwise the conduct of business will be inefficient and productive of unnecessary difficulty. It should go without saying that our respective Embassies and the concerned divisions of the Department of State and the Department of External Affairs should be sufficiently staffed with officers of high quality. Among them should always be some who are especially knowledgeable in Canada-United States affairs through actual service in the other country. It is evident that the situations within the two governments are not identical, for various reasons. Nevertheless, we attach importance to these observations which we believe to have validity on both sides.

45. Over the years, and especially since the early days of World War II, certain joint bodies for the conduct of certain of our affairs have been created by treaty and by executive action. Of the former the International Joint Commission is one which has been of continuing importance to both countries since its establishment by the Boundary Waters Treaty of 1909. Originally designed to prevent disputes arising between Canada and the United States regarding the use of boundary waters and to settle any questions involving the rights, obligations, or interests of either party along the common frontier, this unique institution acts as a single body composed equally of United States' and Canadian members. In our judgment, its solid foundation of law and precedent and its long and successful record in the disposition of problems along the boundary justify consideration of some extension of the Commission's functions. Accordingly, we recommend that the two governments examine jointly the wisdom and feasibility of such a development.

46. Among the bodies established by executive agreement, the Joint Committee on Trade and Economic Affairs is among the most important. Composed of the Cabinet members, on both sides, responsible for foreign affairs, trade and commerce, finance, agriculture and natural resources, it meets periodically to review the economic situation of the two countries and to consult on current problems. Under the general aegis of this Committee special working groups or other consultative arrangements have been established.

47. In this connection, we recommend that the Joint Committee on Trade and Economic Affairs establish a Joint Committee of Deputies which could meet frequently on behalf of their principals and be available at short notice to consider any emergent problem. We make this recommendation because it is unreasonable to expect Cabinet members with all their other responsibilities to come together as often, as systematically and as quickly as is needed.

48. In other areas of common concern similar joint facilities have been set up, among them the Committee on Joint Defense on which sit the Cabinet members responsible for defense, foreign affairs and finance.

49. Below the Cabinet level there is the Permanent Joint Board of Defense established in 1940. Consisting as it does of both civilian and military members, it seems to us that this body could be more fully utilized to the mutual advantage.

50. There is also continuing and valuable interchange between the military services of the two countries.

51. Special mention should be made of the direct consultative arrangement between Parliament and the Congress. Founded in 1959 this Canada-United States Interparliamentary Group is composed of representatives from both Houses in both countries. Any misgivings which may at first have existed as to possible legislative intrusion into the conduct of foreign affairs have been dispelled by the important and positive role which this body has played in broadening understanding between our two countries. The members meet regularly, alternating between the United States and Canada. Their agendas cover a wide range of current topics and their discussions have been characterized by ease, candor and enthusiasm.

52. One could extend this enumeration, for there are many other joint bodies which have been set up to facilitate the process of consultation and the conduct of our joint affairs in different areas. Their importance and utility vary with circumstance. Their activities supplement the scores of daily contacts maintained by the official departments and agencies of the two governments. . . . Added together, all these means of communication must surely constitute the most elaborate and valuable apparatus of consultation existing between any two nations. Not only should these arrangements be utilized but they should be strengthened, revised and expanded as need and convenience may suggest.

53. In view of the complexity and variety of official relationships between the two governments at all levels, it is particularly important that there be maintained between the capitals of Washington and Ottawa passenger air facilities with modern standards of equipment, rapidity and regularity. It is also important that mail deliveries between the two capitals be prompt and frequent.

Guidelines for Consultation

54. We now turn to the essence of consultation and to certain guidelines which, in our judgment, should be observed by our two governments in their dealings with each other:

(a) In the first place, every effort should be made to begin the consultative process sufficiently early to provide reasonable time for each party to consider and give full weight to the views and interests of the other. This will help to satisfy each side that its position on any issue is being seriously examined. It will also improve the chances of resolving difficulties and, where no detours around roadblocks are to be found, it can ease the shock of impending collision.

(b) In certain fields where combined efforts are called for, such as continental air defense arrangements and joint development of resources, there is obvious advantage in having the consultative process begin at the planning stage so as to facilitate concurrent formulation of policy.

(c) There will be in the future — as in the past — cases where, by reason of what is deemed an overriding need for speed or secrecy, the process of consultation must be telescoped. This is a fact of life which must be recognized, but the judgment in such circumstances should be that of the highest authority.

(d) While all crises are not predictable, many — probably most — can be foreseen as possible. For this reason the process of consultation should provide for continuous exchanges of views between the appropriate authorities of the two governments over the whole range of looming problems, including mutual exposure to any relevant contingency planning.

(e) Consultation should be initiated whenever one of the two governments is in the process of formulating important policies or planning actions which would have an appreciable impact on the other. The responsibility for initiating consultation in such cases rests on the party approaching decision or contemplating action.

(f) Existing mechanisms for consultation should be utilized in order to ensure prompt and continuous access by one government to the other.

(g) Many problems between our two governments are susceptible of solution only through the quiet, private and patient examination of facts in the search for accommodation. It should be regarded as incumbent on both parties during this time-consuming process to avoid, so far as possible, the adoption of public positions which can contribute unnecessarily to public division and difference.

(h) Each government has a responsibility to ensure that its own procedure for intragovernmental consideration of subjects which affect the other country operates promptly, effectively and consistently so as to facilitate the consultative process.

55. We recognize that the kind of consultation which we have described has different implications for our respective governments. These derive primarily from the wide disparity in power and international responsibility which we have already underlined. In consultations with the United States, Canadian authorities must have confidence that the practice of quiet diplomacy is not only neighborly and convenient to the United States but that it is in fact more effective than the alternative of raising a row and being unpleasant in public. By the same token, the United States authorities must be satisfied that, in such consultations,

Canada will have sympathetic regard for the world-wide preoccupations and responsibilities of the United States.

56. Such a regime of consultation is difficult — for both sides — but we are convinced that it is fundamental to the maintenance of healthy relations between our two governments and peoples. We believe it can be most effective in the best interests of both if it is conducted along the above lines.

Toward a More Effective Partnership

57. President Kennedy in his address before members of the two Houses of Parliament in Ottawa on May 17, 1961, said:

> Geography has made us neighbors. History has made us friends. Economics has made us partners. And necessity has made us allies.

A little later, in the same speech, he added:

> Thus ours is the unity of equal and independent nations, cotenants of the same continent, heirs of the same legacy, and fully sovereign associates in the same historic endeavor. . . .

Prime Minister St. Laurent, some years earlier, in a Commencement address in the United States, referred to one of the conditions of the partnership in these terms:

> You in the United States obviously have the power and strength to dominate our country. But you also have the wisdom and the respect for freedom to refrain from exercising that power and that strength. The fact that you respect our freedom, the fact that you treat us as an equal partner, make our country a far more potent ally than any satellite could ever be.

58. Wrapped in such eloquence is the core of the problem. How can two free political communities of such unequal strength, living side by side and with so much in common — though with a strong element of contrast in their cultural heritage — reconcile the facts and expanding opportunities of partnership with the preservation and development of the national identity of each?

59. In the first place, the process of reconciliation is a continuing one; it is never "done." It calls for conscious and sustained effort on both sides and at many levels. It requires a large extension of mutual knowledge of one another's affairs. For one thing, a better and wider understanding is needed in both countries of their respective national characteristics, their political institutions and processes, the trends of public opinion and the development of government policies. Americans and Canadians often assume that they know and understand one another instinctively. This is both untrue and dangerous.

60. It will have been abundantly evident from earlier passages in our report that we are persuaded of the mutual advantage which is to be derived from the

development of a more effective working partnership between our two countries. If such benefits are to be fully realized, it will require on the part of both not only a willingness to exploit acceptable opportunities for joint undertakings but also the willingness of each government to examine existing hindrances to cooperation with a view to their removal.

Mutual Respect for National Jurisdiction

61. It is important that each country should avoid efforts, or apparent efforts, to extend its domestic law into the territory of the other. A case in point — the administration of foreign assets control under the United States Trading with the Enemy Act, as it relates to United States-owned branches and subsidiaries domiciled in Canada, occasionally comes into conflict with the laws, regulations and policies of the Canadian Government. We strongly recommend that the two governments examine promptly the means, through issuance by the United States of a general license or adoption of other appropriate measures, by which this irritant to our relationship may be removed, without encouraging the evasion of United States law by citizens of the United States.

62. Each country should respect scrupulously the other's exercise of its sovereign authority in legislation and the functioning of its judicial system. There are clearly identifiable areas where good fences contribute to good neighborly relations.

Projects for Partnership

63. If such fundamentals be accepted on both sides, then the border need prove no barrier or hindrance to a common approach, as partners, in broad areas of the national lives of the two countries. Indeed, this has already been demonstrated in many ways over many years, for example, in the great joint enterprise of the St. Lawrence Seaway and Power Project and in the agreement for the cooperative development of the water resources of the Columbia River Basin. Four areas where the current possibilities of a similar approach seem to us promising and important are described in the following paragraphs.

Energy

64. We have been impressed by the prospects of mutual benefit which might be realized in closer cooperation and coordination between our two countries in the production and distribution of energy, especially electrical energy. Under appropriate conditions, joint planning and development of resources to that end in various regions would appear to afford promising opportunities. For this reason we recommend early and serious study of such possibilities.

65. We have been led to this conclusion by a number of circumstances in the current and prospective situation:

(a) the high and rapidly rising use of energy in the two countries and its increasing importance to our peoples and in the economic development of the regions in which they live;

(b) recent technological advances, especially in extra-high voltage transmission, which create the potential for substantial future reductions in costs;

(c) the economic advantages to both countries of disregarding the boundary for energy purposes, that is, in the development and distribution of energy on a regional north-south basis where this is to the mutual advantage. Such an approach permits the "economies of scale" to operate to reduce costs; planning can be coordinated and efficient; and mutually profitable interchanges and interconnections can be effected, taking advantage of the different time zones and the diversity of climatic conditions which can produce important savings.

66. In any such study, and in any subsequent cooperative arrangements worked out between the competent authorities in the two countries, a number of important points would have to be kept in mind:

(a) the differing situation as between the various sources of energy and their changing importance relative to one another;

(b) the importance of having regard to whole north-south regions at an early stage in the design and development of networks;

(c) the need to establish jointly in advance that significant net benefits would result from joint projects, and that such benefits could be equitably divided;

(d) the wisdom of avoiding situations in which the entities involved in one country become in effect "public utilities" in the other; and,

(e) the protection of the national interests of each country.

67. Primary responsibility for moving ahead, and much of the expertise, particularly in electricity, rests with the system owners — public and private — in the two countries, and much of the authority resides elsewhere, notably within State and Provincial jurisdiction. Nevertheless, we are persuaded that in this area there is opportunity for advantageous cooperative leadership and initiative in the two national governments.

68. We appreciate the variety of differing circumstances which affect the various energy sources in the two countries. There are, for example, special conditions bearing on coal, oil and gas which are not all or equally applicable to electrical energy. Nevertheless, we believe there would be virtue in having a joint look at the energy picture as a whole.

69. We express no opinion as to how such studies can best be undertaken and advanced, whether under the aegis of a joint body or by the coordinated efforts of the appropriate elements and agencies of government in the two countries.

Trade

70. The economies of scale in production and the potential of larger markets justify continuing efforts on both sides to minimize barriers to trade between the two countries. It is to be hoped that the current Kennedy Round negotiations will make significant progress in this direction.

71. Each government should continue to study, for the longer range future, the economic, financial, and political practicability of further progressive reductions in tariffs and other barriers to trade between the two countries with a view to increasing the market for the products of each. This study should go forward on a basis consistent with their obligations under the GATT [General Agreement on Tariffs and Trade] and their common effort to expand and liberalize multilateral trade. There should be frequent consultations on the subject between the two governments. In this connection the possibilities of working out special arrangements of mutual advantage, as was done by the two governments with respect to automobiles and automotive parts, might be worthy of exploration.

Civil Aviation

72. For a variety of historical reasons, the United States-Canada network of air routes and services has failed to keep pace with either the technical development of jet transport or the travel needs of the peoples of the two countries proceeding to and from the other's territory.

73. We recommend that the appropriate authorities of the two countries approach the aviation problem with a view to the development of a continental pattern of air travel which:

(a) would be responsive to the travel requirements of the public of both countries;

(b) would provide for the optimum utilization of modern equipment; and,

(c) would result in opportunity for equitable sharing of air business between Canada and the United States.

Cooperation in Finance

74. The commercial and finanical relationships between Canada and the United States are so extensive and so intimate that each country is bound to be affected if the other finds it necessary to take steps to correct a deficit in its balance of international payments. In a world of convertible currencies, what matters to each country is, of course, the maintenance of an appropriate balance of payments with the world as a whole. But the impact on the other country of the specific measures taken by either to correct a disequilibrium is bound to be affected by the structure of their bilateral trade and financial relationships. Thus, the fact that two-thirds or more of Canada's trade is with the United States and that Canada has a very large current account deficit with the United States makes it inevitable that any measures Canada finds necessary to reduce its overall current account deficit if it gets into exchange difficulties will bear particularly heavily on the United States. On the other hand, if the United States finds it necessary on occasion to limit its exports of capital, or if it should ever find it necessary to curtail imports, the impact of such measures would, in the absence of some special alleviation, fall with particular severity on Canada which is a large importer of capital from the United States and with which it does most of its trade.

75. The very close though asymmetrical relationships referred to in the previous paragraph appear to involve two consequences. The first is that each country, in determining from time to time what policies to follow with regard to its balance of payments with the outside world, should have clearly in mind its bilateral balance of payments with the other, so that the impact on the other of any corrective action which may be needed is recognized. The second is that each side should keep the other fully informed of developments in its balance of payments and the underlying reasons for them, so as to provide opportunity for working out constructive and imaginative solutions to difficulties that may from time to time arise in their bilateral trade and payments flows. In this connection we commend the recent agreement to establish a joint committee to maintain continuous watch over the situation.

76. Thus we see compelling reasons — based upon past experience and discernible opportunities for the future — actively to seek the strengthening of the

partnership, both by removing impediments to its better functioning and by exploring other areas in which the two countries can work together to their mutual advantage.

Some Guiding Principles

77. From the foregoing analysis we conclude that it is feasible to formulate certain guiding principles. These we set out in the following paragraphs.

78. The need is clear for our two governments to confirm the practice of intimate, timely and continuing consultation on all matters of common concern, at the appropriate level, employing such machinery and procedures as are most effective for this purpose.

79. As partners in NATO, and sharing responsibility for the air defense of this continent, Canada and the United States have similar policies and share important common obligations. In the conduct and development of their unique bilateral relationship, however, the two countries must have regard for the wider responsibilities and interests of each in the world and their obligations under various treaties and other arrangements to which each is party.

80. This principle has a particular bearing upon our affairs in relation to the heavy responsibilities borne by the United States, generally as the leader of the free world and specifically under its network of mutual defense treaties around the globe. It is important and reasonable that Canadian authorities should have careful regard for the United States Government's position in this world context and, in the absence of special Canadian interests or obligations, avoid, so far as possible, public disagreement especially upon critical issues. This is not to say that the Canadian Government should automatically and uniformly concur in foreign policy decisions taken by the United States Government. Different estimates of efficacy and appropriateness of degree of risk generate honest differences of opinion among the closest allies. The Canadian Government cannot renounce its right to independent judgment and decision in the "vast external realm." On its part, Canada has special relations and obligations, some of which the United States does not share but of which it should take account, in particular with Great Britain and the other states of the Commonwealth, with France, and with certain other nations.

81. It is in the abiding interest of both countries that, wherever possible, divergent views between the two governments should be expressed and if possible resolved in private, through diplomatic channels. Only a firm mutual resolve and the necessary practical arrangements to keep the totality of the relationship in good and friendly working order can enable our countries to avoid needless frictions and minimize the consequences of disagreement.

82. It is hardly necessary to add that, in these remarks concerning public statements by government spokesmen, we intend of course no reference to all those whose freedom to criticize official policies at home and abroad is clear and equally cherished in both countries.

83. There should be a conscious effort by the authorities on both sides to accept and extend a common approach to additional areas of the two economies

where it can be demonstrated that joint undertakings are to the national advantage of each as well as to the common advantage of both.

84. There is another important principle. This is that the United States should be continuously alert, throughout the entire process of policy-formulation and decision-making, to the potential impact on Canada of United States' actions, especially in the economic area. By this we intend particularly commercial policy — tariffs and quantitative restrictions — and fiscal and monetary affairs. While the necessity for such constant alertness derives primarily from the economic inequality of the two countries, coupled with their close interconnection, it derives also from the different characteristics of the two economies. Decisions taken in this area by the United States can have a disproportionately heavy incidence upon Canada. This vulnerability to United States economic policies is increased by the persistent Canadian deficit on trading account with the United States and the fact that Canada is far more dependent on exports — 16 percent of GNP as compared with 4 percent for the United States. Obviously the United States cannot renounce concern for the protection of its own economic interests, but it should maintain a conscious awareness of Canadian interests to ensure that they are not violated or prejudiced through inadvertence or ignorance.

85. Since Canadian actions and decisions can also seriously harm the United States, there should be a sense of reciprocal obligation on Canadian authorities to give consideration in advance to the potential impact on United States' interests of decisions and actions contemplated in the economic and financial fields.

86. By conclusion, we find the evidence overwhelmingly in favor of a specific regime of consultation between the two governments. We are also convinced that there are large opportunities for mutual advantage in the extension of the partnership of our two countries. Not only is the relationship unique but Canadian-American mutual involvement and interdependence grow daily more evident. For our part, we are satisfied that the process can be as mutually rewarding as it is inevitable.

FOREIGN POLICY FOR CANADIANS, 1970†

Why Review Foreign Policy

Canada emerged from the Second World War on the leading edge of an internationalism which sought to create a rational world order out of the ruins of "isms" of the thirites. Canada hoped then that its future security and well-being could be safeguarded through strengthening international institutions — especially in the United Nations family of organizations — which were to be the basis for maintaining world peace and achieving human progress.

When it became apparent that many of these co-operative efforts were endangered by the rigidities of the cold war, viable alternatives to the new world order were needed. The threat of Communist armed aggression — first against a weakened Western Europe, later in Korea and Indochina — led to the establishment of the North Atlantic Treaty Organization (NATO), then the North American Air Defence Command (NORAD) and other security arrangements. These and subsequent peace-keeping operations, and a rather important group of organizations specifically assembled for financial, trade, development and social purposes, relied for their effectiveness on varying degrees of international co-operation.

Canada's foreign policy was then largely concerned with objectives and obligations arising out of active membership in multilateral organizations. Canada's international role, its influence, its self-expression were seen in the context of those intergovernmental bodies. It was all part of the most striking phenomenon of the post-war period — the increasing interdependence of events and nations.

Canadians as Internationalists

During the post-war decades, Canada and Canadians acquired a certain taste and talent for international activities of various kinds. Canadians took pride in the skill with which their political leaders, their military and civilian peacekeepers, their trade and other negotiators conducted the nation's business abroad. The international reputation Canada had then was earned at a time when Canada enjoyed a preferred position and a wide range of opportunities, as one of the few developed countries that had emerged from the Second World War materially unscathed and indeed politically, militarily and economically stronger than ever. It was a position that was bound to be affected by changes in the world power structure resulting from the post-war rehabilitation of larger countries, including friends and former enemies. The Canadian people had broken out of the isolationism of the thirties and come to the realization that there was an interesting and important world outside where Canada should have a distinctive contribution to make. Canadians developed and exercised a substantial interest in international organizations. They moved in ever-growing numbers into the less-developed parts of the world as technicians, teachers and

†Department of External Affairs, *Foreign Policy for Canadians* (Ottawa, 1970), 5-30.

administrators; they encouraged and accepted foreign scholars, students and trainees to enter Canadian institutions of education; Canadians travelled far and wide in search of business, service and pleasure. The emergence of former colonies as free nations offered new challenges to religious groups, private aid societies, universities, humanitarian groups generally.

This varied activity by Canadians has stimulated and substantiated a deep-seated desire in this country to make a distinctive contribution to human betterment. It manifests itself in the various pressures which have been exerted on successive Governments to do more in such international fields as peacekeeping, development aid and cultural cross-fertilization. This altruistic aspiration seems to be shared generally across Canada. What Canada can hope to accomplish in the world must be viewed not only in the light of Canadian aspirations, needs and wants but in terms of what is, from time to time, attainable.

The Changing World

From the outset of this policy review it was apparent that some of the safe assumptions of the post-war decades were crumbling away as the world changed:

— International institutions which had been the focus and instrument of much of Canada's policy were troubled by internal divergences and by criticism about their continuing relevance in new world situations.

— The world powers could no longer be grouped in clearly identifiable ideological camps, groupings which had conditioned political and military thinking since the War.

— Long-standing human problems in the Third World — which in the post-war euphoria seemed manageable in due course — had crystallized into irresistible demands and expectations for international action to deal with development needs and to put an end to race discrimination.

— Science and technology had produced in spectacular array powerful weapons, computerized industry, instant communications, space travel; but in sum these marvellous innovations raced far ahead of political, economic and social institutions, magnifying the problems they faced and rendering them inadequate in some cases.

— Social attitudes had changed. Civil disobedience and the use of violence became the commonplace of the new confrontation politics. The basic values of most societies were called into question — perhaps nowhere more harshly than in North America.

Canada's Changing Outlook

By the mid-sixties Canada had its own set of difficulties. An over-heated economy, regional differences and disparities, the reverberations of the quiet revolution in Quebec, all added to the stress and strain on Canada's national fibre. They affected the way Canadians saw themselves and the world around them.

Developments in the outside world — the changes already noted — raised questions and doubts in the minds of some Canadians about Canada's foreign policy. Criticism tended to gather in a hard lump of frustration — accentuated by the war in Vietnam — about having to live in the shadow of the United

States and its foreign policy, about the heavy dependence of Canada's economy on continuing American prosperity, and about the marked influence of that large and dynamic society on Canadian life in general.

Canada's "traditional" middle-power role in the world seemed doomed to disappear after the United Nations ordeal in the Congo, in the face of peacekeeping frustrations in Vietnam, following the collapse of the UN Emergency Force (UNEF) in 1967. Western Europe had not only fully recovered from the war but was taking steps toward integration that put strain on transatlantic ties and, combined with changes in the Communist world, called into question the need for continuing Canadian participation in NATO. The renaissance of French Canada, with its direct consequences for relations with French-speaking countries, raised further questions about the fundamentals of Canadian foreign policy.

Policy had not remained static since the war; it had been adjusting to the changing world and to Canada's changing needs. It had served the country well. But an empirical process of adjustment cannot be continued indefinitely. There comes a time for renewal and in 1968 the Government saw that for Canada's foreign policy the time had arrived.

Role and Influence

At times in the past, public disenchantment with Canada's foreign policy was produced in part by an over-emphasis on role and influence obscuring policy objectives and actual interests. It is a risky business to postulate or predict any specific role for Canada in a rapidly evolving world situation. It is even riskier — certainly misleading — to base foreign policy on an assumption that Canada can be cast as the "helpful fixer" in international affairs. That implies, among other things, a reactive rather than active concern with world events, which no longer corresponds with international realities or the Government's approach to foreign policy.

There is no natural, immutable or permanent role for Canada in today's world, no constant weight of influence. Roles and influence may result from pursuing certain policy objectives — and these spin-offs can be of solid value to international relations — but they should not be made the aims of policy. To be liked and to be regarded as good fellows are not ends in themselves; they are a reflection of but not a substitute for policy.

Foreign Policy in Essence

In undertaking this review the Government has been constantly reminded of its need and responsibility to choose carefully aims, objectives and priorities in sufficiently long and broad terms to ensure that essential Canadian interests and values are safeguarded in a world situation where rapid and even radical changes can be anticipated as normal rather than exceptional conditions. Canada, like other states, must act according to how it perceives its aims and interest. External activities should be directly related to national policies pursued within Canada, and serve the same objectives. Diplomatic relations are maintained and strengthened for a wide variety of reasons — among others, trade expansion, collective security, cultural contact, co-operation in development assistance, exchanges in science and technology. Such relationships have to be kept under review to ensure that they continue to serve Canada's objectives effectively. Those may change as both Canada and the world change. In essence, foreign policy is the product of the Government's progressive definition and pursuit of national aims and interests in the national environment. It is the extension abroad of national policies.

National Aims

The ultimate interest of any Canadian Government must be the progressive development of the political, economic and social well-being of all Canadians now and in future. This proposition assumes that for most Canadians their "political" well-being can only be assured if Canada continues in being as an independent, democratic and sovereign state. Some Canadians might hold that Canada could have a higher standard of living by giving up its sovereign independence and joining the United States. Others might argue that Canadians would be better off with a lower standard of living but with fewer limiting commitments and a greater degree of freedom of action, both political and economic. For the majority, the aim appears to be to attain the highest level of prosperity consistent with Canada's political preservation as an independent state. In the light of today's economic interdependence, this seems to be a highly practical and sensible evaluation of national needs.

Basic National Aims

In developing policies to serve the national interests, the Government has set for itself basic national aims which, however described, embrace three essential ideas:

— that Canada will continue secure as an independent political entity;

— that Canada and all Canadians will enjoy enlarging prosperity in the widest possible sense;

— that all Canadians will see in the life they have and the contribution they make to humanity something worthwhile preserving in identity and purpose.

These ideas encompass the main preoccupations of Canada and Canadians today: national sovereignty, unity and security; federalism, personal freedom and parliamentary democracy; national identity, bilingualism and multicultural expression; economic growth, financial stability, and balanced regional development; technological advance, social progress and environmental improvement; human values and humanitarian aspirations.

Pursuit of Canadian Aims

Much of Canada's effort internationally will be directed to bringing about the kinds of situation, development and relationship which will be most favourable to the furtherance of Canadian interests and values. As long as the international structure has the nation state as its basic unit, the Government will be pursuing its aims, to a substantial degree, in the context of its relationships with foreign governments. While Canada's interests might have to be pursued in competition or even in conflict with the interests of other nations, Canada must aim at the best attainable conditions, those in which Canadian interests and values can thrive and Canadian objectives be achieved.

Canada has less reason than most countries to anticipate conflicts between its national aims and those of the international community as a whole. Many Canadian policies can be directed toward the broad goals of that community without unfavourable reaction from the Canadian public. Peace in all its manifestations, economic and social progress, environmental control, the development of international law and institutions — these are international goals which fall squarely into that category. Other external objectives sought by Canada, very directly related to internal problems (agricultural surpluses, energy management, need for resource conservation), are frequently linked to the attainment of international accommodations (cereals agreements, safeguards for the peaceful uses of atomic energy, fisheries conventions) of general benefit to the world community. Canada's action to advance self-interest often coincides with the kind of worthwhile contribution to international affairs that most Canadians clearly favour.

Canada's foreign policy, like all national policy, derives its content and validity from the degree of relevance it has to national interests and basic aims. Objectives have to be set not in a vacuum but in the context in which they will be pursued, that is, on the basis of reasonable assumption of what the future holds. The task of the Government is to ensure that these alignments and interrelationships are kept up-to-date and in proper perspective. In no area of policy-making is this whole process more formidable than foreign policy.

Shaping Policy

The world does not stand still while Canada shapes and sets in motion its foreign policy. The international scene shifts rapidly and sometimes radically, almost from day to day. Within one week an assassination in Cyprus, a decision about another country's import policy, a coup in Cambodia, an important top-level meeting of two German leaders, a dispute in Niamey — while not all such events affect Canadian interest, some have done so, others will.

It is much the same on the domestic scene. An oil-tanker foundering in Canadian territorial waters endangers marine life and underlines once again the need for international co-operation to deal effectively with pollution of the sea as regards both technical remedies and legal responsibilities. A wheat surplus in Western Canada poses very difficult domestic problems and externally requires action to get effective international co-operation in marketing and production policies. A criminal trial in Montreal is considered in a friendly country to have race undertones and causes concern for Canadians and for Canadian business firms there.

The scene shifts constantly, foreign and domestic factors interact in various ways at the same time; they appear quickly, often unexpectedly, as threats or challenges, opportunities or constraints, affecting the pursuit of Canadian national aims. National policies, whether to be applied internally or externally, are shaped by such factors. The trick is to recognize them for what they are and to act accordingly.

The problem is to produce a clear, complete picture from circumstances which are dynamic and ever-changing. It must be held in focus long enough to judge what is really essential to the issue under consideration, to enable the Government to act on it decisively and effectively. That picture gets its shape from information gathered from a variety of sources — public or official — and sifted and analyzed systematically. The correct focus can only be achieved if all the elements of a particular policy question can be looked at in a conceptual framework which represents the main lines of national policy at home and abroad.

The Framework

Broadly speaking, the totality of Canada's national policy seeks to:
- — foster economic growth
- — safeguard sovereignty and independence
- — work for peace and security
- — promote social justice
- — enhance the quality of life
- — ensure a harmonious natural environment.

These six main themes of national policy form as well the broad framework of foreign policy. They illustrate the point that foreign policy is the extension abroad of national policy. The shape of foreign policy at any given time will be determined by the pattern of emphasis which the Government gives to the six policy themes. It is shaped as well by the constraints of the prevailing situation, at home and abroad, and inevitably by the resources available to the Government at any given time.

Policy Themes

The principal ingredients of Canadian foreign policy are contained in the following descriptions of the six policy themes:

— *Fostering Economic Growth* is primarily a matter of developing the Canadian economy, seeking to ensure its sustained and balanced growth. This theme embraces a wide range of economic, commercial and financial objectives in the foreign field, such as: promotion of exports; management of resources and energies; trade and tariff agreements; loans and investments; currency stabilization and convertibility; improved transportation, communications and technologies generally; manpower and expertise through immigration; tourism. It involves varying degrees of co-operation in a group of international institutions — e.g., the International Monetary Fund (IMF), the General Agreement on Tariffs and Trade (GATT), the Organization for Economic Co-operation and Development (OECD), the Group of Ten — vital to the maintenance of a stable and prosperous economic community in the world.

— *Safeguarding Sovereignty and Independence* is largely a matter of protecting Canada's territorial integrity, its constitutional authority, its national identity and freedom of action. Sovereignty and independence are challenged when foreign fishermen illegally intrude into Canadian territorial waters, when Canadian constitutional arrangements are not fully respected by other governments. They may be affected by external economic and social influences (mainly from the United States); or qualified by international agreement, when Canada in its own interest co-operates internationally in trade (GATT) or financial institutions (IMF), for example. Sovereignty may have to be reaffirmed from time to time, especially when territorial disputes or misunderstandings arise, and should be reinforced by insistence on compliance with Canadian laws and regulations and by employing adequate means of surveillance and control to deal with infringement. Above all, sovereignty should be used to protect vital Canadian interests and promote Canada's aims and objectives.

— *Working for Peace and Security* means seeking to prevent war or at least to contain it. It includes identifying the kind of contribution which Canada can usefully make to the solution of the complex problems of maintaining peace, whether through defence arrangements, arms control, peacekeeping, the relaxation of tensions, international law, or improvement of bilateral relations. In essence, peace and security policies are designed to prevent, minimize or control violence in international relations, while permitting peaceful change.

— *Promoting Social Justice* includes policies of a political, economic and social nature pursued in a broad area of international endeavour and principally today with international groupings (the United Nations, the Commonwealth, la Francophonie). It means, in the contemporary world, focusing attention on two major international issues — race conflict and development assistance. It is also related to international efforts: to develop international law, standards and codes of conduct; and to keep in effective working order a wide variety of international organizations — e.g., the UN Development Programme (UNDP), the UN Conference on Trade and Development (UNCTAD), the International Development Association (IDA), the Development Assistance Committee (DAC).

— *Enhancing the Quality of Life* implies policies that add dimension to economic growth and social reform so as to produce richer life and human fulfilment for all Canadians. Many of these policies are internal by nature, but in the external field they involve such activities as cultural, technological and scientific exchanges which, while supporting other foreign objectives, are designed to yield a rewarding life for Canadians and to reflect clearly Canada's bilingual and multicultural character. Part of this reward lies in the satisfaction that Canada in its external activities is making a worthwhile contribution to human betterment.

— *Ensuring a Harmonious Natural Environment* is closely linked with quality of life and includes policies to deal not only with the deterioration in the natural environment but with the risks of wasteful utilization of natural resources. Implicit are policies: to rationalize the management of Canada's resources and energies; to promote international scientific co-operation and research on all the problems of environment and modern society; to assist in the development of international measures to combat pollution in particular; to ensure Canadian access to scientific and technological information in other countries.

Interrelationships

The conceptual framework serves particularly well to emphasize the various interrelationships which enter into the consideration and conduct of Canada's foreign policy. These include, for example:

— the relationship between domestic and foreign elements of policy designed to serve the same national objective (The utilization of energies and resources in Canada is related to international agreements on their export, both elements being pursued to promote economic growth.);

— the relationship between basic national aims and intermediate objectives for furthering their attainment (National unity is related to the external expressions of Canada's bilingualism and multicultural composition.);

— the relationship between activities designed to serve one set of objectives and those serving other national objectives (Cultural and information programmes are related to trade promotion activities.);

— the relationship between and among the six main thrusts of policy (Ensuring the natural environment is related to enhancing the quality of life; both are related to the fostering of economic growth; which in turns relates to the promotion of social justice.)

Hard Choices

Most policy decisions — certainly the major ones — involve hard choices which require that a careful balance be struck in assessing the various interests, advantages and other policy factors in play. As in so many fields of human endeavour, trade-offs are involved. For example:

— In striving to raise national income through economic growth, policies may be pursued which adversely affect the natural environment by increasing the hazards of pollution or by depleting resources too rapidly. Such policies might also cause infringement of social justice (because of inflation, for example) and impair the quality of life for individual Canadians.

— In seeking social justice for developing nations, through trade policies which offer them concessions or preferences, the Government's policy may adversely affect the domestic market opportunities for certain Canadian industries, or it might involve parallel policies to curtail or reorient their production.

— Similarly, if international development assistance programmes require a substantial increase in Canadian resources allocated, the trade-off may be some reduction of resources allocated to other governmental activity, like the extension of Canadian welfare programmes or the attack on domestic pollution.

— Reductions in military expenditure may lead to results difficult to gauge as regards Canada's capacity to ensure its security, to safeguard its sovereignty and independence, and to make a useful contribution to the maintenance of peace; though resources might thereby be freed for other activities.

— The most difficult choices of the future may result from seeking to recapture and maintain a harmonious natural environment. Such policies may be essential to enhance the quality of life (if not ensure human survival) but they may well require some curtailment of economic growth and freedom of enterprise and a heavy allocation of resources from both public and private sources.

Criteria for Choosing Policy

How then is the choice to be made?

First: The Government could arbitrarily decide that it wants to emphasize specific policy themes like Peace or Independence or the Quality of Life in order to create a certain political image at home and abroad. This choice would be based not on any particular forecast of future events, nor on an assessment of the contribution which specific policy themes would make to the attainment of national aims, but on the pursuit of political philosophy largely in a vacuum. Applied alone, this criterion could easily produce unrealistic results.

Second: The Government could base its policy emphasis solely on what Canada's essential needs might be in various situations forecast. This would be largely a matter of deciding which of the policy themes would best serve to attain national aims in such situations. This approach would produce a foreign policy largely reactive to external events, and more often than not to those which posed foreseeable threats to Canadian interests. If this criterion were allowed to dominate, it could be very restrictve on policy choices because forecasts would be more concerned with constraints than opportunities, hampering the Government's initiative and freedom of manoeuvre.

Third: Taking some account of forecasts, and especially the very obvious constraints, the Government could seek to emphasize those foreign policy activities which Canada could do best in the light of all the resources available, and under whichever policy theme such action might most appropriately fall.

In practice, these criteria may have to be applied from time to time in some kind of combination. In specific situations this might produce the best balance of judgment. Nevertheless, the Government regards the three criteria as optional approaches to ranking and has selected the third one as a main determinant of its choice of policy emphasis. The Government's preference stems in part from the conclusion that, since forecasting in the field of external affairs is likely to be more reliable in the shorter term, it will be desirable to assign more weight to forecasts when considering relatively short-term programmes rather than when setting the broad lines of policy. The Government is firmly convinced that Canada's most effective contribution to international affairs in future will derive from the judicious application abroad of talents and skills, knowledge and experience, in fields where Canadians excel or wish to excel (agriculture, atomic energy, commerce, communications, development assistance, geological survey, hydro-electricity, light-aircraft manufacture, peacekeeping, pollution control, for example). This reflects the Government's determination that Canada's available resources — money and manpower, ideas and expertise — will be deployed and used to the best advantage, so that Canada's impact on international relations and on world affairs generally will be commensurate with the distinctive contribution Canadians wish to make in the world.

Foreign policy can be shaped, and is shaped, mainly by the value judgments of the Government at any given time. But it is also shaped by the possibilities that are open to Canada at any given time — basically by the constraints or opportunities presented by the prevailing international situation. It is shaped too by domestic considerations, by the internal pressures exerted on the Government, by the amount of resources which the Government can afford to deploy.

Perspectives for the Seventies

All government decisions on policy questions depend in some degree on the forecasting of events or situations likely to arise in future, whether short- or long-term. Forecasting in a field as vast and varied as foreign affairs is bound to be difficult, complicated and full of uncertainties. The variables of politics are in the broad arena of international affairs exaggerated, multiplied, diversified and often intensified in their impact. The risks of faulty or short-lived predictions run high and are compounded in an era of swiftly evolving events and technologies, even though some technological advances can be used to improve the process of forecasting. Forecasts for foreign policy purposes of necessity must be generalized. They rest on the facts and interpretations of international developments which are both subject to correction and change, and susceptible of widely differing deductions.

All this produces complex difficulties of targeting for any government wishing to set its objectives and assign priorities for policies intended to deal with specific issues arising, preferably before they become critical. The Canadian Government, moreover, must assess its various policy needs in the context of two inescapable realities, both crucial to Canada's continuing existence:

— Internally, there is the multi-faceted problem of maintaining national unity. It is political, economic and social in nature; it is not confined to any one province, region or group of citizens; it has constitutional, financial and cultural implications. While most of its manifestations have a heavy bearing on Canada's external affairs — some have already had sharp repercussions on Canada's international relations — in essence they are questions whose answers are to be sought and found within Canada and by Canadians themselves.

— Externally, there is the complex problem of living distinct from but in harmony with the world's most powerful and dynamic nation, the United States. The political, economic, social and cultural effects of being side by side, for thousands of miles of land, water and airspace, are clearly to be seen in the bilateral context. In addition the tightly mixed, often magnified and wide-ranging interests, both shared and conflicting, bring Canada into contact with the United States in many multilateral contexts. It is probably no exaggeration to suggest that Canada's relations almost anywhere in the world touch in one way or another on those of its large neighbour. This has both advantages and disadvantages for Canada.

The many dilemmas of the Canada-United States relationships, combined with — because they are linked in many ways — the no-less-complicated issues of national unity at home, have created for Canada a multi-dimensional problem of policy orientation and emphasis which few nations have faced in such an acute form. This many-sided problem raises some fundamental questions, for example:

— What are the implications of sharing the North American continent with a super-state?

— What kinds of policy should Canada pursue to safeguard its sovereignty, independence and distinct identity?

— What policies will serve to strengthen Canada's economy without impairing political independence?

— How can foreign policy reflect faithfully the diversities and particularities of the Canadian national character?

It was these questions and others in the same vein which ran like threads through the foreign policy review. They are reflected in a variety of ways in the policy conclusions now being presented to the Canadian people in this set of papers.

Power Relationships and Conflicts

Despite the trends toward a relaxation of East-West tensions, most of the available evidence suggests that Europe in the seventies will continue to be divided, with Germany split as two partly competing entities. This will be a source of strain and potential conflict, even though in Eastern Europe there is likely to be a slow evolution toward more liberal Communism, still under Soviet control however. Accordingly, security will remain one of the fundamental concerns of all European states and will affect almost every aspect of the continent's affairs. The relative stability of the past 20 years is likely to continue since the United States and the Soviet Union both seem convinced of the need to avoid nuclear war, whether by miscalculation or by escalation. The super-power competition in the development and deployment of offensive and defensive strategic weapons systems and nuclear warheads will continue but, if the bilateral U.S.A.-U.S.S.R. talks on strategic arms limitations were to succeed the pace of the arms race would slacken, with proportionate reductions in risks and tensions. Some of these potential benefits may be lost or misplaced through the proliferation of nuclear and conventional armaments or through failure to find the political and economic accommodation needed to allay perceived threats to vital security interests on both sides.

In any event, the Soviet Union will continue to be preoccupied by its relations with China and the Soviet interest in accommodations with other countries may reflect the degree to which the Chinese threat is considered to be credible to the Soviet Union. Any fighting between these two powers will probably be confined to frontier clashes of limited duration and scale, though the strategic nuclear threat posed by China will require a regular assessment of the strategic balance as regards China, the Soviet Union and the United States. Security in Asia may largely depend on the future attitudes and actions of China, whose place in the world power picture is not likely to be fully clarified until China emerges from its isolation, at least partly self-imposed. Its triangular relationship with India and Pakistan, together with their unresolved disputes, provides a source of potential instability. However, United States disengagement from the conflict in Vietnam, plus serious efforts at reconciliation, could bring about better relations between China and the United States. The eventual participation of China in world affairs — in disarmament talks and at the United Nations, for example — will reflect more accurately the world power balance and, at the same time, produce new problems.

There are likely to be significant adjustments in global relationships attributable to the emergence of new great powers, notably Japan and Germany.

The success of the European communities — the European Economic Community (EEC), the European Coal and Steel Community (ECSC) and the European Atomic Energy Community (EURATOM) — has given the countries of Western Europe increased stability and prosperity and enhanced their international influence.

Because it is in the vital interests of the super-powers to contain sources of conflict there, Europe is likely to remain for some time an area of relative peace and stability. In other geographical areas the general situation is very fluid and political instability will continue to be widespread, though to some extent localized and separate as to cause and effect. There could be prolonged difficulty in reaching an early and satisfactory settlement in Vietnam, for example, and the possibility of subversive activities, communal strife and perhaps guerilla warfare in other Southeast Asian countries. The Middle East situation shows no promise of early solution, and could even deteriorate. In Latin America, more political coups, and perhaps limited conflicts between states, are probable. In southern Africa, racial tension is likely to aggravate in the form of terrorism and sabotage since the remaining white regimes seem determined to persist in their racist policies.

Canada cannot expect to exercise alone decisive influence on the kinds of international conflict implicit in these forecasts, especially those involving larger powers. Nevertheless, there is plenty of room for international co-operation and a continuing Canadian contribution to bringing about a relaxation of tensions, encouraging arms control and disarmament, improving East-West relations, maintaining stable deterrence. There could be no further international demands for Canadian participation in peacekeeping operations — especially in regional conflicts. The Government is determined that this special brand of Canadian expertise will not be dispersed or wasted on ill-conceived operations but employed judiciously where the peacekeeping operation and the Canadian contribution to it seem likely to improve the chances for lasting settlement.

American Impact on Canada's Economy and Other Economic Developments

On the assumption that reasonable civil order is preserved in the United States and that such international involvements as the Vietnam war are scaled down and avoided in future, the economic and technological ascendancy of the United States will undoubtedly continue during the next decade, although it will be tempered by the economic integration of Europe and the industrial growth of Japan. This ascendancy will continue to have heavy impact on Canada, with political, economic and social implications. The dependence of Canadian private industry and some government programmes on United States techniques and equipment (not to mention capital) will continue to be a fact of life. United States markets for Canadian energy resources and more advanced manufacturing goods will be of growing significance to the Canadian economy. Increasingly, the Canada-United States economic relationship will be affected by agreements between governments and arrangements by multinational corporations and trade unions.

While such developments should be beneficial for Canada's economic growth, the constant danger that sovereignty, independence and cultural identity may be impaired will require a conscious effort on Canada's part to keep the whole situation under control. Active pursuit of trade diversification and technological co-operation with European and other developed countries will be needed to provide countervailing factors. Improvements in United States relations with the Soviet Union and China — which would seem quite possible within the decade — would enhance Canada's peace and security but would also reduce trading advantages which Canada now enjoys with Eastern Europe and China. In general, United States developments and policies are bound to have profound effects on Canada's position during the seventies, even though there is no reason to believe that the United States Government would consider intervening directly in Canadian affairs.

National incomes will continue to increase at a constant and rapid rate in developed countries. However, there could be disturbances in the interrelated fields of finance, trade and economic activity generally. Individually, countries will probably experience balance-of-payments and other crises. There is a continuing temptation to autarkic policies which could be very unsettling to the varying patterns of trade.

Technological advances can be expected to produce rapidly-changing evolution in the world economic situation. The internationalization of industry, largely in the form of multinational corporations, appears to be a firm feature of the future economic scene and one which governments generally may have to grapple with more consciously and more frequently in future. The international machinery and internal arrangements within the major industrial countries should be able to prevent a major economic crisis from occurring, but developments of sufficient magnitude and duration to disturb Canada seriously could take place. The Canadian Government has a clear interest in sustaining the effectiveness of the international agencies concerned, and in maintaining close relations with governments in the key countries with a view to encouraging the right kinds of policy.

Canada must earn its living in a tough and complicated world. Perhaps the hardest choice in this area of policy — one which arises frequently out of today's economic realities — will be to maintain a proper balance of interest and advantage between Canada's essential needs in ensuring health and growth in its economy and Canada's determination to safeguard its sovereignty and independence. Nor are these necessarily in conflict at all points, for economic growth is essential to sovereignty and independence.

In developing the complex of vital relationships between Canada and the United States, Canadians must choose very carefully if they are to resolve satisfactorily the conflicts which do arise between maintaining their high standard of living and preserving their political independence. They can have both. In an era of heavy demand for energy and other resources, the cards are by no means stacked in one hand.

The Rich-Poor Nation Imbalance

The frustration of developing countries during the next decade will increase as they feel more acutely the limitations of their own technological and material progress, compared with that of industrialized countries. Their sense of impotence to gain quickly and effectively a more equitable distribution of needed resources will become more bitter if the signs of flagging interest and disillusionment on the part of more-developed countries are not reversed. The frustration is likely to manifest itself in various ways. Developing countries will increasingly set aside their political differences to form regional blocs that will urge and put pressure on developed countries to adopt policies that will accommodate the needs of developing countries. If these efforts fail, or do not succeed as quickly as the developing countries hope, recriminations, racial tension and, in some cases, political and economic reprisals against the governments, private investors and nationals of the more-developed countries are likely to increase in magnitude.

The emphasis of development efforts during the coming decade will probably be on human development, including education, social change and control of population. These in turn will lead to a greater awareness of the outside world and a greater appetite for quick change. In addition, a shift of emphasis can be expected from direct development assistance to a range of more sophisticated methods of effecting resource transfers to developing countries and of increasing their export earnings. Industrialized states will be called upon to take meaningful steps to facilitate the access to their markets of products from developing countries, and such other measures as financing unexpected shortfalls in the foreign exchange receipts of developing countries. There is likely to be growing pressure to recognize that a long-term solution to the growing disparity between rich and poor will entail a more rational international division of labour. This in turn would entail developed countries agreeing to make structural changes in their economies that would allow them to absorb the products that developing countries can produce most competitively.

Canada has been contributing to development assistance programmes as long as they have been in existence and increasingly as new nations emerged, in the United Nations, the Commonwealth and la Francophonie. The Government regards development assistance as the major element in its pursuit of Social Justice policies for the benefit of nations less fortunate than Canada. The alternatives in this field are not whether development assistance should be continued on an increasing scale but how and in what amount. Because of their importance, these and other questions are the subject of a separate policy paper in this series. Development assistance is clearly an integral part of Canada's foreign policy and increasingly is being co-ordinated with trade, financial and political policies. It enhances the quality of life not only in receiving countries but in Canada as well, as Canadians gain knowledge, experience and understanding of other people and find opportunities abroad to apply Canadian knowledge and experience to the solution of development problems which rank foremost in the priorities of the world today.

Technological Progress and Environmental Problems

The impact of science and technology on international affairs is becoming increasingly significant and varied as new advances are made. It will be important for Canada to be assured of access to scientific development abroad and to participate in multinational co-operation in scientific undertakings, co-operation which is expanding in scope and complexity. The direct impact of science and technology will bear significantly on such fields as transportation and mass communications, automation and the industrial process, the increasing internationalization of industry, and life in the developing countries (some of which may not be able to make the necessary adjustments with the speed required, widening the gulf between them and the developed countries). The problem of harnessing science and technology to serve human objectives, rather than allowing autonomous scientific and technological advances to dictate the accommodations to be made by man, may prove to be the major challenge of coming decades.

Already modern technology has produced serious social and environmental problems in developed nations and will continue to do so unless remedial measures are taken. This is an argument in favour of vigorous co-ordinated research, an institutionalized sharing of experience in various fields, and co-operative action in sectors of international responsibility. The principal changes in the everyday life of Canadians during the next decade are likely to be caused by scientific and technological changes, and by the social and political consequences which flow from them. There will be increasing demands for action to deal with such consequences by mobilizing science and technology to serve social ends. Legal structures, domestic and international, will have to be developed in tune with those demands.

It is already apparent that the existence of pollution presents complex problems which require effective action at all international and national levels. It is equally apparent that some remedial measures will be costly, complicated and perhaps disrupting to development and will affect the competitiveness of growing national economies. But even the existing threats of ecological imbalance may be among the most dangerous and imminent which the world faces. With about 7 per cent of the world population, North America is consuming about 50 per cent of the world's resources. The rising aspirations of expanding populations will demand that progressively more attention be paid to achieving the optimum economy in the consumption of non-renewable resources. Anti-pollution and resource conservation measures will of necessity have to be linked with others of a social nature designed to deal with acute problems of many kinds arising in the whole human environment — problems of urbanization, industrialization, rural rehabilitation, of improving the quality of life for all age-groups in the population. The problems and their remedies will continue to spill across national boundaries.

Governments at all levels in Canada, Canadians generally both as corporate and individual citizens, are clearly required to act vigorously and effectively in order to deal with a whole range of environmental problems, headed by pollution. There is no question about the high priorities which attach to these urgent problems. They lie squarely within the closely-related policy themes

Quality of Life and Harmonious Natural Environment. The real alternatives which the Government is considering and will have to face increasingly, relate to finding the most effective methods. The international ramifications are obvious, especially in Canada-United States relations, and just as obvious is the need for solid international co-operation.

Social Unrest

Many ideologies will continue in the seventies to exert an influence, perhaps in new forms, but more likely as variants of the contemporary ones. Some of these may become mixed with Canada's internal differences. The most profound effects for the Canadian people could be caused by the continued and widespread questioning of Western value systems — particularly the revolt against the mass-consumption society of North America with its lack of humanism. Powerful influences will undoubtedly come from the United States, but developments in Europe, Latin America and within the Communist group of nations could also have a bearing on the evolution of Canadian society. The implications for foreign policy are varied and not very precise. There might, for example, be some public sentiment in favour of restricting immigration or imposing other controls to ensure national security. Bitter experience of past decades has demonstrated rather conclusively, however, that ideological threats cannot be contained merely by throwing up barriers, military or otherwise. The alternative — and this the Government favours and is pursuing — is to seek as far as possible to pursue policies at home and abroad which convince all Canadians that the Canada they have is the kind of country they want.

The Conduct of Foreign Policy

"One world" is not likely to be achieved in the next decade or so. As suggested earlier, United States relations with either or both the Soviet Union and China could improve, making possible real progress toward more effective instruments for international co-operation, but generally speaking progress in that direction is likely to be slow.

There will probably be a continuing world-wide trend toward regionalism in one form or another. In Western Europe the growth of a sense of shared European identity has expressed itself in a movement toward greater integration, as exemplified by the EEC, which will undoubtedly be carried forward in spite of formidable obstacles. Elsewhere, loose regionalism, ranging from the Association of South-East Asian Nations (ASEAN) in the Pacific to the Organization of American States (OAS) and the Organization of African Unity (OAU), now seems to be an accepted type of grouping for many states but a number of more tightly-knit functional or sub-regional groupings have been growing (Caribbean Free Trade Area (CARIFTA), the regional development banks, or l'Agence de Coopération culturelle et technique for *francophone* countries) adding to earlier international bodies composed of countries with common interests (NATO, Warsaw Pact Organization, OECD and many others).

Nevertheless, international organizations, more or less world-wide in composition or representation, will continue particularly under the United

Nations aegis. The role of those international organizations should gain more substance as there is a greater multilateralization of the policy-formulating process in such fields as communications, outer space, the seabed, anti-pollution, arms control, aid co-ordination, and rationalization of agricultural production. In some fields this need will require new institutional machinery, whereas in others existing institutions can satisfy the requirements, though they will regularly require strengthening or reorientation.

Membership in international organizations is not an end in itself and Canada's effort at all times will be directed to ensuring that those organizations continue to serve a useful purpose to the full extent of their capacity to do so. The trend toward regionalism, on the other hand, poses problems for Canada because its geographical region is dominated by the United States; and because excessive regionalism in other geographical areas complicates Canada's effort to establish effective counterweights to the United States. Nevertheless, the Government sees no alternative to finding such countervailing influences, and this will be reflected in the new policy emphasis on geographical diversification of Canada's interests — more attention to the Pacific and to Latin America, for example — while taking fully into account new multilateral arrangements in Europe.

Challenges Close to Home

If there are no unpleasant political and military surprises on a grand scale, it may not be unrealistic to assume that for the next decade or so the real external challenges to essential Canadian interests could be:

— trade protectionism in the policies of foreign governments or regional groupings which could impair the multilateral trade and payments system developed since the Second World War;

— other developments abroad, including excessive inflation or deflation seriously affecting Canada's economy;

— a sharpening of ideological conflict with a further upsetting influence on Western value systems (the effect of the Vietnam war has been massive in this regard); and/or deteriorating conditions (poverty, race discrimination, archaic institutions) leading to violent disturbances (including civil wars, riots, student demonstrations), which are not only important in themselves but can also be detrimental to trade and investment abroad and to unity and security at home;

— the erosive effect on separate identity and independence of international activities and influences, mainly under American inspiration and direction, in the economic field (multinational corporations, international trade unions). Such activities and influences have yielded many practical benefits, but the degree of restriction they impose on national freedom of action must be constantly and carefully gauged if sovereignty, national unity and separate identity are to be safeguarded.

Coupled with these challenges and also involving international co-operation will be the need to consult closely on the utilization of natural resources, the drive to sustain economic growth and the advances in science and technology, so that they serve to improve rather than impair the quality of life for all Canadians. . . .

THE MULRONEY GOVERNMENT'S POLICY, 1985†

. . . .

Objectives and Policies

It is time to take our bearings and to chart the broad lines of public policy for the coming years. Canadian domestic issues are unavoidably bound up with international developments. Accordingly, the policies we develop — foreign and domestic — must address both Canadian and international realities. The two are inseparable elements of a truly national policy.

In framing our policies, we are pursuing objectives that derive from our values and aspirations:
— unity,
— sovereignty and independence,
— justice and democracy,
— peace and security,
— economic prosperity,
— the integrity of our natural environment.

There are linkages between these objectives; balances must be struck between them. The emphasis we place on them shifts from time to time. At the beginning of the 1930s, for example, our preoccupation was the economy. By 1939, it was security. Today it is both.

A constant of Canadian policy has been the protection of our national sovereignty. We make our own decisions on domestic and foreign policy. The Canadian people rightly demand that their government forcefully advance and protect their interests. But in an age of interdependence, Canadians recognize that sovereignty entails balancing national goals and international responsibilities.

Also constant is the determination of Canadians to make a contribution to a safer, more prosperous and more humane world. . . .

Canada in the World

The dynamics of international life raise issues of direct relevance to our prosperity and security. We cannot isolate ourselves behind barriers; the world will not allow us that luxury. The whole range of international issues — economic, political and security — now extends unavoidably into our daily lives.

The international economy is our economy. None of us is unaffected, not the homeowner renewing a mortgage, not the factory-worker or the small businessman, not the farmer, fisherman or seal hunter, not the large corporation. We are subject to its constraints and open to its opportunities.

Every region of Canada is dependent on exporting to foreign markets. From softwood lumber in British Columbia to oil and gas in Alberta and Saskatchewan, from automotive products in Ontario and transportation equipment in Quebec to lumber and fish in New Brunswick and Nova Scotia, the story is

†Department of External Affairs, *Competitiveness and Security: Directions for Canada's International Relations.* Presented by The Right Honourable Joe Clark, Secretary of State for External Affairs (Ottawa, 1985), 3, 17–36.

everywhere the same. Major industries cannot survive without exports to foreign markets. And those exports mean jobs for millions of Canadians. The only differences are of magnitude. Manitoba, a major producer of wheat, exports 15% of its gross provincial product; while Newfoundland sends fully 70% of its total shipments of goods to foreign markets, including 90% of its major resource products (fish, minerals and newsprint). Prince Edward Island, small as it is, exports to 53 different countries around the world.

Similarly, our security is everyone's security. Conditions abroad touch and change our lives. Tensions between Moscow and Washington, war in the Gulf, a refugee exodus from Indo-China, terrorist murders in London — or Ottawa — all diminish our security and demand our attention. There are few corners of the world which Canadians do not know or care about and few whose circumstances do not affect our welfare.

Shifting international opportunities and constraints demand corresponding changes in Canadian policies. The status quo is not an attractive option and we face some difficult choices. If we are to make the right decisions, we have first to take a hard look at ourselves — our economic competitiveness and our power and influence in international affairs — and at the need to change.

Competitiveness

Our competitiveness in the world economy is vital. It establishes our relative wealth and determines our possibilities for the future. Riding on it are:
— our standard of living;
— the jobs of Canadians in every region of the country;
— the quality of our social system;
— our cultural well-being and our ability to afford national self-expression;
— our influence in the world, as an economic power, as a partner to poorer nations and as a voice on international political and security issues.

Of the seven countries which participate in the annual Economic Summit meetings, Canada is the second most dependent on exports (28 percent of Gross Domestic Product), exceeded only by the Federal Republic of Germany. In contrast, our two main trading partners, the U.S.A. and Japan, depend considerably less on exports. Their domestic markets are much larger than ours and absorb a much greater proportion of their production. In 1984, we exported over $4,000 per Canadian.

Our dependence on trade means that we are economically secure only if we are internationally competitive. It is no simple matter to compare Canada's economic competitiveness with that of other countries. For example, exchange rate movements alone can have a dramatic effect on relative prices and, hence, on competitive positions. (Exchange rates also have a direct impact on real incomes and purchasing power.) But some comparisons can be made and they suggest, despite improvements in the past year or two, that we have some serious causes for concern about the underlying determinants of our international competitiveness.

We were once assured of prosperity because of our privileged position as a world supplier of much sought-after raw materials. But today there is a global oversupply of many raw materials because of reduced demand in the industrialized countries, new production in developing countries and the advent of materials-saving technologies. So our "traditional" comparative advantage in natural resources can no longer be counted on to ensure our prosperity to the extent it once could be. At the same time, our reliance on manufactured exports is increasing steadily.

Between 1970 and 1982, however, our share of manufactured exports to other market economies declined from about 4.8% to 3.6%. The shares of the United States and of the larger European Community countries also declined, but proportionately less than ours, while those of Japan and the rest of the world, on average, increased. For almost all of those years, we had a negative trade balance in manufactured products. The largest components of the deficit were trade in high and medium technology commodities. Although Canadian high technology firms are very export-oriented, the deficit in high technology products continues to widen.

It is a sobering thought that, while in 1968 Canada exported about as much as Japan, today Japan exports twice as much as we do. It is also sobering that, while previously Japan was in a class by itself as an aggressive exporter in certain key sectors, now there are several more — among them South Korea, Hong Kong and Singapore.

Our Productivity

One of the reasons for Japan's strength on world export markets is its remarkable growth in manufacturing productivity. Canada has lagged in this measure of competitiveness. Many factors contribute to productivity such as the character of investment, the effectiveness of management and the efficiency of labour. The quality of supporting public services, education, health, transport, communications and public policies is also an important factor.

Between 1970 and 1981, Canada's growth of manufacturing productivity (defined as GDP per worker) was fifth among the seven Summit countries. For 1982, in the depths of the worst recession since the Thirties, the data indicate a fairly sharp productivity decline. As economic growth resumed in 1983 and 1984, productivity appears to have improved. While Canada's absolute level of productivity, historically, has been quite high, the trend shown here for productivity growth in manufacturing is cause for concern.

From 1960 to 1983, Canada's level of productivity remained below, and grew almost in parallel with, that of the U.S.A. The gap between Canadian and American productivity did not change significantly during this period. Evidence suggests, however, that Japan has drawn ahead of Canada in absolute productivity.

There is also evidence that between 1970 and 1981 Canadian productivity growth in the combined resource category of agriculture, hunting, fishing and forestry was very low. This evidence shows that international competition is becoming stiffer in these traditionally strong Canadian economic sectors.

Our R & D Performance

All industrialized nations and increasing numbers of developing countries see technology and innovation as the most critical elements in today's economic equation. Powerful new technologies are being introduced and exploited in a growing number of countries. These "core" technologies — microelectronics, biotechnology and new materials development — are giving rise to innovations which are increasing productivity and dramatically altering the competitive advantages of countries.

Expenditures on research and development (R & D) are an imperfect indicator of a nation's economic competitiveness, particularly as a good deal of technology is imported. R & D expenditures are, nonetheless, indicative of one aspect of industrial performance and what they suggest is not reassuring.

R & D and the innovative process, as a whole, are crucial factors in achieving improved economic performance. The percentage of our GDP devoted to R & D has recovered to about the same level as it was in 1971, while those of most other major industrialized countries have moved upward significantly. As a proportion of our domestic product, we spend about half of what the U.S., West Germany, Japan and the U.K. do on research. We rank still further down the list of OECD [Organization for Economic Cooperation and Development] countries when our performance in R & D done by industry is compared to that of others. Our record on patent registrations at home and abroad accords with these observations. Relative to other industrialized countries, we have fewer research-intensive industries and we spend less on research. Additionally, there appears to be a disposition in some industries in Canada to look to the government for R & D financing and, in some cases, for R & D itself. . . .

Power and Influence

Nations derive their international influence from the assets at their disposal and their effectiveness in using them; influence is a function both of national assets and of national will. Neither, by itself, is sufficient.

We remain a country of economic weight, the world's ninth largest economy, and one of its premier traders. Our membership in the Economic Summit and in most other key trade and finance groups provides the opportunity to strengthen the multilateral economic system and advance our own economic interests. But if our competitiveness flags, our influence eventually will decline.

Our record on development assistance has been a source of influence, not only because of its generally high quality but also because of the percentage of our GNP which we have devoted to aid. In 1983, we ranked sixth among the 17 OECD aid-giving countries in terms of total Official Development Assistance (ODA). We ranked third among the summit seven countries in terms of ODA as a percentage of GNP, and our ODA contribution was $71 per Canadian.

We are also a country of political consequence, respected by others for our stable parliamentary democracy; our dedication to the rule of law in international relations; our constructive, longstanding support for the UN system; our strong advocacy of arms control and disarmament; our commitment to human rights and environmental integrity; and our training of foreign students and our support of international educational and cultural contacts and exchanges.

Our memberships in such organizations as NATO, the UN, the Commonwealth and la Francophonie are especially valuable assets. Membership in such organizations allows us to influence the policies of larger countries through developing positions which carry the support of all members. As well, our standing with smaller countries rises as we assist them to have their voices heard collectively and, thereby, to carry more weight. In the past ten years, however, allies have sensed less active and creative Canadian participation in some international political institutions.

Our record on peacekeeping has been a particular source of international influence. We have participated in sixteen of seventeen UN peacekeeping operations and in two independent operations in Indochina, at a cumulative cost of approximately $500 million, providing a range of specialized services which few others could. But our capacity to respond is more limited now than it was in the past.

Canada is also a country of military consequence. Our forces are relatively small, but highly professional. We rank 6th among NATO allies in total defence expenditures. Our northern territory and early warning system provide some of the vital strategic depth and reaction time on which the effectiveness and credibility of the American nuclear deterrent depend — on which, in turn, the security of the West depends. Our manpower, national resources and industry remain fully committed to the defence of Western democracy, as we have proved in two world wars at a cost of over 100,000 Canadian dead.

Yet, it is in the area of military capability that our power has been most markedly in decline. We emerged from the Second World War a major military power, with an army of half a million soldiers, a navy of 200 ships, and an airforce comparable to that of Britain. After the war, we set a definite upper limit on our military capability when we ruled ourselves out of the nuclear club, and in the mid-1960s our conventional military power began a steady decline — in respect of both personnel and equipment.

The decline has been most notable in the resources available for surveillance of Canadian air-space and sea approaches, during a period when the security sensitivity of these areas was regarded as relatively low. This assessment has now changed. While air defence capabilities will improve in the next few years, without new policy direction, the capability of Canada's surface maritime forces will continue to decrease until well into the 1990's, even assuming an extension of the Canadian Patrol Frigate (CPF) program.

In recent years, Canada has met its NATO target of a three percent real increase (above inflation) in annual defence spending. In the process, new capital equipment programs, including the acquisition of new long-range patrol aircraft, CF-18's and frigates, have helped to arrest the decline. Some decline was inevitable and normal. Canadians have no history of large forces in peacetime and no tradition of universal military service. Nor are we a continental European state directly under threat from the conventional forces of the Warsaw Pact, or a superpower with global responsibilities. The principal threat to Canada has been from nuclear-armed ballistic missiles, against which the only effective defence has been strategic deterrence. It is now generally recognized, nevertheless, that the decline was allowed to go too far.

The Need for Change

Canada has the capacity to be both powerful economically and influential in the cause of peace and security. There are sectors in which we have done well and in which we should continue to keep pace — agriculture, especially grains, newsprint, pulp, steel and transportation products. There are sectors in which we are at the leading edge of technological development — notably telecommunications and digital technology. But in some areas there is evidence that in various ways our economic competitiveness is slipping. Certainly the competition is getting tougher in virtually every field.

Our competitiveness is measured against international standards, but our ability to compete is in our own hands. We can try to create a climate in which our strong industries will flourish. We can rely less on government protection for those other industries that are not, or cannot be, competitive. We can enhance our human capital through technical education and training. Cooperative education, industry-university research collaboration and the development of centres of excellence and specialization are important factors. And we can remove the unnecessary obstacles to economic growth that have resulted from some government policies over the years.

Our success in advancing the cause of peace and security depends on judgements by us about what we can achieve and how we can achieve it, and judgements by others about our capacity and our seriousness of purpose. Our political and moral standing is high; we can be counted upon to contribute to international progress on the most serious and difficult issues which divide East and West, North and South. Our commitment to collective security remains firm, but we need to examine carefully the ways in which our forces can make their most effective contribution. Our desire to help control and reduce arms is deeply held, but we need to develop ideas that stand up to the most searching scrutiny. Our dedication to helping the world's poorer countries develop their own economies is strong, but we need to look at our government programs and voluntary sector efforts to ensure that they remain effective.

The challenges are real, but so too is the determination of Canadians that Canada make a difference in the world.

Directions for Change

The world is changing and so is Canada. For example, in 1970, when the last full review of Canadian foreign policy was published, the participation rate of women in the workforce was 38%; now it is 52%. In 1970, our interest rates were about 8.0%; now they are about 12.0%. Unemployment then was 5.7%; now it is over 11%. In 1970, most of our immigrants came from Europe; for several years now the principal source has been Asia. In 1970, environmental problems were looked at from a local perspective; today the international dimensions of both problems and solutions are increasingly apparent.

In 1970, a different world seemed to be shaping up from the one that actually emerged. Fifteen years ago American economic preeminence was being challenged, optimism about economic prosperity was widely shared, and detente seemed to hold the key to more fruitful relations between East and West.

Forecasting is as fraught with difficulties today as it was in 1970. American economic performance continues to defy conventional economic thinking. Will it do so indefinitely and, if not, will the change be dizzying or gentle? What does the international revolution in financial services mean to the international economy and to our own? Will the debt problem be resolved? How will the generational shift in Soviet leaders affect USSR policy both at home and towards the West? How will new technologies affect the arms race and strategic doctrines? Are crisis-management mechanisms adequate for the challenge ahead? On these most basic issues that are no certainties. The extent of this uncertainty underscores the importance of flexibility in policy formulation and implementation.

Some things, however, are quite predictable. The United States will remain the world's dominant economic power. It will also remain our most important ally and market. The Pacific Rim will outpace the rest of the world in economic growth. Competition at home and in our export markets will be fierce. The poor and hungry of the Third World will continue to need assistance. Europe will remain divided between East and West for some time to come. Collective security will remain necessary. Interdependence will deepen.

If we are to make our way successfully, we must ask ourselves the right questions about what we want and about what we can achieve. We do not have the resources to do everything. We face tough choices which go to the heart of our national life. To succeed, we need to develop a national consensus on handling the critical international challenges before us.

In some cases, existing policy appears satisfactory. But in a number of important areas, a re-examination of directions appears warranted.

International Economic Affairs

The effects of high interest rates, protectionism, fluctuating exchange rates and lagging productivity are felt by Canadians from coast to coast. Faltering competitiveness means lumber sales in offshore markets are difficult. Subsidized grains production in Europe is competing with our own grains exports abroad. New competitors, new materials and changes in demand are slowing our minerals exports. Highly competitive electronic and automotive imports have captured large shares of our domestic market.

The forces affecting our economic well-being are of both domestic and foreign origin. This section examines several ways in which we can improve our economic circumstances. It looks at Canada-U.S. trade, strengthening the multilateral economic system, the search for competitiveness, investment and exports, and official development assistance.

Canada-U.S. Trade

Trade with the United States dwarfs our trade with any other country. It accounts, in fact, for about three-quarters of our entire trade. The employment of millions of Canadians depends on it.

Protectionist pressures are strong in the United States and could result in new restrictions on the entry of our goods into the American market. The restrictions could reduce the prosperity of Canadians from coast to coast and could have particularly severe regional impacts. They could also diminish the competitiveness of the Canadian industries affected.

For almost every export sector of the Canadian economy except grains, secure and enhanced access to the U.S. market is very important. Efforts to achieve it proceed both multilaterally and bilaterally. The principal rules governing our trade with the United States (and most of our other partners) are contained in the GATT. A new round of multilateral trade negotiations (MTN) could begin under GATT auspices in the next twelve to eighteen months; a preparatory committee could be struck this summer. Progress in those talks would improve our access to the U.S. market.

But multilateral rules, although necessary, may no longer be a sufficient means of managing our most important trade relationship. Canadians are now asking whether, in our own interests, we should consider complementing the multilateral approach by negotiating a special, bilateral trade arrangement with the United States.

A new Canada-U.S. trade regime, incorporating expanded mutual trade obligations, could provide a stable, long-term solution to Canada's vital objectives of secure export market access and enhanced international competitiveness. The arguments for secure and enhanced trade with the U.S. derive from: calculations of economic efficiency and competitiveness; practical experience in post-war economic development, where freer trade has made an indisputable contribution to economic growth; and informed judgement not only on the dangers to Canada of protectionism and intense competition from new sources, but also on the opportunities presented to Canadian exporters by a large market.

There are four broad options for securing and enhancing our trade access to the United States:

1) The Current Approach
2) A Framework Agreement
3) Sectoral or Functional Agreements
4) A Comprehensive Trade Agreement

The current approach entails Canada defending itself from U.S. protectionism by successful lobbying efforts in the U.S., coupled with full exploitation of our GATT rights. This strategy has worked reasonably well to date, although it has given rise to substantial costs to Canadian exporters for legal fees, lobbying, and similar defensive measures. But future success is uncertain, since protectionist pressures are strong and the current approach cannot guarantee secure access.

A bilateral framework agreement on trade relations would establish objectives for improving the trade relationship. Such an agreement could also establish bilateral working groups to examine trade issues and make recommendations to governments. A framework agreement could provide political momentum and be a useful tool but, in itself, would not guarantee access.

The two countries could also examine *special trade arrangements in selected sectors*, as now exist in defence goods and automotive products. There may also be scope for negotiating *specific functional arrangements* which would clarify our respective policies on such issues as subsidization and government procurement. While attractive in some areas, these approaches are hampered by the difficulty of establishing balance and symmetry in the trade interests of the two sides and by the need to square them with our respective GATT obligations.

Finally, the two countries could negotiate *a comprehensive trade agreement* to eliminate most tariff and non-tariff barriers. Such an agreement would have to be consistent with our GATT obligations but could go beyond to cover issues now outside the GATT, such as trade in services. This approach for securing and enhancing market access would be broader in scope than the other options.

A decision on a new type of trade arrangement with the U.S. would not be a marginal one. By 1987, 80% of Canadian goods will enter the U.S. duty-free and 65% of U.S. goods are expected to enter Canada duty-free. Nonetheless, considerable tariff (and non-tariff) protection will remain in each country after 1987. A new agreement to expand access beyond our current GATT commitments could involve giving up a substantial amount of protection.

Policy makers will need to be satisfied that, if Canada-U.S. trade were liberalized further, the benefits would outweigh the costs. For example, would the competitiveness of Canadian companies be advanced or reduced? Policy makers will also need to take account of the potential consequences of a more liberalized trade environment for such areas as taxation, occupational safety, regional development, industrial incentives and environmental regulation. Also, if trade barriers were significantly lowered, would potential investors, Canadian or foreign, set up production in Canada or in the United States?

The negotiation of an international agreement is itself an exercise of sovereignty, even though the outcome may constrain a state's ability to act in certain ways. This is the case for hundreds of international agreements we have concluded. In negotiating an agreement to liberalize trade, those areas of Canadian political, cultural and economic life central to our sense of ourselves as a nation could be excluded from negotiations. It is possible that, if there were a well-defined, mutually-obligating, beneficial treaty governing trade, cultural policy and foreign policy would be less affected by bilateral trade disputes than they are now. Our bilateral trade interests could be shielded from the unintended consequences of U.S. action against the unfairly traded exports of third countries. In effect, with a treaty it may be possible to immunize critical Canadian interests from the effects of unrelated trade disputes.

In the absence of an agreement to secure and enhance trade, U.S. protectionism could seriously hinder the access of Canadian exports to the USA, affecting our prosperity, especially the security of many thousands of jobs. Canada-based companies could increasingly be obliged to set up operations in the USA to reach and serve the U.S. market. Financing the instruments of our distinctive nationality, including our social programs and our instruments for cultural self-expression, could be more difficult.

The Government is seeking the views of all interested Canadians on this issue. How best can we secure and enhance the access of Canadian exports to the U.S. market? Do Canadians believe that an agreement on closer trade relations with the United States entails important economic, cultural and foreign policy advantages or disadvantages? In summary, what kind of relationship with the United States do Canadians want?

The process of consultations with Canadians is already under way. Decisions may need to be taken before the Parliamentary review is completed. At the Quebec Summit Meeting in March of Prime Minister Mulroney and President Reagan, the two leaders agreed to search for ways to secure and facilitate trade and investment flows. A bilateral mechanism to examine all possible and mutually acceptable ways of reducing and eliminating existing barriers to trade was established and the respective ministers responsible for trade were asked to report to the Heads of Government within six months.

Strengthening the Multilateral Economic System

We need the international economic system to conduct our extensive two-way trade and capital investment. That system is being strained by financial uncertainty and trade protectionism. We have an important interest in doing our share, and more, in preserving and improving it.

For the multilateral system to work better, progress will have to be made on macroeconomic and financial cooperation, trade rules, international debt and development assistance. Sound fiscal and monetary policies in the major economies are needed to achieve a stable economic climate for the world as a whole. The U.S. deficit and U.S. interest rates are obviously central factors and U.S. leadership is pivotal. But others, including Canada, also have a responsibility to the larger system and must play their full parts, particularly when setting national macroeconomic, industrial and trade policies.

There are two crucial, related Canadian trade policy objectives: to enhance our companies' existing access to markets and to preserve the integrity of the GATT system. Investors, farmers, businessmen and labour need to know what the ground rules are, what and how they can sell abroad, and what and how foreign producers can sell in our market.

We must judge existing or proposed federal and provincial policies not only on their substantive merits but also on their impact both on the international system and on our own capacity to adjust to international changes and to compete. For instance, the government is currently providing protection against international competition to the footwear, clothing, automotive and certain agricultural sectors. Our financial sector is also shielded somewhat. Might we allow more international competition to prevail?

Canada supports the initiation of a new round of multilateral trade negotiations in the GATT which will offer the opportunity to revitalize the system of rules, to address new and emerging issues such as trade in services, and to restore confidence and predictability to international trade. A new trade round would demonstrate international commitment to the multilateral trading system; the fact of negotiations would, in itself, be a valuable weapon in the battle against protectionism. Efforts will also be needed to reduce the trade-distorting effects of such government practices as subsidies and "Buy National" provisions. Improved rules, of course, would also apply to Canadians and, in certain situations, might make it more difficult for Canadian producers to obtain relief from foreign imports, unless these were unfairly traded. Domestic consultations are under way to define Canadian interests so that we can, in turn, help to establish the negotiating agenda. What do Canadians, especially business and labour, want to see on that agenda?

Competitiveness, Investment and Exports

Improved competitiveness can enhance our economic prospects significantly in the years ahead, help to provide more jobs for Canadians and increase our economic and political influence in the world. Our international competitiveness is, to a large extent, determined by our firms' capacity to invest and their ability to innovate, using their own R & D and applying the best technologies available. It needs to be backed up by economic diplomacy and combined with even more effective export marketing.

Investment is essential to competitiveness. It sustains expansion, creates jobs, generates technological skills and knowledge, provides a capital stock for future expansion and eases and facilitates the process of economic structural adjustment. Our own recent investment performance has been dampened by sluggish growth and soft resource prices. High real interest rates have encouraged many investors to put their money into debt instruments rather than equity. Much of the investment in Canada will be generated at home but we will need more and the competition for foreign investment may be intense. Our ability to attract foreign investment depends on our productivity, our receptivity and the returns investors can expect.

The United States will remain by far our principal foreign source of capital investment and technological expertise. But other sources will also be important, notably Europe, Japan, Hong Kong and the Middle East. Is there scope for closer government-industry-banking cooperation to attract productive investment to Canada? Should the federal government and Canadian industry and banks develop a program to prospect abroad for potential direct foreign investment?

Upgrading our international competitiveness will take time. Science and technology are crucial to that process, especially achieving and maintaining mastery in core technologies such as microelectronics, biotechnology and advanced materials development. This means not just superior technology but superior technology management. Effective cooperation between government and industry is very important in these industrial sectors.

Future industrial competitiveness and growth require complementing our own research efforts with new, best-practice foreign technologies. Acquiring the most advanced technologies from abroad and disseminating them in Canada is sometimes difficult. How best can government programs abroad complement private sector activity? Would Canadian industry lend experienced personnel to the government to identify important new technologies abroad and to direct this information to the companies who need it?

Not all advanced technology is available simply for the buying. In some fields, unless we have our own, complementary programs and can make a contribution to the advancement of the technology, we cannot get access to the most advanced foreign knowledge. This is particularly true where research abroad is stimulated by government programs. Defence programs are one means for Canadian industry to develop high-technology products, particularly in the electronics and aerospace sectors, and to participate in advanced "state-of-the-art" projects. How best can government, industry (including multinational enterprises) and other research centres cooperate to keep abreast of leading-edge technology?

International marketing initiatives, along with efforts to improve our international competitiveness and ensure access to foreign markets, form the principal elements of a national trade strategy. The federal government and the provinces have agreed to work together with the private sector and labour to ensure a more focussed, consistent and dynamic approach to export development. Better sharing of information on trade development activities and better coordination of federal and provincial resources in Canada and abroad will be achieved. Other activities of a longer-term nature, such as the identification of markets of concentration and the development of appropriate mechanisms to assist companies to acquire new technology, will be the subject of further federal-provincial-private sector dialogue over the coming months.

Our approach to trade development must be built on the needs and commitment of the private sector. Together, industry and government must focus on large and dynamic markets. We must also develop better ways of measuring the effectiveness of our trade and investment development activities. The government is moving to bolster trade promotion resources in the areas where trade prospects are most promising, particularly in the Asia-Pacific region. Should more be done? For example, should new posts be opened and, if so, where? And, given budgetary realities, from where should these resources be reallocated?

It is necessary to have a clear idea of the nature and composition of our trade if government programs are to be effective. As multinational enterprises have grown, there has been a corresponding increase in the proportion of international trade conducted within one company. Although figures are difficult to come by, it is estimated that in Canada-U.S. trade over 50% may be intra-corporate and, therefore, not directly affected by government export promotion activities. Trade volumes by themselves may, therefore, be imperfect guides to where the government should focus its efforts. Should we distinguish between that portion of our trade which genuinely requires government support and facilitation and that portion which takes place (and will continue to take place) without any reference to government export programs and activities?

A recently released report found that trading houses account for 13% of total Canadian exports. How can greater use be made of this sector's international marketing expertise, particularly for small and medium-size manufacturers and producers? What roles should the government and private sector play in promoting awareness of trading house opportunities and activities?

There is a need for getting better information to Canadian companies on emerging market opportunities and on changes in trade policies in countries with which we do business. Is a computerized national trade opportunities information system practical?

There are also questions about whether the mix between private effort and public support is right. Could the private sector take over certain trade promotion activities hitherto provided by government? In a climate of fiscal restraint, should business pick up part of the costs of government assistance, perhaps on a fee-for-service basis?

In a number of countries, successful market penetration depends on the establishment of joint ventures with local businesses. Canadian companies will increasingly have to look for foreign partners as a precondition of successful exporting. What are the most effective ways for the government to facilitate the establishment of joint ventures between Canadian and foreign companies?

SECTION 2
CRITICAL
APPROACHES

This section consists of critical approaches to the history of Canadian foreign policy in the twentieth century. The section begins with an essay by James Eayrs of Dalhousie University, the country's leading historian of foreign policy. Eayrs examines the creation of the Department of External Affairs in 1909, focussing on the people involved and the reasons why that seemingly essential department of government was so slow to be formed. The next essay is extracted from one of the best books on Canada's relations with Britain, Philip Wigley's *Canada and the Transition to Commonweath*. Wigley, who recently died in a tragic accident, was a Canadian scholar teaching in Britain, and his book, and this excerpt, looked at the way the Great War provided impetus both for greater Canadian autonomy in foreign policy and, paradoxically, for closer cooperation within the Empire.

The next two essays examine the 1930s, that "low, dishonest decade", as it has been called. Escott Reid, then a young activist and isolationist, examined Mackenzie King's policy and found it wanting in virtually every respect. Two later historians, J.L. Granatstein and Robert Bothwell, with access to almost all the documents, tended to disagree. In their view, King had manoeuvered with great skill to achieve his ultimate goal — bringing a united Canada into the Second World War at Britain's side.

The war, as we have seen in the section on policy statements, changed much. Not least, it altered the way Canada had to look at and deal with the world. The United Kingdom clearly was not going to be a great power after the war; the United States, without doubt, was going to be the strongest nation of all. Sharing a continent with the Americans, doing most of its trade with them, Canada had relatively few options, and Robert Bothwell and John English examine them in their essay on war and postwar trade policy. Escott Reid, by the postwar years a senior Canadian diplomat, looked at the Canadian role in creating the North Atlantic Treaty of 1949. This too was a search for options, an attempt to call up Europe to redress the imbalance in relations between the two North American nations; it was also necessary to stiffen Europe's spine to resist the onrush of Soviet Communism.

NATO worked, but it did not and could not make relations between Ottawa and Washington easier to manage. That was particularly true in the Diefenbaker years from 1957 to 1963 when a Conservative Prime Minister allowed his mistrust of the "Pearsonalities" in the Department of External Affairs and of President Kennedy in Washington to bring Canadian-American relations to their lowest point in the twentieth century. This subject is studied here by John Hilliker, a historian in the Department of External Affairs. But when the Liberals came back into power, relations stayed difficult, this time thanks to the Vietnam War. John Holmes, a distinguished former diplomat and political scientist, looked at the Vietnam War and its impact on Canada in a paper first presented in 1970. A few years later, the publication of the Pentagon Papers released a flood of American documents on the war, including some, published originally in Canada in the *Canadian Forum*, on Ottawa's role as an "intermediary" between the United States and North Vietnam.

Three essays conclude this section. J.L. Granatstein offers one of the very few critical overviews on the Canadian penchant for and practice of peacekeeping. Why did peacekeeping become so popular? Why did it lose its hold on the public's (and the government's) imagination? Thomas Hockin, a political scientist and, since 1984, a Conservative member of Parliament, looked at the way in which Canada's experience of federalism shaped its practice of foreign policy. Harald von Riekhoff, a political scientist at Carleton University, studied the impact of Pierre Trudeau's sometimes vigorous but often reticent and almost isolationist foreign policy.

Many issues and many aspects of Canadian foreign policy have necessarily been left uncovered here. There is nothing on defence policy, nothing on the Bennett government, nothing on Pearson's role in resolving the Suez Crisis of 1956, nothing on the law of the sea, sovereignty, or the Trudeau peace initiative. The "further readings" section will point to works that treat some or all of these subjects.

ORIGINS OF THE DEPARTMENT OF EXTERNAL AFFAIRS†

On June 1, 1959, Canada's Department of External Affairs may look back upon a history of half a century's duration.[1] Even so it is not the oldest foreign ministry in the overseas Commonwealth. That distinction belongs to the Australian Department of External Affairs, which became one of the original departments of the new federation created in 1901. The Canberra innovation seems not to have excited the slightest interest in Canada, despite the appearance during the same year of a book by a Canadian author containing what is probably the earliest written advocacy of separate foreign ministries for the self-governing colonies or dominions. In *The Canadian Contingents and Canadian Imperialism*, W. Sanford Evans[2] developed at considerable length the case for "the creation in Canada, and in each of the other self-governing Colonies, of a Ministry of Imperial and Foreign Affairs."[3] It was, however, far from his intention to provide machinery for conducting a foreign policy distinct from and perhaps in defiance of that of the mother country. Evans was a staunch supporter of imperial federation, who looked on his project as a means of strengthening the imperial connection by adding to the power and influence of the centre. The ministers of imperial and foreign affairs from the self-governing colonies (together with their premiers if these did not themselves hold the new portfolio) were to meet in London as "a Council of the Empire," "a Cabinet of Cabinets," determining by majority vote imperial policy "on all of a large class of questions" (p. 347). The creation of a ministry, he continued,

> whose business it is to promote our external interests would merely show our intention to treat an important part of our interest seriously. . . . The existence of a Minister who is responsible to Canadians for the conduct of foreign affairs, in as far as Canada has a voice in them, would merely be supplying the machinery by which Canada could, in a regular and systematic way, express her views. It would be a movement toward the rounding off of our system of self-government, and yet would be neither a challenge for independence in these matters, nor a submission to continual dependence . . . (pp. 348-9).

The new portfolio might be held "conjointly with another, but it should be as distinct from any other as the portfolio of Agriculture from that of Finance" (p. 340). If, as might be said, "the Premiers of the Colonies now practically fill this position," it was still "advisable to name and definitely locate this part of their functions" (pp. 340-1). Some objection could be anticipated on the ground "that if a Minister was appointed for such a department he would, from a common weakness of human nature, be anxious always to have something to show as a proof of his energy or wisdom, and that, as a consequence, new obligations would continually be forced upon us. . . ." To this Evans responded:

†James Eayrs, "The Origins of Canada's Department of External Affairs," *Canadian Journal of Economics and Political Science* XXV, 2 (May 1959): 109–128.

If enough legitimate and necessary business cannot now be found for the constant employment of a Minister, then join the portfolio to some other. But with preferential trade, the Pacific Cable, the Alaskan boundary, and other issues with the United States, our interests in an American trans-isthmian canal, German discrimination against our goods, the desirability of securing more favourable terms from many other countries, and the South African War, we have surely had problems enough during the past few months to have kept a Minister out of mischief. And there is not likely to be any lack in future. Our external relations have not been cultivated as they might have been, and the ambition of a Minister, whom we would call to account when we would, might not be an unmixed evil . . . (pp. 349–50).

Soon after the publication of Evans' book, if not before, the idea of creating a Canadian foreign office had occurred to one of the country's most influential civil servants. Joseph Pope had been private secretary to Sir John A. Macdonald from 1882 to 1891; assistant clerk of the Privy Council; and, since 1896, Under Secretary of State. "In official circles," a contemporary wrote, he was known as " 'the man with a pull,' " "the Chesterfield, as it were, of the Laurier Government."[4] As Under Secretary of State he attended to a wide range of governmental business, much of it relating to external affairs. He was the only public servant who cared deeply about points of protocol, and thus became indispensable when important personages visited the country; if they embarked on a tour of the Dominion, as did the Prince and Princess of Wales in 1901, Prince Arthur of Connaught in 1906, and Prince Fushimi of Japan in 1907, Joseph Pope was invariably in attendance.[5] In 1893 he served on the staff of the British agent at the Behring Sea Arbitration in Paris; in 1898-9 he was Canada's agent at the International Commission in Washington and Quebec; and in 1903 he was an associate secretary at the Alaska Boundary Tribunal in London. He took a keen and solitary interest in the fate of official documents, striving to rescue them from oblivion and to arrange them in some sort of order for future reference. "I have got some ferrets at work in the Archives," Earl Grey, the Governor General of Canada, wrote to James Bryce, the British Ambassador at Washington, about negotiations over fisheries that were pending in 1907,

> and I hope they will be able to bold out some statements from American authorities which will more than counter balance the quotation from Lord Salisbury made use of in Mr. Root's despatch of June 30th. We are much handicapped here by the want of any organized Department for the coordination and reproduction of information bearing on the relations between Canada and the U.S. It happens that Mr. Pope the Under Secretary of State has taken a personal interest in this question and he has got together from time to time a certain, but no means complete, collection of papers.[6]

Finally, Pope's unique experience and close association with the Prime Minister enabled him to suggest lines of policy and to draft dispatches for their execution in the manner of a permanent under secretary in a foreign office. "Will you allow me to remind you," he wrote to Sir Wilfrid Laurier on February 26, 1907, about a memorandum he had prepared on the Newfoundland Fisheries, that this paper was written for the confidential perusal of yourself and Lord Grey alone. It should not be sent, *no matter how confidentially*, to anyone in England. I mention this because His Excellency rather hinted that with a little toning down, it might do Sir E. Grey good to read it. It was not however written with that object in view. Indeed its style and phraseology make this plain. While the Home Government's treatment of Newfoundland was not such as we are accustomed to, it would not do to say this with the directness and freedom I have employed in a confidential paper which I thought at the time was for your eye alone. If you think my criticisms generally sound, and you decide that Canada should take a hand in the controversy (the expediency of which I venture to think is doubtful) I should be ready to try my hand, if you so wished it, at clothing in diplomatic language the sentiments expressed in my memorandum.[7]

It was, therefore, with slight if any exaggeration that Earl Grey wrote to James Bryce that "Mr. Pope . . . is the non-official Foreign Office of the Canadian Govt."[8]

Pope's first formal advocacy of the project of making the "non-official Foreign Office" into a separate department of government was contained in a submission to the Royal Commission on the Civil Service. It bears the date May 25, 1907, and is sufficiently important to be reproduced here in its entirety:

I desire, with the permission of the commissioners, to offer a few observations upon a matter akin to the subject of their inquiry in respect of which I had not an opportunity of inviting their attention when recently before them. I refer to the desirableness of establishing a more systematic mode of dealing with what I may term, for want of a better phrase, the *external affairs* of the Dominion.

It is commonly supposed that such matters are now administered by the department of which I am deputy head, but this is a misapprehension. The Secretary of State is primarily and principally the official mouthpiece of His Excellency the Governor General in respect of Canadian affairs; he is the channel of communication between the Dominion Government and those of the Provinces, towards which he occupies somewhat the same relation that the Colonial Secretary does towards the Colonies. All communications which reach the Secretary of State for transmission to England or to a foreign country, are forwarded by him to the Governor General with a recommendation that he would be pleased to transmit the same to their destination. All despatches from the Colonial Office are addressed to the Governor General and by His Excellency are sent, for the most part, to the Privy Council where they are referred to the heads of those departments which they particularly concern. Much of this correspondence relates to domestic matters, and with it I have no concern here. Much, however, bears upon what I have called external affairs, that is to say, questions touching our relations with foreign countries, as the Behring Sea Seal question, the Alaska Boundary, the Atlantic Fisheries, International boundaries, and other pending controversies with the United States; or, it may be, with questions whose scope and bearing, though within the empire, extend beyond the bounds of the Dominion; such, for example, as the difference with Newfoundland over the boundary in Labrador. Let us say the Imperial government have occasion to communicate with the government of Canada, in respect of any one of these subjects: The Colonial Minister addresses a despatch to the Governor General; that despatch is forwarded by command of His Excellency to the Privy Council, which means with us the cabinet. The Privy Council refers it to the minister at the head of the department to which it relates, who causes to be prepared a reply in the form of a report to the Privy Council thus:

"The undersigned to whom was referred a despatch from the Secretary of State for the Colonies dated . . . . on the subject of . . . . has the honour to report that . . . ."

That report, when it reaches the Privy Council, is turned into a minute, preserving the sense, and even the phraseology unchanged. It has, as it were, merely been given a head and tail, thus:

"The Committee of the Privy Council have had under consideration a despatch from the Secretary of State for the Colonies dated the . . . . . . The Minister of . . . . to whom the said despatch was referred, reports that (here follows the minister's report verbatim).

"The Committee concur in the foregoing observation of the Minister of . . . . and advise that a copy of this minute, if approved, be transmitted to the Secretary of State for the Colonies for the information of His Majesty's Government."

This minute, when approved by the Governor General, is forwarded to England. If it is an important despatch, the policy of the Government in regard to the principle involved is, no doubt, discussed and agreed to in Council; but the terms of the report are almost invariably left to the department to which the despatch was originally referred. Under this mode of dealing with official correspondence there is no uniformity of system or continuity of plan.

The preparation of despatches is a technical acquirement, attained only after special study of the questions involved, and by assiduous practice in drafting. It may happen; it must sometimes happen; that the official to whom these Imperial despatches are referred (for it cannot be expected that a busy Minister has time to attend to such matters personally, calling for much study, and a large acquaintance with intricate details) while fully competent to deal with the merits of the question in its present aspect, is not familiar with the past history of the controversy or skilled in the framing of State papers. There are moreover certain questions which relate partly to one department and partly to another, so that it may not be easy to tell at first sight to whom a new despatch should be referred. The earlier communication may have related to one department, and a later despatch on the same subject to another. Neither department having any knowledge of what has been referred to the other, the consequence is that both departments, *quoad* this particular subject, are working more or less in the dark.

In the early years of Confederation, when these questions were few, the inconvenience of which I speak was not so greatly felt, as the Prime Minister of the day kept them pretty much in his own hands; but with the growth and development of the Dominion this is no longer possible.

The practical result of the system in vogue is that there does not exist to-day in any department a complete record of the correspondence to which I have alluded. It has been so scattered, and passed through so many hands that there is no approach to continuity in any of the departmental files. Such knowledge concerning them as is available, is, for the most part, lodged in the memories of a few officials. I fear too that in Downing Street, Canadian despatches are noted for diversity rather than for elegance of style. As the Dominion grows this state of things must always be getting worse. If some reform is not soon effected it will be too late. Even now, I am of opinion that it would be an extremely difficult task to construct from our official files anything approaching to a complete record of any of the international questions in which Canada has been concerned during the past fifty years. To give one illustration: Thirty-five years ago the question of ownership of the Island of San Juan, long at issue between Great Britain and the United States, was decided by the Emperor of Germany in favour of the latter. That surely is a matter of important historical concern to the Dominion, yet I should be at a loss to know to-day to what department of the government to turn for any information as to this arbitration. Indeed, I am quite confident that it does not exist in any of them.

My suggestion is, that all despatches relating to external affairs should be referred by the Privy Council to one department, whose staff should contain men trained in the study of these questions, and in the conduct of diplomatic correspondence. These officials should be in close touch with the other departments, from which they could draw all necessary information, the raw material, as it were, of their work; but the digesting of this information, and its presentation in diplomatic form, should rest with them, through, of course, the same channels as at present; for in this suggestion there is no thought of change in that regard. Every effort should be made to collect from the beginning all papers bearing on the questions I have indicated, from the office of the Governor General, the Privy Council office, the various departments and the Foreign and Colonial offices. I wish most earnestly to impress upon all concerned that if this work is not soon systematically begun it will be too late. The few men throughout the service conversant with these questions are growing old, and must soon disappear. So far as I know they will leave no successors. Much of the early history of these subjects, so far as Canadian records are concerned, will thus be lost. I recommend that a small staff of young men, well educated and carefully selected, be attached to the department whose creation I have advocated, and that they be specially trained in the knowledge and treatment of these subjects. In this way we shall acquire an organized method of dealing with international questions which at present we wholly lack.

I have spoken of the creation of another department, but I see no reason why this work should not be done under the supervision of the Secretary of State, whose present department might be divided into two sections, one for Canadian, and one for External affairs.

All of which is respectfully submitted.[9]

All of which, too, had been carefully pondered; and it must have been disconcerting to Pope to receive from J. M. Courtney, the chairman of the three-member Royal Commission to which his memorandum was submitted, nothing but the briefest acknowledgment promising "proper consideration," and suggesting as an afterthought that "possibly the missing San Juan papers are amongst the Archives of British Columbia."[10] Provoked by so blatant a misunderstanding of his argument, Pope replied: "I merely referred to San Juan papers by way of illustration. I have a set of them that I obtained from the Foreign Office; but my point is that this is a personal asset of my own, and in no wise connected with the official records. To look for anything of the kind in the departmental files would be, I am sure, perfectly hopeless."[11]

Copies of the Pope memorandum were sent to various members of the Government. There is record of only one response, this from L. P. Brodeur, the Minister of Marine and Naval Defence, who wrote to say that he was "very favourably impressed with your arguments, and they are exactly in accord with my own views."[12] An opportunity to influence another member of the cabinet came later in the year when Pope accompanied Rodolphe Lemieux, who was both Minister of Labour and Postmaster General in the Laurier Government, on his mission to Japan with the object of negotiating a "Gentlemen's Agreement" regarding the number of immigrants which the Japanese Government would allow to proceed to Canada. During such appropriate intervals as may have presented themselves in the course of their "long stormy passage across the Pacific, the worst our Captain had known on that route,"[13] Pope informed Lemieux of his difficulties in the past and of his hopes for the future. Lemieux was not unreceptive, and his experience while conducting negotiations in Tokyo only strengthened the force of Pope's arguments. "En lisant la correspondance échangée entre Tokio, Londres et Ottawa depuis 1894," Lemieux wrote from Japan,

> il est malheureusement trop évident que nous n'avons suivi, au Canada, les négociations d'assez près. Nous pouvions — au début — obtenir des *Concessions* et c'est à peine si nous avons répondu par un accusé de réception aux propositions avantageuses qui nous étaient faites! Nous manquons absolument de tradition et de correction. L'affaire de tout le monde n'est l'affaire de personne. J'en ai long à vous dire la-dessus. Je n'ai pu obtenir à Ottawa que des bribes de documents et de corresondances, ce rapportant à ce traité. Il faut voir au contraire comme les *records* du F.O. à Londres sont parfaits et comme la genèse du traité en est complète. J'ai pu mettre la main sur ces records (12 *vols.* semblables aux factums de la Cour d'Appel). "*Forewarned is forearmed*". C'est en consultant tout cela que j'ai cause, tout en évitant d'aborder ceux qui nous étaient défavorables. Il faudra que Sir W. [Laurier] réorganise dans le service public tout ce qui a trait à la correspondance officielle. Il ne faut plus qu'elle soit repartie entre les différents ministères. Tout devrait être remis au Secrétaire d'Etat et nous aurions alors des *Records* intelligibles.
>
> Tout ceci pour dire que si, comme j'en ai maintenant la certitude, je réussis à régler cette affair, il faudra se garer à l'avenir.[14]

Lemieux's interest in Pope's project was sustained following his return to Canada by the reply to a letter written by him to the British Foreign Secretary to ask "if it could be possible for me to obtain a complete series of the Foreign Office confidential print: 'Correspondence respecting the revision of the treaty of 1894 between Great Britain and Japan' "; he had "found the record of the British Embassy . . . [in Tokyo] very useful during my negotiations with Count Hayashi, as it contains some important despatches concerning Canada's attitude in the matter." He suggested that the documents be sent directly to Ottawa, and promised that their confidential character would be respected by the Canadian Government.[15] Sir Edward Grey replied:

> I have given my careful consideration to the request which you made. . . .
> I am afraid it will not be possible to issue completed volumes of the series owing to the strict rules we are obliged to observe with regard to their distribution and to the principle involved in these rules; but if you will specify what special documents you may wish to have, I will gladly do my best to meet your wishes.[16]

Lemieux sent this letter to Pope for his comments. "I return Sir E. Grey's letter," Pope wrote,

> which I think calls for no answer. Not merely every volume, but according to my recollections nearly every page of the Confidential Prints, contains some reference to Canada. The series is a whole, and portions of it would be of no use.
> What a commentary this affords on our lack of system! If my suggestion had been listened to years ago, we should not have to ask anybody for these papers to-day, for we should have had them ourselves.[17]

Lemieux persisted, however, in the attempt to extricate the documents from the Foreign Office files and, contrary to Pope's advice, wrote in answer to Grey's letter:

> At this moment it is a little difficult, nay, impossible, for me to specify any particular documents, as the file has running through it references to Canada, and it is the documents containing these references that I desire in particular. I can assure you, however, that I shall be only too pleased to observe, with the greatest care, any obligation of secrecy which the possession of these documents might impose, should you find it possible under the circumstances to permit me having the complete volume.
> I am sending this letter by Mr. Mackenzie King, who is to have the pleasure of conferring with you while in London, and who will be better able to explain the precise nature and purpose of my request than it is possible for me to do in a written communication. You may safely entrust to Mr. King's care any documents which you feel at liberty to allow me to have, and I shall indeed be grateful if, under the circumstances, you may still find it possible to allow me to be supplied, for purposes of confidential record, with the complete print.[18]

So reasonable a procedure could hardly have been refused by the British Government without causing serious offence; and it may perhaps be presumed from the favourable impression made upon Mackenzie King by the British Foreign Secretary[19] that King returned to Ottawa with a copy of the Foreign Office print in his possession. But the incident served to illustrate the inadequacy of relying henceforth upon Foreign Office sources of information, and so emphasized the need for Canada to acquire its own collection of diplomatic documents for future reference.

Rodolphe Lemieux thus became Pope's principal ally within the cabinet, and the latter sought to keep his enthusiasm for the proposed Department of External Affairs alive and active. Soon after their return from Japan, Pope sent Lemieux a copy of his memorandum of May 25, 1907. "I repeat to you," he remarked in his covering letter,

> that if something is not done before long in the way I have suggested, it will be too late. . . . The Foreign Office confidential papers which I obtained for your use in Tokyo afford an apt illustration of the system we should have. There is no reason why records of international questions in which we are concerned should not be equally available here, but as you know, not only are they not so available, but there is no attempt made to collect them together. They are scattered through half-a-dozen departments, and a complete record nowhere exists. As I have asked myself over and over again, how can an official be expected to have a proper acquaintance with these subjects when he cannot even get at the papers that treat of them? There ought to be a system under which officials should have these questions at their fingers' ends, ready whenever they may come up for adjustment. At present when an arbitration or anything of the sort comes on, everything is hurry-skurry, and we start off on our mission with perhaps half the papers, and that half ill-digested. Believe me it is a very important subject and well worth a few hours' consideration on the part of the Cabinet.[20]

And two days later:

> I venture to point out that my suggestion looking towards the establishment of a special branch of the Public Service to deal with Canada's External Affairs, is rather a far reaching one, and would involve considerable reorganization (or organization; for at present there is none) of the method of conducting our external relations. It cannot be disposed of simply by referring a few despatches to this department. The whole subject will require to be carefully thought out. If such a work is to be assigned to this department, I must have more room and some additional clerks. . . . What I aim at is the gradual establishment of a sort of Foreign Office. I am inclined to think such a scheme might require legislation. . . .[21]

To this supporter within the Government, Pope could add an even more influential supporter in the person of Earl Grey. No governor general has taken a more active interest in the affairs of the nation, and in the policies by which these are directed; none has so fully exploited the trinity of his prerogatives, to be consulted, to encourage, and to warn.[22] As the channel of communication between the Canadian Government, the British government, and its Embassy at Washington, Grey became increasingly occupied with the conduct of Canada's external affairs and, towards the end of 1907 and throughout 1908 — a period of unprecedented diplomatic activity — increasingly concerned at the confusion attending it. Like Joseph Pope, he attributed much of the confusion to the want of a separate department of government to which would be assigned responsibility for making adequate preparation for negotiations involving Canadian interests. In March, 1908, he wrote on this subject to the Colonial Secretary:

> Bryce's difficulties in conducting the negotiations [with the United States Government] have, I am sorry to say, been increased by the chaotic condition of the Administration here *qua* External Affairs. There is no Department, no official through whose hands all matters dealing with external affairs must go. Consequently there is no record, no continuity, no method, no consistency.

I have represented all this to Laurier, who agrees with every word I say. I regret that he did not, when he came into office 11 years ago, create a Department. Well it is not too late. Do it now, I urge. I fear that must wait until after the Elections, he replies.

I trust I may be able to overcome this fatal procrastination. We have only three men in the Government Service who have any knowledge of details connected with Canada's foreign relations. One drinks at times, the other has a difficulty in expressing his thoughts, and conversation is as difficult as it is to extract an extra tight cork, and the third is the Under Secretary of State, Pope — a really first class official. Not a day should be lost in putting him in charge of a Department of External Affairs under Sir Wilfrid Laurier, and in a short time he would be able to train one or two young men who would take up his work after he has gone. He would have the papers on every question in good shape. Sir W. Laurier's work would be ever so much facilitated, and Canada would be prompt and satisfactory to deal with, instead of the swollen impossible cork, the extraction of which almost bursts a bloodvessel. The results of Bryce's visit will I hope enable me to overcome Laurier's procrastination. There is no one who will benefit from the change more than he will.[23]

The third of Pope's allies was James Bryce, the British Ambassador at Washington. Formally, and to a great degree practically, responsible for the settlement of Canadian-American differences, Bryce had ample opportunity for experiencing at first hand the woefully inadequate facilities that Ottawa provided for the purpose. Too frequently was he on the point of reaching agreement with the State Department on some matter of importance to Canada only to discover with concern and chagrin that the Canadian Government had changed its stand on the issue, or had allowed it to lie unattended while disposing of other business, or, indeed, had altogether forgotten about it.[24] After a series of frustrating episodes of this kind he had written to Earl Grey:

All this shows once more the frightful inconvenience of not having in Ottawa a Dept. of External Affairs. Knowing how Sir Wifrid is worked . . . I entirely understand his difficulties. But the loss of time which this constant breaking the chain of negotiations and then trying to rivet the sundered links afresh involves is so great that really nothing seems so urgent as to create at once the needed department. Will you not continue to press for the doing of this?[25]

It was in fact Bryce who first raised the matter with authorities in the United Kingdom, writing in the first instance to the Colonial Secretary to urge, as Lord Crewe informed Earl Grey, "rather keenly" that a Department of External Affairs be created at Ottawa. This proposal seems to have been at the outset treated with reserve at Whitehall, perhaps with some apprehension as well. "It seems to me," Crewe wrote to Earl Grey,

to be a matter requiring no little consideration before it is decided upon. I daresay, as I think I told you before, that the existing arrangements are somewhat haphazard, and may lead to dilatory action, but I should rather dread the establishment of a regular Foreign Department with a Minister all to itself, which might be likely to undertake or at any rate to attempt independent action in matters upon which we here, and the Foreign Office in particular, ought to have a preliminary word. On the other hand, if it were a question of fitting out the Prime Minister with a small Foreign Bureau containing one or two experienced permanent officials who would give their whole time to these questions and to nothing else, and who would be able to put pressure on the Prime Minister to deal with such matters when they were urgent, instead of postponing them to other matters of domestic interest, I think that nothing but good would result. Perhaps you will think this over and let me know your opinion. Bryce, of course, placed where he is, is naturally disposed to consider the discussion of these international questions the most important work that your Government has to do, but we must not lose sight of the possible danger which I have indicated.[26]

Earl Grey hastened to reassure the British Government that nothing so radical as a breach in the diplomatic unity of the Empire would be in prospect as a result of the proposed innovation, and that all that was desired was, as he put it, "that the Prime Minister should have attached to his office a small Department of External Affairs, containing one or two experienced permanent officials, who will give their whole time to External Affairs and nothing else, and who will keep him properly posted."[27] This attempt to minimize the constitutional significance of the project seems to have allayed initial misgiving in London. "The C.O. has been uneasy as to this," wrote Bryce to Earl Grey, "lest it should relax the connection with C.O. and F.O., but they now appear to see that it is indispensable, and that in the form not of a separate Ministerial Department but of a secretariat attached to the Prime Minister it need not do any harm."[28]

These representations of Pope, Lemieux, Earl Grey, and Bryce had by this time had their desired effect; henceforth they would be preaching to the converted. "Sir Wilfrid Laurier agrees that [the Department of External Affairs] is needed," Earl Grey wrote Lord Elgin on July 14, 1908, "and so do all the members of his cabinet. Mr. [W.S.] Fielding [the Minister of Finance] has assured me that he will make no objection to finding the money for the additional salaries required."[29] On September 9 Joseph Pope was "told . . . that Sir Wilfrid Laurier had informed the Cabinet of his resolve, immediately after the elections, to erect a Department of External Affairs such as I have long advocated and to place me in charge of it. This the Cabinet unanimously agreed to do. If they really mean this, it is a welcome piece of news. To tell the truth I have been feeling discouraged and disheartened over the apathy with which my suggestions have been received. . . ."[30]

"In accordance with your request," Joseph Pope wrote to Laurier on February 6, 1909, "I send you a draft of a proposed Act establishing a Department of *External Affairs*. It is only a first attempt and is no doubt susceptible of improvement, but it may serve as a basis for discussion of the subject."[31] The changes undergone by Pope's draft before it became law and his conception of the new department may be shown by reproducing collaterally (1) Pope's original draft of February 6, 1909,[32] which, notwithstanding his note to Laurier that it was "only a first attempt," set forth, as he later wrote, the act "as I wanted it"; (2) the bill in the form to which royal assent was given on May 19, 1909; and (3) Pope's proposed amendments of (2),[33] "those I thought of suggesting in mitigation of the changes the Bill was undergoing, but [which] I never had a chance to pass. . . ." Thus:

An Act respecting the Department of External Affairs	An Act to create a Department of External Affairs	[As in (2)]
His Majesty, by and with the advice and consent of the Senate and House of Commons as follows:	His Majesty, by and with the advice and consent of the Senate and House of Commons of Canada, enacts as follows:	[As in (2)]
1. There shall be a department of the Public Service of the Government of Canada, which shall be called the Department of External Affairs, over which the Member of the King's Privy Council for Canada, recognized as the First Minister, for the time being shall preside with the title of Secretary of State for External Affairs.	1. There shall be a department of the Government of Canada to be called the Department of External Affairs, over which the Secretary of State for the time being shall preside.	[As in (2)]
2. The Governor in Council may appoint an officer, by Commission under the Great Seal, who shall be styled the Under-Secretary of State for External Affairs, and who shall be the Deputy Head of the Department; and may also appoint other such officers, clerks and servants, as are requisite for the due administration of the business of the department, all of whom shall hold office during pleasure.	2. The Governor in Council may appoint an officer who shall be called the Under Secretary of State for External Affairs, and who shall be the deputy head of the department, and may also appoint such other officers and clerks as are requisite for the due administration of the business of the department, all of whom shall hold office during pleasure.	[As in (2)]
3. The Secretary of State for External Affairs shall be charged with the direction of all matters relating to the external affairs of the Dominion, including the conduct and management, in so far as appertains to the Government of Canada, of such international and intercolonial negotiations as are now pending, and others whch may, from time to time, arise. All communications from the Secretary of State for the Colonies, or from any other authority within the Empire, or from His Majesty's Ambassador to the United States, or other member of His Majesty's diplomatic or consular service abroad, touching matters others than those of internal concern, shall be referred to the Secretary of State for External Affairs, and be dealt with by him.	3. The Secretary of State, as head of the department, shall have the conduct of all official communications between the Government of Canada and the Government of any other country in connection with the external affairs of Canada, and shall be charged with such other duties as may, from time to time, be assigned to the department by order of the Governor in Council in relation to such external affairs, or to the conduct and management of international or inter-colonial negotiations so far as they may appertain to the Government of Canada.	3. The Secretary of State, as head of the Department, shall have the supervision of all matters in connection with the external affairs of Canada, and shall be charged with such other duties as may, from time to time, be assigned to the department by order of the Governor in Council.

4. The administration of all matters relating to the foreign Consular Service, and also those connected with the grant of passports, now dealt with by the present department of the Secretary of State of Canada, shall be transferred to the Department of External Affairs, as well as any matters which the Governor in Council may hereafter decide should more conveniently be assigned to that department.	4. The administration of all matters relating to the foreign consular service in Canada shall be transferred to the Department of External Affairs.	"I struck this [paragraph] out, because they [the Government] struck out 'passports'. I thought this gave undue prominence to consuls" [marginal comment by Pope].
5. Section 2 of Chapter 76 of the Revised Statutes of Canada 1906 is hereby amended by providing that the member of the King's Privy Council now known as the Secretary of State of Canada, shall in future be designated as the Secretary of State for Canada, and also that the officer heretofore known as the Under-Secretary of State of Canada, be styled the Under-Secretary of State for Canada.	5. The Secretary of State shall annually lay before Parliament, within ten days after the meeting thereof, a report of the proceedings, transactions and affairs of the department during the year then next preceding.	5. [As in (2), but queried by Pope: "?"]
	6. This Act shall come into force on a day to be fixed by a proclamation of the Governor in Council.	6. [As in (2)]

Among these versions may be found a number of discrepancies of substance as well as of style, three of which are significant. In the order of their appearance in the documents these are as follows: (i) In Pope's original draft, the prime minister is designated as the minister in charge of the new Department; in the bill, the secretary of state is so designated. (ii) In Pope's original draft, the minister in charge of the new Department is to be styled "Secretary of State for External Affairs"; in the bill, the additional function is not made explicit by a new title, and the minister remains simply the secretary of state. (iii) In Pope's original draft, the minister in charge of the new Department is described as being responsible for "the *direction* of all matters relating to the external affairs of the Dominion. . . .."; in the bill, for "the *conduct* of all official communications. . . .."; while in Pope's proposed but unimplemented revision, for "the *supervision* of all matters in connection with the external affairs of Canada . . .." (my italics). Each of these discrepancies requires further examination.

The provision in the bill placing the new Department under the secretary of state, Pope wrote in his diary, was "a *great* mistake. It should be under the Prime Minister."[34] Similar views had been expressed that day in the House of Commons by Conservative critics. "You have a more simple, economical and thorough manner of dealing with the matter," George Foster had declared, "if you attach a little body of expert clerks to the Privy Council, put them under the Prime Minister, where, I think, these things ought to be, and let them do all this work of keeping the records. . . ."[35] "If we are to concede what the Prime Minister has argued for," remarked R. L. Borden, ". . . then I say that the department should be under the control of the Prime Minister and not under the control of the Secretary of State"; and he cited the Australian precedent in support of this contention.[36] Just why the new Department was placed under the secretary of state remains obscure. In debate, Laurier brushed the criticism aside. "It does not matter," he insisted, "under which Minister the Department of External Affairs may be placed. . . ."[37] Pope later wrote that his original draft of the bill in this respect "was changed at the last moment" for "some reason of which I am ignorant." He pointed out, however, that despite the bill's assignment of responsibility to the secretary of state, it was Laurier as Prime Minister rather than Charles Murphy as Secretary of State upon whom the burden of the new Department fell. "Sir Wilfrid Laurier even in the beginning," Pope pointed out in a memorandum written for Borden in 1912,

> was so impressed with the necessity for having supervision over the
> Department that he added to the draft Minute of Council a provision that a
> duplicate of all despatches should be sent to him.
> All important subjects of negotiation were . . . laid by me before the
> Prime Minister, according to Sir Wilfrid's instructions. He discussed them
> with me, and when he had decided on a line of action (which might or
> might not be in accordance with the view of the Department immediately
> concerned, or perhaps before the despatch had reached that Department) I
> would, after acquainting that Department with the Prime Minister's wishes,
> prepare a report to be signed — not however by the Prime Minister, but by
> the Secretary of State, whose first knowledge of the subject was thus a cut
> and dried report set before him to sign.[38]

Following the defeat of the Laurier Government in 1911, Earl Grey wrote to James Bryce that he had already told Borden "that I think it is imperative in the interests of the Crown that the External Affairs Department should be removed from the Secretary of State's Department to his own."[39] During the transferring of power there seems to have been some talk of placing the Department under the president of the Privy Council. If, as was ordinarily the case, the prime minister was also president of the Privy Council, the result desired by Pope and Grey would be achieved. But, as Pope promptly pointed out to Borden, "of your seven predecessors in the office of Prime minister, three never held the office of President of the Privy Council when Premier, and a fourth was successively Minister of Justice, Interior and Railways. To transfer the External Affairs from one portfolio to another, would not tend to [increase] its prestige or importance. I still venture to hope that you may see your way to take this office under you as Prime Minister."[40] Borden, who in the 1909 debate on the bill to create the Department of External Affairs had urged that the prime minister be placed in charge, was easily convinced by Pope's arguments. Accordingly, on April 15, 1912, assent was given to "An Act respecting the Department of External Affairs," of which the second and third paragraphs read as follows:

> 2. There shall be a Department of the Government of Canada to be called
> the Department of External Affairs, over which the Secretary of State for
> External Affairs shall preside.

> 3. The Member of the King's Privy Council for Canada holding the
> recognized position of First Minister shall be the Secretary of State for
> External Affairs. . . .[41]

As his original draft of the Act of 1909 makes clear, it had been Pope's intention that the minister in charge of the new Department should receive the title "Secretary of State for External Affairs." But the Act placed the Department under the secretary of state, creating no new portfolio with which the bearer of the additional responsibility might be invested, even though it had created the position of an under secretary of state for external affairs. This anomaly irritated Pope's sensibilities. "Does not the existing statute," he wrote to Borden,

> in creating the office of "Under Secretary of State for External Affairs",
> appear to contemplate that there shall be a Secretary of State for External
> Affairs? I do not quite see how there could be an Under-Secretary of State
> for External Affairs without a Secretary of State for External Affairs, but if
> there were, such official would popularly be regarded as in some sense
> amenable to the jurisdiction, not merely of *the* Secretary of State, but also
> (as is more or less the case at the present moment) of the officer at present
> known as "*the* Under Secretary of State".
>
> The existence of two Secretaries of State, one for *Home*, the other for
> *External* affairs is so reasonable in itself and so accordant with British usage
> that I feel it would speedily commend itself to public opinion, in so far as
> public opinion has any interest in such matters.[42]

Moreover, despite the perverse wording of the Act of 1909, the Secretary of State, acting in his capacity as the Minister in charge of the new Department, had been directed by none other than the Prime Minister to use the title which Pope had originally suggested. "The first recommendation I laid before him [Laurier]," Pope wrote to Borden, "was prepared for signature as 'Secretary of State'. Without any suggestions on my part he added, with his own hand, the words 'for External Affairs' and directed that that title should be always used."[43] This direction was duly carried out, for the diplomatic correspondence of the period 1909-11 bearing the signature of Charles Murphy describes him as "Secretary of State for External Affairs," an office not recognized by law until the Act of 1912 removed the anomaly, greatly to Pope's satisfaction.

No part of the legislation creating the Department of External Affairs caused as much controversy at the time of its enactment as its third paragraph. "I do not like the expression: 'shall have the conduct of all official communications between the Government of Canada and the Government of any other country,' " Pope wrote to W. H. Walker[44] on March 10, 1909:

> That would rather imply that the Government of Canada can conduct
> direct negotiations. It is quite evident from the Prime Minister's speech [in
> the House of Commons on March 4] and that of Mr. Murphy, that they do
> not mean this. It is just a bit of clumsy drafting. Can you think of any
> qualifying phrase that might be inserted, such for example as, after the word
> "communications", "through the usual channel", or something of that
> sort?[45]

Walker replied:

> I cannot bring myself to interpret the phrase "conduct of communications",
> even if qualified as you suggest, to mean anything else than an actual

carrying on of correspondence by the Secretary of State.

Personally I am not prepared to criticize the policy involved in such an interpretation. It might be supported on grounds of constitutional theory as well as of convenience; and possibly might be sanctioned by H.M. Government.

But assuming that this is not the Government's policy it seems to me that the language of the Bill might be brought more into harmony with what I believe is your own view, and the view which I understand Sir Wilfrid to advance in his explanation, by substituting "direction" or "superintendence" for "conduct". I can quite see that neither substitution is altogether satisfactory, for, in view of the procedure now followed, according to which His Excellency actually makes the communications, both are open to the objection of implying an inversion of the relative positions of Governor and Minister and a control exercised over the former by the latter.[46]

The Governor General himself was quick to sense and to attempt to forestall the possibility that the wording of the bill might weaken the authority of his office. "His Excellency is much worked up over the wording of the External Affairs Bill as brought down," Pope wrote on March 12, "particularly Sect. 3. . . . I merely said that in the circumstances I could not do anything, and that His Excellency ought to see his Ministers on the point."[47] Promptly Earl Grey did so, and wrote to Lord Crewe of the result:

I called the attention of Sir Wilfrid as soon as it was drafted to the fact that the word "conduct" in clause 3 did not correctly interpret the speeches made by himself and Mr. Aylesworth in the debate on the introduction of the Bill: that to give the Secretary of State the "conduct" of official communications between the Government of Canada and other Governments, would be regarded as an improper attempt to shelve the Governor General; that I was aware that this was not his intention, and that the substitution of the word "care" for the word "conduct" was all that was required. He unreservedly agreed with all I said, and undertook that the word "care" should be substituted. Although he made a note at my request in his pocket book, he must have forgotten to give any instructions in the matter, with the result that the bill has passed the Commons and the second reading of the Senate in its unamended form.

I saw the Secretary of State [Murphy], Sir Wilfrid Laurier and the Minister of Justice [Aylesworth] this morning and pointed out to them the importance of amending the bill in this direction in Committee of the Senate. They all three promised that it should be done, so I hope that matter is all right. If Sir Wilfrid Laurier had allowed the bill to be passed in its original form I should have had to request him to bring in an amending act, in order to avoid men of the Ewart stamp[48] from . . . deducing from it that the Governor General was a superfluous and unnecessary official.[49]

Whatever promise Laurier may have made to alter the bill in the manner desired by the Governor General, he did not keep it. The bill became law, and the Minister of the new Department became responsible for the "conduct" rather than the "care" of diplomatic correspondence. Grey was still determined that the offending phrase should not affect his position as the channel of communication with the governments of other countries. He wrote to the British Ambassador at Washington:

> There is no reason why you should not at once start a correspondence with the External Affairs Department, but with the view of preventing the office of Governor General drifting into a subordinate and undignified position, I must ask you to send me, for purposes of filing in my office, copies of any private communications you may send to the Secretary of the Department for External Affairs; and on my return from England I think it would be as well if the correspondence went as much as possible through the Governor General, in order that he should know exactly how things are moving. Apart from the principle involved it should often be in the power of the Governor General to help matters forward by private non-official talks with men like the Chief Justice or other members of the Cabinet, besides the Prime Minister.[50]

Bryce replied:

> With all you say about the new External Affairs Department I agree. It was my own feeling that the Embassy ought to correspond with you, not with the "External Affairs", not merely because that is the proper constitutional course but also because it is the course most likely to advance business and to secure impartial interests. The Governor General ought to know all that is passing. The Ambassador can say things to him he would not say equally well to the Prime Minister and can consider with him the general Imperial bearings of what is passing. . . . Sometimes it may be well for the Embassy to jog the memory of the Cabinet through "External Affairs", sometimes to ask External Affairs what is passing— but the really important correspondence ought in my view as in yours to be, still and always, with the Governor General.[51]

"Still and always" proved in fact to mean the two remaining years of Earl Grey's governor generalship. By 1912 the office of his successor, the Duke of Connaught, informed the British Embassy at Washington of its view that "to prevent direct correspondence between the Embassy and the First Minister . . . would be as impossible to do as it would be undesirable."[52] But Grey never lost hope. As late as 1910 he was still asking Laurier to amend the Act. The Prime Minister did not do so, possibly because he had been impressed by Charles Murphy's argument that as the new Department was "not popular with some of my colleagues, and still less so with many of the Government supporters," it was well to avoid "attracting the attention of Council or Parliament to unimportant details that are sure to excite opposition and suspicion." An equally plausible explanation is that by this time Laurier had become wholly impatient with Grey's persistent intrusions into Government policy. In any event, as Murphy did not fail to point out, "Earl Grey will be leaving Canada in a couple of months, the matter is not one with which he is particularly concerned and his successor will never dream of raising such an objection."[53] This prediction proved wholly correct.

"I am in the most extraordinary position," wrote Joseph Pope on the fourth day of his new career, "— a deputy head without an office or a staff."[54] To the extent that the second of these deficiencies went unremedied Pope had especial reason to feel aggrieved, for, as he wrote some years later, "when Sir Wilfrid asked me to undertake the organization of the new Department, I told him frankly the only condition upon which I could assume the responsibility was that I should have the benefit of Mr. Walker's assistance."[55] Within a month, however, this condition had been satisfied. Walker joined the Department as the senior of two "chief clerks"; he was, in effect, the Department's Assistant Under Secretary, although it was not until 1911 that an order in council was passed authorizing him to sign for the Under Secretary in the absence of that officer. The battle for clerical assistance had begun on the first day of the Department's existence. "We are starting a Department with nothing," Pope wrote to his Minister. "We have to design books, forms, and in fact to think out a whole system in detail."[56] For this purpose he requested two "typewriters" (typists), and these were duly acquired, though their assistance was only temporary.[57]

The Act creating the new Department of government could not as easily bring into being the offices in which it might be installed. During the first weeks of his new responsibilities, Pope not only stayed in his old office but was required to share it with the official succeeding to his duties as Under Secretary of State. He presented at this time a somewhat pathetic spectacle. "Mr. Pope," Earl Grey wrote to James Bryce, "has not even a table to write on, or a chair to sit in; no cupboards in which to put his papers and his books, and as he is a gentlemen who moves with dignity and deliberation some time must elapse to enable him to settle down comfortably in the midst of his new surroundings."[58] During the summer he occupied some vacant rooms in the House of Commons, but the return of the legislators forced another evacuation. Space above a barber shop on Bank Street was all that could be found, and it was here that Grey, returning to Ottawa in October from a trip to the Canadian West, found the entire staff of a branch of government to which Laurier had promised to attach "the dignity and importance of a department by itself."[59] The Governor General turned at once upon his Prime Minister. "I cannot refrain from expressing to you my great disappointment," he wrote to Laurier on November 3.

> You will remember that when we discussed the location of these offices during last session you took the view that the public convenience demanded that the offices of the Department of External Affairs should be in the same building as the offices of the Governor General, the Prime Minister & the Secretary of State. It was on an assurance from you that this would be arranged that I consented to my office being weakened by the transfer of Mr. Walker to the newly created Department. It was arranged with Mr. Pope that my office should have the power of consulting freely at all times with Mr. Walker re the drafting of despatches &c. It is hardly necessary for me to point out that Mr. Walker in his Bank St. office is almost as useless to my office as if he were in Calcutta![60]

Laurier assured Grey that the Department's accommodation in Bank Street was only temporary, and that when new offices were ready it would be moved into the East Block. But the new offices were not completed until 1914, and only then was realized the original conception of placing the Department of External Affairs in physical proximity with the office of the prime minister.

Amidst all the confusion, the work of the new Department was begun. A necessary first step was to cast about for some principles of organization. A study was made of the Australian Department of External Affairs, but to Pope and Walker this did not seem to offer a useful model. "Their Department seems to have a much wider sphere of activity than is contemplated for the Canadian one," Walker wrote, "and while the information supplied is interesting as far as it goes it does not seem to me very helpful towards establishing an organization or procedure for the new Depart."[61] No attempt was made to ascertain the workings of the Department of State at Washington, or, indeed, those of any foreign ministry other than the Australian and the British. While in London some years earlier, Laurier (as he later told the House of Commons) "took pains to learn how these things were dealt with there";[62] it was accordingly to London that he decided to send Pope in 1910, "to look into the Foreign Office system and to collect back records . . . ," wishing, as Pope noted in his diary, "the foundations well and truly laid."[63] Armed with letters of introduction to Sir Edward Grey and Lord Crewe, Pope set out for Whitehall in the spring of 1910; on May 5 he reported to Laurier that he had found "every facility afforded me for carrying on my work."[64]

Ten weeks were sufficient to complete the assignment. On returning to Ottawa his next task, undertaken "at the request of the Prime Minister," was to compile "a set of all treaties affecting Canada from the beginning," thus "laying the foundation for the periodical issue of a series of Canadian State Papers somewhat on the lines of the British and Foreign State Papers, which are issued regularly from the Foreign Office."[65] It was, he wrote, "a long job and involves considerable research";[66] it was also, and obviously, a labour of love. "I am naturally desirous to carry the date of our beginning as far back as possible," he confided some weeks after the project had got under way, "and I do not see why I should not start with . . . the Commission to Jacques Cartier from Philippe Chabot, Admiral of France, dated 30th October 1534. . . ."[67] It may be that these antiquarian pursuits absorbed at this early stage of its history too much of the attention of the Department of External Affairs, for Bryce complained that its creation "has not, so far, accelerated business."[68] But the tribute paid by Bryce's successor some years later would seem to confirm the wisdom of Pope's appointment in 1909, if not as yet the wisdom of founding the Department over which he was to preside until 1925. "One of the chief reasons why, as I believe, Canadian interests are very well looked after in Washington now," wrote Sir Cecil Spring-Rice to Sir Robert Borden in 1918,

> is that Sir Joseph Pope who is persona gratissima there, was always ready to come down and settle questions by direct personal negotiations. His relations with his own Embassy [sic] were as cordial as they were with his old friends in the Departments, and owing to him we were always able to get into direct touch with the U.S. officials who always regarded him with confidence and respected him as having the full authority of the Dominion Government.[69]

Notes

1. The Act creating a Department of External Affairs was brought into force by a proclamation issued on the evening of 1 June 1909, by authority of Order in Council P.C. 1227 of 1 June 1909.

2. A Manitoba Conservative, a journalist and financier, Mayor of Winnipeg 1909-10.

3. London, 1901, 340. Evans' early advocacy of separate foreign offices for the overseas dominions has been pointed out in F. H. Soward, *The Department of External Affairs and Canadian Autonomy, 1899–1939*, Canadian Historical Association Booklet no. 7 (Ottawa, 1956), 5.

4. Henry James Morgan, *The Canadian Men and Women of the Time: A Handbook of Canadian Biography of Living Characters* (Toronto, 1912), 910.

5. For his services during the Canadian tour of Prince Fushimi, Pope was awarded the Japanese Order of the Sacred Treasure (Second Class). Another prince was both less generous and less gracious; see *A King's Story: The Memoirs of the Duke of Windsor* (New York, 1947), 140–3.

6. 14 Jan. 1907, Grey Papers (Public Archives of Canada), box 14, folder 12a.

7. 26 Feb. 1907, Laurier Papers (P.A.C.), 120623–4.

8. 28 Nov. 1907, Grey Papers, box 7, folder J.

9. "Memorandum for Consideration of the Civil Service Commissioners, 25 May, 1907," Civil Service Commission 1908: Minutes of Evidence, I, 48–50, *Sessional Papers of Canada* XLII, no. 15, 1907–8.

10. Courtney to Pope, 28 May 1907, Under Secretary of State: Semi-Official Correspondence (P.A.C.), folder 191.

11. Pope to Courtney, 28 May 1907, *ibid.*

12. Brodeur to Pope, 21 Oct. 1907, *ibid.*

13. Pope to Laurier, 15 Nov. 1907, Laurier Papers, 132091–2.

14. Lemieux to Sir Louis Jetté, 4 Dec. 1907, Lemieux Papers (P.A.C.), 397–8.

15. 13 Dec. 1907, *ibid.*, 534.

16. 11 Feb. 1908, *ibid.*, 888.

17. 24 Feb. 1908, *ibid.*, 977.

18. 5 March 1908, *ibid.*, 889–90

19. R. MacGregor Dawson, *William Lyon Mackenzie King: A Political Biography*, I, *1874–1923* (Toronto, 1958), 161.

20. 10 Feb. 1908, Under Secretary of State: Semi-Official Correspondence, folder 191.

21. 12 Feb. 1908, Lemieux Papers, 878.

22. "He was, indeed, a frequent cause of annoyance to the Government. . . . On one occasion (1909) when Grey's enthusiasm for proportional representation threatened to become embarrassing, Laurier 'wished Earl Grey would mind his own business,' and King in his diary added: 'The truth is His Ex. is getting into too many things.' " Dawson, *William Lyon Mackenzie King*, 174–5. This propensity could explain Laurier's refusal, during the latter half of 1908 and early 1909, to be much moved by Grey's entreaties to act with speed to establish the Department of External Affairs.

23. Grey to Lord Elgin, 28 March 1908, Grey Papers, box 14, folder 25.

24. Some measure of the frustrations Bryce encountered in negotiating with the United States on Canada's behalf is provided by the following episode, related by Bryce in a letter dated 30 June 1908, to Earl Grey: "Your letter of the 22nd June enclosing Minute of P.C. [Privy Council] illustrates admirably the need for an External Affairs Dept. in your Govt. Laurier suggested to me that instead of 3 arbitrators for the Pecuniary Claims Arbitration we should have two Arbitrators with power to appoint an Umpire when they disagreed. I conveyed this suggestion unofficially to [Elihu] Root [the United States Secretary of State]. Root accepted it and redrafted the Convention to meet Laurier's view. Now after all these months [Allen] Aylesworth [the Canadian Minister of Justice] prepares and the P.C. approves a Minute disapproving Root's draft because it embodies Laurier's suggestion! Aylesworth would seem never to have heard of Laurier's view, tho' I put it into a Memorandum of my talks wh. Laurier initialled and approved. Now where are we? Are we to tell Root that the P.C. disapproves Laurier's own suggestion which he adopted?" (Grey Papers, box 8, folder W). A few months later, on 7 January 1909, Bryce complained to Earl Grey: "The letters and Minutes that come from Canadian Ministers sometimes ignore our communications simply because these

have been forgotten, or mislaid, or perhaps never seen by the person who writes to us" (*ibid.*, box 9, folder B).

25. 11 May 1908, *ibid.*, box 8, folder U.

26. 4 July 1908, *ibid.*, box 15, folder 29.

27. Grey to Elgin, July 14, 1908, *ibid.*, box 15, folder 30.

28. 10 Aug. 1908, *ibid.*, box 8, folder X. This faint-hearted and grudging response was typical of the character of the Colonial Office at the time, as revealed in a recent and authoritative study: "What . . . was wrong with the Office? Briefly, it lacked inspiration. . . . Moreover, it was imprisoned in its environment. The culture of London seemed so polished that it was hard to treat with perfect seriousness the aspirations of Toronto or Auckland, Lagos or Belize. To the men of Whitehall the civilisation of the colonies, whether newly contrived by expatriated Britons or the child of the primordial jungle, was not merely different to their own, it was inferior to it. Colonial peoples were like children and were to be treated with all the kindness and severity of the Victorian parent." R. B. Pugh, "The Colonial Office, 1801–1925" in *The Cambridge History of the British Empire*, III, *The Empire-Commonwealth, 1870– 1919*, edited by E. A. Benians, Sir James Butler, and C. E. Carrington (Cambridge, 1959), 768. Nor was the personality of its Minister of a kind to dispel these failings. Lord Elgin's tenure, a critic has cruelly written, was "undistinguished. His part in conferences on Colonial matters was often said to consist in tugging at his beard in silence, and on one occasion when he was expected to sum up he surprised his colleagues by carefully putting the end of it into his mouth." John Pope-Hennessy, *Lord Crewe: The Likeness of a Liberal* (London, 1956), 64.

29. Grey Papers, box 15, folder 30.

30. Pope Diary, entry for 9 Sept. 1909.

31. Under Secretary of State: Semi-Official Correspondence, folder 375.

32. *Ibid.*

33. *Ibid.*

34. Pope Diary, entry for 4 March 1909.

35. Canada, House of Commons, *Debates*, session 1909, I, 4 March, col. 1988.

36. *Ibid.*, col. 2002.

37. *Ibid.*, col. 2003.

38. 10 Jan. 1912, Borden papers (P.A.C.), OC 552.

39. 26 Sept. 1911, Grey Papers, box 11, folder D.

40. 30 Dec. 1911, Borden Papers, OC 552.

41. 2 George V, c. 22.

42. 30 Dec. 1911, Borden Papers, OC 552.

43. 10 Jan. 1912, *ibid.*

44. A graduate of the University of Toronto and Osgoode Hall, served in the Governor General's office before entering the Department of External Affairs in June, 1909. He became Assistant Under Secretary in 1911, and remained in that post until his death in 1933.

45. Under Secretary of State: Semi-Official Correspondence, folder 375.

46. 12 March 1909, *ibid.*

47. Pope Diary, entry for 12 March 1909.

48. A reference to J. S. Ewart, whose collected essays, *The Kingdom of Canada . . . and Other Essays* (Toronto, 1908), had appeared the previous year.

49. 3 May 1909, Grey Papers, box 15, folder 36.

50. Grey to Bryce, 2 June 1909, *ibid.*, box 9, folder R.

51. 10 June 1909, *ibid.*

52. Col. Henry C. Lowther to Eustace Percy, 13 March 1912, Borden Papers, OC 39.

53. Murphy to Laurier, 22 April 1910, Laurier Papers, 170261-2.

54. Pope Diary, entry for 4 June 1909.

55. Pope to W. L. Mackenzie King, 27 Dec. 1922, King Papers (P.A.C.).

56. Pope to Murphy, 30 June 1909, Murphy Papers (P.A.C.).

57. The Foreign Office was at the time scarcely better equipped. Its official historian offers as an explanation rather than an excuse that as "Her Majesty altogether declined to read typewritten documents . . . there were for some time after 1893 only one or two typists. . . . When we had deciphered or ciphered our telegrams we made copies for distribution in what was known as 'blueing ink' on a 'jelly'. The first copy

was naturally the best, and this was always destined for the Queen." Sir John Tilley, *The Foreign Office* (London, 1933), 135–6. The young Robert Vansittart, beginning his diplomatic career in 1904 or 1905, "was told off to . . . copy out telegrams in violet ink and rub them into scores on stacks of decomposing 'jellyfish'. . . . Once I sought escape, for under a tarpaulin like the gun at Dover Harbour was a typewriter; but as I sat down to explore it, the Head of the Department burst in exclaiming: 'Leave that thing alone! Don't you know we're in a hurry.' " *The Mist Procession: The Autobiography of Lord Vansittart* (London, 1958), 43.

58. 2 June 1909, Grey Papers, box 9, folder R.
59. Canada, H. of C., *Debates*, session 1909, I, 4 March, col. 2004.
60. 3 Nov. 1909, Laurier Papers, 206367-9.
61. Walker to Pope, 13 May 1909, Under Secretary of State: Semi-Official Correspondence, folder 375.
62. Canada, H. of C., *Debates*, session 1909, I, 4 March, col. 1983.
63. Pope Diary, entry for 16 Jan. 1910.
64. Laurier Papers, 170643-52.
65. Pope to H. P. Biggar, 25 Oct. 1910, Under Secretary of State: Semi-Official Correspondence, box 39.
66. Pope to James White, 6 July 1910, *ibid*.
67. To H. P. Biggar, 25 Oct. 1910, *ibid*.
68. Bryce to Grey, 4 July 1910, Grey Papers, box 10, folder Q.
69. 21 Jan. 1918, Borden Papers, OC 169.

CANADA AND THE TRANSITION TO
COMMONWEALTH†

For the Canadian government the outbreak of war brought an immediate end to the spell of barren inactivity occasioned by their abortive naval policies. Overnight, an enervating political stalemate was transformed into an earnest political truce, the unconditional terms of which Laurier, for the opposition Liberals, announced to the House of Commons when they assembled in August 1914 for an emergency session:

> This session has been called for the purpose of giving the authority of parliament and the sanction of law to such measures as have already been taken by the Government. . . . I hasten to say that to all these measures we are prepared to give immediate assent. If in what has been done or in what remains to be done there may be anything which in our judgement should not be done or should be differently done, we raise no question, we take no exception, we offer no criticisms, and we shall offer no criticisms so long as there is danger at the front. . . .
> It will be seen by the world that Canada, a daughter of old England, intends to stand by her in this great conflict. When the call comes our answer goes at once, and it goes in the classical language of the British answer to the call of duty: "Ready, aye, ready." [1]

The Liberal leader's remarks epitomized the mood in which the dominion went to war. They reflected the unreserved determination with which volunteers were already flocking to the military recruiting posts; they were promised, furthermore, on the widely held belief that the war would not be a long one. Guided by this assumption, government policy needed no detailed elaboration: Canada would simply supply whatever military assistance was needed to bring the conflict to its conclusion. [2] And so in much the same way as Laurier offered his unconditional support to the government, Borden offered the dominion's support to Britain. The control, the command, the deployment of the Canadian expeditionary forces were placed without question in the hands of the War Office. (For what they were worth, two old cruisers that the Laurier government had purchased in 1910 for training purposes were put at the Admiralty's disposal.) The notion of relating Canada's commitment to the war to the larger question of a dominion voice in imperial affairs did not arise. Like the expenditure for dreadnoughts planned for 1912, wartime assistance was thought of as an emergency contribution to a short-term problem, with no immediate connection to the development of empire relations.

Such was the unqualified nature of Canada's entry into the war that her troops, in effect, were dispatched to England on terms practically identical to those governing her earlier participation in the Boer War. Certainly they were accepted in England as coming from a willing colonial assistant, for use in another such war. The outbreak of the war, in fact, had stimulated strongly regressive attitudes in

†Philip Wigley, *Canada and the Transition to Commonwealth: British-Canadian Relations 1917–26* (Cambridge: Cambridge University Press, 1977), 21–44.

the British government. The military command, in making arrangements for a single imperial army — and more spectacularly in planning a campaign dominated by the cavalry[3] — were indeed thinking of a Boer War. But the civilian administration also, particularly with regard to imperial relations, showed similar inclinations to fall back upon traditional patterns of conduct. Never mind that they had so recently tried to encourage the overseas governments to send representatives to the C.I.D. [Committee of Imperial Defence], and indicated a willingness to begin, at least, to explore the difficulties of joint consultations. The war once begun, the C.I.D. was prorogued, and throughout Whitehall the accent became one of strict constitutional propriety, marked by an implacable deference to the dominions' colonial autonomy. The freedom with which the overseas governments offered Britain their support, it seemed, must not be compromised by any thought of inter-imperial discussions about the war. Collaboration of this sort might turn unsolicited aid into an obligation, and threaten thereby the free association on which the empire's internal relations were founded. For the best of reasons, therefore, consultation during the war was calmly ruled out by the British government. It was not even felt necessary to provide regular information for the dominions about the course of the fighting.

No doubt the dominions were initially grateful to know that their assistance was entirely their own affair. As the war progressed, however, and the scale of dominion support rose to a degree never envisaged, such persistent acknowledgement of their autonomy became irritating, and before long utterly perverse. In Ottawa the Canadian government were soon encountering severe financial and economic difficulties in their attempt to meet the demands of war production; they were also greatly angered when despite their protests the British government placed far more orders for equipment with the United States than with Canada.[4] Of the war at the front they knew little more than that their troops were suffering appalling losses.[5] Yet as late as October 1915 the British government, far from providing information, would not even ask Borden officially to supply more troops. Such requests continued to be transmitted (through the acting high commissioner, not the Colonial Office) as an indirect suggestion. Thus Perley could only tell Borden that "authorities here say they cannot urge on Dominions sending more men but that they are much needed and would be very welcome".[6] It says much for the prime minister's loyalty that two days after receiving this message the authorized limit for Canadian military personnel was raised by 100,000 to a quarter of a million men.

The isolation in which Borden was obliged to conduct the dominion's war effort was by then almost intolerable, the prime minister having meanwhile discovered to his cost that even a personal visit to London could bring him no closer to information or policy. In May 1915 the formation of a Liberal-Conservative coalition government in Britain had seemed a hopeful sign, and Borden had thoroughly approved when Andrew Bonar Law, leader of the Conservative party and a Canadian besides, had accepted the post of colonial secretary under Asquith. It was shortly after this reconstruction that he decided to cross the Atlantic and deal with British ministers at first hand. He made speeches, saw the king, visited military hospitals, dined with any number of the British establishment — he even attended a cabinet meeting; but after six weeks he had uncovered no helpful official information relevant to the war effort, and only by a bald threat to Bonar Law that further Canadian assistance might be withheld did he at last secure an interview with Lloyd George, minister of munitions and a central figure in British war operations. Lloyd George impressed the Canadian prime minister with frank attacks against the military authorities and his own departmental staff (a technique of assimilating and deflecting dominion criticism he would employ again when prime minister) but though Borden was encouraged by such ministerial candour he was still unable during the visit to establish any regular flow of information from Whitehall to Ottawa, and returned home to carry on in remote frustration.

It was news from Perley in October 1915, to the effect that a "small war council having special powers" was to be set up by the British government, that gave Borden good reason to make a fresh appeal to London.[7] "The overseas Dominions", he insisted to the colonial secretary, "have large responsibilities to their own people for the conduct of the war, and . . . the Canadian Government deem themselves entitled to fuller information and to consultation respecting the general policy of war operations." He made it plain that he wished this to be provided by the new war council. In the face of this forthright claim, Bonar Law could hardly invoke the sanctity of colonial autonomy as an excuse for not discussing the war with the dominion governments. However, he could easily retreat to a second line of defence. He would not deny, he told Perley candidly, that Canada had every right to information and consultation about the war. The problem unfortunately, was that he could think of no feasible way that either could be provided for the Canadian prime minister. (The suggestion of dominion access to the war committee was simply ignored.) And he added rather sharply that unless Borden's government had practicable suggestions of their own to make, it was "very undesirable that the question should be raised".[8]

Borden was bitterly annoyed with Bonar Law's curt dismissal of his appeal, which so politely recognized his rights in principle and so bluntly rejected them in practice. Confined to bed with painful lumbago over the week of the new year, the prime minister must have brooded sourly over the British government's cavalier response to Canada's war efforts, and he sent off a vehement letter to his acting high commissioner:

> During the past four months since my return from Great Britain, the Canadian Government (except for an occasional telegram from you or Sir Max Aitken) have had just what information could be gleaned from the daily press and no more. As to consultation, plans of campaign have been made and unmade, measures adopted and apparently abandoned and generally speaking steps of the most important and even vital character have been taken, postponed or rejected without the slightest consultation with the authorities of this Dominion.
>
> It can hardly be expected that we shall put 400,000 or 500,000 men in the field and willingly accept the position of having no more voice and receiving no more consideration than if we were toy automata. Any person cherishing such an expectation harbours an unfortunate and even dangerous delusion. Is this war being waged by the United Kingdom alone or is it a war waged by the whole Empire? If I am correct in supposing that the

second hypothesis must be accepted then why do the statesmen of the British Isles arrogate to themselves solely the methods by which it shall be carried on. . . .

. . . if we are expected to continue in the role of automata the whole situation must be reconsidered. . . .[9]

The prime minister's anger quickly cooled, however, and his letter was overtaken by a cable telling Perley to "take no further steps at present". The "reconsideration", as Borden obviously knew, would have to come from London.

For several reasons, the hoped-for change in imperial wartime relations did not come while the Asquith coalition government held office. In the first place the colonial secretary quite wantonly lacked any personal interest in imperial problems.[10] This in turn only served to reinforce a strong official distaste for making procedural or constitutional innovations in time of war. At first, as we have seen, the autonomous status of the dominions had provided some justification for this passive and conservative outlook, though very soon the scale of dominion support made such deference to status seem wilfully evasive. Thereafter, however, the problems of the war itself — about which the overseas governments were so anxious for enlightenment — were held up as an insuperable barrier to imperial discussions. As early as June 1915, when Bonar Law learned that Borden might persuade the premiers of Australia and New Zealand to accompany him on his trip to London, he had pleaded with the Canadian prime minister that the arrangements for any such gathering of overseas leaders would be impossible. He continued thereafter to forestall any dominion initiatives. . . .

In the closing weeks of 1916 the Asquith coalition government was brought to an end by a struggle for political power organized from within the British cabinet. The prime minister tendered his resignation, confident that he alone could reconstruct the administration; but after two days of negotiations a combination of ministers was successfully put together under the leadership of Lloyd Geroge. Promised mixed but adequate parliamentary support the new regime took office on 7 December, with Lloyd George as prime minister. This second change of government since the start of the war was ostensibly not unlike the first: a shuffle and reallocation of portfolios without recourse to a general election. . . .

The British war cabinet settled into its duties in the second week of December 1916, a committee of five made up of Lloyd George, Lord Curzon, Lord Milner, Arthur Henderson and Bonar Law, and in support Hankey's proven secretarial machinery from the Committee of Imperial Defence. Of the five ministers Bonar Law alone continued "regular" duties as chancellor of the exchequer and war cabinet spokesman in the House of Commons. Apart from this one necessary concession to the lower house, the war cabinet was to work in isolation from the legislature. It was quickly realized that this new cabinet was also to work in isolation from what had hitherto been understood as the executive — that is, the twenty-odd heads of department meeting in cabinet to determine government policy. In Lloyd George's reorganization this most established of unofficial institutions of government was prorogued *sine die*. Each department of state would have its minister still, but he was permitted to attend the war cabinet only when summoned, and then only for the particular item of business for which his views were required. These moments apart, he and his colleagues, deprived of their collective responsibilities, were soon enough confined to carrying out orders from above, delivered in the form of war cabinet "conclusions", and carefully kept track of by Hankey or one of his assistants. Exhorted to administer rather than to govern, stranded and somewhat confused by the new channels through which executive power now began to flow, Lloyd George's ministers found themselves the handmaidens — at best the ladies-in-waiting — of the self-made monarch from Wales.

One minister who felt strongly and at once the loss of his prerogatives was Walter Long, colonial secretary in the new coalition. Courteous but easily annoyed, old fashioned and uncomplex, Long was not the easiest man to reconcile to the new order. He had supported Lloyd George's bid for power, but he expressed his apprehensions to the new prime minister on the day the government took office:

> I cannot conceal from myself that we are running grave risks in the abolition of the old constitutional system of governing by Cabinet. For instance, India and the Colonies may very well complain when they learn the simple fact that the Ministers who are charged with the care of their interests in the Imperial Government are no longer members of the Cabinet.[11]

It was a valid point for Long to make. He needed no intimacy with his new portfolio to know that the dominions were stretching to the limits their economies and their manpower, and even so had little knowledge of the direction or progress of the war in Europe. But if he hoped in this way to call in the new world to redress the balance of the old, he was disappointed. Two days later the war cabinet assembled without him, and continued to exclude him from their meetings.

Long was soon back with a more modest proposal for Lloyd George, suggesting that the dominions be sent a weekly cable of information about the war. Possibly this idea sprang from self-interested motives, for the regular dispatch of confidential news would enable the colonial secretary to see a wide range of war cabinet documents, and thus be kept in touch with government policy — in the new order of things a privilege not to be lightly discounted. At any rate, whatever the motives, the suggestion promised considerable advantages for the overseas governments. Lloyd George, however, was already thinking on much broader lines than his colonial secretary. Long wanted cablegrams. In reply Lloyd George announced his intention to hold a full-scale Imperial Conference at the earliest opportunity. The dominions, he reminded Long,

> have made enormous sacrifices, but we have held no conference with them as to either the objects of the war or the methods of carrying it out. They hardly feel that they have been consulted. As we must receive even more substantial support from them before we can hope to pull through, it is important that they should feel that they have a share in our councils as well as in our burdens.[12]

The colonial secretary, it seemed, was cautiously preaching to a prime minister already fully converted to the cause. Indeed, it appears that Lloyd George had determined at once on a conference with the dominions without securing the full approval of even his own war cabinet, with the result that two weeks later Maurice Hankey was still wondering about his chief's decision, noting in his diary, "As a matter of fact the war cabinet have not a notion of what they are to discuss, and as Bonar Law said, 'When [the dominion prime ministers] are here you will wish to goodness you could get rid of them'."[13]

Yet for all Hankey's nervous worries about not having an agenda, and Bonar Law's sour reluctance — an apt reminder of his unhelpful attitudes while colonial secretary — there were many men close to Lloyd George who from the outset of his regime offered enthusiastic support for any moves towards closer co-operation with the overseas governments. In the war cabinet the imperialist viewpoint was weightily represented by Lord Milner; Philip Kerr, another charter member of the Round Table group, added his influence as the prime minister's private secretary; at the Cabinet Office Leopold Amery, one of Hankey's assistants, was also well placed to inject the imperial element into relevant matters of policy. And in his calmer moments Hankey himself must count as a promoter of fuller imperial ties. As an ambitious career civil servant in a new and untried post he was cautious to a fault about being identified with any interest group, and particularly in these opening months of his job was distinctly cool towards Amery, whom he considered "foisted on me by Milner".[14] But his own earlier hopes for the creation of consultative machinery capable of giving the dominions a voice in imperial affairs were still alive, provided only that he could remain at the administrative centre of control. To none of these men, in their enthusiasm for empire and their privileged access to Lloyd George, were the anxieties of the colonial secretary of great concern, except perhaps as an expression of the traditional patterns of organization that now needed clearing away.

Lloyd George's decision to call an Imperial Conference thus checked Long's own initiatives. Nonetheless he could assume that the Colonial Office, which had organized such affairs since their inception in 1887 (and incorporated a conference secretariat within their department in 1907), would again be given the job of running the conference and in this way have an ample opportunity to manifest their involvement with imperial policy. Yet six years on from the last Imperial Conference such credentials looked far from convincing. Long was forgetting that even in 1911, the Committee of Imperial Defence had been used as an alternative forum for British-dominion discussions, and but for the war might have revealed further potential in this role. When the war cabinet came to discuss arrangements for the forthcoming meetings, in any event, it became clear that Colonial Office claims were not at all secure. Milner strongly opposed sticking to established procedure, and the colonial secretary, called in on this occasion to be given his say, found himself the only advocate of a conference on conventional lines. After a clearly heated debate it was settled that the dominion prime ministers should discuss the problems of war directly with the war cabinet. A cable was drafted to the overseas governments informing them

> that what His Majesty's Government contemplate is not a session of the ordinary Imperial Conference. They invite your Prime Minister to attend a series of special and continuous meetings of the War Cabinet.[15]

Long was not easily deterred, however. An appeal lodged two days later found the cabinet still determined "to supersede the idea of a Conference on former lines", but an important concession was now implied when they accepted that topics other than the war might be discussed outside the war cabinet — though "it was preferable not to invite such discussions". By dint of strenuous lobbying (particularly with Austen Chamberlain, secretary of state for India and keen to give Indian representatives as large a role as possible at the London talks) the colonial secretary had within a week fashioned this conciliatory gesture into a fully-fledged subsidiary conference, the war cabinet reluctantly letting him have his way. Thus after a tense confrontation of the old establishment with the new the main lines of the 1917 imperial meetings were laid down. Strategic problems of the war and possible peace terms were to be dealt with in the war cabinet, and secondary matters would be left to the Colonial Office. While dominion premiers would alone be members of the war cabinet, they would be able to bring to London whichever other colleagues they considered necessary.

The concession of a conference was a welcome fillip to the colonial secretary, although it did little to mitigate his hostility towards the proposed sessions in the war cabinet — a cabinet whose methods of government he continued privately to disparage.[16] It was clear that most of the important business with the dominions would be transacted in the war cabinet, and Long was anxious to reduce if possible the exclusiveness of those meetings. In this he was unwittingly helped by the dominion representatives themselves. By early March the delegations from Canada, New Zealand and Newfoundland had arrived in England, and in advance of the scheduled imperial meetings the government decided to open discussions by inviting the three prime ministers to the war cabinet. W. F. Massey of New Zealand, however, insisted that his colleague, Sir Joseph Ward (with whom he had formed a coalition government), must also attend — whereupon Borden, jealous of his rights, demanded a second seat for Canada. It was a problem the colonial secretary did nothing to resolve; indeed the increased size of this meeting provided justification for his own attendance. Considerations of protocol were thus allowed to jeopardize the intended format, and to set a most important precedent for the main sessions to come.[17] Three days later the war cabinet made a second attempt to secure a measure of intimate contact with a dominion prime minister, proposing that Borden alone should be invited to discuss questions concerning the United States. But Long was quick to complain about this to the foreign secretary, Arthur Balfour:

> I am compelled to ask that the invitation you contemplate extending to Borden alone shall be given to the others . . . The only sound principle seems to me to be to invite all or none.[18]

Rather than give the colonial secretary a chance to create further difficulties the war cabinet dropped the invitation altogether.

When, therefore, the Imperial War Cabinet began its regular meetings, it was attended by the Dominion prime ministers and their ministerial colleagues (an impending election in Australia prevented Hughes from participating), by eight British ministers, three Indian representatives and the military and naval service chiefs[19] — these latter possibly to keep British delegates in a majority, for fear of an adverse vote. Under the weight of such numbers intimacy had to give way to formality, and it was impossible to conduct these gatherings, as originally intended, as "special and continuous sessions of the War Cabinet". The day-to-day running of the war had perforce to be carried out by the British war cabinet, which continued to meet at least once a day throughout the weeks that the larger body was in session.

Despite the formal nature of the proceedings in the Imperial War Cabinet, the British government were at last able to give the overseas leaders the thorough briefing about the war that they had lacked for so long. Over the course of fourteen meetings, daily summaries of the military situation were followed by more general reports on a wide range of problems, covering manpower, material resources, finance, diplomacy, and economic strategies. This comprehensive survey not only gave the dominion ministers their first over-all picture of the war effort, but also convincingly demonstrated the urgent attempts of the Lloyd George ministry to co-ordinate and control that effort. The British prime minister's strategy of candid revelation struck exactly the right balance. On the one hand the manifest difficulties facing the empire, as he made clear, required even greater efforts from the dominions; on the other, his own resolute determination inspired the prime ministers to meet these new demands with every means possible. After only three meetings, the Imperial War Cabinet resolved that the empire "should put forth the whole of its military strength in 1917", and if need be "throughout 1918". Behind this simple affirmation lay a sense of common and dedicated purpose that had not been known since the opening months of the war.

British leaders brought the Imperial War Cabinet to terms with the increasing demands of the war through a straightforward exposition of the outstanding problems. There was little by way of forward-looking consultation on these issues, in part because it was obviously difficult to foresee what demands would be made as the war progressed — if indeed it was progressing at all, given the stalemate of attrition on the western front and Russia's collapse into revolution on the east. Even allowing for a future clouded with forbidding uncertainties, however, there were other more contingent restraints upon consultation in 1917. For one thing, there was still a palpable gap between war cabinet planning and the execution of fighting strategy in the field. Four months of power had not sufficed to gain Lloyd George's civilian administration the working control over military affairs necessary to bring the generals under their surveillance, a shortcoming that compromised any policy discussions in London. Yet in any case, it was plainly evident at the Imperial War Cabinet that even amongst themselves, the British authorities were far from agreed on over-all military priorities. Against Lloyd George's unwavering commitment to total victory — a stand that was strongly endorsed by Borden — Milner and his associates argued that the empire stood to benefit far more from a limited paramountcy over Germany, based on the expropriation of her colonial possessions. The Imperial Cabinet's agreement to make full effort throughout 1917 and 1918 represented success for the viewpoint of the two prime ministers — but equally, the lack of specific details in that resolution was an acknowledgement that firm strategic decisions had yet to be reached. The overseas leaders had no option but to trust the British government to do the right thing. For the moment it was enough that they had been brought up to date with the general situation.[20]

A more rewarding opportunity for tangible British-dominion consultations came at a later stage of the Imperial War Cabinet's proceedings, when after three weeks of appraising military affairs, the discussion turned to a consideration of possible conditions for a future settlement of peace. From the British point of view, consultation about peace terms was a practical necessity. Since any final peace treaty would be the product of an international conference, at which the dominions would understandably not be represented, it was essential to ascertain their views in advance, and in fact promises to this effect had been made to the overseas governments as early as 1915. For this purpose, therefore, two sub-committees of the Imperial Cabinet were established under Milner and Curzon to examine the empire's economic and territorial interests as they might relate to the eventual terms of peace.[21] Here, it seemed, a type of imperial executive had at last been constituted: two small groups of British and dominion ministers, meeting to derive an imperial consensus in advance on basic questions of policy.

Yet it is apparent, even so, that what passed for consultation in these two committees was little more than dominion ratification of British conclusions. Nor was this a matter of chance, however much overseas ministers might pride themselves on meeting their British colleagues on equal terms. In these or any other imperial gatherings the British delegates enjoyed one incomparable advantage, in having the administrative support of Whitehall's civil service. Whatever intramural antagonisms Lloyd George's regime might have created amongst his ministers there was no escaping the fact that the British departments of state, together with Hankey's secretarial bureau, constituted an establishment whose resources of information, planning and talent the dominion governments could never hope to match. (It might be added that however badly they argued amongst themselves, the ministers and civil servants of the mother country were nearly always prepared to present themselves as a firmly united interest *devant les enfants*.) Here was a fundamental structural inequality which weighed strongly in the balance between Britain and the dominions, and which would continue to exert an important influence over the evolving forms of their imperial association.

In the particular case of the Curzon and Milner committees, certainly, the initiative and control of the discussions rested squarely with the home ministers. Thus Curzon's group on territorial questions, far from taking up these matters as if for the first time, was conveniently provided with the report of an earlier British government inquiry into the same subject, conducted in late 1916[22] — and in the limited amount of time available the sub-committee could do little but ratify the conclusions already reached. The overseas representatives were no doubt gratified that Curzon's final report spoke of the need for further imperial consultations before any territorial bargains could be made with Britain's war allies. The sub-committee's conclusions, for all that, were a carefully prepared *fait accompli*.[23]

As discussions in the Imperial War Cabinet progressed from the immediate problems of the military conflict to the possible terms for peace, a variety of other issues less directly concerned with the war was examined in the Imperial War Conference, which assembled under the chairmanship of the colonial secretary on alternate days to the Imperial Cabinet. Although a good deal of time was taken up here with matters of secondary interest, there were a number of items on the conference's agenda that were of the highest priority, notably the empire's future economic objectives, post-war imperial defence policy . . . and constitutional relations. Like economics and defence this latter subject was also necessarily one for future planning—there was no desire to revise the constitutional basis of British-dominion relations during the war. Nonetheless, on several grounds constitutional matters demanded some attention in 1917. In the first place the overseas governments, in the light of the acknowledged importance of their war efforts, were anxious to consolidate their claims with the British authorities to a future voice in imperial policy-making, and thus were keen to examine possible methods for improving inter-imperial consultation. Closely tied up with any discussions about consultation, of course, was the Imperial War Cabinet itself, an innovation whose function and significance remained to be fully assessed. These matters in turn inevitably encouraged wider speculations about the future course of imperial relations. On all sides of the conference table ministers were concerned to know under what auspices they were gathered together.

Of all the parties to the constitutional discussions in 1917, the man most determined to seize and hold the initiative was Lord Milner, who brought to the study of imperial relations a long-standing interest and single-minded commitment. His importance for the 1917 talks is worth a moment's consideration. For ten years and more Milner and his ex-South Africa disciples, the Kindergarten, had been at the centre of an extensive campaign for the closer organic union of the empire, endeavouring privately to create "an immense nexus of influence and patronage for directing public policy in imperial and other matters".[24] Before the war they had little enough to show for their efforts; but the onset of hostilities offered fresh possibilities for the Milnerite cause. Admittedly on the theoretical side their major project, to build a federal constitutional model for the empire through joint negotiations between British and dominion imperialists, had to be shelved (and when Lionel Curtis, the project's director, went on to complete a model, he was obliged to publish it under his own name and without the imprimatur of the Round Table organization).[25] In practical terms, however, the strains placed by the war on imperial co-operation were regarded as telling evidence in support of federalist arguments. At first the Round Tablers thought it best to marshal these arguments for use at a post-war imperial conference — by which time the overseas governments would be thoroughly discontented with the existing constitutional relationship. But by 1916 Milner appeared ready for a much bolder step forward—into the open arena of British politics. With an eye to the manifest weakness of the Asquith-Bonar Law coalition he wrote to a colleague (who had suggested the revival of the Imperial Federation League, defunct for over twenty years) in March of that year:

> My hope rather is that out of the present political chaos, there may emerge a new party, which will make the organic unity of the Empire one of the planks of its programme. I think this would advance matters quicker than the formation of a League of a non-party character.[26]

The level of activity, he thought, could also be stepped up overseas. A month later he was telling a leading Canadian member of the Round Table movement: "My own view is that the time has come, or is very near at hand, when definite proposals for Imperial unification ought to take the place of the somewhat vague general propaganda."[27] Eight months later Milner was in office, if not with a new political party then at least with many of his friends around him. In Canada, Sir Wilfrid Laurier certainly overstated the case in claiming that the dominion "is now governed by a junta sitting in London, known as the 'Round Table' ";[28] but a London newspaper article was less far from the truth in seeing that a "new bureaucracy" had come to power, "whose ideas were not those of Mr. Lloyd George . . . but of Lord Milner".[29] The new format of the 1917 imperial discussions bore witness to the influence of the group. And it was Milner's intention not merely to see that the hybrid Imperial War Cabinet survived, but to make it the point of growth of a federated structure linking Britain and the dominions.

Nonetheless, despite the impressive political advantages that Milner with his associates now enjoyed, his campaign for imperial federation still lacked the essential support of his prime minister. Lloyd George acknowledged a personal and political sympathy for Milner.[30] He also well appreciated the collective strength of the Milnerites in his government — though the influence they enjoyed through their informal chain of connections could hardly compare with the power and control available to Lloyd George through the cabinet secretariat (where Hankey, moreover, kept a careful eye on Milner's friends). The prime minister, in any event, had called these men into office for their administrative talents and their commitment to a total war effort, not for their constitutional ideas. The same priorities held true for the 1917 imperial discussions. The overseas leaders had been summoned to London because a greater contribution to the war was needed from the dominions, and though constitutional questions were on the agenda they were only tangential to Lloyd George's major preoccupations. He was certainly not prepared to jeopardize the chance of an increased imperial war effort by committing the British government to Milner's constitutional designs.

Thus in the end it was in a personal capacity only that Milner presented his case for imperial federation to the Imperial War Conference. Initially, it seems, he offered something close to an ultimatum, threatening to sabotage the conference's proceedings unless federation was agreed upon — a striking manifestation of his major premise that the empire must either federate or disintegrate.[31] In a more concerted attempt, however, to convince the dominion ministers of their case, Milner and his friends removed the discussions from the conference table to the more congenial atmosphere of the dining table, where at "a series of little dinners . . . overseas men have met a number of us belonging to the Home Government".[32] Dominion reactions, even so, were not encouraging. Massey, as expected, was "very Imperialistic and determined to force the issue",[33] but neither Borden nor Jan Smuts of South Africa would endorse imperial federation. Smuts would have made his point by simply refusing to consider constitutional revisions during the war. Borden, while supporting this argument against wartime change, was prepared to answer the federalist position more directly by putting forward counter-proposals for the approval of the Imperial War Conference. The initiative now switched from Milner to the Canadian prime minister, who proceeded to canvass opinions amongst the overseas delegations for constitutional measures of his own.

The whole weight of Borden's experience as prime minister of the senior dominion placed him firmly against the proponents of imperial federation, and impelled him to define and promote an alternative conception of imperial development. He himself, of course, was no stranger to federalist ideas by 1917. His visit to London five years earlier in 1912 had brought him up against the Round Table persuaders. A year later his newly-appointed adviser on external affairs, Loring Christie, had soon revealed that he too subscribed to the "either-or" school of thought, and was bent on converting the prime minister. A policy review by Christie in late 1913 argued strongly that the dominion had only two feasible options for its foreign affairs: to be fully independent, or to gain sufficient control of a truly integrated imperial foreign policy so as to meet Canadian requirements.[34] There was soon established a dominion Round Table group to drive home the logic of these alternatives, and to create popular support for closer imperial union.[35] Yet the movement in Canada had never achieved a commanding influence. In the pre-war period, there was little need for any official response to the fledgling federalist organization, and Borden appears to have taken scant notice of it amidst his other preoccupations. And the stimulus of war itself failed to create any wider measure of support for imperial federation in Canada. For all attempts to play up the war for their own purposes (or to turn anti-French Canadian feelings into pro-empire loyalties) the local Round Tablers found that their federalist doctrines had to work across the grain of a growing Canadian nationalism. (The publication in 1916 of Curtis's *Problem of the Commonwealth* was in this respect a distinct embarrassment to the Canadian faithful, who tried to dissociate themselves from its ruthless imperial logic.) Canada's active and total commitment to war, in short, was marked by a decided deepening of national sentiment — and at the very centre of the war effort, Borden himself was no less untouched. As the fighting took its course through 1915 and 1916, his own appreciation of Canada's place in the empire — and in the war — revealed a distinctly nationalist outlook. His conviction that Canada had a right to be consulted in the making of imperial foreign or military policies was one aspect of this new perspective. But by March 1916, for instance, Borden was also thinking that the next governor general for the dominion might well be a Canadian.[36] As he was preparing to leave for London eleven months later, he was readily able to satisfy the staunchly nationalist J.W. Dafoe, editor of the *Manitoba Free Press*, that he held no brief whatever from the advocates of federalist integration of the empire. Like Dafoe, Borden with an increasing assurance had come to regard Canada not as an adjunct to the war but as a principal in her own right, not as a colonial assistant but an imperial partner. "I should like to think", Dafoe wrote after their interview, "that Canadians can rely upon him to stand up to his position under the pressures which will be put upon him when he reaches London".[37]

In reaction to those pressures, but equally in response to his own nationalist impulses, it thus came about that Borden assumed the leading dominion role in constitutional affairs in the Imperial War Conference. Closest to him in spirit in the creation of an overseas consensus was Smuts, though in view of the excessive credit given to the South African in subsequent accounts of the 1917 negotiations,[38] it is worth emphasizing that even he needed persuading at first, particularly as regards the extent of possible dominion participation in the making of the empire's foreign policy. A telling entry in Borden's diary for 22 March 1917 reveals:

> had an hour's discussion with Smuts and Massey as to agenda and as to resolutions to be moved respecting constitutional relations. I insisted on a clause declaring our right to an adequate voice in foreign policy. Smuts fears this may involve responsibility for financial aid in defence, etc.[39]

Five days later, in any event, all the overseas leaders had come round, and with the approval and support of the colonial secretary Borden was able to put the finishing touches to a draft resolution.[40] The results finally appeared on 16 April, as conference resolution IX.

Conceding that the war precluded any immediate revision of imperial relations, resolution IX made no specific recommendations. It offered instead a statement of principles, to serve in effect as the terms of reference for a post-war constitutional conference. Even in these general terms, however, it effectively discounted imperial federation as a future possibility. Although there must be stronger connections — a voice in foreign policy, and continuous consultations — between Britain and the dominions, the keystone of the imperial structure was not to be organic unity, but the national autonomy of the dominions:

> any [constitutional] readjustment, while thoroughly preserving all existing powers of self-government and complete control of domestic affairs, should be based upon a full recognition of the Dominions as autonomous nations of an Imperial Commonwealth, and of India as an important part of the same, should recognize the right of the Dominions and India to an adequate voice in foreign policy and foreign relations, and should provide effective arrangements for continuous consultations in all important matters of common Imperial concern.

In resolution IX, the overseas ministers declared their intention to pursue a constitutional course between federation and independence, a choice that Milner and his associates had tried to prove was not legitimate. In essence, the federalists argued that status and function, the two components of constitutional development, could not be held for long out of alignment: they must point either to integration or to the break-up of the empire. The supposition behind this argument was that the dominions' willing commitment to the imperial war effort would guide them towards integration. Here in particular, however, the federalist analysis was too narrow. Far from producing any such predominant impulse the war had given rise to a wide range of feelings in the dominions, confirming imperial loyalties but at the same time encouraging local nationalism. It was precisely this complexity of response that Borden was able to translate into resolution IX, in which the federalist alternatives were transcended. It was the dominions' declared purpose now to integrate themselves functionally in imperial affairs — not simply by continuing and expanding their material contributions to the war effort, but by gaining meaningful access to the executive centre of imperial affairs. The Imperial War Cabinet was an obvious manifestation of the new order of things. Yet this new integration was to be based on a full acceptance of their status as autonomous communities of the empire.

For all the ready acceptance of resolution IX, it nonetheless remained to be seen whether this statement of intent represented a genuine way forward, or merely an unstable compromise between imperial unity and national independence. In April 1917, in any event, its effect on the scope of constitutional speculations in official circles was negligible. Smuts was happy to think that imperial federation had been "negatived by implication". The Colonial Office, for their part, were somewhat puzzled as to the shape of things to come.[41] Even Milner found no cause for dismay. From the constitutional conference, he forecast, the dominions would emerge with

> some permanent representation in an Imperial Cabinet dealing with Defence, Foreign Affairs and Communications; and would undertake to provide in their own way for a certain definite proportion of the cost of the Navy and the Consular and Diplomatic Service. It would be a lop-sided sort of arrangement, but might carry us on for a bit. Nothing could, in fact, be more lopsided than the present temporary Imperial War Cabinet, which, nevertheless, has I think, served a useful purpose.[42]

Clearly he hoped that the practical implications of joint consultation and policy making might be such as to undermine the strength of dominion autonomy.[43]

For the moment, however, the most important question was the future of the Imperial War Cabinet, whose 1917 session was drawing to a close. On the eve of its final meeting, the British war cabinet met to consider the results of various informal ministerial soundings on this subject. One suggestion was that Smuts, who was about to take up temporary membership of the British war cabinet, might act as spokesman for all the dominion governments, an idea Lloyd George had put to Borden but which had not been well received by him. A second idea was that a minister from each government might remain in London and the Imperial War Cabinet be kept in semi-permanent session; but here again the colonial secretary had to report that the overseas prime ministers were not enthusiastic. The resistance to both schemes, of course, hinged on the need to delegate responsibility in imperial affairs from the dominion premiers to nominated representatives — an essential pre-requisite of any well-integrated constitutional structure, but one that in 1917, at least, overseas leaders were not prepared to confront. The only alternative that found general support, therefore, was a plan for an annual session of the Imperial War Cabinet, and at their final session for 1917 this policy was officially endorsed.

It is worth noting that Borden, who had worked hard to secure the necessary acceptance for this policy, was clearly pleased at the prospect of yearly meetings of the Imperial Cabinet — and small wonder, given that leave of absence from Ottawa could be organized with far less administrative disruption than was possible for the other dominion leaders. Canada's relative proximity to Britain, in this respect, was a critical advantage for the senior dominion, and one that possibly had already begun to exert a subtle but powerful influence over Canadian attitudes. At the threshold of a new co-operative venture in imperial affairs, with the door to high-level consultations beginning to open, Borden would be well placed to respond to calls to London for conferences — and by extension would feel a keener sense of frustration were such calls not to be issued. His fellow prime ministers, based as they were in the southern hemisphere, could hardly fail to have a different perspective: where a minimum of twelve weeks had to be invested in any consultations in London, the temptation to leave things to Whitehall would be understandably much greater. Whitehall, it would soon enough emerge, would often feel the same.

Notes

1. Canada, House of Commons, *Debates*, 19 Aug. 1914.

2. From London, acting high commissioner Perley wrote that the war "cannot go on for very many months", though he reported that Kitchener's estimate was from eighteen months to two years. Perley-Borden, 15 Aug. 1914, *Documents on Canadian External Relations* (hereinafter *DCER*), vol. I, *1909-18* (Ottawa, 1967), 22.

3. See A. J. P. Taylor, *English History, 1914-45* (Oxford, 1965), 59.

4. G. Smith, "Canadian External Affairs during World War One", in Keenleyside, *The Growth of Canadian Policies in External Affairs* (Durham, N.C., 1960), 38-40.

5. An inquiry from Borden in March 1915 as to when British ministers thought the war might end produced the following speculations: Harcourt (Colonial Office) 18 months, Grey (Foreign Office) 8 months, Kitchener (War Office) 12 months. The betting at Lloyds showed even odds for a finish by the New Year! Perley papers: Perley-Borden, 17 March 1915.

6. Perley-Borden, 28 Oct. 1915; *DCER*, I, 92.

7. The British government had established a war council in November 1914, which became the Dardanelles committee in June 1915 and the war committee in November 1915. In each of its manifestations, however, it was no more than a cabinet sub-committee, responsible to that body.

8. Bonar Law-Perley, 5 Nov., Perley-Borden, 5 Nov. 1915; *DCER*, I, 96-7.

9. Borden diary, Jan. 1916; Perley papers: Borden-Perley, 4 Jan. 1916. Aitken (Lord Beaverbrook, 1917) was a Canadian, owner of the *Daily Express*, and at the time a British Conservative MP. He provided an informal liaison for the Canadian government with both the overseas Canadian forces and Whitehall.

10. A lack of interest accepted and endorsed by Bonar Law's biographer and indeed extended by him to cover the whole range of Colonial Office wartime administration. See R. Blake, *The Unknown Prime Minister* (London, 1955), 261.

11. Lloyd George papers: Long-Ll. G., 7 Dec. 1916.

12. Lloyd George papers: Ll. G.-Long, 12 Dec. 1916, printed in D. Lloyd George, *War Memoirs*, 2 vols. (London, 1938), I, 1026.

13. Hankey diary; S. Roskill, *Hankey, Man of Secrets* (London, 1974), I, 348.

14. Hankey diary; *ibid*, 349, 352-3. "He is a scheming little devil", he wrote, "and his connection with *The Times* would make it possible for him to oust me".

15. CAB 23/I: WC 15, 21 Dec. 1916.

16. W. Hewins, *The Apologia of an Imperialist*, 2 vols. (London, 1929), II, 104. Lloyd George, hearing of Long's complaints, told Hankey "he didn't give a d—n if Walter Long resigned or not, and would rather welcome a row in the House and a General Election". Roskill, *Hankey*, I, 359.

17. Hankey noted in his diary, "Lloyd George decided the whole caboodle must be asked but was very bored." Lord Hankey, *The Supreme Command*, 2 vols. (London, 1961), II, 568.

18. Lloyd George papers: Long-Balfour, 5 March 1917.

19. CAB 23/40: IWC I, 20 March 1917.

20. A fuller treatment of the range of strategic discussion at the 1917 meetings is provided by G. Cook, "Sir Robert Borden, Lloyd George and British Military Policy, 1917-18", *The Historical Journal* XIV, 2 (1971).

21. The minutes of the Milner committee are in CAB 21/71; those of the Curzon committee are in CAB 21/77.

22. CID, sub-committee on territorial changes. Minutes and interim reports of the committee are in CAB 16/36.

23. See 44 ff.

24. C. Quigley, "The Round Table Movement in Canada, 1909-1938", *Canadian Historical Review* (hereinafter *CHR*) XLIII, 3 (1962), 304; cf. J. Eayrs, "The Round Table Movement in Canada, 1909-1920", *CHR* XXXVIII, I (1957). The sixtieth anniversary issue of *The Round Table* 240 (1970), contains useful general articles on the beginnings of the movement.

25. L. Curtis, *The Problem of the Commonwealth* (London, 1916).

26. Milner papers: Milner-Sidney Low, 24 March 1916.

27. Milner papers: Milner-Sir Edmund Walker, 22 April 1916. *The Round Table* also took a more assertive tone in its promotion of imperial federation. See "The Imperial Dilemma", *The Round Table* 24 (Sept. 1916); "The Growing Necessity for Constitutional Reform", *ibid.*, 25 (Dec. 1916).

28. Quoted in J. D. Milner, *Richard Jebb and the Problem of Empire* (London, 1956), 23.

29. *The Nation*, 24 Feb. 1917. See P.A. Lockwood, "Milner's Entry into the War Cabinet, December 1916", *The Historical Journal* VII, 2 (1964), an excellent study of Milner's political activities in 1916.

30. "He is a poor man and so am I. He does not represent the landed or capitalist classes any more than I do. He is keen on social reform and so am I." Quoted in K. Morgan, "Lloyd George's Premiership: A Study in 'Prime Ministerial Government,' " *The Historical Journal* XIII, 1 (1970), 132. For an interesting insight on the affinity between democratic socialism and imperialism in these years, see Enoch Powell, "The Myth of Empire", *The Round Table* 240, (Nov. 1970), 440.

31. W. Hewins, *Apologia*, II, 134, 144. No record of Milner's threat appears in the minutes of the conference, a draft unedited print of which is in CO 532/97.

32. Milner papers: Milner-A. Glazebrook (a Canadian member of the Round Table movement), 21 April 1917.

33. Lloyd George papers: Long-Ll. G. (April 1917).

34. Memorandum cited by R. C. Brown, "Sir Robert Borden, The Great War and Anglo-Canadian Relations", in *Character and Circumstance*, edited by J. Moir (Toronto, 1970).

35. See V. Massey, *What's Past is Prologue* (London, 1963), 35 ff.

36. Perley papers: Borden-Perley, 14 March 1916.

37. Dafoe-Sir Clifford Sifton (his publisher), 12 Feb. 1917, quoted in Eayrs, "Round Table Movement", 18.

38. Leopold Amery felt that Smuts was the "main author" of the War Conference's constitutional resolution; *My Political Life*, II: *War and Peace, 1914–1929* (London, 1953), 109. Smuts' biographer accepted this view without further evidence; W. L. Hancock, *Smuts*, I: *The Sanguine Years, 1870–1919* (Cambridge, 1962), 429.

39. Borden diary, 22 March 1917.

40. *Ibid.*, 27 March 1917. A detailed examination of the various rejected drafts put up by the other prime ministers is provided by R. C. Brown and R. Bothwell, "The Canadian Resolution", in *Policy by other Means*, edited by R. C. Brown and R. Bothwell (Toronto, 1972).

41. CO 532/98: minutes, May 1917.

42. Milner papers: Milner-Glazebrook, 21 April 1917.

43. *The Round Table* accepted resolution IX though insisting that short of full integration no constitutional organization would work satisfactorily: "While welcoming the changes let us not suppose that they will in themselves solve the fundamental problem which lies at the root of the politics of the Empire." *The Round Table* 27 (June 1917).

CANADA AND THE THREAT OF WAR†

The tragic and inescapable fact about the present world situation is that we are living in the shadow of an impending war. Another first-class war may not yet be inevitable. A miracle or a succession of miracles may remove that shadow. There can be no doubt, however, that the probability of another first-class war in the near future is very great.

It is with the near future that a statesman in office must be mainly concerned — not with the distant future nor with the immediate or distant past. When the world is stumbling daily from crisis to crisis and is in danger of stumbling any day from crisis to catastrophe, a minister for foreign affairs must be mainly concerned not with who or what is responsible for the present international anarchy, nor with the long-run objectives of foreign policy but with what his country's policy should be to-day, to-morrow, or during the next twelve months.

What is a good rule for the foreign minister is perhaps a good rule for the foreign minister's contemporary critic. The critic ought not to waste his time crying over the milk that was spilt during the Sino-Japanese dispute, the Chaco war, the Italo-Abyssinian campaign. That is the historian's job: to apportion the blame between this country and that — between Japan and the United States, between Canada and Italy, between France, Germany, Great Britain, and so on; between this person and that — M. Poincaré, President Wilson, Herr Hitler, and Mr. Mackenzie King; between capitalism and communism, socialism and fascism, stupidity and malevolence. The most useful thing a critic of Mr. Mackenzie King's present foreign policy can do is to ask whether his is a desirable policy for Canada to follow in the near future.

Mr. King's foreign policy, as deduced from his statements and actions since his reassuming office on October 23, 1935, can be summed up as follows:[1]

1. The guiding principle in the formulation of Canada's foreign policy should be the maintenance of the unity of Canada as a nation.

2. Canada's foreign policy is, in the main, not a matter of Canada's relations to the League, but of Canada's relations to the United Kingdom and the United States.

3. Canada should, as a general rule, occupy a back seat at Geneva or elsewhere when European or Asiatic problems are being discussed.

4. Canada is under no *obligation* to participate in the military sanctions of the League or in the defence of any other part of the Commonwealth.

5. Canada is under no *obligation* to participate in the economic sanctions of the League.

6. Before the Canadian government agrees in future to participate in military or economic sanctions or in war, the approval of the parliament or people of Canada will be secured.

7. Canada is willing to participate in international inquiries into international economic grievances.

†Escott Reid, "Canada and the Threat of War. A Discussion of Mr. Mackenzie King's Foreign Policy," *University of Toronto Quarterly* VI (Jan. 1937): 242–253.

1. *The guiding principle in the formulation of Canada's foreign policy should be the maintenance of the unity of Canada as a nation.*

With the first of these principles it is difficult to quarrel. The purpose of the Canadian government's policy — whether foreign or domestic — ought, of course, to be to promote the welfare of the people of Canada. The normal assumption upon which a Canadian government must work is that the welfare of the people of Canada would be promoted by the continued existence of the Canadian nation, held together not by force but by common consent. The guiding principle in the formulation of Canada's domestic and foreign policy should, therefore, be the maintenance of the unity of Canada as a nation. This means that a government should not adopt a policy on a matter of overwhelming importance, involving deep differences of opinion between Canadians, unless this policy is supported not merely by a substantial majority of Canadians but by substantial majorities in each important section of Canada. Otherwise there will develop between different groups of the Canadian people cleavages so great that the continued existence of the Dominion of Canada may be gravely endangered.

The argument in favour of this first principle of Mr. King's foreign policy can be put another way. One may believe that the main objective of Canada's foreign policy should be the maintenance of the integrity of the British Empire, or of the U.S.S.R., or the defence of democracy, socialism, or the rule of law. It does not follow from this that in the event of an attack on the British Empire, the U.S.S.R., democracy, socialism, or the rule of law, the Canadian government should try to come to their defence with all the forces at its command, if an attempt to intervene on such a scale would provoke so serious a civil disturbance that any effective intervention would be rendered impossible. The maintenance of a substantial degree of Canadian unity is an essential prerequisite to the effective carrying out of any foreign policy.

2. *Canada's foreign policy is, in the main, not a matter of Canada's relations to the League but of Canada's relations to the United Kingdom and the United States.*

Under present conditions this statement is a mere truism. Collective security does not exist. The League has still, as Mr. King has said, "a long-range importance;" but in a world which is on the brink of war, our relations with the United Kingdom, and the United States, are of more immediate importance, if only for the one reason that we shall not become involved in war unless one of those two countries first becomes involved.

3. *Canada should, as a general rule, occupy a back seat at Geneva or elsewhere when European or Asiatic problems are being discussed.*

The main purpose of this "back seat" policy is to give Canada as much freedom of action as possible in the event of war by trying to ensure that Canada does not in advance, by her actions at Geneva or elsewhere, become involved in a "moral" obligation to send armed forces overseas to participate in war or in the application of other forms of force. She might well become involved in a "moral" obligation if her representatives at Geneva, London, or elsewhere were responsible for initiating a policy, which, when adopted by other nations, led to war. In December, 1935, for example, it was possible that the application of an oil sanction against Italy might have led to war. The risk was perhaps worth running, and Canada was prepared to join with other nations in imposing an oil sanction. But she was not prepared to involve herself in advance in an obligation to send armed forces overseas to participate in war. The Canadian government, therefore, made it clear that Dr. Riddell's proposal on oil sanctions "was not the Canadian government's proposal, but that it was simply the proposal of an individual member of a committee."[2] If the Canadian government had not done that, it would have been held responsible for initiating the oil sanction, and if war had ensued from its application, many people both inside and outside Canada would have held that Canada was under a "moral," though not a legal, obligation to send armed forces overseas to participate in that war.

If one believes that the Canadian parliament or people should, if war breaks out, be as free as possible from "moral" obligations to participate, so that they may be able to decide for themselves in the light of all the circumstances at the time whether or not they should participate, then one must be in favour of the "back-seat" policy.

Another argument in favour of the "back-seat" policy is that a "front-seat" policy would do us harm and the world no good. "Any general war [in Europe] would be a calamity to civilization that would drag us downward with that part of the world from which we sprang; but in the present aspect of affairs we cannot help to prevent it, for it rests upon conditions there which we cannot change, upon the inability of European nations to act with harmony enough to settle their dissensions by peaceful means."[3] Lawrence Lowell's statement about the inability of the United States to exert any serious constructive influence in Europe to-day applies with much greater force to Canada.

4 and 5. *Canada is under no obligation to participate in the economic and military sanctions of the League or in the defence of any other part of the Commonwealth.*

The main argument in favour of this policy is the desirability, under present international and domestic conditions, of Canada's keeping a free hand, so that she can, if she wants to, refrain from intervening in an overseas war. She obviously will have tied her hands in advance if she is legally committed to participate, in certain circumstances, in the sanctions of the League or in the defence of the Commonwealth.

The argument for the free hand is in large measure domestic. Canada must be able to pick and choose between the various types of war in which she may be invited to take part. There are certain conceivable wars in which for Canada to take part would be to invite almost certain civil war. Participation in other sorts of war might not so seriously endanger Canadian unity. Of late the foreign policy of the Vatican seems to be growing increasingly pro-fascist and anti-communist. Certainly dominant groups in French Canada seem increasingly to be flirting with fascism and becoming more embittered against communism. Four out of every ten Canadians are Roman Catholics. Three of those four Roman Catholics are French. What would this forty per cent of the Canadian population and fascist sympathizers in English-speaking Canada do if a Canadian government decided to participate actively on the side of communist Russia and "socialist" France against fascist Germany, Austria, and Italy? Many of them would certainly not be convinced by the argument that the war was not a war "between economic systems, between social philosophies, . . . between religious faiths,"[4] but was instead a war in defence of the rule of law, the collective system, or the British Empire.

The possibility of maintaining the national unity of Canada demands that the Canadian government be under no obligation to participate in the application of force overseas.

6. *Before the Canadian government agrees in future to participate in military or economic sanctions or in war, the approval of the parliament or people of Canada will be secured.*

Since the question of participation by Canada in war or in other forms of force is a matter of life and death to many Canadian citizens, to their friends and families, it would seem only right that the citizen or his representative in parliament should, if possible, be consulted before the government takes positive action. The pledge to consult parliament or the people is obviously not intended to apply to the remote contingency of an armed attack on the territory of a neutral Canada. In such circumstances the Canadian government would certainly not wait till parliament were convened before taking steps to repel the invader by force of arms.

Using this as an analogy, critics of parliamentary or popular control over declarations of war say that the Canadian cabinet should also be prepared to shoulder the responsibility for immediate armed intervention overseas. They argue that if we are going to intervene at all we should intervene at the beginning of the war when our assistance would be of most value. Some, indeed, go so far as to say that since the war will be short and sharp, our only chance of helping our allies will be to intervene immediately with as much force as we can bring to bear. To advocate this in Canada comes close to advocating irresponsible government. If a major war broke out involving Great Britain — and this is the war which we all have in mind — it is most unlikely that any Canadian cabinet would be unanimous in favour of immediate armed intervention on the largest possible scale. A substantial number of cabinet ministers would resign if the majority tried to put such a decision through. The cabinet would have to be re-formed. Until it met parliament and received a vote of confidence, no one could be certain that it had the support of a majority in the House of Commons and was therefore able to continue in office without a new election. It is possible that the following series of events might take place: the interventionist majority in the cabinet sends Canadian armed forces to Europe; it convenes parliament to ratify its decision; it is defeated in parliament; it dissolves the House; it is defeated in the general election; and it is succeeded by a non-interventionist government, which immediately recalls the Canadian troops.

That is not a pleasant prospect. For one thing the passions of the opposition during the election would be raised to white heat by the thought that Canadian troops had been sent to Europe by a government which did not have the confidence of parliament, and that at the very moment the election was taking place those Canadian troops were being killed. In equal measure the withdrawal of Canadian troops by the new Canadian government would infuriate the supporters of intervention.

A debate in the Canadian House of Commons, or a general election, to decide the question of participation in war would be a nasty business calculated to strain Canadian unity almost to the breaking point. A debate or an election to ratify the action of a government which had already sent Canadian troops overseas, would be an even nastier business provided, as is likely, there were a substantial number of the Canadian people opposed to intervention. It might well strain Canadian unity to the breaking point.

A compromise policy is, of course, possible. A Canadian government might say that it was prepared to participate in economic sanctions without securing the approval of the parliament or people of Canada. This was, in fact, the policy followed by Mr. Mackenzie King, in October, 1935, in respect of the application of economic sanctions against Italy. This is the policy which Mr. King, in view of his experience during the Italo-Abyssinian crisis, has decided to give up. One of his reasons appears to be that economic sanctions and military sanctions are very similar in that they are both means by which one state (or group of states) endeavours to impose its will on another state. A sharp distinction between the two is therefore unwarranted. Secondly, the application of effective economic sanctions may lead to war. Whether economic sanctions "will progress into military measures is not necessarily within the control of the powers that impose them; that may depend on the calculation of advantage and disadvantage made by those against whom the test of will is directed."[5] To participate in economic sanctions is thus to participate in what may be the initial stages of war. Participation in the initial stages of war renders more difficult non-participation in the war that may follow. Therefore, if parliamentary or popular control over questions of participation in war is to be real and effective, it must apply equally to economic and to military sanctions.

7. *Canada is willing to participate in international inquiries into international economic grievances.*

Certainly if the danger of war is to be lessened the economic grievances of the dissatisfied powers must be investigated, regardless of whether, to begin with, we believe that there is, or is not, an economic basis for those grievances. It would be hard to find any intelligent person who would criticize Mr. King for going too far when he declared in the House of Commons last June: "Inquire we should into any question, raw materials, population movements, labour conditions, that is felt as a grievance. . . . Within the measure of our power we must pursue the attempt to bring international trade gradually back to a sane basis, to lessen the throttling controls and barriers."[6]

An examination of the seven points of Mr. King's foreign policy thus demonstrates (to one critic at least) how well each point, taken by itself, is suited to present conditions. But the adequacy of the policy as a whole is a different matter. Mr. King has certainly not provided an answer to many pressing questions about Canada's foreign policy. It will be sufficient to indicate what some of these questions are.

1. He has said that Canada is under no *obligation* to participate in war or in other forms of force. He has not stated whether he is in favour of Canada's participating in certain circumstances and to a certain extent — and if so, in what circumstances and to what extent.

2. He has pledged himself to consult the parliament or people of Canada before his government agrees to participate in war or in other forms of force. He has not let us know whether it is to be parliament or the people, and if the people, whether by general election or by plebiscite.

3. He must envisage the possibility of a great war in which neither the United Kingdom nor Canada is engaged. In such a war what sort of neutrality policy is he in favour of Canada's pursuing: the old-fashioned neutrality of trying to sell as much as possible at as high a price as possible to as many belligerents as possible; or the new-fashioned neutrality of embargoes on the export of arms and munitions to all belligerents, and on the public floating of loans by all belligerents?

4. If he envisages the possibility of Canada's taking no active part in a great war involving the United Kingdom, does he favour a state of passive belligerency for Canada or one of complete neutrality[7] — and if complete neutrality, is it to be old-fashioned or new-fashioned neutrality?

5. He has emphasized the fact that Canada's relations with the United States are of great importance. He has not said whether, if a great war breaks out in which the United States is neutral, Canada is going to co-operate with the United States in an attempt to ensure that the purpose of its neutrality legislation is not frustrated. Nor has he given any inkling of what he would recommend Canada's doing if the United States should become involved in a war with Japan.

6. And just because he has not answered all these questions he is unable to define what Canadian defence policy he favours.

7. He has said that he favours Canadian participation in international inquiries into international economic grievances. He has not indicated how far his government might be willing to modify Canadian policies in the light of the recommendations made by such international inquiries.

Mr. King has put forward a seven-point foreign policy. If he wants to give the Canadian people a fairly complete picture of his foreign policy, he will have to emulate President Wilson and give us a fourteen-point programme. But if Mr. King were to give unambiguous answers to the seven questions he has left unanswered, he would raise a tremendous political storm in Canada. Parties would split. Passions would be aroused. The national unity of Canada would be subjected to severe strains. If war should break out, such a crisis will probably be inevitable. It is human not to wish to hasten the arrival of the inevitable, if the inevitable is unpleasant — and perhaps dangerous.

The argument in favour of provoking the crisis now instead of waiting, is much the same as the argument for the "preventive" war. A crisis now would settle the question, and as a result there would be no crisis of any importance when war did break out. A crisis to-day would not be as severe as a crisis during a war. In other words, a crisis to-day would be a "preventive" crisis. But democracies and democratic statesmen hate both preventive wars and preventive crises.

Notes

1. For a detailed presentation see my "Mr. Mackenzie King's Foreign Policy, 1935–1936" *Canadian Journal of Economics and Political Science* III (Feb. 1937).

2. Canada, House of Commons, *Debates* Feb. 11, 1936, 110.

3. A. Lawrence Lowell, "Alternatives before the League," *Foreign Affairs* (Oct. 1936), 109–10.

4. League of Nations Assembly, Sept. 29, 1936, Verbatim record, 2. Speech by Mr. Mackenzie King.

5. House of Commons, *Debates*, June 18, 1936, 4187.

6. *Ibid.*, pp. 4195–96.

7. For a statement of some of the difficulties in the way of either alternative see P. E. Corbett, "Isolation for Canada?" *Quarterly* VI (Oct. 1936), 120–31.

CANADIAN FOREIGN POLICY, 1935–1939†

"If you were to ask any Canadian," Stephen Leacock wrote in 1939, " 'Do you have to go to war if England does?' he'd answer at once, 'Oh, no.' If you then said, 'Would you to go war if England does?' he'd answer, 'Oh, yes.' And if you asked, 'Why?' he would say, reflectively, 'Well, you see, we'd have to.' "[1]

Leacock's typical Canadian of 1939 had solved the conundrum that confronts the historian of Canadian foreign policy between the wars: support for Britain was first a moral duty, and a political duty, if it was at all, a long way after. The subject of long and complicated constitutional struggles, Canadian autonomy once achieved turned out to be like free will: it existed to enchance the righteous choice. Neutrality, like the devil, was there to provide a colourful background and to ensnare unsophisticated French Canadians, occasionally fractious academics and some unwary Englishmen.

What did puzzle Canadians in the last prewar years and long after was where Prime Minister W.L. Mackenzie King stood on the question of Canada's "duty to Great Britain". Critics at the time dealt only in terms of probabilities, for until the sticking point of September, 1939, neither King nor fate presented them with a clear, irretrievable decision. The fluidity of Mackenzie King's policy in external relations has continued to bedevil historians looking for clarity and consistency, if not on the public level then at least in the confidential memoranda that underlay and presumably expressed the thought of the Canadian government.

The result, however, is a more private and confidential expression of the same vagueness and imprecision that blurred King's public persona. It is, however, possible to discern certain self-contradictory rather than complementary themes in King's conduct of foreign policy. Pre-eminent was his distaste for war and fear of Canadian involvement in any future world conflict. Accompanying this wholly reasonable position was the realisation that neither Canada's international nor her internal situation would permit isolation from a major European war. Responding to these two imperatives, King's policy between 1935 and 1939 veered and wobbled according to the interpretation that he put on the international situation of the day. But as a contemporary observer recognised, King had always believed "that if Britain became engaged in a serious struggle Canada would again bleed and impoverish herself on Britain's behalf".[2] The profundity of this conviction and King's knowledge of the damage that another war could do to Canadian national unity defined his efforts—not to keep Canada out of any war, which he knew to be virtually impossible, but to encourage the possibilities of peace.

The prime minister's chosen policy for peace was appeasement. The abandonment of the restraints imposed upon Germany by the Treaty of Versailles, the reunification of the German *Volk*, the end of the pompous legalities of the League of Nations, all these commended themselves to Mackenzie King. They were objectives that could be achieved without violence, through deliberate negotiation.

†J.L. Granatstein and Robert Bothwell, " 'A Self-Evident National Duty': Canadian Foreign Policy, 1935–1939," *Journal of Imperial and Commonwealth History* III, 2 (Jan. 1975): 212–233.

King had made his career out of industrial and political negotiations, and he was, as the British high commissioner in Ottawa correctly observed, "temperamentally as well as politically attracted by a policy of settlement by negotiations".[3]

King's predilections were powerfully reinforced by his domestic circumstances. The Liberal Party, which he again led to victory in 1935, had traditionally based its appeal in Quebec on its opposition to imperial adventures and, more recently, to conscription for overseas service. The leader of the federal Liberals in the province, Ernest Lapointe, was King's right-hand-man and indispensable in the cabinet. At one point, King had promised Lapointe the post of secretary of state for external affairs, and the latter was disappointed when King relegated him to the Ministry of Justice in 1935 and kept External Affairs for himself. Even so, Lapointe retained his interest in foreign policy and acted as a restraint on King's initiatives in the field.[4] None of King's other ministers, however, showed more than sporadic interest in questions of foreign policy.

As secretary of state for external affairs, King headed a department of exceptional intellectual distinction. The under secretary, Dr. O.D. Skelton, had been his hand-picked choice in 1923 to direct Canada toward autonomy. Skelton could be relied upon to suspect and resist British schemes to involve Canada in imperial adventures.[5] Like Skelton, the department's counsellor, Loring Christie, was a confirmed isolationist, who believed that Canada's sovereign interests could only be damaged by irresponsible foreign adventuring when the vital task was to build up Canadian strength at home. Christie even went so far in his resistance to foreign entanglements as to suggest autarky as a desirable end of Canadian policy.[6] Both of these men worked to keep Canada neutral and, in particular, neutral in a British war. Under Skelton and Christie, some members of the department, such as Norman Robertson and Scott Macdonald, could nevertheless argue for Canadian support for the failing democracies of Western Europe. Skelton encouraged their criticism but ignored it. Other officers, such as J.W. Pickersgill and Hugh Keenleyside, were close to the Skelton line and still others, including L.B. Pearson, then serving in London, defy categorisation.[7]

Information flowing to and about Canada derived from Canadian missions abroad and foreign missions in Ottawa. Canada's two principal external posts, London and Washington, were both headed by political appointees, Vincent Massey in London and Sir Herbert Marler in Washington. While Massey was prominent and sometimes influential, he was not trusted by his prime minister who viewed him, correctly, as Anglophilic in the extreme. Massey was strictly ordered to abstain from any gesture that might give credence to Canadian participation in a common imperial foreign policy.[8] Marler, ageing and ill, was no heavyweight in diplomacy, but his inclinations reflected and even exaggerated Mackenzie King's public attitudes.[9] Both Marler and Massey soon learned that King looked on their offices as decorative post-boxes, and at no time between 1935 and 1939 was either man given significant authority to represent or interpret the views of the Canadian government. Indeed, neither was even informed of crucial changes in Canadian policy. In Marler's case this did not prove particularly significant, but in Massey's there were important consequences.

Marler's weakness was partially compensated for by the ability of the American minister in Ottawa, Norman Armour. Armour's dispatches reflect his considerable ability and effectiveness. He was on good terms with Mackenzie King and regularly furnished President Franklin D. Roosevelt with information and analyses of the Canadian scene.[10] When he left Ottawa in January, 1938 he was replaced by a series of short-term political appointees, none of whom had any particular impact on the Canadian scene.

The British were represented by two high commissioners during this period, Sir Francis Floud and Sir Gerald Campbell. Both were conscientious, but neither was an intimate of Mackenzie King and neither was particularly well-informed on Canadian matters. Their isolation was reflected in their despatches home, full of their dislike for Mackenzie King and their mistrust of his intentions and bonafides. In the case of Campbell, his prior knowledge of Canada can best be epitomised by his self-description at the time of his arrival in Ottawa: "I had mighty little idea . . . of what it means to a Dominion to be independent of all control from the country it once called Mother."[11]

The prime minister worked in a situation where all effective decision-making power was concentrated in his own hands and where, with the possible exception of Armour, no foreign diplomat had real influence. The government's willingness and ability to convey its thoughts on external policy to other governments was dependent entirely on the prime minister who alone could express the views of the administration. If he didn't, no one else could.

Mackenzie King's involvement with the darkening European crisis began as soon as he took office in October, 1935. Italy had just invaded Ethiopia, and the Canadian government with the rest of the League had appeared to take a strong stand against aggression through the imposition of sanctions. But sanctions, as King well knew, could lead to war. His unease was reinforced by warnings of a hostile reaction from Quebec, conveyed by Ernest Lapointe. Dr. Skelton, who regarded the League as a creature of Britain and France, vigorously opposed Canadian participation in irrelevant European entanglements. Mackenzie King's subsequent exit from the sanctions dilemma was hasty and undignified: Canada would follow where others led, knowing they would not lead. The brief "Canadian initiative" of oil sanctions was disavowed.[12]

The oil sanctions were the first victim of King's preoccupation with internal tranquillity. He believed that the League and its supporters could easily lead the world to war while judicious negotiations could preserve peace. An insistence on the international status quo, symbolised for him by the League's committment to defend its members against aggression, could jeopardise attempts to reach a more equitable, if less legalistic, settlement of grievances. The prime minister was prepared to see the League linger on, if its fangs were pulled, as a forum for international negotiation and conciliation. Such an approach, he argued, might even lure more members to Geneva, and thus create for the first time a truly universal organisation.[13] But sanctions were anathema and the thought of them could provoke King into extreme statements. In 1937, for example, he treated Sir Ronald Lindsay, the British ambassador in Washington, to "a diatribe . . . against sanctions . . . .He said that Canada was resolved to maintain neutrality in any war at any price, and that on no account would she be dragged into any hostilities."[14] As far as Lindsay was concerned, King's "attitude corresponded very closely to that generally adopted in America."[15] For certain aspects of Canadian policy, especially where O.D. Skelton was concerned, this observation was just. As a summation of Mackenzie King, it leaves something to be desired.

King was fully aware that his background and conduct left him open to the charge of being a pro-American isolationist and, as he told the American minister in Ottawa, some called him "the American."[16] But given Canadian political and racial difficulties, what could be more natural than for King to emulate the policies of his American neighbour and remain aloof from European conflict? This interpretation gains plausibility because of King's close relationship with Roosevelt. The two met once or twice a year after 1935 for friendly consultation on Canadian-American and international problems. Moreover, when King returned to office, he told Armour "that he wanted to choose 'the American road' if we made it possible for him to do so." At the same time, Dr. Skelton emphasised that Canada had come to "a very important crossroads," nor only economically but politically as well.[17]

For his part, Armour pointed out to his superiors "the wisdom of the development of an increasingly close economic and political relationship with Canada which will protect it from the vicissitudes which might flow from the adventure of all-British economic imperialism." The dangers of standing off from Canada were "not only of an economic but also of a political nature."[18] King also told Armour that "we must stand together on all these questions" that might affect North American "mutual interest and well being,"[19] and the prime minister still cherished what assistant secretary of state William Phillips called his "pet idea that Canada can play a useful role as an intermediary between the United States and Great Britain."[20]

King's policy of close relations with the United States had a British dimension, of course. He wanted to bring the two countries together as a force for peace, for if the British and the Americans could achieve economic and then political co-operation, his hopes for world stability would be greatly enhanced. King told Armour in 1936 that he was trying to impress on the British "the importance of trying to meet our [American] views . . . . It was up to them," he said, "to join with Canada and the United States in presenting a united front, etc., politically and economically."[21]

King's emphasis on economic agreement reflected the preoccupation of the 1930s with economic recovery as a priority of foreign as well as domestic policy. World recovery through freer trade was a staple belief of some members of the Roosevelt administration, one that King apparently shared. This economic peace would have to apply outside the Anglo-American-Canadian triangle, too, and just before the 1937 imperial conference, Roosevelt and King concocted a plan for universal economic appeasement through a world conference to be held in Geneva. Its aim would be to dispose of the "evils (economic and social) . . . which are the *fundamental cause of war*."[22] In brief, King hoped to involve the United States in a programme of economic appeasement.

At the same time, he believed that international conditions were steadily deteriorating. Affairs in Europe, King told secretary of state Cordell Hull, "were continuing very confused and improving but little, if any in numerous ways while they were becoming worse in other ways." He was "very discouraged."[23]

The Americans had nothing to offer except preachings of economic appeasement and words of good will. In these circumstances King found "the American road" increasingly difficult to reconcile with the possibility of war, war in which Canada might be involved.

The imperial conference did nothing to reassure him. Although King had presented himself to Roosevelt and Hull as the interpreter of their views to the British, and although Armour had reported that the Canadian delegation would press for economic appeasement,[24] the conference did not turn out this way. Britain's new prime minister, Neville Chamberlain, was impatient of what he saw as the American penchant for words without deeds[25] and King does not seem to have struggled to alter his mind. The Canadian accepted an agenda that placed economic questions on the sidelines and, in addressing the assembled prime ministers of the empire, he confined himself to mentioning that, "Both the President and the Secretary of State are firmly convinced of the value and possibility of a policy of economic appeasement as a constructive means of lessening political tension. Their reciprocal tariff policy," he lamely concluded, "is a step in this direction. . . ."[26] The "Permanent Conference on Economic and Social Problems" over which King and Roosevelt had enthused in March was buried. That line of Anglo-American co-operation was dead and, as far as King's policy was concerned, so was economic appeasement. In the future, political appeasement would be King's principal hobbyhorse.

In the depressing state of the world in 1937, political appeasement seemed a necessity if war was to be averted. Certainly King's advisers were uniformly bleak in their world view. From London, Lester Pearson had written that "if I were responsible for Canadian policy, I would assume that war in Europe is certain within five years . . . ." In his view, Canada's "chief interest now is to avoid being involved in any circumstances," although, he added, "I admit we may not be able to avoid it."[27] Loring Christie had also reached that conclusion. Writing to Lord Lothian in 1936, he predicted an inevitable war into which Canada would be dragged. Worse, the decision for war lay with England alone, not Canada.[28] But despite his assumption of futility, Christie continued to struggle against Canadian involvement right up to September 1939. His chief, Dr. Skelton, was less definite on the inevitability of war but even more convinced about the necessity of Canadian neutrality.

The problem for Mackenzie King was that despite his best efforts defence was becoming an important issue in Canadian politics. The American minister reported in May 1937 that "defence has been the dominant political question in Canada, no other subject even approaching it in sustained interest or importance."[29] The same thing was true at the imperial conference, of course.

There the British wanted to discover how far Canada would go toward setting up common defence facilities and planning for a joint economic war effort. The answer was not different than it had been at earlier imperial conferences: not very far at all. The minister of national defence, Ian Mackenzie, explained the Canadian position to the conference:

> . . . Canadian public opinion would not, under present conditions, support any larger appropriations than those voted this year by Parliament. . . .

> Canadian public opinion was definitely opposed to extraneous
> commitments . . . . The most important contribution they could render at
> this time, when dark shadows seem to be hovering over the world, was, as
> far as possible, to preserve *unity* in their councils. . . .

The minister concluded by urging the conference not to weaken the links of empire "by placing too much strain on them. . . ."[30]

The effect of Canada's determination to resist "strains" was to weaken Britain's rather fragile enthusiasm for any kind of forward policy in defence. In fact, Britain's attitudes to Canada during these years were an odd mélange of scepticism and hope. In December 1934, as the British slowly began to rearm, Sir Maurice Hankey reported that he had found only "calculating aloofness" on a visit to Ottawa. The secretary of the Committee of Imperial Defence felt compelled to raise "the brutal question of whether Canada would come to our assistance in another's war," a question that Hankey resolved satisfactorily by discounting the influence of the " 'highbrows', isolationists, French Canadians, Irish disloyalists . . . [and] intellectuals" and by asserting that "the men of action", whether or not they were a majority, "would be sufficiently numerous to stampede the country."[31] Two years later, with Mackenzie King in power, Hankey was less confident: "We realise that in the present state of Canadian opinion no Canadian Government could commit itself to active participation in a war . . . ." The Dominions secretary, Malcolm MacDonald, added a minute to suggest that "We do not want Mackenzie King to think that we really contemplate Canada not being in a war with us."[32]

From the British point of view, King was being extremely difficult. Repeated attempts to secure Canadian co-operation in munitions production came to naught,[33] and when Ian Mackenzie and his prime minister held to this position at the conference, Hankey was seriously disturbed: "all our efforts at the conference failed to obtain from Canada any really satisfactory assurance that we should be able to count with certainty on obtaining supplies from her in time of war." This was vital, for "It would be clearly disastrous if we laid our plans on the assumption that we could count on Canada, and then when the day came we found that we had been building upon false premises."[34]

The major effect of the conference was to drive home to the British the need to handle Canada with care. First, since some of the information supplied by the imperial government seemed to excite opposition among the dominions, certain confidential material was withheld from the visitors. Then, the British gave in to Canadian demands (backed by South Africa) and agreed to a communiqué that was virtually meaningless wherever it touched on defence and foreign policy. Chamberlain was directly responsible for these expedients. With them he bought a façade of empire unity without which, as he told a London audience, Great Britain would be merely "a fourth-rate Power."[35]

If the British were discouraged by the results of the imperial conference, King was not. Although he indefatigably resisted British schemes at every such meeting, he was nonetheless always deeply stirred by the trappings of Empire, particularly prominent in 1937 because of the coronation of George VI. Norman Armour, for one, had shrewdly allowed for an irrational factor in King's behaviour. As he wrote in May, the prime minister "is emotional and warm-hearted. He is, for his own peace of mind in political life, too easily hurt by criticism and apt to be influenced by his surroundings . . . ." He did not, Armour said, "wish to give the impression that Mr. King will be swept off his feet during the forthcoming conference," but it was a possibility.[36]

Armour was right. King left the heady atmosphere of the conference for Berlin where he had an audience with Herr Hitler. Before leaving, he had told Malcolm MacDonald that he would inform the Nazi leader "that if Germany should ever turn her mind from constructive to destructive efforts against the United Kingdom all the Dominions would come to her aid and that there would be great numbers of Canadians anxious to swim the Atlantic!"[37] King was as good as his word in his interview with the Fuehrer,[38] and British newspapers reported that he had made a public commitment in a speech in Paris on 2 July:

> We have our own representation in other countries [and that] is evidence of that great liberty and freedom, which, above all, we prize, and were it imperilled from any source whatever [this] would bring us together again in preservation of it.[39]

King's staff were appalled at what their master had done. Christie told Lothian that he doubted King himself knew what he meant in Paris.[40] Skelton reminded his prime minister that "no government of a free country can determine what course its people will follow in years to come and under circumstances which no one can now envisage, and . . . it would be futile to rely on such undertakings . . . ."[41]

The British, of course, were delighted by King's interview with Hitler (although the high commissioner in Ottawa doubted King had been as forceful as he claimed)[42] and by his Paris remarks. Chamberlain referred to the latter as a "remarkable speech" meaning "that in case of any threat toward England, it would bring Canada at once to her side."[43] Still, the British were not entirely certain of Canada, however optimistic Chamberlain might sound in public statements. Late in 1937, the Dominions Office concluded glumly that the Canadian position was doubtful in the event of war. If "democracy" were threatened and if the Canadians could be sustained by a sympathetic American attitude, then Canada might come to the aid of the mother country.[44] But the doubts were real, and there were grounds for them.

Most Canadians, the American Legation reported in mid– 1937, wanted "continued membership in the British Commonwealth, and in the League of Nations, with avoidance of entanglements that might lead Canada into another overseas war."[45] How entanglements could be avoided while membership was retained was unclear, but Skelton was certain in his own mind that "From the military standpoint there can be little question that today our connection with the United Kingdom . . . is, on a balance of advantages, a net liability rather than asset."[46] The chief of the general staff, however, did not see things that way. He was pleased that his officers could plan to defend Canada, "and, incidentally, to make some contribution toward the defence of all those countries that may some day necessarily associate themselves for the purpose of preserving their liberties . . . ."[47] That prospect gave External Affairs nightmares. Skelton and Christie persistently assaulted the defence estimates between 1937 and 1939 on the grounds that the military were secretly preparing an expeditionary force. If the plans were prepared and the occasion offered, the Canadian reaction would be a foregone conclusion: an expeditionary force like that of 1914.[48] Ironically, at this juncture the British themselves were still hoping to avoid sending an army to the continent. The prevailing philosophy of "limited liability" prescribed a small army and a concentration on air defence and sea power.[49]

As for Mackenzie King, he had left London in 1937 with confidence in Neville Chamberlain's sincerity and ability. "Limited liability" was a concept that appealed to him, as did Chamberlain's determination to seek a peaceful accommodation with Hitler.[50] During the winter and spring of 1937–8, therefore, there was no change in King's attitude or in the policy of the government. The internal debate continued, but no external occasion arose to disturb the tranquil surface of events. As the British government acquiesced in the *Anschluss* and prepared to sacrifice Czechoslovakia to Hitler, Canada was peaceful.[51]

The Sudetenland crisis woke the dreamers on both sides of the Atlantic, and the British again began anxiously to watch developments in the dominions. The high commissioners were their ready source of information, and Sir Francis Floud summed up the position of King and Canada in a long letter to Sir E.J. Harding, the permanent under secretary at the Dominions Office. Mackenzie King, the high commissioner said, wanted to keep his eye "on what he considers to be the main objective, viz. the preservation of Canada's unity" and thus he was content "again and again to insist on the supremacy of Parliament as the interpreter of the people's wishes if and when the time comes." The prime minister "resolutely refuses to take any other line," Floud continued, "and it is clear that however unsatisfactory this may be for those who are charged either here or at home with working out anything in the nature of Imperial defence plans, we cannot hope, under the present regime, to get any further." Moreover, in Floud's view, Canada seemed legally "well equipped at least to avoid getting herself entangled unofficially as it were in a war in which we were engaged." This was not a view that many Canadians shared.[52] Still, the high commissioner was guardedly hopeful as he wound up his letter:

> Since it is inconceivable to you and to me that we shall embark on an aggressive war, and that any war in which we do ever get engaged will be other than a war of direct self-defence after an unprovoked attack, or a war which we are bound to wage in fulfillment of express undertakings shared by Canada or a war in which our undertakings are not actually shared by Canada but which is manifestly equivalent to a war of self-defence, it is surely equally inconceivable that Canada will not be with us in the end. All I myself really fear is a period of hesitancy, and I am afraid that we cannot necessarily count on Canada being in with us from the very beginning. There might be a delay of days, and those days might lengthen into perhaps two or three weeks . . . . After all, what is the alternative? Personally I think that whatever Canada's own attitude may be, she would be brought in on our side in any case by the enemy's own action.[53]

To have Canada back into war in such a fashion was not particularly palatable to many Englishmen — or to many Canadians.

But as the Czech crisis developed British fears should have ceased. At first Mackenzie King carefully refrained from public statements, but in private he had made up his mind even before the press reports of German threats and Sudeten riots alarmed the public. On 31 August, he confided to his diary:

> I made it clear to both Mackenzie and Power [the Minister of National Defence and the Postmaster General] that I would stand for Canada doing all she possibly could to destroy those Powers which are basing their action on might *and not on* right, *and that I would not consider being neutral in this situation for a moment. They both agreed that this would be the Cabinet's view* . . . .

Dissension in Quebec was predictable, but King made it clear that this would not deter him. His Quebec ministers would simply have to lead the province in seeing its obligation to participate. In that other hive of isolationism, the Department of External Affairs, Dr. Skelton told the prime minister that he agreed "that the Government could not, without suffering immediate defeat," adopt non-intervention as its policy. As Skelton read the national mood, Canada "would be strong for intervention and even for participation by a possible expeditionary force . . . ."[54]

This assessment did not deter Skelton from doing his best to hold King to the straight and narrow. He reminded the prime minister on 11 September that, "we are the safest country in the world — as long as we mind our own business." He recognised the internal factors that would make it difficult for Canada to resist "the call of the blood" particularly from "the older and middle aged generations which control public opinion in English Canada."[55] King's response, set out in his diary, was that Skelton's memorandum was

> Excellently done, but all the way through referring only to self-interest of each part as determining its action, and leading to a sort of isolationist attitude so far as Canada is concerned. I believe myself that whilst care must be taken as to determine the part that Canada may be called upon to play, and the steps toward that end, that our real self-interest lies in the strength of the British Empire as a whole, not in our geographic position and resources. That not to recognize this would be to ultimately destroy the only great factor for world peace, to lose the association of the United States and the British Empire and all that it would mean for world peace. That it would place Canada in an ignominious position.
>
> I am clear in my own mind that cooperation between all parts of the Empire and the democracies is in Canada's interests in the long run and in her own immediate self respect. The only possible attitude to be assumed.[56]

The attitude King now criticised in Skelton was precisely that which he had recently allowed to be sent out over his name. Quite evidently, King too felt "the call of the blood."[57]

King reaffirmed his stand repeatedly in conversations and correspondence with his ministers. To Charles Dunning, the minister of finance, he wrote on 3 September that "My mind is wholly clear as to the course we should pursue."[58] He spoke to Norman Rogers, the minister of labour and, some said, King's favourite among his ministers, and recorded that

> We both agreed that it was a self-evident national duty, if Britain entered the war, that Canada should regard herself as part of the British Empire, one of the nations of the sisterhood of nations, which should cooperate lending every assistance possible, in no way asserting neutrality, but carefully defining in what ways and how far she would participate.[59]

The next day, 14 September, Chamberlain's decision to fly to Germany to see Hitler was announced. It is doubtful that King knew of this in advance, but it is abundantly evident that he approved of Chamberlain's dramatic gesture. "I am sure," his public statement proclaimed, "the whole Canadian people will warmly approve this striking and noble action on the part of Mr. Chamberlain. Direct personal contact is the most effective means of clearing away the tensions and misunderstandings that have marked the course of events in Europe in recent months . . . ."[60] King thus reinforced Chamberlain's peace policy, but he did not go far as to indicate in public what Canada would do if Chamberlain's mission failed.

There was no one who could tell London of Canadian policy for the prime minister did not confide his thoughts on Canada's "self-evident national duty" to Vincent Massey. As the high commissioner later wrote, he received no messages of any kind from King in this period.[61] Massey had his own views, however, and he criticised the "timid and isolationist Canadian Government" and its "inert" prime minister, at the same time as he assured the editor of *The Times* that he personally was "all against a world war fought with the object of keeping large dissident minorities under Czechoslovak rule."[62] A few days earlier, however, he had told the dominions secretary that "he had no doubt that if Great Britain got involved in war, Canada also would be in the war."[63] As the crisis developed, Massey was sent a copy of King's statement of 17 September, in which the Canadian government expressed its appreciation for Chamberlain's "efforts to preserve the peace of Central Europe." Beyond that, the statement did not commit Canada to a predetermined course of action in "hypothetical contingencies."[64]

For a while it seemed that Chamberlain's first visit to Hitler had achieved the basis of a peaceful settlement. His second visit on 22 and 23 September was far less hopeful and war again seemed close. In Ottawa, the prime minister met with his cabinet to decide if the government should issue a statement of its intentions should Chamberlain's mission fail. Mackenzie King had envisaged "as expressive of our position" a statement that, " 'The world might as well know that should the occasion arise, Canada will not stand idly by and see modern civilisation ruthlessly destroyed.' " Skelton was predictably "greatly shocked at this", King recorded, "and felt it was going back on my whole position with respect to having Parliament decide, etc. I told him I thought we would have to indicate long before Parliament met what our policy would be, though Parliament itself would decide whether that policy should be carried out." In cabinet, King found that W.D. Euler from Ontario was flatly against any statement and against war, and at least one other minister insisted that parliament should really decide Canada's course.[65] From Geneva, Ernest Lapointe also discouraged a statement and deplored the turn of events.[66] Under the circumstances caution won out and King decided to withhold his statement although, as Christie later told a friend, "he felt like a cad" in so doing.[67]

The crisis grew worse over the next few days as the British government struggled to find a way out that would at once preserve peace and the appearance of peaceful concession while still satisfying Hitler. Massey reported on 26 September that he along with the other high commissioners had spent most of an hour with Chamberlain "and heard from him intimate accounts of his efforts . . . . My impression is that he and his Government feel that they have exhausted every means of avoiding catastrophe and that they are none too confident that it can be averted."[68]

The Canadian cabinet met again on 27 September. Mackenzie King presented another draft statement for approval, this one being less specific and noting only that Canada was in complete accord with Chamberlain's policy. There was still dissension, however, and King tried to counter it by remarking that

> I doubted if the British would send an expeditionary force to Europe; did not think an expeditionary force would be expected from Canada. That our part would probably consist in supplying munitions, air pilots, etc., and looking after our own defences.

Reflecting on the meeting, King characteristically sounded a high note:

> Personally, I feel very strongly that the issue is one of the great moral issues of the world, and that one cannot afford to be neutral on an issue of the kind.[69]

The statement was approved and duly issued, simply urging the country to "keep united" and adding that the government "is in complete accord with the statement Mr. Chamberlain has made to the world today."[70]

King's public statements were all the British had to go on in their estimates of Canadian policy. From the uninformed Massey, they gathered that Canada would be a reluctant combatant at best. From Ottawa, Sir Francis Floud had predicated "hesitancy" but eventual participation. But descriptions of the climate of opinion were far different from official promises. Lacking reliable reports on Canada, the British seem to have lumped it with the other dominions into something called "Dominion opinion". The result has been that from 1938 on historians have regularly invoked the dominions as "obscure but important factors."[71] There was no more obscurity than importance from the Canadian side. At no point did King threaten Chamberlain by withdrawing his support; at no time did he encourage him by openly promising it. The influence of such a non-policy lies entirely in the eye of the beholder.

American observers in Ottawa had no doubt which course Canada would follow. The legation reported that "as the crisis became more acute, Canadian opinion fell strongly behind the line of action taken by Mr. Chamberlain. This was demonstrated not only in the press but also by the expression of officials in Ottawa."[72] Certainly this was an accurate reflection of the prime minister's attitude. But there were others, including some who shared the prime minister's readiness to back Britain, who were sceptical of the vocal interventionist support. Dr. R.J. Manion, the Conservative Party chief and the leader of the opposition, characterized the pro-British enthusiasts to his son as "the usual crowd of old bachelors and childless parents."[73] Dr. Skelton, too, was convinced that opinion in Canada was shaped by middle-aged Anglo-Saxon enthusiasts. Youth, he hoped, would be on the side of peace.[74]

Almost everyone was relieved by the dénouement at Munich. The American legation reported "great relief,"[75] while Mackenzie King publicly rejoiced and privately buried the potential divisions in his cabinet. Almost a year later he admitted to the governor-general that he had had serious doubts about his ability to bring a united cabinet and country into a war in September, 1938.[76] Some Canadians, however, saw the Munich settlement with a jaundiced eye. Four days after the agreement, Skelton pointed out that, "The settlement is not one to be proud of in itself."[77] Christie was pleased that peace was preserved but he saw danger from the east. Russia, he argued, would try to provoke a war between Germany and the Western powers.[78] From London, Lester Pearson predicted another crisis:

> I am pessimistic enough to think that an armaments race is not necessary to cause trouble: the nature of the German state, the aggressive spirit of Nazi-ism, the feeling of triumph through power from recent successes, and the equally strong feeling of British and French impotence, should be enough to cause another crisis before long.[79]

But for the time being there was peace, and King and Skelton took the opportunity for a vacation cruise in the Caribbean. Naturally, they refought the events of the past few months, and Skelton used the opportunity once again to press his autonomist theories on his chief. His arguments were familiar enough, but King's reactions were not. In Kingston, Jamaica, the prime minister summed up his under secretary as "a Canadian, pure and simple, [who] did not feel British connection meant anything except the possibility of being drawn into European wars; thought the younger generation were all against it."[80] And when Skelton stated that Canada relied for its security on the United States, King was perturbed:

> I do not like to be dependent on the U.S.; change of leaders there might lead to a vassalage so far as our Dominion was concerned. There was more real freedom in the British Commonwealth of Nations, and a richer inheritance. This I truly believe.[81]

In fact, King found himself fundamentally in disagreement with Skelton:

> . . . I felt more and more—the materialistic "scientific" point of view which Skelton had in all things—a critical frame of mind, also a "republican" attitude. I felt his negative viewpoint and inferiority complex in so many things—a real antagonism towards monarchical institutions, and Britain, a sort of communist sympathy—lack of larger view in reference to world affairs—an isolated Canada—which I cannot accept. It told on me and him, and raised a sort of wall of separation between us. He seeks to dominate one's thought, is intellectually arrogant in some respects . . . .I can see I must control policy and be the judge of my own conduct and other affairs— to lead and not be controlled, while in many ways he is the best of Counsellors and guides . . . .[82]

Yet for months after Munich, King's public policy was scarcely distinguishable from Skelton's private opinions. In cabinet, however, he seldom deviated from his decision at the time of Munich to come to Britain's aid if need be. He told the defence committee of the cabinet that the "gangster nations" were a threat and that Canada had to be prepared against them.[83] (Not so prepared, however, as to indulge in reckless spending after the "emergency" had passed. Defence estimates were still watched closely and pared to the bone.[84]) In December, King emphasised the dangers of the situation to cabinet "to show [them] the necessity of Canada joining with other nations in impressing Dictators with the determination of the Democracies to make themselves more powerful to resist aggression."[85] One 16 January he quoted Sir Wilfrid Laurier's 1910 dictum to the House of Commons:

> If England is at war we are at war and liable to attack. I do not say we will always be attacked; neither do I say that we would take part in all the wars of England. That is a matter that must be guided by circumstances, upon which the Canadian parliament will have to pronounce and will have to decide in its own best judgment.

Later that day King wrote that, ". . . I simply developed what had been most in my mind and particularly in regard to Canada's relations to Britain in time of war, made up my mind that I would not allow myself to take the one sided view that I was crowded into, speaking on External Affairs, last session which ignored the possibility of Canada being at war when Britain was at war." Finally with a new scare filling the telegrams from London, King told his ministers at the end of January that Canada would be attacked if Britain was at war. Lapointe conceded that Canada would indeed be involved in such a war, but the minister of justice urged delay in making any pronouncement until public opinion matured further. King agreed.[86]

Political realism might dictate delay but it also prescribed the policy that eventually emerged. Christie remarked cynically that, "A Government does not determine its own activities — its activities are determined for it by the course of events."[87] The Canadians now had only to wait for the course of events to manifest itself. In the meantime King sternly rejected all attempts by Skelton to lead him back to belief in the old policy of "no commitments." His "only mistake" so far, he wrote in his diary, had been in not saying "what was the real position about the reality side of things, thereby letting it be assumed that I was indifferent to this aspect, and was holding solely to the academic position — crisis or no crisis."[88]

A crisis there soon was. On 15 March 1939 Hitler seized what remained of Czechoslovakia. Two days later, Chamberlain was forced to denounce the German action and mentioned in his remarks that the dominions supported Britain. He was, his biographer noted, "informed by strong representations as to opinion in the House, the public, and the Dominions . . . ."[89] Mackenzie King was annoyed by the implication that he had been consulted on the shift in British policy to a harder line. "I wish very much that he had made no mention of other parts of the British Empire," he wrote, "as it immediately raises the most difficult question with which we are faced in Parliament. It gives the jingos a chance to press for a clear cut statement on standing by Britain, and [it is] more difficult to make clear the wisdom of giving no blank cheque with respect to wars."[90]

Skelton seized the opportunity to warn King once more of the folly of relying on Chamberlain. The British leader's qualities, whatever else they were, were not those of a diplomat: "He is a self-confident to the point of arrogance, intolerant of criticism, and at the moment sore because he thinks in the eyes of the world Hitler has made a fool of him." Worse, he was descended from the hereditary enemy of all Liberals:

He is also a Chamberlain, born and bred in a Tory imperialist school, and cannot imagine that any part of the British Empire has any choice but to halt when he says halt and march when he says march. Hence his references, unconscious or deliberate, to turning to our partners in the British Commonwealth, to having the approval of the whole British Commonwealth for declarations of which they knew nothing in advance . . . . Hence also other British Ministers calmly announcing what "our Dominions" will do. They are not men to whom blank cheques may safely be given.[91]

King's mood was cautious, therefore, in the last week of March. When Sir Gerald Campbell, Floud's successor at the High Commission in Ottawa, came to call on 24 March, King read him a lecture. The prime minister was worried, Campbell reported, that Canada might be invited to join an alliance between England and eastern European countries. "This he said would cause grave embarrassment and in particular he expressed regret that it should apparently have been necessary for the United Kingdom to associate herself with the U.S.S.R." A "Balkan dispute" would not be a sufficient *casus belli* for Canada, King warned. The high commissioner concluded that King was "if anything less disposed to cooperate with other countries in the defence of democracy than is the Government of the United States."[92]

Campbell's harsh words were understandable, but he seemed to be neglecting King's long-contemplated public statement of Canada's position in the event of war on 20 March. In it, the prime minister went further than ever before, telling parliament that if there was any danger of bombs raining in London, Canada would step forward to Britain's aid.[93] But after marching two steps to the front, King characteristically took one pace back when on 30 March he spoke again to the House of Commons. He worried beforehand that his remarks would not be "as immediately helpful to Britain as I should like . . . but, in the long run, [it is] the kind of thing that will keep this country together, and enable us to do most effectively in the end whatever may be decided upon."[94] The speech was Skeltonian both in conception and in phraseology:

> The idea that every twenty years this country should automatically and as a matter of course take part in a war overseas for democracy or self-determination of other small nations, that a country which has all it can do to run itself should feel called upon to save, periodically, a continent that cannot run itself, and to these ends to risk the lives of its people, risk bankruptcy and political disunion, seems to many a nightmare and sheer madness.[95]

The prime minister's policy clearly was to balance bellicosity with caution; the requirements of the domestic scene demanded this.

King's careful speech of 30 March was balanced the next day by a vigorous attack on the idea of Canadian neutrality from Ernest Lapointe. Taken together, the two helped lay the ghost of conscription at the same time as they reassured those unduly concerned over King's firmness ten days before. The prime minister accurately gauged the effect of the speeches. He would "suffer . . . from an impression of aloofness so far as relations between Canada and Britain are concerned," but with Lapointe's, the two speeches amounted to "a sort of trestle sustaining the structure which would serve to unite divergent parts of Canada, thereby making for a united country."[96]

The long-run significance of King's position in March 1939 lies more in the hidden diary than in the public utterances. King wanted to support Britain, and his statement on March 20 was an accurate reflection of everything he had been saying since the Imperial Conference of 1937, if not before. His concern on March 30 was to bind up national unity, then as always his fundamental preoccupation. It was a classic case of *reculer pour mieux sauter*.

Still, British policy could infuriate him, and Skelton's analysis of Chamberlain's underlying attitude to the dominions was proving more and more perceptive. On 31 March Chamberlain extended an unconditional British guarantee to Poland and Rumania. In effect, Canada was now committed to support Poland in precisely those hypothetical circumstances against which Skelton and Christie had always warned. And if Chamberlain's record of perspicacity in foreign affairs was uninspiring, it positively shone when compared with the Poles'. King was properly provoked at not having been consulted. "This, a conditional declaration of war was made certainly without anything in the nature of consultation or the possibility of consultation with Canada or any of the Dominions."[97] In London, the new dominions secretary, Sir Thomas Inskip, helpfully explained to the high commissioners that he had thought their governments "would not have wished that the United Kingdom should invite them to share responsibility for the decision."[98]

A month later when Sir Gerald Campbell called on King to propose a blanket statement of support for British policy, King's resentment boiled over. According to the high commissioner's account of the interview, the prime minister had said that there was

> considerable opposition in Canada to the manner in which the United Kingdom appears to be becoming entangled with Balkan and East European countries and above all with Russia. There were many people in Canada including some Ministers, and I gathered this included him, who disliked entanglements of this kind . . . . He could not forecast in advance of Parliament what line Canada would take if the United Kingdom went to the help of one of these countries and as a result were herself attacked.[99]

To make matters worse for the confused Campbell, King and Skelton agreed the same day that "Germany knew quite well that Canada would go into the fight if Germany were in any way an aggressor."[100]

In a curious way, King's relationship with the high commissioner was almost symbolic in nature. It was as if Campbell was there to expiate in person all the crimes and follies of Great Britain's foreign policy. The abuse and hectoring under which he suffered, however, did not mean very much, for once Campbell was disposed of King went on to indulge in an orgy of royalist and Anglophile feeling during the spring tour of George VI and Queen Elizabeth.

The royal tour evoked a fervent display of loyalty from Canadians. As L.B. Pearson wrote from London at the time, the visit "does make even more complicated certain complicating features of Canada's imperial relationship." The British public now had the "conviction that all this talk of Canadian isolation and neutrality is academic eye-wash, and that the reception given by Canada to

the King has proved, if it needed proving, 'the great heart of Canada is sound.' "
Pearson seemed concerned with the problem of "eradicating" this impression,[101]
but time had run out.

Word arrived on 21 August that the Soviet Union would sign a non-aggression
pact with Germany. Mackenzie King, who had been thinking of a fall election,
abandoned his contemplations for the time being and prepared for war.[102] Dr.
Skelton, who a month before had judged Lord Halifax to be "the best British
Foreign Minister in years," now deplored "the greatest fiasco in British history."[103]
And in his diary, King criticised the "blundering there has been in England's
foreign policy all along the way."[104] None the less, democracy was at stake and
the prime minister was prepared to meet the challenge.

It remained only for Dr. Skelton to write the epitaph for Canada's foreign
policy as he had conceived and sporadically implemented it. On 25 August he
minuted that

> The first casualty of this war has been Canada's claim to control over her
> own destinies. If war comes to Poland and we take part, that war came as a
> consequence of commitments made by the Government of Great Britain,
> about which we were not in one iota consulted, and about which we were
> not given the slightest inkling of information in advance.[105]

Skelton was writing about his conception of foreign policy, and however closely
it correlated with Mackenzie King's on certain points, it had never been the
official, authorised foreign policy of the government. For both men, delay and
obfuscation had been instrumental — but instrumental for different reasons. King
believed that Canada would perish if it did not go to war, while Skelton believed
the exact opposite. After reading Skelton's anguished memorandum, however,
King felt the need to console his "best of Counsellors." He telephoned his under
secretary to say "how wholeheartedly he agreed with the memorandum of 25
August. If we get through this, Mr. King stated, there will be an Imperial Conference at which there will have to be some very plain speaking."[106]

This account of certain aspects of Canadian foreign policy between 1935 and
1939 has attempted to refute the legend of Mackenzie King the isolationist and
neutralist. It has concentrated on the events of 1937 and 1938 because these
were in a sense dress rehearsals for September 1939. The plot was the same, but
refinements to the script were required, and some of the actors needed extra
coaching. But when the prologue was ready for the audience in August 1939, it
achieved its purpose.

At no point was King an isolationist in his basic conception of Canadian relations with the Empire. Between 1935 and 1939 he was convinced that events
abroad would necessarily affect the peace and well-being of Canada. If collective
security proved dangerous, then the world, not Canada alone, must abandon it.
If economic appeasement proved ineffective, then King would support its political
manifestation. The Prime Minister sought a close relationship with the United
States at least partly because he thought he could influence British policy in that
way, and bring Britain and the United States into a harmonious relationship —
and one with stabilising consequences for the world. When, in 1937, he decided

that Canada would have to tread a road the United States could or would not, he effectively postponed his preoccupation with bringing the United States into a "North Atlantic triangle." While relations with Roosevelt remained close, the influence of the United States on Canadian policy from 1937 to 1939 must be adjudged slight.

In many of his opinions on foreign policy, King revealed himself to be unreasonably optimistic, prejudiced and unrealistic. But in his basic perception that foreign policy can be no more effective than one's internal strength will support, he was profoundly right. King's backing and filling, his evasions and hesitations do not make inspiring reading. But his actions, particularly between 1937 and 1939, indicate his sure grasp of the public mood and his recognition that public opinion cannot be wished into existence simply because one course of action or another is "right." When King took a united Canada into a second world war, he gave Canadians a policy that not only was right to him, but one that seemed right to them.[107]

Notes

1. Stephen Leacock, "Canada and Monarchy," *Atlantic Monthly* (June 1939), 735.

2. J. Pierrepont Moffat to Secretary of State, 21 Dec. 1940, in Nancy Harvison Hooker, *The Moffat Papers* (Cambridge, Mass., 1956), 342. An excellent assessment of King's concern with national unity in the late 1930s is H. Blair Neatby, "Mackenzie King and National Unity," in H.L. Dyck and H.P. Krosby, *Empire and Nations* (Toronto, 1969), 54 ff. For a contrary view, see K.W. McNaught, "Canadian Foreign Policy and the Whig Interpretation," *Canadian Historical Association Report*, 1957, 43ff.

3. Prem. 1/242 (Public Record Office, London), High Commissioner, Ottawa, to Dominions Office, 27 Oct. 1938.

4. See F.W. Gibson, "The Cabinet of 1935," in *Cabinet Formation and Bicultural Relations*, edited by F.W. Gibson (Ottawa, 1970), 115 ff.

5. Cf. Norman Hillmer, "The Anglo-Canadian Neurosis," a paper presented at "Britain and Canada: A Colloquy," Windsor Great Park, England, 3–5 Sept. 1971.

6. Christie wrote many lengthy memoranda on Canadian foreign policy. Those that best express his thoughts are "The Canadian Dilemma," Nov. 1938 and "Responsible Government: The Last Stage," 1926, both in the Loring Christie Papers (Public Archives of Canada), 23.

7. The best published account of the pre–1939 history of the Department is Gilles Lalande, *The Department of External Affairs and Biculturalism* (Ottawa, 1969), 3ff.

8. See Vincent Massey, *What's Past is Prologue* (Toronto, 1963), 231ff; Cab. 21/494 (P.R.O.), High Commissioner, Ottawa to Dominions Office, 24 March 1939.

9. For an assessment of Marler by the British Ambassador, see F.O. 371/ 22820/A4461/250/45 (P.R.O.). For an appraisal by a shrewd Canadian reporter, see Lothian Papers, 17/381/241–2 (Scottish Record Office), Grant Dexter to Lothian, 4 April 1939.

10. See, for example, the remarkable series of memoranda by Armour from October 1935 on the subject of King and trade negotiations in F.D. Roosevelt Papers, PSF, Box 33 (Roosevelt Library, Hyde Park, New York).

11. Sir Gerald Campbell, *Of True Experience* (New York, 1947), 97.

12. Cf. R. Bothwell and J. English, "Dirty Work at the Crossroads: New Perspectives on the Riddell Incident," *Canadian Historical Association Report*, 1972.

13. For King's 1936 speech at Geneva, ushering the League "out into the darkness," see Nicholas

Mansergh, *Survey of British Commonwealth Affairs: Problems of External Policy, 1931-1939* (London, 1952), 119-120.

14. F.O. 371/20670/A2182/2082/45, Lindsay to Vansittart, 8 March 1937.

15. *Ibid.*

16. Roosevelt Papers, PSF, Box 33, King to W.D. Robbins, 17 Dec. 1934, encl. with Robbins to Roosevelt, 18 Dec. 1934. Robbins added that King "is inclined . . . to play the game with us."

17. *Ibid.*, Armour to Phillips, 22 and 24 Oct. 1935.

18. *Ibid.*

19. *Ibid.*, Memorandum by Armour, 25 Oct. 1935.

20. *Ibid.*, Phillips to Roosevelt, 7 Nov. 1935.

21. State Department Records (U.S. National Archives), 842.20/37½, Armour to J. Hickerson, 13 Nov. 1936.

22. Roosevelt Papers, PSF, Box 33, King's "Permanent Conference on Economic and Social Problems — Notes," 6 March 1937. An almost identical version appears in James Eayrs, *In Defence of Canada* (3 vols. to date; Toronto, 1964-72), II, 223-5. See A.A. Offner, *American Appeasement* (Cambridge, Mass., 1969), chapter 7, for American preoccupations at this time.

23. State Department Records, 500.A19/61, Hull's Memorandum of conversation, 5 March 1937.

24. *Ibid.*, 841.01 Imperial Conference 1937/28, Armour to Secretary of State, 5 May 1937.

25. See esp. Keith Middlemas, *Diplomacy of Illusion* (London, 1972), 54-5.

26. John Munro, ed., *Documents on Canadian External Relations* (7 vols. to date; Ottawa, 1969-74), VI, Baldwin to King, 18 Nov. 1936, 121-2; Baldwin to King, 23 Jan. 1937, 124-5; King's speech to Imperial Conference, 21 May 1937, 161. (Cited hereafter as *DCER*, VI).

27. Department of External Affairs Records (Public Archives of Canada), file 4-1, Pearson to Skelton/?/, n.d. The letter bears the notation "late 1935 or early 1936."

28. Lothian Papers, 17/327/218-22, Christie to Lothian, 20 Oct. 1936.

29. State Department Records, 841.01 Imperial Conference 1937/28, Armour to Secretary of State, 5 May 1937. For examples of public discussion, see "The Folly of Canadian Rearmament," *Canadian Forum* (Feb. 1937), 6-7; "Armaments Expenditure," *ibid.* (March 1937), 3; G.M.A. Grube, "Pacifism: The Only Solution," *ibid.* (June 1936), 9-10; and *Canada: The Empire and the League* (Toronto, 1936) for discussion of Canadian policy by various politicians and intellectuals in the summer of 1936.

30. *DCER*, VI, 203.

31. Cab. 63/81, "Impressions of Canada," Dec. 1934.

32. Cab. 21/671, Hankey to Baldwin, 22 Oct. 1936 with minutes by MacDonald.

33. E.g., see *DCER*, VI, 175-6; External Affairs Records, vol. 42, file 241-1, "Procedure Respecting British Munitions Contracts in Canada," 26 June 1937; Eayrs, *In Defence of Canada*, II, 116.

34. Cab. 21/670, Hankey to Sir E.J. Harding, 9 May 1938.

35. See R. Tamchina, "In Search of Common Causes: The Imperial Conference of 1937," *Journal of Imperial and Commonwealth History* I (Oct. 1972), 79-105.

36. State Department Records, 841.01 Imperial Conference 1937/28, Armour to Secretary of State, 5 May 1937.

37. Cab. 23/88, Cab. Conclusion 34(37) 5, 16 June 1937.

38. Eayrs, *In Defence of Canada*, II, 226ff.

39. Reported in *Montreal Gazette*, 3 July 1937.

40. Lothian Papers, 17/346/157-157a, Christie to Lothian, 10 July 1937.

41. External Affairs Records, vol. 9, file 59, Memorandum to Prime Minister, 17 July 1937.

42. Prem. 1/334, Floud to Sir H. Batterbee, 9 Aug. 1937.

43. Reported in *Montreal Gazette*, 9 July 1937.

44. D.O. 35/543/D28/5 (P.R.O.), "Probable Attitude and Preparedness of Dominions in Event of War," n.d.

45. State Department Records, 842.00/504, "Canada, Political Estimate," 1 June 1937.

46. External Affairs Records, vol. 2, file 4-3, "Note re Canada's Foreign Policy, Particularly in Relation to the United Kingdom," n.d.

47. C. G. Power Papers (Queen's University, Kingston, Ontario), General Staff memorandum, "The Defence of Canada — A Survey of Militia Requirements," 7 Jan. 1938.

48. External Affairs Records, vol. 8, Christie's "Notes on General Staff Paper," 17 Jan. 1938. Cf. C. P. Stacey, *Arms, Men and Governments* (Ottawa, 1970), 71.

49. See Peter Dennis, *Decision by Default* (London, 1972), 81-140 and Michael Howard, *The Continental Commitment* (London, 1972), 96-120.

50. Eayrs, *In Defence of Canada* II, 60-1.

51. See Middlemas, *Diplomacy of Illusion*, chapter 7. For the quiescence of Canadian press opinion, see State Department Records, 842.00 P.R., periodical reports for the summer months of 1938.

52. See, e.g., the discussion in R. A. MacKay and E. B. Rogers, *Canada Looks Abroad* (Toronto, 1938), chapter 15.

53. D.O. 35/543, Floud to Harding, 21 June 1938.

54. Mackenzie King Diary, 31 Aug. 1938, quoted in Stacey, *Arms, Men and Governments*, 7.

55. External Affairs Records, vol. II, file 66-2, "Central European Situation," 11 Sept. 1938. See also Christie's memo, ibid., "Re Ideological Crusading," 4 April 1938 and Skelton's, ibid., "Re Chamberlain's Policy," 14 April 1938.

56. W. L. M. King Papers, (P.A.C.), Diary, 12 Sept. 1938.

57. See *DCER*, VI, 1085-7.

58. Charles Dunning Papers (Queen's University, Kingston, Ontario), King to Dunning, 3 Sept. 1938.

59. King Papers, Diary, 13 Sept. 1938.

60. *DCER*, VI, 1090. The Canadian people did agree, for the American legation reported "strong support for the British stand" and no sentiment for neutrality. State Department Records, 842.00P.R./136, "Periodical Report on General Conditions in Canada," 17 Sept. 1938.

61. Massey, *What's Past is Prologue*, 262.

62. *The History of the Times* (London, 1952), IV, part II, 938.

63. Prem. I/242, memo by M. MacDonald, 13 Sept. 1938. "He also told Lord Halifax that 'the majority' in Canada would be against 'action' at this point in the hope of avoiding war." Middlemas, *Diplomacy of Illusion*, 342.

64. *DCER*, VI, 1093-4.

65. King Papers, Diary, 23 Sept. 1938.

66. Eayrs, *In Defence of Canada*, II, 68.

67. Norman Lambert Papers (Queen's University, Kingston, Ontario), Diary, 10 Oct. 1938.

68. *DCER*, VI, 1096-7.

69. King Papers, Diary, 24 Sept. 1938.

70. *DCER*, VI, 1097.

71. Middlemas, *Diplomacy of Illusion*, 5, is the latest; see also Keith Feiling, *The Life of Neville Chamberlain* (London, 1946), 371-2.

72. State Department Records, 842.00 P.R./137. Periodical Report, 3 Oct. 1938.

73. R. J. Manion Papers (P.A.C.), vol. 16, Manion to James Manion, 7 Oct. 1938.

74. See above n. 55. Cf. External Affairs Records, vol. 2, file 4-4, H. Keenleyside's memorandum "Western [Canadian] Opinion and the European Crisis," November [?], 1938; ibid., vol. II, file 66-2, for a collection of varying reactions to the crisis, and MacKay and Rogers, *Canada Looks Abroad*, 249-324.

75. State Department Records, 842.00 P.R./137, Periodical Report, 3 Oct. 1938.

76. Stacey, *Arms, Men and Governments*, 7.

77. External Affairs Records, vol. 54, file 319-2, "After the Munich Agreement," 3 Oct. 1938.

78. Ibid., file 254-36, "Re the Russian Game in the European Crisis," 10 Dec. 1938.

79. Ibid., file 319-1, Pearson to Skelton, 4 Nov. 1938.

80. King Papers, Diary, 24 Oct. 1938.

81. *Ibid*.

82. *Ibid*., 14 Nov. 1938.

83. *Ibid*., 13 Nov. 1938.

84. *Ibid*., 7 Oct. 1938.

85. *Ibid*., 2 Dec. 1938.

86. Canada, House of Commons, *Debates*, 16 Jan. 1939, 52; King Papers, Diary, 27 Jan. 1939. Cf. Massey, *What's Past is Prologue*, 273-6.

87. External Affairs Records, vol. 721, file 47, "Re: Defence Estimates," n.d.

88. King Papers, Diary, 27 Jan. 1939.

89. Feiling, *Neville Chamberlain*, 400.

90. King Papers, Diary, 17 March 1939. Arnold Heeney believed that 15 March ended King's last hopes for peace, Arnold Heeney, *The Things that are Caesar's* (Toronto, 1972), 55.

91. External Affairs Records, vol. 2, file 4–5, "As to a Statement of the International Position," 20 March 1939.

92. D.O. 114/98, Campbell to Dominions Office, 24 March 1939.

93. Canada, House of Commons, *Debates*, 20 March 1939, esp. 2043.

94. King Papers, Diary, 29 March 1939.

95. Canada, House of Commons, *Debates*, 30 March 1939, 2605–13. Cf. Bruce Hutchison, *The Incredible Canadian* (Toronto, 1952), 242–6.

96. King Papers, Diary, 31 March 1939.

97. Ibid.

98. F.O. 371/22969/C5265/15/18, Hankinson to Harvey, 30 March 1939 encl. notes of the meeting. Massey was there but with no right to speak on behalf of the Canadian government. For Massey's reaction, and for reasons why King was right not to trust his judgment, see Massey, *What's Past is Prologue*, 236ff. Cf. Lester B. Pearson, *Mike: The Memoirs of the Rt. Hon. L. B. Pearson*, I: 1897–1948 (3 vols.; Toronto, 1972, 1973, 1975), 105–6.

99. D.O. 114/98, Campbell to Dominions Office, 26 April 1939.

100. King Papers, Diary, 24 April 1939.

101. External Affairs Records, vol. 48, file 265, Pearson to Skelton, 9 June 1939.

102. Hon. J. W. Pickersgill interview, April, 1970; Hutchison, 248–9.

103. External Affairs Records, vol. 54, file 319–2, Memoranda 19 July 1939 and 22 Aug. 1939.

104. King Papers, Diary, 22 Aug. 1939.

105. External Affairs Records, vol. 54, file 319–2, "Canada and the Polish War: A Personal Note," 25 Aug. 1939.

106. *Ibid.*, memo, 28 Aug. 1939.

107. See Lester Pearson, "Forty Years On: Reflections on Our Foreign Policy," *International Journal* 22 (Summer 1967), 67 which offers Pearson's comment that after being a prime minister concerned with national unity he had more understanding of Mackenzie King's difficulties.

CANADIAN TRADE POLICY, 1943-1947†

"Canadian trade with both the United Kingdom and the United States is of a complementary nature, and is a classic example of a basically sound division of labour," the Rowell-Sirois Commission wrote in 1940. It continued: "Canada's position is similar to that of a small man sitting in a big poker game. He must play for the full stakes, but with only a fraction of the capital resources of his two substantial opponents; if he wins, his profits in relation to his capital are very large, and if he loses, he may be cleaned out."[1] In the 1930's, this economic equation had not worked very well for Canada. Buffeted by an unfavorable international economic climate, Canada in 1938 possessed a standard of living lower than that of Great Britain; it went without saying that the American standard of living was an unattainable height for most Canadians.[2] The small man in the poker game had been nearly cleaned out, a fact which few Canadian officials or economists dared forget in the years that followed.

Canadian trade policy during the 1940's was conditioned by the dismal experience of the 1930's. The spectre of depression was ever-present, and to exorcise it the small Canadian poker-player was driven back to the trading table, to gamble with his larger partners, the United States and Great Britain. During the war years, the Canadians occasionally suggested modifications in the rules of the game to afford some protection against bankruptcy. They discovered that the problem was greater than it had been, since now another player, Great Britain, was also in serious straits. As a direct consequence, Canada turned more and more often to the American side in the game, pursuing the goal of a "sound division of labour" — and a sound bank balance. In this game, Canada had no choice: it was the only game in town, and Canadian officials were constrained to anticipate, and counter, their American partner's changes of mood. It was in this spirit that Canada entered the world of trading negotiations in the 1940's.

The war produced a phenomenal rise in Canadian exports, particularly to the United Kingdom. Canada's problem of the 1930's, the lack of export markets, vanished; so, too, did Canadian unemployment. Canadian officials knew, however, that the war was only a palliative for Canada's export problems, a palliative which, by weakening Britain's external economic position, would make the post-war cure more difficult. Unfortunately for the Canadians, the new exports would be an early casualty of the peace: they were almost entirely munitions, foodstuffs, and raw materials to feed the British war effort. Moreover, these exports rested on a hastily-constructed foundation of loans, credits, and temporary wartime financial expedients. This foundation rested, in turn, on the Hyde Park Agreement of 1941 between Canada and the United States, by which American money was made freely available to keep Canada's war industries alive. After 1941 Canada herself had to finance most of her exports to the United Kingdom.[3] The fact was, in Lord Lothian's breezy phrase, "Boys, Britain's broke."[4]

†Robert Bothwell and John English, "Canadian Trade Policy in the Age of American Dominance and British Decline, 1943-1947," *Canadian Review of American Studies* VIII, 1 (Spring 1977): 54-65.

That Britain was broke was often concealed behind the facade of heroism and endurance, but for Canadian and British officials, there could be no escape from wrestling with the very real economic disasters of the war and with the obscure economic prospects for the peace. In this atmosphere of ambiguity, Canadians sought security: all agreed that secure trading patterns were desirable, but how these patterns would be obtained was unclear. Fearing a return to peacetime poverty, Canadian public opinion, if the polls are to be trusted, looked to economic union with the United States as the preferred solution. Even a majority of upper income Canadians, traditionally insulated by the tariff from personal concern about depressions, seem to have favored this course. Among middle and lower income Canadians, the percentages were much higher.[5] The politicians and officials, however, did not have the simplistic choices which Gallup presented. There was, it is true, an apparent choice between "bilateralism" — special agreements between trading partners — and "multilateralism" a universal regime of orderly trading, a system which the United States strongly promoted for reasons of economic self-interest and classical liberal ideology.[6] Committed by the Atlantic Charter and Article VII of the Lend-Lease agreement, the British too knelt before the altar of multilateralism, but, in their hearts, scepticism and suspicion remained. Unless there was some solution to Britain's international financial problems she "would be unable, after the losses of the war, to take the risks of an international economy organized on liberal lines."[7] There remained as well an emotional commitment on the part of many Britons to the Imperial, bilateralist faith of the past. The path to the multilateralist heaven had very many thickets.

The Canadian wartime and postwar pursuit of economic stability and security, like most episodes in Canada's international history, is also a story of Anglo-American endeavor. Indeed, for much if not most of the time Canada was very much in the position of simply seeking recognition that it had something to say in shaping its own economic destiny. As long as the war was on, Canadians recognized that they had some leverage by reason of their war exports, and it was decided early in the war that this leverage must be used to the best possible purpose, but, unfortunately, it was not always certain what that purpose was. Like the Americans, and generally for the same reasons, the Canadians favored multilateralism. Thus, in May 1943, the Economic Advisory Committee to the cabinet, a group made up of the government's most senior economic advisers, recommended "the negotiation of a multilateral convention of commerce, providing for tariff reductions and limitations and the removal of other barriers to the exchange of goods" as the soundest method of securing satisfactory conditions of trade between nations after the war. It was, the Committee emphasized, "especially in Canada's interest" that this be done.[8] But Canadian policy had its defensive, preventive side as well as its "multilateral," idealist aspect. Memories of American sky-high tariffs during the 1920's and 1930's and of American economic instability and political unpredictability were still fresh, and the Ottawa Agreements of 1932, establishing an Empire preferential system, were highly regarded in some Canadian circles, agricultural as well as manufacturing.[9] The Canadians were perturbed by the zeal of American multilateralists, and, in particular, by the fashion in which the Americans exacted a promise from the British and other Lend-Lease recipients to abandon discriminatory trade policies in return for supplies and other aid. As Norman Robertson, the Undersecretary of State for External Affairs, put it, the Americans "were really pressing for payment, not at the expense of the United Kingdom but at the expense of the other parts of the Empire which enjoy a preferred position in the British market."[10] There was little that the Canadians could do but accept the situation. Although they remained isolated in their refusal to take Lend-Lease aid — the psychological risk in becoming a pensioner of the United States was too great — they did sign the "multilateral" pledge for fear that they might be isolated in any trade concessions reached between the Lend-Lease recipients and the United States.[11]

It is clear, therefore, that neither the Americans nor the British faced the same political and economic imperatives as the Canadians. When a senior Canadian economist described to an American audience the principles of Canadian trade policy, he invoked the image of a "split [Canadian] personality," one "in which complexes [would] arise only if she [were] forced to choose between Britain and the United States."[12] Canadians worked to prevent a situation where such a choice was necessary. When the British convened a meeting of Commonwealth representatives in London in June 1943 to pore over proposals for future trade, the Canadians' contribution was to suggest that an American observer be present, to forestall any impression that Britain and the Dominions were "ganging up" on the United States.[13] Conversely, the Canadians gently reminded the Americans of Britain's special fears and circumstances and of the gap between American promises and deeds. "[B]old or even heroic action is needed," Robertson warned an American diplomat, if a "broad multilateral agreement" was to be achieved. Americans should take advantage of the war while special interests were disoriented: if the Americans would remove their own protective tariff, Empire preferences could be abolished. But if boldness were lacking, if multilateralism failed, Canada, Robertson claimed, would seek a bilateral pact with the United States, ignoring any protectionist schemes the British might promote.[14]

Trade was not merely considered at the level of tariffs and quotas. By mid-1943, proposals for a stable international financial system were freely circulating, with the Canadians characteristically trying to bridge the gap between British and American ideas. After a round of Anglo-American discussions in September 1943, the American government approached the Canadians to sound out Canada's views on post-war trade, and the Canadians were most eager to talk. Robertson portentously explained to Prime Minister King that "what we do, or leave undone, in these next few months may determine the whole course of international economic relations." In December 1943, he proposed a bilateral agreement with the United States, not as a second-best to a multilateral accord, but as a first, exemplary step in that direction; as he put it, "a comprehensive and thoroughgoing trade agreement with the United States . . . could be the first major instalment of the multilateral programme which nearly everyone recognizes as the desirable goal."[15]

What was described as Robertson's "free trade kite" was flown in January 1944 in a series of "highly confidential conversations," word of which quickly leaked into the press. United States Ambassador Atherton took matters a little too far when he advocated an eventual mutual elimination of tariffs in a speech in Hamilton, Ontario, and was admonished by an alarmed State Department, which feared a nationalist Canadian reaction.[16] The flowers of winter withered in spring, and the only result of the Canadian-American talks was a greater understanding by both sides of what their respective positions would be, in certain hypothetical circumstances, and good feelings on both sides. Secretary of the Treasury Morgenthau remarked to his staff, "I think the Canadians are unique in the way they have conducted themselves. I wish the British could learn from them."[17]

In fact, the Canadians had learned much about the British position, and the Robertson remarks can best be understood in light of the Canadian understanding of British attitudes and circumstances. The British anticipated that the end of the war would allow them to reduce their North American liabilities and return to normal channels of supply. Their object was to conserve scarce Canadian and American dollar exchange. This presented a proportionately greater problem to the Canadians than to the Americans, whose trade with Britain had not been a large percentage of American exports at any time in the twentieth century. For Canada, however, the situation was crucial. It was beyond hope that Canada could continue to export wartime volumes to the United Kingdom in peace, but the government did hope to preserve traditional, pre-war markets and to continue to ship foodstuffs and raw materials to the British. Canadian officials pointedly reminded their British opposite numbers of Canada's financial sacrifice for the common cause. Instead of the tangible gratitude which they expected, they were confronted with a new accounting formula which "proved" that Canada's war effort was not as great proportionately as the British, and that Canada's apparent surplus on the British account could also be viewed as a deficit.[18]

This placed the Canadian government in a potentially embarrassing position, since Canadian officials felt (and told the British) that there was a "certain impression" that the United Kingdom was exploiting Canada to pay off its sterling debts to the rest of the Empire and Egypt. Deputy Minister of Finance Clifford Clark had already warned the British that there was "a growing feeling in Parliament and the country that 'Canada was being had for a sucker'."[19] Equally bluntly, Keynes told the Canadians that a reduction in credits to the United Kingdom not only would reduce Canada's immediate exports but also would impair long-term trade relations. Canada's unexpected acceptance of Keynes' accounting mechanism saved the day: it kept Canadian credits flowing to Britain and obviated further domestic criticism by subsuming the transaction under the excuse of payment of the full cost of Canadian troops in Europe.[20]

The Canadians nevertheless realized that Keynes had made no idle threat. By the end of 1944 Canadian officials were nervously noticing that Canadian exports to sterling area countries had diminished through those countries' desire to reduce their sterling balances and preserve their dollar reserves. Australia, for example, stopped importing Canadian cyanide, and there were other cases as well. The Canadian High Commission in London summed it up in November, agreeing with Ottawa that "the future of Canadian exports would not be cleared up until some major decisions on post-war trade policy were made."[21] These decisions would be, to a large extent, political, and they might have to await a British general election. This the Canadians could not afford to do. Besides, they had political concerns of their own which the British often forgot but which Mackenzie King never did.

King had been outraged when Lord Halifax, speaking in Toronto in January 1944, had called for a strengthening of defence, economic, and foreign policy ties within the British Commonwealth. To King, the proposal was "like a conspiracy on the part of Imperialists to win their own victory in the middle of the war."[22] His anger grew as Conservative newspapers hailed Halifax's message and French-Canadian newspapers denounced it. This was important, for as J.L. Granatstein has pointed out, "On foreign policy questions, his area of expertise, King was more likely to insist on his views being followed."[23] Moreover, most of his advisers on foreign policy also tended to bear some resentment towards the British attitude. When Britain's most avid defender among Canadian diplomats, High Commissioner Vincent Massey, complained about "the perennial search for conspiracies against our sovereignty" in British actions, Hume Wrong replied that "There is a feeling [in Ottawa] that the U.K. is very prolific with its requests on Canada and much less prolific with its appreciation of what we have done."[24] This feeling existed not only among the advisers but also within the cabinet, especially, although not exclusively, among the members from Quebec. While there was great admiration for what Britain had done and, on the whole, a willingness on the part of the government and the general public to assist Britain in her post-war recovery, distrust lingered.[25]

This was the setting when, early in 1945, the responsible ministers and their senior officials convened for a gloomy meeting to consider the economic consequences of victory. Clifford Clark, always the leader in such discussions, informed his ministerial superiors and his civil service colleagues that "the developing prospects . . . appeared to be so serious . . . that they justified the Canadian Government doing what it could at the present time to improve matters." Recent information as to the state of official economic thinking in Britain indicated that the British were at least considering "a cordon sanitaire" around the sterling area, "and would endeavour to develop and expand trade within that area and restrict it between that area and the rest of the world." This projected policy seemed to some Canadian observers to resemble "the policies worked out for Germany by Dr. Schacht," although the British professed that they were not intended to be "so extreme." The Governor of the Bank of Canada, Graham Towers, warned that if Britain chose the option of restriction, "the outlook [could] only be described as terrible." Worse even than the impact of these policies was the possibility of American retaliation, of which the "political and economic consequences must be left to a vivid imagination." Towers told his colleagues that when Keynes last visited Ottawa in December 1944, he had sounded him on the possibility of a Canadian loan to the United Kingdom. Keynes had deprecated such an offer at that time: "it would be regarded as unacceptable because Canada and the U.S. would probably ask the U.K. as a *quid pro quo*, not to discriminate against imports from them." The excuse for Keynes' demurral was Britain's huge debt to the other dominions, India, Egypt, Iraq, and the crown colonies. The Canadians, Towers concluded, must oppose all British steps which led towards a sterling "cordon sanitaire."[26] If the world divided into two opposing trading blocs, there was no doubt where Canada would end up; and Canada's happy split trading personality would become permanently unhinged.[27]

To avert this drastic fate, the Canadians in February 1945 tried to devise a seductive bait to lure the British towards a more equitable attitude to trade with Canada. The notes eventually sent expressed "the gravest concern for the future of the Commonwealth," and warned that "the general reaction in North America would be one of bitter recrimination and disillusionment" if the British went in for a discriminatory trade policy of "sterling area isolationism." A financial carrot accompanied this political stick: Canada offered a long term credit repayable starting ten years after the end of the war. If the British balance of payments fell beneath a certain level in any given year, no repayment would be required in that year. Then the Canadians sat back, apprehensively, to see what reaction they had stirred up. Initial reports were of an "excellent impression" at the official level, but the Canadians were not told the full story.[28] Sir Wilfrid Eady, the second secretary at the Treasury, summarized the major British consideration, one which endured throughout the war and into the peace: "Every move we make with Canada has to be very carefully related to our much bigger problem with the U.S.A." He suggested that the Canadian slate be kept clear until the British knew what the Americans were doing.[29] Sir John Anderson, never an admirer of Canada, wrote that the Canadian "aim is really the break-up of the sterling area." Keynes at least was more perceptive, commenting that "the bilateralism is their object." Although all the British commentators recognized the overwhelming importance of the United States, and by corollary, the impossibility of any separate deal with Canada, they were divided as to what their own immediate reaction should be.[30] The British emphasis on the practical necessity of dealing jointly with the Canadians and Americans, and on the practical identity of Canadian and American trade attitudes, was the mirror image of suggestions inside the Canadian government that Canada should reach its own agreement with the United States as a prelude to a general multilateral settlement. In the end, the British reaction was as tentative and ambiguous as the Canadian policy.

The British were prepared to exchange views with the Canadians on an unofficial level. Meeting at Cambridge, Canadian civil servants and Treasury officials heard Lord Keynes declare that the United Kingdom would not choose "starvation corner," the policy most dreaded by his transatlantic audience. To avoid "starvation corner," Britain intended to seek a $5 billion loan from the United States and $500 million from Canada. Replying for the Canadians, W.A. Mackintosh of the Reconstruction Department said that "he was pleased to see that on the whole there was agreement between authoritative Canadian and United Kingdom opinion on final objectives." Towers warned that if the British policy failed, "Canada would be inevitably thrown more in the direction of the United States." On a practical level, the negotiators agreed that, in return for a Canadian credit of $1.25 billion for fiscal 1945-46, expected to be the last year of the war, the British would permit token imports from Canada in areas where Canada had been a traditional supplier before the war.[31] The Americans were not informed of the token import agreement, an agreement which symbolized Canada's traditional claims on the British market. Though insignificant themselves, the token imports were a promise that Canadian trade would find a secure haven, somewhere, when conditions returned to normal.[32]

The paramount concern for security was also apparent in the trade discussions which the Canadians and the Americans held in Ottawa in the summer of 1945. In those meetings, the Canadians argued "very insistently and forcefully their view that the only adequate and effective means of attacking the trade barrier was through a multilateral horizontal tariff cut." When the Americans explained that this proposal was impractical, the Canadians responded by suggesting "a series of bilateral trade agreements among the leading nations." They did not tell the Americans that they had already experimented with such an agreement, although not of the type they were now proposing.[33] Had they known, the Americans might not have been as sympathetic as they were towards what they termed "the Canadian question." An official in the Ottawa Embassy had already suggested the possibility of a peace-time Hyde Park agreement, pointing out that "Canadians are interested in a measure of postwar collaboration so far as industry is concerned." The official, J.G. Parsons, added: "You know the Canadian fears in regard to their United Kingdom market after the war. These fears give them an added interest in economic collaboration with us." These sentiments fell on fertile ground in Washington. W.L. Batt, one of the top war production officials, announced: "I am authorized to take the position for the State Department that to treat Canada like any other foreign Government would be contrary to our policy. It is their view that the Canadian economy should be treated as nearly as possible like our own in peacetime as well as in war, based always on mutual reciprocity."[34] But when peacetime came, the promises of the spring and summer subsided. The Hyde Park agreement, which applied to defence purchases, was no longer so beneficial when the Japanese war came to an unexpectedly sudden end, and the carefully constructed edifices of Lend-Lease and Mutual Aid came tumbling down.

The blast of peace found the trading world unprepared with either multilateral agreements or workable bilateral schemes. The British hesitated in their commitments to multilateralism and showed resentment for the North American zeal to sell them consumer goods. "The Americans," *The Economist* complained, "with their usual impetuosity to make a million overnight are looking for a lusty and healthy partner in putting two motor cars in every European barn and a chicken in every Zulu's pot."[35] But the enthusiasm of Canadian exporters soon waned as they realized that Europe's political instability and military insecurity would not end after V-E Day; it would continue and would produce and reflect economic insecurity. The first sign that things were not well was the misfiring of the token import agreement: Canadian manufacturers soon complained, with reason, that the British were obstructing Canadian trade with Britain. Acrimonious discussions soon followed between the Canadians and the British, in which the British were acutely aware that the Canadians held a financial whip hand. For the British once again needed a loan.[36]

The Canadians were prepared to bargain hard, but the even harder line taken by the United States generated both public and governmental sympathy for Britain in Canada. When an American official suggested that Canada increase the tariff against British imports as a means of re-establishing the pre-war "equilibrium position" between American and British imports, Robertson replied that such an action would be completely unreasonable: "That equilibrium had, in fact, been completely and perhaps irretrievably upset, and to the advantage of the United States, by the fact of the war itself, which had severed many Canadian-United Kingdom trade connections and increased our dependence on domestic and American sources of supply."[37] Proof for this claim was soon available in the terms which the Americans imposed upon the British in exchange for a loan. As a British official in Ottawa observed, the Canadians considered "the terms not only harsh in themselves but out of keeping with the real fundamentals and spirit of the case when looked at from the broadest viewpoint."[38] An American official spoke of the Canadian "carping at the United States for being so miserly on the British loan . . . ." Canadians believed, the official continued, "that we struck a hard bargain with a man who was down."[39] Nevertheless, the Canadians could do no better: the prior American negotiations and the terms of the loan itself meant that Canada could not offer more favorable or radically different terms.

The Canadians, knowing a loan was insufficient to sustain their export markets, were willing to forsake multilateralism in specific cases if bilateralism offered security. The clearest example of this is the wheat agreement entered into in 1946. During the war Canada had concluded bulk sales of foodstuffs to Britain, and Canadian farmers rejoiced in high prices and secure markets. The Department of Agriculture, too, had been involved in negotiations looking towards the formation of a multilateral marketing system; like other, similar wartime projects these talks had ended in stalemate. The Minister of Agriculture, Jimmy Gardiner of Saskatchewan, was concerned with the stability of farm incomes, and as a rural politician, he should have been. He was also an intense anglophile, and a believer in the future, as well as the past, of the British Empire. After satisfying himself that no progress was likely in international wheat negotiations, Gardiner began discussions in London for a bilateral wheat contract, to last five years, providing for bulk purchasing by the British of a large proportion of Canada's wheat crop. Gardiner's cabinet colleagues let him have his way, and, over-ruling his civil service advisers, he concluded the agreement in June 1946, on British terms. Even the British were incredulous at Gardiner's determination to have this agreement come what might.[40]

At Prime Minister King's insistence, Canadian ratification of the wheat agreement was postponed while one last approach was made to the Americans for a multilateral alternative. The American government, however, "had no alternatives to offer."[41] The Canadian-British wheat agreement accordingly came into force, a practical testimony to Canada's overriding concern for trading security; if multilateral principles could not provide it, then bilateralism would have to do. Self-interest dictated immediate action while wartime memories were fresh, but as one British negotiator warned: "Contracts made in abnormal times are rarely much good for ordinary times." The wheat agreement was no exception.[42]

The negotiations for the British loan had already educated Canadian officials in the abnormality of the times. Originally there was some feeling that Britain should be forced to liquidate British investments in Canada before a loan could be granted. The British, however, warned that the liquidation of investments was a price too high to pay. Cobbold, the Governor of the Bank of England, claimed that Britain could live without American and Canadian loans, but "it would mean that she would have to direct her trade to those countries which had quantities of sterling in England and exercise a rigid direction of industry, commerce etc. It would probably be disastrous for Britain, but equally disastrous for other countries." King, speaking in reply, indicated how intimately economics and politics intermingled. If the consequences Cobbold foresaw became realities, King pointed out, "there was a further one which would certainly follow, which would be that if this continent became dependent on herself, Canada would soon be out of the British Commonwealth of Nations." Later, King privately confided . . . in Louis St. Laurent, his French Canadian lieutenant, his fears for his nation's future: "I felt the great menace was from the U.S.S.R. and of having [sic] little doubt that the fear of Russian aggression would create a strong continental feeling which might inevitably make this continent one. I felt pretty sure that in the next war Canada would become the battlefield in an attempt at conquest of the world by the U.S.S.R. . . . It is an appalling prospect and one hates to entertain it. It is not looking realities in the face to fail to do so." In this case, "looking realities in the face" meant approval of a loan in the amount of $1.25 billion. When the loan agreement was presented to Parliament, there was no "mother country" rhetoric, only a grim appreciation of Canada's desperate need for markets. Despite fear of French-Canadian and other opposition, the critics were few. For the officials, the loan negotiations had clearly revealed, in Finance Minister Ilsley's words, "that Britain is no longer a wealthy country."[43]

Although Britain was no longer a wealthy country, Canada had not yet given up on her: indeed, the wheat agreement and the loan were wagers on a successful future for the United Kingdom. The loan, it was hoped, would sustain the British economy through reconstruction and would shore up Britain's foreign exchange reserves until the traditional markets for her exports were recovered. Canadians expected a gradual drawing on the Canadian credit which would not overstrain Canada's capacity to pay. There was, in short, much optimism in the air in 1946, despite international difficulties, and one indication of this was the restoration of parity between the Canadian and American dollars. According to *The Financial Post*, the move was an expression of faith in Canadian industry. Most Canadian businessmen favored it, believing that it would restrain domestic inflation at little cost to Canadian exports.[44]

Unfortunately, the faith in British recovery and the revalued currency was ill-founded. In November 1946, Sir Stafford Cripps worried aloud that the American and Canadian loans were being expended too rapidly.[45] The depletion of the loans that had been intended to tide the British over the transitional period in turn jeopardized or made irrelevant various international trade measures planned for 1947; notable among these were the return of the British pound to convertibility in July and multilateral trade discussions in Geneva. Canada attached great importance to these talks, which later produced the General Agreement on Tariffs and Trade, but the dwindling of Canada's American dollar reserves at a rate of $100 million per month dampened Ottawa's enthusiasm. Already by April 1947, Dean Acheson could observe that Canada had made a mistake by prematurely re-establishing parity between the Canadian and American dollars.[46] In June, with convertibility of the pound only weeks away, Canada tightened the terms on which Canadian goods would be made available to the British. In Ottawa, officials freely discussed the possibility of "imminent economic catastrophe and a collapse of world trade."[47] General Marshall's Harvard speech on June 5 offered hope, but, for the immediate future, not much more. By the time the British were forced off convertibility, in mid-August, it was clear that the expedient policies designed to tidy up the financial aftermath of the war had failed, and that another set was now urgently required.

For Canada, this meant stringent import controls and an emergency loan of $300 million from the Export-Import Bank of Washington. Because, as the Minister of Finance told Parliament, the dollar crisis had occurred on account of a shortage of American dollars, rather than a deterioration in Canada's competitive position, the Canadian dollar was not devalued. The Americans accepted discriminatory restrictions on exports to Canada because of the self-evident gravity of the crisis; at the same time, imports from non-dollar sources were increasing.[48] Ironically, the Minister of Finance's statement followed immediately after the Prime Minister announced the results of the Geneva negotiations. Canada agreed to reduce rates or grant other concessions on roughly one thousand items. In return, Canada's exporters obtained better access to foreign markets, especially those of the United States. Canada and the other Commonwealth countries accepted that no new preferences could be created and that the remaining preferences were negotiable. This meant, in the words of an American summary of the time, that "in all future tariff negotiations between the United States and Canada or between the United States and the United Kingdom, either of those two countries can negotiate with [the United States] with respect to their most-favored-nation tariff rates free of any contractual obligation to the other to maintain preferential margins."[49]

A recent study describes the Geneva agreement as a "new Calvinistic Confession of Faith," and explains it as the culmination of "Canada's credulous faith in the new American commercial orthodoxy." Canada, the author concludes, "had left one trading world forever; and for good or ill, had committed itself irrevocably to another."[50] Both this analysis and this conclusion may be questioned. The impact of Geneva on preferential margins was not dramatic. What was important was that British trade with Canada was relatively much less than it had been before the war, and the fate of British preference was proportionately less significant.[51]

Circumstances, not ideology, dictated Canada's position at Geneva. As our study has indicated, there was no fixed Canadian position on international trade between 1942 and 1947. Canadian civil servants were well aware of the conventional wisdom that prescribed multilateral trade as a nostrum for the nation's economic ills. Some, particularly Norman Robertson, subscribed wholeheartedly to this proposition. Nonetheless, between 1942 and 1947, the Canadian government pursued at least three policies: the protection of the British preference, bilateral trade, and multilateralism. The actions of the Canadian government belie its ostensible devotion to a multilateral panacea that not even Robertson believed could reach immediate fruition. Canadian policy of necessity was reactive, not creative, and common prudence dictated a policy for each possible circumstance.

The experience must have been instructive. The vast horizons of wartime planning shrank under the impact of politics and uncertainty. Optimism was replaced by the more prosaic emotion of fear — fear that the multilateral trading economy of the prewar years was gone, never to return. To the extent that it could, the Canadian government promoted the non-American side of Canadian trade through extensive credits. Its motives were certainly not altruistic: the Anglo-Canadian Wheat Agreement, besides being an exercise in prewar nostalgia, was also an attempt to shore up Canadian wheat prices at the eventual expense of the British consumer, a hallowed Canadian tradition. Unfortunately, as events proved, the British were no longer able to afford this role. Instead the Canadian government had to turn to another form of bilateralism which it had contemplated as early as 1942, customs union with the United States. Donald Creighton has described metaphorically Canada's position in this period as that of a traveller facing a forked road. A better metaphor would be that of a wayfarer confronting a maze.

Notes

1. Rowell-Sirois Report, quoted in J.B. Brebner, *The North Atlantic Triangle* (Toronto, 1966), 315.

2. *The Economist*, 3 Nov. 1945, reported that before the war the average per capita purchases of all consumer goods and service was less in Canada than in Britain. The Canadians expected to lag behind the U.S., and they did.

3. See J.L. Granatstein, "Settling the Accounts: Anglo-Canadian War Finance, 1943–1945," *Queen's Quarterly*, 83 (1976): 234–49; and also, R.S. Sayers, *British Financial Policy, 1939–1945* (London, 1956), 337ff.

4. Quoted in Gordon Wright, *The Ordeal of War* (New York, 1968), 168n.

5. Such a union was favored by 67%; 17% opposed it; and 16% "didn't know." Gallup Poll, *Montreal Star*, 2 June 1943.

6. See John Lewis Gaddis, *The United States and the Origins of the Cold War, 1941–1947* (New York, 1972), 18–23. Gaddis writes: "Classical liberals had always viewed commerce as the main bond between nations, and most State Department economists adhered to this position" (p. 19). For general background on Anglo-American attitudes and negotiations, Richard N. Gardner, *Sterling-Dollar Diplomacy: Anglo-American Collaboration in the Reconstruction of Multilateral Trade* (Oxford, 1956), is invaluable.

7. This summary of Lord Keynes' attitude is found in D.E. Moggridge, *Keynes* (London, 1976), 140.

8. "Report of the Advisory Committee on Economic Policy on Trade Policy," 14 May 1943, Finance Department Papers (RG19), v. 3592, file L-11-E, Public Archives of Canada (PAC).

9. The Minister of Finance, J.L. Ilsley, was very sensitive to any disturbance of the preference on apples, a crop grown in his Nova Scotia constituency.

10. Norman Robertson to Prime Minister King, 3 Oct. 1941, King Papers, J4, C2 50326-7 (PAC).

11. On the issue of lend-lease, see Clifford Clark (Deputy Minister of Finance) to A.F.W. Plumptre, 4 June 1942; and Plumptre's reply, 11 June, in External Affairs Papers, series B3, v. 2148 (PAC). On the Canadian agreement to sign, see Adolf Berle diary, 10 June 1942 (Franklin D. Roosevelt Library). The State Department *Bulletin*, after prodding from Canada, published a statement on 16 July 1944 stressing that Canada was not a recipient of Lend-Lease, although Canada did subscribe to the multilateral principles.

12. Louis Rasminsky, "Anglo-American Trade Prospects: A Canadian View," *Economic Journal* 65 (1945): 161–178.

13. King to High Commissioner in United Kingdom, 19 and 25 June 1943, King Papers, J1, v. 346, (PAC).

14. John Hickerson to Cordell Hull, 29 July 1943, U.S. State Dept. Papers, 611.0031/134, National Archives.

15. Robertson to King, 12 Dec. 1943, King Papers, J4, v. 334, file 3584, (PAC).

16. Kenneth R. Wilson, "Ottawa is Sceptical of Free Trade Feeler," *Financial Post*, 6 Nov. 1943; "Talk Tariff Elimination U.S.-Canada," *ibid.*, 29 Jan. 1944; and Hickerson to J.G. Parsons (U.S. Embassy, Ottawa), State Dept. 611.4231/3075½, National Archives.

17. Morgenthau Diary, 15 March 1944, Roosevelt Library.

18. Alexander Clutterbuck, Dominions Office, to D.H. Robertson, Treasury, 24 April 1944; Robertson to Clutterbuck, 28 April 1944; and Keynes, "Suggestions for a Revised Formula Governing Relations Between Canada and the U.K. after March 31, 1945," 8 Aug. 1944. T160/ 1376/F17969/1013/2, Public Record Office (PRO).

19. High Commissioner in Canada to Dominions Office, for Treasury, 3 July 1944, T160/1376/X/101365 (PRO).

20. Sayers, *Financial Policy*, 357, argues that the tough British attitude during these negotiations proved to be a salutary awakening for Canadian departments other than Finance; to this we would add their evident concern with post-war trade. R.B. Bryce, "Notes on Meeting in Office of Minister of Finance to Discuss United Kingdom Financing—August 1, 1944," External Affairs Papers, file 154, Dept. of External Affairs Archives.

21. *Ibid.*

22. Quoted in J.W. Pickersgill, *The Mackenzie King Record*: Volume 1, *1939-1944* (Toronto, 1960), 637-38.

23. J.L. Granatstein, "King and his Cabinet: The War Years," in *Mackenzie King: Widening the Debate*, edited by J.R. English and J.O. Stubbs (Toronto, 1978).

24. Quoted in Vincent Massey, *What's Past is Prologue* (Toronto, 1963), 390-92.

25. *Ibid.*, chs. 10 and 11.

26. "Notes of meeting of ministers and officials in office of Minister of Finance, Jan. 18, 1945, to discuss immediate post-war commercial policy outlook," External Affairs Papers, file 154(s), Dept. of External Affairs Archives.

27. Rasminsky, "Anglo-American Trade Prospects", 163.

28. The notes were numbers 45, 46 and 47, 23 Feb. 1945, External Affairs Papers, file 154(s). First British reaction is reported in F. Hudd to Robertson, 28 Feb. 1945, *ibid.*

29. Eady to Mullins, 24 Feb. 1945, T160/1377/F17969/ 024/1 (PRO).

30. Eady to Tucker, 6 March 1945; Halifax to Foreign Office, 7 March 1945; Cherwell to Anderson with minute by Anderson, 23 March 1945; and Eady to Keynes with minute by Keynes, 26 March 1945, T160/1377/F17969/024/2.

31. Records of the meetings, which took place on 19, 20 and 28 May in Cambridge and London, are in DO35/1219/T665/ 101 (PRO).

32. K.R. Wilson, memorandum accompanying articles submitted to *Financial Post* editorial contest number 4, 15 Nov. 1945. K.R. Wilson Papers (privately held); and Macintosh to R.G. Munro, 22 June 1945, Finance Dept. Papers, v. 3579, file L-15A (PAC); and Colonial Secretary to the Officers Administering All Colonies, 16 July 1945, DO35/1219/T665/101 (PRO).

33. Herbert S. Marks, "Report on Ottawa Trip," 18 July 1945, State Dept. 611.4231/7-1845, National Archives.

34. J.G. Parsons to Hickerson, 21 April 1945, State Dept. 842.20 Defense/4-2145; and Wm. Batt to Edward Browning and Robert Turner, 27 April 1945, *ibid.*

35. *The Economist*, 3 Feb. 1945.

36. K.R. Wilson, memorandum, 15 Nov. 1945, Wilson Papers; Pickersgill and Donald Forster, *The Mackenzie King Record*: Volume III, *1945-1946* (Toronto, 1970), 159-60.

37. Robertson, "Memo for the Prime Minister," 18 July 1945, King Papers, J4, v. 334, C230360-1.

38. R.G. Munro, "Note on Forthcoming United Kingdom-Canada Financial Negotiations," 15 Dec. 1945, DO35/1219WT665/110 (PRO).

39. Clark to Parsons, 28 Dec. 1945, State Dept. 842.00/12-2845, National Archives.

40. This account is drawn from Charles F. Wilson, "Review of Government Grain Policy," unpublished manuscript, part IV (Ottawa, mimeo, 1974), 1299ff.

41. Lester Pearson to Robertson, 27 June 1946, cited in Wilson.

42. James Rank to C.D. Howe, 15 July 1946; and Howe to Rank, 18 July 1946, C.D. Howe Papers, v. 171, file 90–6 (PAC).

43. Ilsley to Power, 19 March 1946, External Affairs file 1893–40, v. 2. The account of the loan negotiation draws heavily upon Pickersgill and Forster, *Mackenzie King Record*, III, ch. v.

44. *Financial Post*, 6 and 13 July 1946.

45. Canadian High Commission, London, "United Kingdom Fortnightly Summary," no. 15, 22 Nov. and 5 Dec. 1946. External Affairs file 154 (s).

46. Acheson, "Memorandum for the President," 22 April 1947, State Dept. 842.00/4–2247.

47. K.R. Wilson, "Shadows over World Trade," *Financial Post*, 24 May 1947.

48. See Paul Wonnacott, *The Canadian Dollar, 1948–1962* (Toronto, 1965), 48–56 on the dollar crisis.

49. Pickersgill and Forster, *Mackenzie King Record*, III, 90; and Memorandum by the Chairman of the Committee on Trade Agreements, (Brown) to President Truman, Geneva, 17 October 1947 in *Foreign Relations of the United States, 1947*; Volume I, *General; The United Nations* (Washington, 1973), 1016.

50. D.G. Creighton, *The Forked Road: Canada, 1939–1957* (Toronto, 1976), 126–27.

51. See John Young, *Canadian Commercial Policy* (Ottawa, 1957), 54–56.

THE CREATION OF THE NORTH ATLANTIC ALLIANCE, 1948–1949†

To comprehend the creation of the North Atlantic Alliance and the part which Canada played under the leadership of St. Laurent and Pearson it is necessary to try to put oneself inside the minds of those who conducted and directed the negotiations.[1]

The years from 1929 to 1948 had been apocalyptic for those who lived through them. It is not surprising that many of us became apocalyptic in our dreams and visions. We had learned that civilization was fragile; we believed that the war had made international relations malleable. We believed that the times demanded and made possible revolutionary changes in the relations between nations if civilization were not to collapse.

Here are some illuminating examples drawn only from the United States, Britain, and Canada of ideas current in government circles at that time which a quarter of a century later might be dismissed with such pejoratives as unrealistic, idealistic, doctrinaire, grandiose, and rhetorical.

An official British report of 1943 recommended that all international airlines be owned and operated by an international agency. An official Canadian report of 1944, signed by Norman Robertson, Under-Secretary of State for External Affairs, W.C. Clark, Deputy Minister of Finance, and H.J. Symington, head of Trans Canada Airlines, recommended the establishment of an international air transport board which alone would be competent to grant licenses to international airlines. Dean Acheson, Under-Secretary of State, proposed in 1946, in association with D.E. Lilienthal, Chairman of the Tennessee Valley Authority, "a plan under which no nation would make atomic bombs or the material for them. All dangerous activities would be carried on — not merely inspected — by a live, functioning international authority . . . ."[2]

At the beginning of February 1948, more than a month before the British proposed tripartite discussions on a North Atlantic treaty, Hume Wrong, the Canadian Ambassador in Washington, had a talk with J.D. Hickerson, then director of the Office of European Affairs in the State Department, about Ernest Bevin's proposals of January which finally resulted in the Brussels treaty. Wrong reported that

> some in the State Department have visions of a much more extensive union [than that proposed by Bevin which led to the Brussels treaty] based not only on a defensive alliance, but also on a customs union, perhaps with common citizenship. . . . [T]he United States and Canada might be included in such a union.

On April 7, 1949, three days after the signature of the North Atlantic treaty, I reported to Pearson that Hickerson had told me the day before that he personally was in favour of the proposals by Mr. Justice Roberts, of the Supreme Court,

†Escott Reid, "Canada and the Creation of the North Atlantic Alliance, 1948–1949" in *Freedom and Change: Essays in Honour of Lester B. Pearson*, edited by Michael Fry (Toronto: McClelland and Stewart, 1975), 106–35.

William L. Clayton, former Assistant Secretary of State for Economic Affairs, and others for the immediate formation of a federation of the North Atlantic countries. At about the same time George Kennan

> had visions of a world-trading, maritime bloc, to include not only the British, the Canadians, and ourselves but certain of the Commonwealth nations and possibly some entities of the Scandinavian and Iberian peninsulas as well, to be based on a single currency, to develop eventually into a federal union with a common sovereignty, and to flank in this capacity a similar grouping on the continent.[3]

In January 1948, Gladwyn Jebb (later Lord Gladwyn), then Under-Secretary at the British Foreign Office, hoped that it might be possible

> to construct a "Middle Power" consisting of Western Europe plus the bulk of Africa which, while remaining friendly with the U.S.A. would no longer be economically dependent on that country and hence capable of pursuing an independent foreign policy.[4]

In such an atmosphere is it surprising that at the beginning of October 1948, the Canadian government shared Pearson's view that the proposed North Atlantic alliance would create a new international institution which would, as he said.

> . . . have within itself possibilities of growth and of adaptations to changing conditions. The North Atlantic Community is today a real commonwealth of nations which share the same democratic and cultural traditions. If a movement towards its political and economic unification can be started this year, no one can forecast the extent of the unity which may exist five, ten or fifteen years from now.

In 1944 and 1945 the Western powers did not have high hopes of cooperation with the Soviet Union in dealing with the problems of the post-war world. They did not, however, assume that the borderline in Europe between the Soviet troops advancing from the east and the Western troops advancing through France and Italy would become a border-line between a Soviet empire and the Western world. They believed that a buffer zone would be created between the two spheres consisting of Poland, Czechoslovakia, Hungary, Rumania, and Bulgaria. These states would be friendly to the Soviet Union but they would not be dominated by it. In 1947 and the first few months of 1948, however, these states fell one by one under Soviet domination in a pattern which became frighteningly clear: first, a government of national unity; then a popular front government; then a communist government; and finally a purge of communists who were not considered reliable by the Soviet government, which usually meant liquidating those who had not spent the war years in the Soviet Union. Thus Soviet power in Europe advanced right up to the ceasefire line. The communist takeover of Czechoslovakia on February 25, 1948, seemed final, conclusive proof that the Soviet Union was not content with friendly states on its borders, but demanded that the border states should become satellite members of its empire. The death of Jan Masaryk on March 10, 1948 was an intense emotional shock.

Western leaders became afraid in the first three months of 1948 that the pattern of the Soviet Union's take-over of countries east of the ceasefire line would be reproduced west of the line, especially in countries such as Italy and France where the communist parties were strong and subservient instruments of the

Soviet government.[5] It seemed that an increasing number of influential people in Italy and France had concluded that the accession to power of a Soviet-controlled communist government in their country was inevitable, that Soviet power was the wave of the future, and that they had better ingratiate themselves with, or at least not offend, those who would take control very soon and who would then liquidate any opponents of importance. The fear at the time, as Charles Bohlen has put it, was less an "all out military attack" by the Soviet Union "than the use of Soviet armed force to encourage and give direct support to the Communist parties of Western Europe in case of an attempted [Communist] take-over."[6] This increasing fear of Soviet power was accompanied by mounting revulsion against the nature of Soviet rule, as the West learned more about the atrocities of Soviet armies in occupied territories, Soviet treatment of their own people returning from German prisoner of war and displaced persons camps, their treatment of leaders of social-democratic and agrarian parties in eastern Europe, and the nature of the society which had been created in the Soviet Union.

Our embassy in Moscow gave us a clear picture of that society in a cable in April 1948. After stating that the end professed by Communism, a society in which each man is rewarded according to his needs, was by no means incompatible with our liberal, democratic Christian tradition, the message went on to say that the fallacy in the philosophy of the Communists was that they thought that to achieve their end they could establish a ruthless but temporary dictatorship, lie, cheat, and employ the most up-to-date method of tyrannies old and new. The Communists did not recognize that all men, not just capitalists, landlords, and grand dukes were corrupted by absolute power. The Communists had created the most omnipotent and pervasive state in history. They had taken over the worst feature of Tsarist tyranny, the secret police, and had expanded it. The security forces of the MVD had multiplied to such proportions that they virtually formed a state within the state with their own private army. The men who had set out to elevate the working man were now depending to an increasing extent on forced labour to achieve their economic goals. It was the eight to twenty million political prisoners living like cattle in forced labour camps who had built the White Sea-Baltic canal and some of the other achievements attributed to Soviet labour. The ideals of equality which had inspired the early Communists had been abandoned. The officials of the Soviet Union formed a caste with extraordinary privileges, and with complete control over every aspect of Soviet life.

To understand the mood in Ottawa at the time of the negotiation of the North Atlantic treaty, it is necessary also to comprehend how our feelings about the United States and about our own country differed from feelings a quarter of a century later. The United States of 1948 and 1949 was the pre-imperial United States; the United States government was interested in and influenced by the views of friendly governments. The United States presidency was the pre-imperial presidency; the State Department was powerful under George C. Marshall, Robert A. Lovett, and Acheson. Canada was just emerging from the period when it was the third most important country in the "free world."

Sometime in February 1948, before the Soviet coup in Czechoslovakia, the British government sent Gladwyn Jebb to Washington to sound out the United States on how far it might be prepared to go to support a Western European defensive pact. He was recalled before speaking to the Americans "since the moment was deemed unpropitious."[7] Within the next few weeks developments took place which persuaded the British government that the propitious moment had arrived. It can reasonably be assumed that these developments were the Soviet coup in Czechoslovakia on February 25, the opening of the discussions on the Brussels treaty on March 7, and a message from the Norwegian government on March 8 that it feared that Norway might soon face Soviet demands for a pact which would reduce Norway to the level of a satellite.

On March 11 Attlee proposed to the United States and Canada that officials of the three countries should meet without delay to study the establishment of a regional North Atlantic pact of mutual assistance under Article 51 of the UN Charter. All the countries threatened by a Soviet move on the Atlantic could participate — Norway, Denmark, Iceland, Ireland, France, Portugal, Great Britain, the United States, Canada, and Spain, once it established a democratic regime. Attlee, as Pearson records, "warned that 'failure to act now may mean a repetition of our experience with Hitler.' "[8] We received Attlee's proposal on March 11. That same day, Mackenzie King, after consulting Louis St. Laurent, Secretary of State for External Affairs, Brooke Claxton, Minister of National Defence, and Lester Pearson, Under-Secretary of State for External Affairs, cabled Attlee, accepting his proposal.[9]

The British had prepared the way for their initiative by sending us an appreciation of the dangerous international situation. This took the form of a message from P.J. Noel-Baker, Secretary of State for Commonwealth Relations. It bears a marked resemblance to Gladwyn Jebb's assessment of February 1948, the gist of which he sets forth in his memoirs.[10] From this I assume that he was the principal draftsman of the Noel-Baker message.

Mackenzie King was shocked by the news of Jan Masaryk's death. He wrote in his diary that night, March 10: "One thing is certain. It has proven there can be no collaboration with Communists."[11] The next day he was greatly impressed by the British appreciation of the dangers of the international situation. He read it on March 11 and 12 to the leaders of the three opposition parties and on March 15 to the Cabinet.[12]

Clearly, the British Labour government, not the Truman administration, launched the tripartite discussions which resulted in the North Atlantic treaty. A British, not a United States, appreciation of the dangers of the international situation in March 1948 provided the background against which the Canadian government decided to participate in those discussions. The British pressed persistently for a North Atlantic treaty during the first six months of the intergovernmental discussions when opinion in the United States administration was divided and support in Western Europe was lukewarm. The one thing the North Atlantic treaty of 1949 is not is an example of Canada being persuaded by the United States to support its Cold War policies.

Mackenzie King, St. Laurent, Claxton, and Pearson, who were responsible for the decision on March 11 to accept the British proposal to participate in discussions on an Atlantic security pact, had lived through two world wars. They were convinced that Canada could not escape being an active belligerent in a third world war.[13] They had come to believe that the First and Second World Wars would not have broken out if Germany had known that it would eventually face a coalition of the United States, Britain, and France. They concluded that the way to prevent a third world war was to convince Stalin that in such a war he would face from the outset an even stronger coalition than the coalitions of 1917 and 1941. The grand coalition, therefore, should be created before and not after the outbreak of war. If created before it might deter Stalin; if created after, all it could do would be to defeat him. This belief was put succinctly by Truman at the signing of the treaty:

> It is a simple document, but if it had existed in 1914 and in 1939, supported by the nations which are represented here today, I believe it would have prevented the acts of aggression which led to two world wars.[14]

 The intergovernmental discussions and negotiations in Washington on the North Atlantic treaty were spread over twelve months, from March 22, 1948 to March 15, 1949. The discussions went through three phases. The first was confined to representatives of the United States, Britain, and Canada. It lasted from March 22 to April 1, 1948 and was kept secret from the public and possibly from the United States Congress and the French government.[15] In the second and third phases France, Belgium, and the Netherlands also took part. Luxembourg was represented by Belgium in the second phase and participated directly in the third phase. The second phase lasted from July 6 to September 10 (the day Pearson entered the cabinet)[16]; the third phase from December 10 to March 15, 1949.[17] Norway joined the talks on March 4 and the treaty was made public on March 18. It was signed on April 4 by Denmark, Iceland, Italy, and Portugal as well as by the countries which had participated in the discussions: Belgium, Britain, Canada, France, Luxembourg, the Netherlands, Norway, and the United States. It came into force on August 24, 1949.

Canada pursued four main objectives. The first was that there should be a treaty and not just a declaration by the President of the United States, even a declaration accompanied by a congressional resolution and followed by massive arms aid to Western Europe. The second was that the guarantee article in the treaty should be strong, and the third that there should be a strong article on non-military cooperation. The fourth was that Italy should not be a member of the alliance and that the guarantee provisions of the treaty should not extend to Algeria; on these last two issues St. Laurent, when he became Prime Minister, took a stronger line than Pearson. In the first phase of the discussions Pearson expressed reservations on another issue, Portuguese membership. He opposed Portuguese membership, however, even less firmly than he opposed Italian membership. In a marginal note on a memorandum of mine at the end of October 1948 Pearson wrote: "Surely we cannot insist on the exclusion of Portugal against U.S. opposition."

A fifth Canadian objective was that the North Atlantic treaty should contain an undertaking by the parties to submit to the International Court of Justice all justiciable disputes which they might have with each other. We hoped for an unqualified acceptance of the jurisdiction of the Court over justiciable disputes between the parties; the Brussels treaty made possible the continuance of reservations to that jurisdiction.

We succeeded in our first objective in the negotiations; there was a treaty. We had only limited success in our second and third objectives; the guarantee clause and article 2 were not nearly as strong as we wanted them to be. We failed to realize our fourth and fifth objectives. On the first objective we were lined up alongside the British and part of the State Department. On the second we were aligned with the Brussels treaty powers (Britain, France, and the Benelux countries). On the third we were toward the end of the negotiations isolated, though we continued to receive covert support from the two key officials in the State Department.

Bohlen and Kennan were two of the leading members of the State Department at the time of the discussions on the treaty. Kennan was head of the policy planning staff and Bohlen was Counsellor, which at that time meant that he was in charge of relations with Congress. In the hierarchy of the State Department, they both ranked above the two officers who were working on the treaty — J.D. Hickerson and T.C. Achilles. Hickerson told me on April 6, 1949, two days after the treaty was signed, that both Bohlen and Kennan had never been converted to the North Atlantic Treaty; they had opposed him on every point of importance in the negotiations, but without success.

According to Achilles, Bohlen's "opposition was due to his belief, pretty much a conviction, that the Senate would never consent to ratification of a military alliance."[18] Hume Wrong reported on May 8 that Bohlen believed that all that was required was for the United States to back Western Europe by some form of unilateral guarantee and by supplying arms. Bohlen, however, in his memoirs says:

> NATO was simply a necessity. The developing situation with the Soviet Union demanded the participation of the United States in the defense of Western Europe. Any other solution would have opened the area to Soviet domination . . . . Had the United States not inaugurated the Marshall Plan or something similar and had the United States not departed from its historical tradition and agreed to join NATO, the Communists might easily have assumed power in most of Western Europe.[19]

Kennan in his memoirs states that his reason in March 1948 for opposing the conclusion of the North Atlantic treaty was that he did not

> see any reason why . . . the development of new relationships of alliance between this country [the United States] and European countries was required to meet . . . the Communist behavior — the strikes in France and Italy, the Czech coup and the Berlin blockade.
>
> These were defensive reactions on the Soviet side to the initial success of the Marshall Plan initiative and to the preparations now being undertaken on the Western side to set up a separate German government in Western Germany.

The farthest he was prepared to go, and that with reluctance because he saw "no real necessity" for it, was that the United States, "in partnership with Canada, if Canada were willing," would give countries which joined the Brussels Treaty a unilateral political and military guarantee plus a "readiness" to extend to these countries "whatever was necessary in the way of assistance in military supplies, forces, and joint strategic planning."[20] The report which reached us in Ottawa at the time was that Bohlen and Kennan wanted the extension of the Monroe doctrine to Western Europe.

In the first tripartite phase of the discussions the pro-treaty group in the State Department won a victory over the anti-treaty group. But immediately the first phase was over the anti-treaty group started pressing their views. The result was that on April 12, only eleven days after the end of the first phase, Pearson was seriously concerned at

> the possibility that the United States Government might decide that no pact of any kind is necessary and that the situation can be met by a unilateral guarantee of assistance by the President . . . to a selected group of states [in Western Europe] . . . given after Congressional approval. . . .

Pearson asked me to prepare a memorandum setting forth our reasons for believing that a treaty was preferable to a unilateral guarantee. The memorandum was revised by Wrong and Pearson and became the brief for our discussions with the United States. Later we incorporated most of the memorandum along with additional arguments in letters of instruction to our ambassadors in Paris, Brussels, and The Hague. St. Laurent incorporated parts of the first draft of the memorandum in his speech in the House of Commons on April 29.

In May Wrong had Kennan to lunch to argue our case. Kennan came to Ottawa at the beginning of June where, after a dinner given by the United States ambassador, Pearson, Claxton, John W. Pickersgill, Special Assistant to the Prime Minister, and others launched at him the reasoning set forth in the memorandum. The main argument ran as follows. Because a treaty would have to be ratified by the Senate it would commit the United States much more firmly. It would embody the element of mutual assistance. Why should the United States and Canada come to the assistance of European countries if those countries were not willing to accept similar obligations to us? A unilateral guarantee gave unnecessary prominence to the dependence of the European states and seemed to underline the satellite character of their relationship to the United States. As such, it might unnecessarily offend their pride. Moreover, the United States and Canada needed the assistance of the Western European democracies just as they needed ours. A Russian conquest of Western Europe would mean for us war and war on most unfavourable terms. A unilateral guarantee smelled of charity (in the worst sense of the word); the Western European democracies were not beggars asking for our charity, but were potential allies whose assistance we needed in order to be able to defend ourselves. A pact would be an important demonstration that security arrangements could be worked out under the Charter, in this case under Article 51. Eventually other arrangements could be negotiated for other areas until all free countries might be brought in. Most important of all, a unilateral guarantee would be nothing more than a pledge of military assistance.

Pickersgill added two specifically Canadian arguments. In the last two world wars Canada had gone to war two years before the United States; a treaty commitment by the United States would be more likely than a presidential declaration to lessen the danger that this would happen again. Second, Canada and a number of other North Atlantic countries would find it politically easier to grant defence facilities to a North Atlantic alliance than to the United States.

In my telegram of June 3 to Hume Wrong, I reported that Kennan had said that he was impatient with the pressure from the United Kingdom and the Western European states to make a formal treaty commitment. Those states did not seem to realize that if the United States gave this guarantee it would be doing something which would be in the interests of Western Europe but not necessarily in the interests of the United States itself, since it could at any time make a deal with the Soviet Union.

> We naturally took him up on this and he withdrew from this exposed position. However it did give me a feeling that if you scratch almost any American long enough, you will find an isolationist. They suffer, and you can hardly blame them, from a homesickness for isolation.

When we debated with Kennan in Ottawa, we did not know that on May 24, a week before he came to Ottawa, Kennan had informed Marshall, the Secretary of State, that St. Laurent's speech of April 29 had added "a new and important element" to the problem and that, in the light of this speech and of arguments advanced by Ernest Bevin in a confidential message of May 14, "we must be very careful not to place ourselves in the position of being the obstacle to further progress toward the political union of the western democracies."[21]

By the time the second phase of the negotiations opened in Washington on July 6, the United States administration was pretty well convinced of the advantages of a treaty over a unilateral guarantee, though they were still not firmly committed. Now we became afraid that the trend of thinking in the State Department in the direction of a treaty would be reversed if France and Belgium continued to take a hesitant and negative attitude in the discussions in Washington.

The French, in the summer of 1948, or at least most of those who considered themselves to be members of the policy-making elite, were very naturally obsessed with the dangers to France and to themselves personally of a Soviet military occupation of France. They believed that France would probably never recover from such an occupation, and that they themselves would be liquidated. They feared that a treaty might be considered by the Soviet government as provocative and thus might increase the chances of a Soviet military response. France's prime concern was not a treaty but two concrete and immediate questions: first, obtaining military equipment from the United States, and second, the development of an allied strategy which would ensure active United States cooperation in stemming the tide of Soviet invasion, whether on the Rhine or farther east. These views were shared to some extent in Brussels and The Hague.

In the middle of August, therefore, we instructed our ambassadors in Paris, Brussels, and The Hague to outline our reasons for believing that French, Belgian, and Dutch national interests would be served by a treaty. Some of the arguments were the same as those we had put to George Kennan. Others were specially tailored to meet the objections and fears of the Western European countries.

We argued that the wide differences between the right-wing Republicans who controlled the House of Representatives and the Republican supporters of a bi-partisan foreign policy emphasized the importance of a multilateral agreement binding the United States for not less than ten years. Such an agreement would commit the whole Republican Party and considerably reduce the range within which the compass needle of United States policy could swing. (We shared the general assumption that Dewey would defeat Truman in the elections in Nov-ember.) We agreed that there was a danger that the United States might press the Soviet Union too hard and too fast, and not leave the Soviet Union a way out to save its face.

> To lessen this danger the Western European powers will have to exert a steady and constructive influence on Washington. The establishment of a North Atlantic union will give them additional channels through which to exercise this moderating influence. . . . [It will establish] at least in outline, a semi-constitutional structure of the North Atlantic powers.

We then cited Arnold Toynbee:

> In an even semi-parliamentary international forum, the political experience, maturity, and moderation of countries like [Great Britain, the continental Western European countries and the Dominions] will weigh heavily in the balance alongside the grosser weight of Brennus sword. In a pure power-politics world, on the other hand, these highly civilized but materially less powerful states will count for nothing compared with the United States and the Soviet Union.[22]

Hume Wrong showed the State Department our letters to Paris, Brussels, and The Hague, and the State Department, with our permission, sent them to the United States ambassadors to help guide their talks with the governments concerned. Gladwyn Jebb argued the case for the treaty with the French.

The result of all this was that the French, Belgian, and Dutch ambassadors in Washington received instructions to give full support to the idea of a treaty. The interventions of Britain, the United States, and Canada, and second thoughts in Paris, Brussels, and The Hague, removed a stumbling block to the conclusion of the treaty. (In order to go some distance to meet the fears of Europe about invasion and occupation by the Soviet Union, Truman, within a few hours of signing the ratification of the North Atlantic treaty on July 25, 1949, sent to Congress a request for military aid which resulted in the transfer of $1,130 mil-lion of military equipment and assistance to France, the Benelux countries, Denmark, Norway, and Italy.)

Canada's second objective in the discussions on the North Atlantic treaty was that the guarantee article in the treaty should be strong. In order to reduce the possibility of opposition in the Senate, the United States wanted a guarantee article as close as possible to that in the Rio treaty which the Senate had already approved.[23] The United States therefore suggested the following text:

> An armed attack by any state against a Party shall be considered as an attack against all the Parties and, consequently, each Party undertakes to assist in meeting the attack in the exercise of the inherent right of individual or collective self-defence recognized by Article 51 of the Charter.

The European representatives wanted a text as close as possible to that in the Brussels treaty and suggested.

> If any Party should be the object of an armed attack in the area covered by the Treaty, the other Parties will, in accordance with the provisions of Article 51 of the Charter, afford the Party so attacked all the military and other aid and assistance in their power.

I suggested to Pearson, in a memorandum which I gave him just before the first phase of the discussions began on March 22, 1948, that the guarantee article in the North Atlantic treaty should combine the best features of both the Rio and the Brussels treaties. It should read:

> The Atlantic Nations agree that an armed attack by any state against any Atlantic Nation is an attack against all the Atlantic Nations. In accordance with Article 51 of the Charter, each Atlantic Nation undertakes to give immediately to any other Atlantic Nation which is attacked by any state all the military, economic and other aid and assistance in its power.

When Pearson returned to Ottawa just before the first phase of discussions ended he reported that he had recommended this text and that it had been accepted. He spoke too hopefully. At the end of the first phase of discussions the United States, as a result of what was called "indirect Congressional soundings," retreated from this text to a formula even weaker than the Rio formula. They proposed that the Rio formula should be followed by a provision that each contracting party should determine for itself whether there had occurred an armed attack within the meaning of the agreement.

Pearson sent a message to Wrong strongly objecting to this provision. "It will," he said,

> be interpreted as reducing to almost nothing the obligatory character of the obligation. I realize that the determination of whether an armed attack has in fact taken place is the right of the individual signatories but surely that can be left implicit rather than made explicit.

Whether because of this message or for other reasons the United States withdrew the provision but still insisted on the Rio formula.

The deadlock remained even at the end of the second phase of discussions on September 10. The United States continued to press the Rio formula; the Brussels treaty powers still preferred the Brussels formula; and Canada wanted the compromise it had put forward in March. In a message in August to Wrong, Pearson had said:

> The advantage of the Brussels formula is that the parties promise to fight an all-out war if one of them is attacked. They obviously will have to fight an all-out war so why not say so. . . .

On December 24, 1948, four weeks before Acheson became Secretary of State, the ambassadors' group in Washington had tentatively agreed to a compromise which represented a substantial weakening of the Brussels treaty formula. After using the Rio treaty language of an attack on one being an attack on all, the parties to the treaty would undertake to

> assist the party or parties so attacked by taking forthwith such military or other action, individually or in concert with the other parties, as may be necessary to restore and assure the security of the North Atlantic area.

On February 14, while Acheson was in the process of trying to secure the agreement of the Senate Foreign Relations Committee to this formula, a storm burst on the floor of the Senate. Acheson describes the storm in his memoirs.[24] Senators feared that the treaty would automatically involve the United States in war, thus trenching on the power of the Congress to declare war. In the Senate debate, Tom Connally, the Democratic Chairman of the Foreign Relations Committee, said that the treaty should contain neither a moral nor a legal commitment to go to war in defence of an ally. This and other statements made by senators in this impromptu debate depressed and discouraged the State Department, the ambassadors' group in Washington, and their governments. Wrong said:

> If the type of reservation is written into the treaty which Senator Connally's remarks would imply, it will, of course, seriously reduce the effectiveness of the treaty as a deterrent to aggression and will also assist Soviet propaganda in belittling the value of the pledge.

He requested us in Ottawa to send him a restatement of our views on the guarantee article, leaving him, as he put it, "wide discretion in employing this statement." Pearson replied on February 17 in a long message, approved by St. Laurent.

This message was a forthright statement of why we believed that the language of the treaty should make clear that "the signatories are determined to resist by all necessary means any further encroachments by the Soviet Union" in the North Atlantic treaty area. The

> purposes of the treaty are not going to be fulfilled by an undertaking which is so watered down that it does not create even a moral obligation to take effective action, but is put forward as a charitable donation from the United States. This is reducing the proposed North Atlantic treaty almost to the level of a Kellogg-Briand peace pact.
>
> If there is no satisfactory pledge in the treaty, and if that treaty is interpreted by the Senate merely as a mechanism for getting the European states out of difficulties which really don't concern the United States directly, then its value is greatly reduced and we might have to re-examine our whole position. It might be that in the light of such re-examination we will be compelled to decide that the Canadian national interest involved in this kind of treaty interpreted in this way by United States opinion, is not sufficiently direct and immediate to warrant the government recommending to Parliament our adherence to it. We would do this, of course, with the greatest regret, but we might, in the circumstances, conclude that it is better to have no treaty at all than to have a treaty which is so weak and ambiguous as to be meaningless and therefore mischievous, especially since the conclusion of such a treaty might render less likely the conclusion of a really effective arrangement in the future.

In order to make it impossible for Senator Arthur Vandenberg, the Senior Republican member of the Senate Foreign Relations Committee, to oppose a firm pledge on constitutional grounds, we quoted the pledge in the draft treaties on the disarmament and demilitarization of Germany and Japan which the United States had publicly proposed in 1946, a pledge based on Vandenberg's speeches in the Senate on January 10, 1945 and in Detroit on February 5, 1945. We also quoted from those speeches. We said that those draft treaties had been public for almost three years and "so far as we know have not been attacked in responsible quarters in the United States as being unconstitutional." We quoted the pledge in these treaties:

> The high contracting parties will, by common agreement, take such prompt action — including action by air, sea or land forces — as may be necessary to assure the immediate cessation or prevention

of a violation of the treaty. If the United States insisted on a much weaker pledge in the North Atlantic treaty hostile critics might say that the United States "puts strong pledges [only] in treaties which it knows have no chance of coming into force."

Before Acheson met the Foreign Relations committee on February 18, Wrong brought to his attention, through Hickerson, that part of our telegram which referred to Vandenberg's position in 1945 and to the draft treaties on the demilitarization of Germany and Japan. How far Wrong used the other arguments in the telegram in speaking to Hickerson or Acheson I do not know; he reported on February 21 merely that "the change in the situation here made it unnecessary for me to use a number of your arguments."

The "change in the situation" was that Acheson had, on February 18, persuaded the Senate Foreign Relations Committee to accept the December 24 draft of the guarantee article with one change. The words "as it deems necessary, including the use of armed force" were substituted for the words "such military or other action . . . as may be necessary." The article as agreed to thus read:

> The Parties agree that an armed attack against one or more of them in Europe or North America shall be considered an attack against them all; and consequently they agree that, if such an armed attack occurs, each of them, in exercise of the right of individual or collective self-defense recognized by Article 51 of the Charter of the United Nations, will assist the Party or Parties so attacked by taking forthwith individually and in concert with the other Parties, such action as it deems necessary, including the use of armed force, to restore and maintain the security of the North Atlantic area.

The pledge of the Rio treaty was "to assist in meeting the attack"; the measures of assistance "on which the Organ of Consultation may agree" included "use of armed force"; however, "no state shall be required to use armed force without its consent" (Articles 3, 8 and 20). On balance the pledge in the North Atlantic treaty was somewhat stronger than the pledge in the Rio treaty. After eleven months of negotiation, Canada, the British, and the Western Europeans had won a partial victory. How far Canada contributed to that victory and, in particular, how far Ottawa helped Acheson to resist more erosion of the pledge than that which took place, is impossible to say.

On November 6, 1948, I drew up a memorandum in which I summarized as follows the arguments for effective non-military provisions in the North Atlantic treaty which St. Laurent and Pearson had put forward in public speeches, in private memoranda to Cabinet, and in instructions to Wrong:

> The Canadian Government believes that one of the chief obstacles today to the creation by the Free Nations of an overwhelming preponderance of military, economic and moral force over the Soviet states is the despair, the apathy and the doubt which is so widespread in the western world. The existence of this despair, apathy and doubt makes it essential that the North Atlantic democracies make a bold and imaginative move sufficient to raise in the hearts and minds and spirits of all those in the world who love freedom that confidence and faith which will restore their vigour. In our opinion this means that the North Atlantic Pact must be more than a mere military alliance or a negative anti-Soviet pact; it must be the outward and visible sign of a new inward and spiritual unity in the Western world. . . . [The treaty] should provide a basis not only for political, economic and military cooperation against Soviet threats but also for what might be called either a "spiritual mobilization" of the liberal democracies or "an ideological counter-offensive" to counter the demoralizing and insidious propaganda weapons of Soviet diplomacy. . . . [T]he members of the North Atlantic Alliance should be bound together not merely by their common opposition to totalitarian communism but also by a common belief in the values and virtues of Western civilization, by a common concept of democracy and a positive belief in it and by a determination to make their kind of democracy work for the promotion of mutual welfare and the preservation of peace, for others as well as for themselves.[25]

We also believed that if the members of the North Atlantic alliance were constantly quarrelling over such matters as tariff and non-tariff barriers to trade, competitive currency devaluations, aviation rights, and access to raw materials, they would be less likely to be willing and able to cooperate in political and security matters to the extent necessary to make the military guarantees credible. We therefore considered that pledges of military cooperation should be accompanied by pledges of economic cooperation.

Mackenzie King, at the very outset of the discussions on the treaty, and Norman Robertson, then High Commissioner in London, at the very end of the discussions, put forward the consideration that an undertaking in the North Atlantic treaty to reduce or remove restrictions to trade within the North Atlantic area would assist Canada in its trade negotiations. King was thinking of trade negotiations with the United States; Norman Robertson was thinking of trade negotiations with Britain.

Mackenzie King states in his diary that on March 22, 1948, the day the first phase of the discussions opened in Washington, he informed the half dozen Cabinet ministers and officials involved in the top secret discussions in Washington on a reciprocal free trade arrangement with the United States that he

> felt trade proposals might be made to fit as it were into the larger Atlantic Pact. That if, for example, the Atlantic Security Pact were agreed upon and were brought before Parliament and . . . passed as it certainly would be, we might immediately follow thereafter with a trade agreement as being

something which still further helped to further the object of the Pact, namely the removal of restrictions to trade within the area arranged by the Pact.[26]

King thus assumed that the North Atlantic treaty would contain an undertaking by the parties to remove restrictions to trade between them.

In the middle of February 1949, Norman Robertson reported that, in an effort to secure British support for an economic clause in the treaty, he had argued that an economic clause might acquire substantive importance as a basis for positive economic and financial cooperation between the United Kingdom and Canada, which would balance and complement the obligations assumed by the United Kingdom towards the European countries, participating in the OEEC [Organization for European Economic Cooperation]. "The United States," he said,

> must share, in degree, our long-run worries of the effect on trans-Atlantic trade of methods now being employed to bring the [Western] European economy into balance with the rest of the world. Inclusion of the clause we are advocating could provide a useful leverage for modifying policies required for European recovery so that their end result will permit resumption of multi-lateral clearings and achievement of non-discrimination. . . . It seems to me that the interest and position of the United States in relation to Western Europe generally are substantially similar to our more concentrated interests in the solution of this problem as it affects the United Kingdom particularly.

Because of this, Robertson attached particular importance to the inclusion in article 2 of the sentence in our draft:

> The parties concerned agree to make every effort in common to eliminate conflict in their economic policies and to develop to the full the great possibilities of trade between them.

(He suggested the addition of "international" before "economic.")

Robertson's argument was weighty. It was directed to London and to Washington — perhaps to Hume Wrong who was not keen on article 2. It was not, however, a determinant of Canadian policy. Canada had decided to support an article 2 eleven months before Robertson brought forward his argument.

Our belief that a North Atlantic treaty which contained a strong article 2 would start a movement towards the political and economic unification of the North Atlantic community is the one which has properly received the most attention in discussions of the Canadian approach to the treaty. What has received insufficient emphasis was our belief that the farther the North Atlantic Community moved towards political and economic unification the more protection it would give Canada from the power of the United States. We believed that the more developed the constitutional structure of the Community became the more the power of the United States would be restrained by the influence of its allies, especially Britain and France. The alliance would provide for Canada a countervailing force against the United States; the alliance would call in Britain and Western Europe to restore the balance in North America. As Pearson put it in his memoirs: "[I]n one form or another, for Canada, there was always security in numbers. We did not want to be alone with our close friend and neighbour."[27]

There was another motive for Canadian insistence on article 2, which was not mentioned in public speeches by St. Laurent and Pearson, but which was pressed hard in the private discussions in February 1949 between Wrong and Acheson, and between St. Laurent and Truman. This motive was that the treaty would secure much more public support in Canada if it were more than a military alliance. From my knowledge of St. Laurent and Pearson I think it is highly likely that this consideration did not even occur to them during the first six months or so of the discussions on the treaty. During those six months they constantly emphasized, in all their public speeches, the importance of these non-military aspects because they believed in them for reasons not connected with the political necessity of getting public support in Canada for the treaty. They gradually came to realize that their emphasis on the non-military aspects was one of the reasons for the widespread support for the treaty in Canada. This enabled St. Laurent, in his talks with Truman in February 1949, when all other arguments had failed, to bring forward an argument which was appropriate for one practical politician to put to another, the argument that the realities of domestic party politics in Canada made it essential for him to have substantial non-military provisions in the treaty.

In the memorandum which I gave Pearson just before the first phase of the discussions began on March 22, 1948, I included a draft, not just of an article on economic and cultural cooperation, but of a whole chapter. It read as follows:

> (1) The Atlantic Nations agree so to organize their economic activities as to produce the greatest possible returns by the elimination of conflict in their economic policies, the co-ordination of production and the development of commercial exchanges.

> (2) The Atlantic Nations undertake to make every effort in common, both by direct consultation and in the United Nations and the specialized agencies, to promote the attainment of a higher standard of living by their people and greater economic and social justice, and to develop on corresponding lines the social and other related services of their countries.

> (3) The Atlantic Nations undertake to make every effort in common to lead their people towards a better understanding of the principles which form the basis of their common civilization and to promote cultural exchanges between themselves.

> (4) In order to attain as rapidly as possible the objectives set forth in this Chapter, and thus to create in the Atlantic Community the economic and moral basis on which to build an overwhelming superiority of force on the side of peace, the Atlantic Nations undertake to use their best efforts to secure those amendments to the international instruments setting up the specialized agencies as are necessary to ensure that the agencies become the most effective possible instruments for the speedy attainment of the objectives set forth in this Chapter.

The first three articles were taken almost verbatim from the first three articles of the Brussels treaty.

At the end of the first phase of the discussions, Pearson reported that there was general agreement that the treaty might include a provision to the effect that the signatories would make every effort, individually and collectively, to promote the economic well-being of their peoples, and to achieve social justice, thereby creating an overwhelming superiority of moral, material and military force on the side of peace and progress.[28]

The draft treaty prepared by the State Department at that time contained an article in almost exactly this language.

The draft agreed to on December 24 was a compromise between the Brussels treaty powers, which did not want an article on economic, social, and cultural cooperation, and the United States and Canada which wanted a strong article. The compromise was:

> Article 2 (General Welfare). The parties will encourage co-operative efforts between any or all of them to promote the general welfare through collaboration in the cultural, economic and social fields. Such efforts shall, to the greatest possible extent, be undertaken through and assist the work of existing international organizations.

The United States delegation inserted the words "promote the general welfare," a phrase from the United States constitution.

Pearson instructed Wrong at the beginning of January 1949 to continue his efforts to strengthen the December draft, possibly by including between the two sentences of the draft some such words as, "The parties agree to make every effort in common to eliminate conflict in their economic policies and to develop the great possibilities of trade between them." Wrong, however, reported on January 5, that "we shall not be able to secure agreement on strengthening its [Articles 2's] language."

Acheson took office as Secretary of State on January 20, 1949. He was not able to look at the papers on the North Atlantic treaty discussions until January 29. Early in February he informed the negotiating group in Washington that the United States was opposed to any article 2. In reporting this Wrong said that he had learned that Acheson did not like article 2 because it meant "next to nothing," and that Senators Vandenberg and Connally, whom Acheson had consulted, might wish to have it deleted.

On February 7 Wrong reported that,

> We are now the only party to the negotiation that really favours the inclusion of anything in the treaty about social and economic collaboration outside the general reference in the preamble.

Faced with the possibility of complete defeat we took three steps to strengthen our position. On February 8, at a meeting of the ambassadors' group in Washington, Wrong, on Pearson's instructions, formally proposed the addition of not one but two sentences to the December draft. The first additional sentence was along the lines of that which Pearson had sent to Wrong at the beginning of January; the second was:

> The parties also undertake to make every effort in common to promote the attainment of a higher standard of living by their people and greater economic and social justice, and to bring about a better understanding of the principles which form the basis of their common civilization.

If he failed to get agreement on the addition of these two sentences Wrong was authorized to retreat to the following compromise text of the whole article which he had himself drafted:

> The parties agree to make every effort to bring about a better understanding of the principles which form the basis of their common civilization, and to develop to the full possibilities of trade between them. To this end they will encourage collaboration between all or any of them in the cultural, economic and social fields. Wherever it may be appropriate, action to give effect to this article shall be undertaken through and shall assist the work of existing international organizations.

Second, St. Laurent on his visit to Washington on February 12, put to Truman the practical domestic political Canadian arguments for article 2. He said that,

> it was most important to him that the treaty should not be a military alliance only, but should hold out the prospect of close economic and social collaboration between the parties. An article to this effect would be of the greatest value to him politically in securing the full acceptance of the treaty by the Canadian people.

Third, Norman Robertson in London, and the Canadian ambassadors in Paris, Brussels, and The Hague, were instructed to try to persuade the government to which they were accredited to support our position on article 2. We were informed of British, Dutch, French, and Belgian support on February 11, 18, 19, and 24 respectively. The Belgians appear to have put off telling us their views until the Consultative Council of the Brussels treaty powers had, at its meeting on February 23, unanimously agreed to support the Canadian draft of article 2. (By this they meant our maximum demands not our compromise or fall-back position.)

Wrong discussed article 2 with Acheson, Bohlen, and Hickerson on February 19. (By this time he knew that we had British and Dutch support.) Believing, however, that the stronger version "would only increase his [Acheson's] difficulties with the senators," Wrong gave them the compromise text. On February 22, Wrong had talks with Hickerson and Achilles, and a draft was agreed to for submission to Acheson. In his telegram to Pearson, Wrong reported that he had "told Hickerson that unless we could get an article on these lines in the treaty, the Canadian Government would have to review its position towards the whole project." He

> also pointed out that if no article appears in the treaty, and if we accept it without such an article, we shall have to make it clear publicly that the omission of any pledge on these lines has been caused by the resistance of the United States alone, since we have received assurances of support for our position from nearly all the other governments concerned.

Wrong gave these warnings after a telephone conversation with Pearson. One must assume that Pearson not only gave firm instructions to Wrong to say this but that the language was Pearson's, and that on a matter of this importance Pearson would have secured St. Laurent's concurrence.

At this point Hickerson must have decided that he needed support in his efforts to persuade Acheson to accept the revised draft. According to his story,

the day he [Acheson] finally agreed [February 24] he was in bed with the flu
and Bob Lovett [former Under-Secretary of State] and I went out to his
house in Georgetown and he on one side and I on the other side [of the bed]
beat the poor sick man over the head,[29]

until he accepted the draft with minor modifications.

After Acheson had given his approval, Ernest Gross, Under-Secretary of State
in charge of Congressional Relations, informed the Senate Foreign Relations
Committee. The next day Acheson reported at a meeting of the ambassadors
that he was "much surprised at Mr. Gross' success with the senators when he
put the case [for article 2] to them yesterday."

One cannot avoid suspecting that Gross might have been successful in persuading
the senators to accept an even stronger article 2, and that Acheson, who, as
Hickerson says, "didn't like it [article 2] worth a damn,"[30] exaggerated the
opposition of the senators. Certainly in the debate in the Senate on the North
Atlantic treaty, Vandenberg said of article 2, "Unless this treaty becomes far
more than a mere military alliance, it will be at the mercy of the first plausible
Soviet peace offensive."[31]

Two weeks before Acheson took office Wrong had reported that "we shall
not be able to secure agreement on strengthening" the December compromise
draft. Five weeks after Acheson took office he agreed to the following text (the
text in the treaty):

> The Parties will contribute toward the further development of peaceful and
> friendly international relations by strengthening their free institutions, by
> bringing about a better understanding of the principles upon which these
> institutions are founded, and by promoting conditions of stability and
> well-being. They will seek to eliminate conflict in their international
> economic policies and will encourage economic collaboration between any
> or all of them.

Acheson has claimed that he "defused" the Canadian draft of article 2.[32] A
comparison of the two texts demonstrates that he was mistaken. Acheson did
not defuse the Canadian draft of article 2; by the vigour of his opposition he
helped to infuse new life into it.[33]

It is clear that without Canada there would have been no article 2 in the North
Atlantic treaty. But Canada's efforts might well have failed if, within the State
Department, the two principal United States negotiators, Hickerson and Achilles,
had not strongly favoured it "as the basis upon which a true Atlantic Community,
going far beyond the military field, could be built."[34] They would have liked a
stronger article 2 than that which finally emerged from the discussions.

When I look back after a quarter of a century on the discussions which led to
the North Atlantic treaty, I am perplexed by many questions.

The first is, was an opportunity lost in April 1948 to rush the treaty through
quickly while the sense of urgency was so great? Pearson, in his memoirs, out-
lines the agreement which was reached by the end of March. It contains, as he
says, "the basic features of what was to become the North Atlantic treaty."[35]
The United States negotiators had the complete text of a treaty drawn up at that
time. This first draft of the treaty was made by Achilles; according to him, "The

eventual North Atlantic treaty had the general form, and a good bit of the language, of my first draft but with a number of important differences."[36] The United States could have put this initial draft of April 1, 1948 before a conference of the Brussels powers, Canada, and themselves in April. Indeed on March 15, 1948, Pearson informed Mackenzie King that, in order to check the communists in Italy, he considered that it might be essential to have the treaty concluded and published a week or more before April 18, the date of the Italian elections. He had been ambassador in Washington only a year and a half before, and, nevertheless, he believed that the Administration would be able to get a North Atlantic treaty ratified by the Senate even though consultation between the Administration and the Senate during the negotiations had been severely limited because of the need for haste.

Another question concerns the two articles to which we attached the most importance; the guarantee clause (article 5) and the main non-military clause (article 2). Would it have been possible for the Brussels treaty powers and Canada to have persuaded the United States to accept a stronger guarantee clause? Would it have been possible for Canada, once it had succeeded in getting the support of the Brussels treaty powers, to have persuaded the United States to accept a stronger article 2? (Whether success in these efforts would have made any difference to the course of subsequent events is another matter.)

I put one aspect of this question to Pearson in a memorandum to him of August 30, 1972, commenting on the first draft of the two chapters on the North Atlantic treaty, which became chapters three and four of the second volume of his memoirs. I said:

> Could you somewhere discuss a thesis of mine that ambassadors in a capital, and especially ambassadors in the capital of an important power, should never be used in multilateral negotiations on an issue which is important to the country to which they are accredited, and where the views of the government to which they are accredited are likely to be at variance on important points with the views of their own government. Ambassadors to the U.S., for example, are peculiarly subject to pressure by the U.S.; they have other fish to fry than the multilateral negotiations; they don't want to damage their good relations with the President or the State Department by being tough in the multilateral negotiations. Did we not possibly make a mistake in agreeing that the Washington draft of October 1948 [I should have said September] should be referred to a conference of ambassadors in Washington? A conference of special representatives in, perhaps, London would have been less subject to U.S. pressures and might have produced a better treaty.

(Pearson revised the draft chapter in the light of this comment.)[37]

When I said this to Pearson I was thinking of the way in which the United States delegation under Adolf Berle had bullied some ambassadors to Washington who represented their countries at the international civil aviation conference in Chicago in 1944, and of the subservience to the United States of some ambassadors to Washington (not Pearson) at the San Francisco Conference in 1945. I was also thinking of Wrong's decision not to press our maximum demands on article 2 at his meeting with Acheson on February 19 on the ground that this would increase Acheson's difficulties with the senators. Wrong's task was to get the strongest possible language for article 2. Whether this increased Acheson's difficulties with the senators was relevant only if the additional burden on Acheson would deter him from attempting the task. Wrong had great respect for Acheson. They thought very much alike; they were friends and Acheson's friendship was of central importance to Wrong in carrying out his ambassadorial duties. It was entirely natural that Wrong would not want to increase Acheson's difficulties with the senators.

I am not criticizing Wrong.[38] By making Acheson's task easier on this occasion he may have made his own task easier over many issues in the next three years, when he had to defend and advance Canadian national interests in arguments with Acheson. What I am criticizing is the use of ambassadors in Washington as representatives in multilateral negotiations on an issue important to the United States, where the views of the United States and of Canada are likely to be at variance on important points.

Almost immediately after his election to Parliament, Pearson went as head of the Canadian delegation to the U.N. General Assembly which met in Paris that year. His attendance there, following on his absence from Ottawa to fight the by-election, meant that from October 7 to December 17 he was in Ottawa for only three days (October 27 to 29). This was the period when we were planning for the third and final phase of the discussions on the treaty, discussions which, after repeated delays, finally began on December 10. I had to prepare a detailed memorandum to Cabinet on the treaty which would be acceptable to Claxton, the acting Secretary of State for External Affairs, and to Pearson, and which would, if possible, be agreeable to Wrong and Norman Robertson. In addition to the formal memorandum there were such supplementary papers as a commentary on the Canadian position and a draft of the treaty. If Pearson had been in Ottawa, the memoranda would have been improved. They would also have been ready in time for us to send a statement of our views to the other governments well before the talks resumed, thus increasing the chances of Canada influencing their attitudes.

Pearson, like everyone else, liked doing what he did best. He enjoyed taking part in U.N. General Assemblies; he was very good at it. He liked to get away from his desk in Ottawa.

The treaty might have been a slightly better treaty if I had not had to work so hard during the six months I was acting Under-Secretary, following Pearson's appointment to the Cabinet on September 10, 1948. The pressure on me at the beginning of my tenure was particularly acute since, when Pearson became Minister, he kept the office and the staff he had had as Under-Secretary. It was uphill work getting a new office going, especially since during that period the mass of difficult problems facing the department was exceptionally great, and the experienced staff was small. All this exacerbated my weaknesses as a diplomat: I was a perfectionist and displayed *trop de zèle*. If I had not set my sights for the treaty so high, and if I had not displayed so much zeal in advocating my views, I might have been able to convert Hume Wrong to a less restrictive view of the treaty. By perfectionism and zeal, I probably made him more obdurate in his belief that the non-military aspects of the proposed alliance were non-essential.[39]

The non-military provisions in the final treaty were substantial. They were contained not only in article 2 but also in article 4. These articles set forth three distinct but related undertakings, dealing with democracy, economic collaboration, and consultation.

Each of the allies undertook in article 2 to

> contribute toward the further development of peaceful and friendly international relations by strengthening their free institutions [and] by bringing about a better understanding of the principles upon which those institutions are founded.

These principles were defined in the preamble as "democracy, individual liberty and the rule of law."

The second non-military undertaking, also set forth in article 2, was to "contribute to the further development of peaceful and friendly international relations . . . by promoting conditions of stability and well-being," to "seek to eliminate conflicts in their international economic policies," and to "encourage economic collaboration between any or all of them." The preamble made clear that the reference to conditions of stability and well-being was to conditions "in the North Atlantic area."

The third non-military undertaking was set forth in article 4. Each of the allies undertook to "consult together whenever, in the opinion of any of them, the territorial integrity, political independence or security of any of the Parties is threatened." This required all the allies, at the request of any one of them, to consult together on any threat which an ally perceived in any part of the world to its territorial integrity, political independence, or security. The threat might arise from indirect aggression by the Soviet Union or any other country anywhere in the world, or unwise action by the United States or any other member anywhere in the world. Article 4 of the North Atlantic treaty has nothing to do with routine consultation on questions of interest to the alliance. It has to do with consultation on threats real or apprehended to the territorial integrity, political independence, or security of one or more of the allies. If this kind of consultation is to be effective, it must take place in a small room with not more than about twenty people present, and with no records made of the discussions. To implement the obligation which the allies assumed under article 4 of the treaty it would be necessary for the alliance, when article 4 was invoked, to hold a meeting at which there would be present only one representative from each country (presumably the Head of Government or the Foreign Minister), the Secretary-General of the alliance, one or two interpreters, and no stenographers or tape recorders.

The North Atlantic treaty did not establish two sets of obligations; one a military set to be taken seriously and the other a non-military set to be taken lightly. One set of obligations is as binding as the other.

The inclusion of Portugal in the alliance made a mockery of the reference in the preamble to the freedom of the peoples of the alliance, founded on the principles of democracy, individual liberty, and the rule of law. It did not, however, render inoperative Portugal's undertaking to become more democratic. The Development Assistance Committee of O.E.C.D. requires its member nations to report every year on the nature and extent of their development assistance, and each national report is subjected to scrutiny by the other members. The annual report of the D.A.C. discusses what each member country is doing. The members of the North Atlantic alliance could have set up the same sort of system of annual report, investigation, and publicity on what each member state was doing to carry out its treaty obligation to strengthen its free institutions. Other members might have made clear to a recalcitrant Portugal that its failure to carry out this treaty obligation might result in their concluding that Portugal's breach of treaty obligations released them from their obligation to assist it if it were attacked.

The coming into force of the North Atlantic treaty did not result in any substantial increase in the defence expenditures of the allies. In the United States, in the spring of 1950, the highest figure suggested for the defence budget was $14 billion.[40] In the year ending March, 1950, Canada's expenditures on defence were $385 million. The creation of the North Atlantic treaty did not result in Canada sending armed forces to Western Europe, nor did it result in the creation of a military structure for the alliance. Rather, the Korean wars precipitated these developments. This was because the North Atlantic countries believed that North Korea would not have attacked South Korea without at least the blessing of the Soviet Union, and that Stalin must have realized how shocked the West would be by this first attempt to change by force of arms the *de facto* boundaries between them. The North Atlantic countries, therefore, concluded that the attack on South Korea demonstrated a dangerous willingness on the part of the Soviet Union to risk a general war. The willingness of the Soviet Union to run such risks would, it was thought, be diminished if the Western powers were to rearm; rearmament would be a deterrent. The Korean war, therefore, led to vast rearmament in the North Atlantic countries. Their total defence expenditures increased from $20 billion in 1950 to $64 billion in 1953.[41] Canada's outlays increased from $30 million a month in June 1950 to $150 million a month in June 1952.

The Korean war also led to United States insistence on the admission of Greece and Turkey to the alliance, on the rearmament of Western Germany and its inclusion in the alliance, on the creation of a military structure for the alliance and the appointment of a supreme commander; in fact on the metamorphosis of the North Atlantic alliance into the North Atlantic Treaty Organization. The Korean war led to what Bohlen in his memoirs calls "the militarization of NATO,"[42] to what Pearson in July 1951 called "the growing NATO concentration on the military aspects of the alliance."[43] Without these developments, there might have been a world war in the 1950s. With these developments, the chances of the North Atlantic alliance providing a starting point for the economic and political unification of the North Atlantic community became remote.

Pearson's realization of this resulted in his casting about in July 1951 for a substitute for the North Atlantic alliance as a starting point for such unification. His memoirs[44] describe how, on a visit to Western Europe in July 1951, he thought aloud about this, and threw out some ideas very tentatively when talking to the British, Dutch, and Norwegian governments, and to the United States representative on the North Atlantic Council. Two treaties would be substituted for the North Atlantic treaty. The first would be purely military and would be open to any member of the U.N. which was prepared to accept the obligations of military collective action. This would mean a return to the idea of an optional protocol to the U.N. Charter, the suggestion which Pearson put in St. Laurent's speech to the U.N. General Assembly on September 18, 1947.[45] The second treaty would promote political, economic, social, and cultural cooperation, and would be restricted to countries which were, in fact, members of the North Atlantic Community. Switzerland and Sweden would be included but not the Mediterranean countries; possibly, though he did not say so, Portugal would be excluded. This second treaty would replace existing agreements for Western European cooperation on non-military matters such as the Organization for European Economic Cooperation (OEEC) and the Council of Europe. The response of Dirk Stikker, Foreign Minister of the Netherlands, and Halvard Lange, Foreign Minister of Norway, was encouraging, but nothing more was heard of the idea.

This incident suggests that from the summer of 1951 on, a mere two years after the North Atlantic treaty had come into force, Pearson had virtually given up hope that the alliance could provide a starting point for the political and economic unification of the North Atlantic community. He still, however, believed that it could provide Canada with opportunities to influence the foreign policies of the United States.[46]

Notes

1. United States documents on the negotiations in 1948 were published in February 1975 and presumably the 1949 documents will be published in 1976. The British documents, under the thirty-year rule, will not be published before 1978 and 1979. The Canadian documents may be published in 1978. The documents of France, Belgium, the Netherlands, and Norway, to say nothing of the Soviet Union, present further problems. Gladwyn Jebb, the principal British architect of the treaty, was not allowed to consult the Foreign Office files on the negotiation of the North Atlantic treaty when he wrote his memoirs. His American counterpart, J.D. Hickerson, has not written memoirs, while T.C. Achilles has written only a draft for private circulation. Both Hume Wrong and his assistant in Washington, T.A. Stone, died without writing memoirs. Neither Oliver Franks, the British ambassador in Washington, nor F. Hoyer-Millar, his second-in-command, have published their accounts. Donald Maclean participated in the first phase of the discussions and the beginning of the second phase; he presumably kept the Soviet government fully informed. His reports must have reassured the Soviet leaders that the West did not wish to launch a pre-emptive strike against Russia. Dean Acheson was present only on the sixth day of the creation of the treaty. One must treat recent interviews with participants with caution because memory is errant when it is not refreshed by consulting the documents of the period. Even though the Department of External Affairs gave me permission to refresh my memory, I am conscious of several problems; the files are voluminous, quotation from Cabinet documents and from unpublished non-Canadian documents is prohibited, and I have no knowledge of most of the numerous oral exchanges between Hume Wrong and Pearson.

2. Dean Acheson, *Present at the Creation* (New York, 1969), 153.

3. George F. Kennan, *Memoirs, 1925–1950* (Boston, 1967), 458.

4. Lord Gladwyn, *The Memoirs of Lord Gladwyn* (London, 1972), 225.

5. Bohlen, in his memoirs, says, "In 1947, every Communist party in the world not only was patterned after that of the Soviet Union but was also the subservient instrument of Moscow policy." (Charles E. Bohlen, *Witness to History* [New York, 1973], 261.) Starobin, in his book on the communist party of the United States published in 1972, states that Duclos, in his famous article in *Cahiers du Communisme*, April 1945, was a spokesman for the Soviet Communist Party, and that in his article, "He was suggesting, if taken literally, that the whole of Europe was bound to be the arena of Soviet as well as native Communist ambitions." (Joseph R. Starobin, *American Communism in Crisis, 1943-1957* [Cambridge, Mass., 1972], 81.)

6. Bohlen, *Witness to History*, 267.

7. Gladwyn, *Memoirs*, 214.

8. Lester B. Pearson, *Mike: The Memoirs of the Rt. Hon. Lester B. Pearson*, II (Toronto, 1973), 42.

9. J.W. Pickersgill and D.F. Forster, *The Mackenzie King Record*, Volume IV, *1947-1948* (Toronto, 1970), 166.

10. Gladwyn, *Memoirs*, 211-13. He says the assessment was made early in February 1947, but it is clear that he meant early in February 1948.

11. Pickersgill and Forster, *Mackenzie King Record*, 165.

12. *Ibid.*, 165-68.

13. On June 30, 1948, Mackenzie King, according to his diary, said in Cabinet: "I felt it was quite certain that if war broke out, between the three great powers and Russia, Canada would wish to come in instantly. The Cabinet agreed with that. They felt that there could be no two views on that score." (*Ibid.*, 192.)

14. "The signing of the North Atlantic treaty," Department of State Publication, 3497, June 1949, 33.

15. Secrecy enabled the United States government to pretend to Congress that the second phase grew out of the Vandenberg resolution, adopted by the Senate on 11 June, whereas in fact the State Department was securing by that resolution *ex post facto* legitimation of the results of the first phase of the discussions. Secrecy also enabled Britain, Canada, and the United States to pretend to France and the Benelux countries that they had participated in the negotiations from the outset. As part of this pretence, the "heads of agreement" of 1 April were drafted in the form of tentative proposals by the United States government. On balance, I feel that secrecy aided the negotiations. Publicity about disputes between the negotiators might have helped produce a better treaty; it probably, however, would have resulted in no treaty.

16. This phase resulted in an agreed statement dated September 9 "on the nature of the problems discussed and the steps which might be practicable to meet them"; and an annex outlining possible provisions for inclusion in a North Atlantic Security Pact.

17. The Presidential elections delayed the start of this phase. Until the treaty was almost in final form, the participating governments insisted that no formal negotiations were taking place.

18. Theodore C. Achilles, *Draft Memoirs* (unpublished), 427G.

19. Bohlen, *Memoirs*, 267-68.

20. Kennan, *Memoirs*, 401-3, and 406-7.

21. *Foreign Relations of the United States*, 1948, Vol. III, 128

22. Arnold Toynbee, *Civilization on Trial* (New York, 1948), 137.

23. From April 1948 the State Department was constantly sounding out Senatorial opinion, especially through Senators Vandenberg and Connally. Dean Acheson, in February and March 1949, conducted two sets of formal negotiations, one with governments and the other with the Senate Foreign Relations Committee. The State Department was justifiably concerned with Senate opinion, but, in my view, made more concessions than were necessary to ensure Senate ratification.

24. Acheson, *Present at the Creation*, 280-82.

25. Up to the eve of the third phase of the discussions, I pressed Pearson to include, as one objective, the establishment of a North Atlantic parliamentary assembly. Initially I favoured a body with quasi-legislative powers; by November 1948 I called for merely a deliberative body. Wrong opposed the idea and Pearson agreed with his assessment.

26. Pickersgill and Forster, *Mackenzie King Record*, 264.

27. Pearson, *Memoirs*, II, 32-33.

28. *Ibid.*, 46.

29. Interview with J.D. Hickerson, Oct. 27, 1969. (York University, Oral History Project.)

30. *Ibid.*

31. *Ibid.*

32. Acheson, *Present at the Creation*, 277.

33. By January 1951, Acheson had come to believe that the North Atlantic treaty "was more than a purely military treaty," that it was "a means and a vehicle for closer political, economic and security cooperation with Western Europe." He told Eisenhower this when he briefed him on his appointment as the first commander of North Atlantic forces in Europe. (Acheson, *ibid.*, 493.)

34. Achilles to Escott Reid, Aug. 9, 1972.

35. Pearson, *Memoirs*, II, 45–46.

36. Achilles, *Draft Memoirs*, 418G.

37. Pearson, *Memoirs*, II, 54.

38. Wrong had a profound knowledge and understanding of the situation in Washington, and enjoyed wide discretionary powers. We agreed on most aspects of Canadian foreign policy, but disagreed fundamentally on the North Atlantic treaty. There was tension of a different kind between Pearson and Wrong. Pearson considered Wrong to be his "superior in intellect" (Pearson, *Memoirs*, I, 192.). Wrong shared this opinion. I cannot accept James Eayrs' view (in the *Toronto Star*, Oct. 22, 23, and 24, 1969), that Wrong told the Americans or the international negotiating group in Washington everything he was instructed or authorized to tell them, and that he used the often blunt language of the telegrams from Ottawa. I am confident he did not. He would decide whether it would be wise to put forward the proposal at all and, if wise, whether it would not be prudent to tone down the blunt language. He might be sufficiently sure of himself to go ahead without clearing with Pearson or he might telephone Pearson. If Pearson insisted, he would, of course, do what he was told and do it forcefully and elegantly.

39. In his memoirs, Pearson says of Wrong, "nor was he ever personally convinced that the non-military aspects of the proposed alliance were essential" and he "was not much in sympathy with Reid's views on this subject or with the intensity of his expression thereof." (Pearson, *Memoirs*, II, 47 and 57.)

40. Bohlen, *Witness to History*, 287.

41. *NATO Facts and Figures* (Brussels, NATO Information Service, 1970), 224–25.

42. Bohlen, *Witness to History*, 304.

43. Pearson, *Memoirs*, II, 70.

44. *Ibid.*, 70–73.

45. *Ibid.*, 41.

46. When re-assessing Canadian foreign policy in 1951 in the light of the Korean war, he and I believed that the best hope of restraining the United States from pursuing impatient or provocative policies lay in strengthening the procedures for consultation in the North Atlantic alliance. We believed that the North Atlantic alliance provided a check and balance on the United States.

DIEFENBAKER AND CANADIAN EXTERNAL RELATIONS†

When the Progressive Conservatives came to power in Ottawa under John Diefenbaker on 10 June 1957, they inherited, in the Department of External Affairs, a foreign policy establishment with an impressive reputation.[1] It was an asset, however, to be viewed with some caution by a new government, for it had grown to maturity during twenty-two years of Liberal rule. During about half that period, moreover, it had been under the direction, first at the under-secretarial and then at the Cabinet level, of the outgoing minister, Lester Pearson, who, soon after the election, succeeded to the leadership of his party and hence of the parliamentary opposition. At worst, members of such a department might be suspected of giving clandestine help to Pearson and his political colleagues. Even if that possibility were dismissed as fanciful, there remained the more subtle danger that reliance on the department's capability and expertise might make the new government captive to priorities and policies established under Pearson rather than setting new ones of its own. These suspicions and anxieties are part of the background to the term "Pearsonalities" which Diefenbaker coined to describe members of the Department of External Affairs.[2]

There is a good deal of testimony that members of the Department of External Affairs upheld the principle of nonpartisanship and indeed took considerable care to avoid even innocent social relationships with Pearson, which, if misunderstood, might give rise to suspicion.[3] While not all ministers were satisfied with the adjustment made by the department, the cause seems to have been nothing worse than insensitivity on the part of some officials.[4] Nor did members of the department expect that prevailing assumptions would survive unchallenged. Rather, according to an assistant under-secretary of the time, it had to be assumed that all decisions of the outgoing government were subject to revision. And even if they had wanted to mount a campaign of indoctrination, the resources were lacking. The department was short-staffed in the senior ranks in Ottawa;[5] there were no arrangements for comprehensive background briefing of the new ministers; and the style in departmental memoranda, developed to meet the requirements of an experienced minister and adhered to after his departure,[6] was to present not single-minded policy recommendations but a variety of options in the expectation that the minister himself would take the decision.

Diefenbaker did not rely on these constraints to operate unaided. Much concerned to preserve the autonomy of the elected executive, he made sure that Cabinet, rather than ministerial or interdepartmental committees, remained very much the locus of discussion and decision-making. In Cabinet, associates were aware, he kept a particularly close watch on those who seemed insufficiently independent of their civil-service advisers. At the same time, he maintained resources of his own to guide his judgement, for he kept in touch with and added to a broad acquaintance of informal advisers across the country which he had

†John F. Hilliker, "The Politicians and the 'Pearsonalities': The Diefenbaker Government and the Conduct of Canadian External Relations," Canadian Historical Association, *Historical Papers 1984*: 152–67.

built up over his years in politics. External Affairs was affected by these practices in some ways more than most departments. Diefenbaker had preeminence in matters involving other heads of government and, for the first three months of his administration, had direct responsibility for the department as well, since he retained the portfolio himself. His conduct at that time was an indication of the division of labour he thought appropriate between the elected executive and officials in External Affairs. According to an assistant under-secretary who dealt with him then, Diefenbaker recognised that he could not expect to master the minutiae of the External Affairs portfolio and, especially on the technical side, would have to rely on the guidance of officials. His interest in substantive involvement was in major issues affecting the direction of the new government's policy.

There were good reasons for Diefenbaker to take this approach. While there was a considerable measure of agreement on foreign policy between the new government and its predecessor, for example on the usefulness of Canada's middle-power role in times of international tension, the recent election campaign had also revealed significant differences. In particular, such controversies as the previous government's conduct in the Suez crisis of 1956 and its handling of economic relations with the United States had enabled the Conservatives to exploit their traditional position as the party defending Canada's autonomy in North America while upholding the British and Commonwealth connection. As well, Diefenbaker, whose personality was the centrepiece of Conservative publicity, was identified with certain principles, such as concern for human rights, applicable to international as well as to domestic affairs. The campaign, however, did not produce a comprehensive programme for the conduct of external relations. Rather, it left latent contradictions in the party's declared objectives and failed to anticipate some of the significant changes in the international situation which took place while the Conservatives were in office. External relations, therefore, were likely to provide a challenging test of the decision-making process under Diefenbaker.

The new prime minister got off to a rather uncertain start as a result of two episodes which caused the government some embarrassment: his suggestion that steps would be taken to shift 15 percent of Canada's imports from United States to British sources, and his approval of joining the United States in an integrated North American air defence command (NORAD) without insisting on an intergovernmental agreement. In taking these actions without consulting cabinet or departmental officials beforehand,[7] Diefenbaker no doubt was the victim of inexperience, and the risks involved in ill-considered action were soon appreciated.[8] A potentially more serious problem was communication with External Affairs. Diefenbaker, those around him realised, had little patience with the shaded language of diplomacy, and he did not have either the time or the experience to deal with lengthy expositions of issues. What he needed was guidance, expressed succinctly, which alerted him to the implications of decisions he was being asked to take. But, despite advice on his requirements,[9] much of the paper reaching him remained more suited to a politician experienced in foreign affairs. The same was true of speech material. Diefenbaker, noted a contributor, wanted his speeches on foreign policy as on other matters to have relevance to the ordinary

Canadian voter, but what he got from External Affairs often seemed to be pitched to the more specialised and elitist audience favoured by Pearson and his prime minister, Louis St. Laurent.

These differences of style were another reason for Diefenbaker to regard members of the Department of External Affairs as "Pearsonalities." They affected not only the rank and file but also, an observer of their relationship has recalled, the under-secretary, Jules Léger, despite the high regard the prime minister had for him personally.[10] As a result of this problem in communications and his suspicion of the department as a creation of his political opponents, Diefenbaker at first tended to keep his distance from it in handling foreign affairs, excluding its representatives from his meetings with foreign leaders, omitting debriefing afterwards,[11] and neglecting to refer to it important communications which he received on international subjects. To overcome this problem, R.B. Bryce, Clerk of the Privy Council and Diefenbaker's most trusted civil-service adviser, arranged for the appointment of an experienced foreign service officer as special departmental assistant in the Prime Minister's Office. The first incumbent, Basil Robinson, who remained in place until 1962, became, on the basis of the confidence he earned from Diefenbaker and his associates, a highly effective means of communication between the prime minister and the department.[12] He also tried to educate the department about Diefenbaker's requirements, but some subjects had to be dealt with in complex and subtle terms. As a result, Diefenbaker some years later still remembered the departmental style for "decorative uncertainty."[13]

Another means of getting around the problem of communication between Diefenbaker and the Department of External Affairs of course was the appointment of a full-time minister. In September of 1957 Diefenbaker filled the position by going outside the Conservative caucus to choose Sidney Smith, president of the University of Toronto. Diefenbaker, however, kept in touch with the portfolio through copies of important telegrams and other communications from posts abroad, a daily summary of significant international developments,[14] and private communication which he encouraged with officials whose ideas he thought might be useful. Smith's performance probably caused the scrutiny to become more intense than it would otherwise have been. Although his reputation as a university administrator earned him a warm welcome from the press and the Conservative caucus,[15] it proved to be insufficient compensation for his inexperience in both electoral politics and foreign affairs. As a result, he was not a very effective spokesman for his area of responsibility, and Diefenbaker was concerned as well that he was overly reliant on his officials.[16] This concern no doubt increased after Norman Robertson, whom Smith favoured, succeeded Léger in the autumn of 1958, for the relationship between the prime minister and the new under-secretary was never better than strained.[17] It was not unusual, one writer has observed, for a secretary of state for external affairs to enjoy less latitude than Pearson had had under St. Laurent but, while Smith held the office, prime ministerial involvement was sufficiently evident to leave the impression that there were two centres of decision-making.[18] Equally important, Smith's weakness in cabinet meant that his department's expertise was not always brought forcefully to bear on decisions to which it was relevant.

It was while Sidney Smith was secretary of state for external affairs that Diefenbaker's government took most of its decisions on acquiring weapons systems with nuclear capability for the Canadian armed forces. With encouragement from Léger,[19] Diefenbaker at the same time gave high priority to "the search for disarmament with the Soviet Union,"[20] but without anticipating the potential for conflict between the two courses of policy which was to be a source of difficulty for his government later on. One reason may have been the inexperience and comparative weakness of the secretary of state for external affairs. According to the Cabinet conclusions, diplomatic objectives did not feature in discussions of equipment for the armed forces, which concentrated on strategic, economic and domestic political considerations.

The sudden death of Sidney Smith on 17 March 1959 brought more forceful ministerial leadership to External Affairs in the person of Howard Green, whom Diefenbaker, after resuming the portfolio himself in the interim, named to take over in June. Formerly minister of public works, Green brought to his new office long experience in the House of Commons, a solid position in Cabinet, and the confidence of the prime minister.[21] While some members of his new department were disconcerted by gaps in his knowledge of international affairs and by his lack of subtlety in negotiation,[22] his shrewdness and firmness were much admired by one of the most experienced diplomats in the service, Charles Ritchie at the United Nations.[23] At headquarters, he worked closely and confidently with the under-secretary[24] and other senior officers, but his habits were such that he did not give up his independence to them. He placed a good deal of confidence in his senior departmental assistant, Ross Campbell, who was by no means reluctant to raise considerations additional or contrary to those produced by the flow of advice from the department. Green also established direct contact with individual officers, down to the desk level, who were dealing with subjects that particularly interested him. He was careful to keep control himself of areas of policy he considered to be of special importance and, although he moderated his opinions and developed new interests to take account of his experience in office, he did not change his mind readily once he had made a commitment. Additionally, he tended to specialise, concentrating his energy on a limited range of issues which seemed to him of paramount importance.

The most important of these issues was nuclear disarmament. Closely related was Green's opposition to the acquisition of nuclear arms by Canadian forces and even more to their location within the country's borders, a condition which he feared would affect the credibility of his campaign for disarmament. These concerns were shared by Robertson, who had informed Diefenbaker of his views before Green took over External Affairs.[25] But Green, influenced by his memories of the First World War and reinforced by encouragement from his wife, a biochemist, and his friend C.J. Mackenzie, chairman of the Atomic Energy Control Board,[26] came to his own conclusions without prompting by Robertson. About a week after taking office at External Affairs, Green signalled his doubts about nuclear weapons[27] and it was only some time later, at the end of July of 1959, that Robertson set out his own position for the minister.[28] Green, moreover, remembered as the decisive influence on his thinking, not Robertson's submission, but the discussion, at the United Nations General Assembly in the autumn of 1959, of fallout from nuclear tests.[29] Robertson in fact did not at first always recommend as uncompromising a line on nuclear questions as Green favoured[30] or respond as promptly as the minister would have liked to requests for resources for work on disarmament. The minister, however, made sure that the got what he wanted, for these were subjects over which he maintained close personal scrutiny. An officer who felt the effects has recalled that pressure from the minister's office produced not only the creation of a Disarmament Division[31] but a noticeable diversion of energies to that subject from other parts of the department as well. In due course, Robertson, particularly as a result of shared concern over tendencies in United States policy, moved towards the minister's position, so that together they constituted, a worried observer noted, "a negative force of great importance" on the nuclear question.[32] But it was not an equal partnership, for throughout the pace was set by the minister rather than the undersecretary or other officials.

While Green had objectives of his own, he was also willing to serve as a vehicle for initiatives originating in his department. It was as a result of such an initiative and the minister's support that the Diefenbaker government decided to provide economic assistance to countries in francophone Africa. The suggestion originated with the deputy under-secretary, Marcel Cadieux, who was concerned about criticism in Quebec of the Commonwealth bias of Canadian aid programmes.[33] He therefore suggested a new scheme of educational development directed to the francophone states of Africa which became independent in 1960. Other interested agencies, including the one directly responsible for overseas assistance, the External Aid Office, had doubts about this proposal. The principal concern, according to a leading critic, was whether the federal government could mount a programme in French without further preparation. Cadieux's arguments, however, carried the day with Green, whose ministerial jurisdiction included the aid office as well as External Affairs. But Green did not accept them completely, for he feared that the proposed outlay, $600,000, would be considered too high by cabinet, and at his suggestion it was reduced by one-half.[34] This was a judgement founded on experience, for there were a number of objections recorded in the Cabinet Conclusions to this kind of expenditure, especially on nonfood aid to countries outside the Commonwealth. In this instance, cabinet, no doubt influenced by "informal representations" which some ministers had received in favour of such a scheme, gave its approval, but only with the observation that even the amount of $300,000 might be "disproportionately high when compared with the amounts allocated for other programmes."[35]

Notwithstanding the strength and the independence of bureaucratic control that Green displayed in handling such issues as disarmament and aid, the prime minister remained a potent force in the determination of foreign policy. By the time Green became minister, Diefenbaker was well equipped to assert his authority, for his normal experience of office had been reinforced by his world tour at the end of 1958. He also kept up his independent sources of information. The Prime Minister's Office received copies of all departmental memoranda to the minister, and later it requested copies of telegrams signed by Green and the under-secretary on certain sensitive subjects, including disarmament and nuclear tests.[36] Diefenbaker did not use these resources to become involved across the board in Green's area of activity, but he was active on a limited range of issues which interested him personally or were relevant to his role as prime minister.

Diefenbaker's personal interest and style, the product of his concern for democratic rights, his sensitivity to the views of Canadians of Eastern European origin and his fondness for direct and forceful language, had a marked effect on his government's approach to East-West relations. The Department of External Affairs favoured the soft line taken by the previous government and at first continued under Diefenbaker. This position, it was noted, was agreeable to Green because of his desire to promote an accommodating attitude towards disarmament in the Soviet Union. Diefenbaker, however, came to prefer a more vigorous approach, to which he gave expression in his address to the United Nations General Assembly in 1960. The effect of his involvement is clear from the evolution of the text, which started life in External Affairs in the expectation that it would be given by Green. While expressing concern about recent deterioration in the international situation, his version did not assign blame to either side, and about half the text dealt with disarmament and related matters.[37] Diefenbaker then supplanted Green because of the decision of Khrushchev and a number of other heads of government to attend. Even before he was aware of Khrushchev's text, Diefenbaker was contemplating an attack on the Soviet Union's policies towards the Ukraine, the Baltic states and the European satellites.[38] Notwithstanding Khrushchev's denunciation of Western colonial policies, the officers in External Affairs responsible for drafting the speech were unenthusiastic about this approach. While they responded to Khrushchev by putting the onus for international tension on the Soviet Union,[39] they thought the speech would have the most useful effect if Diefenbaker took on the role of peacemaker. When he was unwilling to give up the offensive, the speechwriters saw their task as marrying the prime minister's desire for pungent language with a text that would not itself become a cause of further deterioration in relations with the Soviet Union. This they did with reasonable success. A contributor remembered that Diefenbaker was pleased with the result, the speech was well received at home, and reports to the Department of External Affairs suggested a friendly response from Canada's allies.[40] Even so, by incorporating a stern critique of "Soviet colonialism" as a major theme, the speech marked a significant departure from past practice, and introduced an important new component into the Diefenbaker government's position on East-West relations.

Two actions followed from Diefenbaker's speech of 1960. One was his decision to acknowledge the consular status claimed by representatives of the Baltic states, strongly indicated during the election campaign of 1962. This went against the advice of External Affairs, which feared complications in dealing with the power in control of the territories, the Soviet Union, on matters of interest to Canadians.[41] Diefenbaker, who remembered the department for insensitivity to "the terrible persecutions behind the Iron Curtain," may well have regarded this advice as bureaucratic obstruction, part of a pattern going back to his expression of interest in the Baltic states early in his administration.[42] Certainly he suspected that such obstruction was a factor in the difficulties encountered in achieving his second objective, a resolution by the United Nations General Assembly in 1962 based on his earlier attack on Soviet policies.[43] In response to his criticism, the department made an intense effort to promote the resolution in friendly nations, but the response was negative and in due course cabinet decided that the initiative ought to be dropped.[44] Diefenbaker settled instead for a campaign of speechmaking, but he made certain that it was based upon the tone he had favoured in 1960. While the opening salvo by Green was fairly mild, the climactic speech, delivered by his parliamentary secretary, Heath Macquarrie, was not. The first version of Macquarrie's speech, when submitted to the prime minister for approval, was rejected as "pusillanimous;"[45] as redrafted, it was described by the mission in New York as "the harshest and most direct attack ever levelled against Soviet colonialism in the UN."[46]

Diefenbaker's personal interests came together with his responsibility for dealing with other heads of government in the matter of South Africa's continued membership of the Commonwealth after it became a republic. As a civil libertarian with a rather stark view of right and wrong, Diefenbaker was not entirely comfortable with advice from the Department of External Affairs that Canada seek to avoid confrontation with South Africa over apartheid in the hope that, if lines of communication were kept open, the moderate forces in the country might operate to some effect.[47] Diefenbaker's party, however, was also identified with support of the old Commonwealth, and he did not feel strong pressure to depart from the course favoured by External Affairs until the Sharpeville massacre of 21 March 1960.[48] Even then there was no clear alternative. Bryce hoped that, to ensure the survival of the Commonwealth as a multiracial organisation, Canada might take the lead in pressing for the exclusion of South Africa, but there was not sufficient support from the Canadian cabinet or other Commonwealth leaders for Diefenbaker to take this line at the meeting of heads of government in 1960.[49] Instead, circumstances encouraged him to follow the recommendation of External Affairs that he try to exploit Canda's potential as a conciliator between South Africa and her critics[50] and to exercise his favourite strategy of playing for time in the hope that the problem would be overtaken by events. With material assistance from Diefenbaker, the heads of government agreed to postpone their decisions on South Africa's continued membership until a referendum on republican status had been taken there.[51]

Diefenbaker's position was no easier when the Commonwealth heads of government met again in March of 1961, after the referendum held in South Africa had approved a republic. Most ministers in Ottawa wanted South Africa readmitted, while the position of a number of other heads of government was difficult to predict.[52] Diefenbaker was attracted by the possibility of postponing a decision yet again, on the ground — supplied by his high commissioner in London, George Drew — that no action was necessary until the constitutional change in South Africa, not due until after the Commonwealth meeting, had actually taken place.[53] By this time, however, Diefenbaker may well have developed a fall-back position: the creation of a situation which would force South Africa to solve the problem itself by withdrawing from the Commonwealth rather than accept onerous terms for continued membership. He had suspected, since his first heads of government meeting in 1957, that "South Africa did not want to remain long in the Commonwealth,"[54] and he had reason to believe that a declaration in support of racial equality, favoured by External Affairs as a means of placating South

Africa's critics,[55] might be a means of getting her out. External Affairs had alerted him to this possibility, and a recent speech by Prime Minister Verwoerd suggested that he might be preparing his people for withdrawal if he could not remain in the Commonwealth on the terms he wanted.[56]

Diefenbaker was not able to take the initiative in promoting this solution because cabinet was against Canadian sponsorship of a Commonwealth declaration of rights. Such action, ministers believed, "would probably provoke ridicule" at home since the Canadian Bill of Rights had not yet been tested.[57] But the idea remained useful when, the day before the discussion of South Africa was to begin, Diefenbaker learned that India, not hitherto expected to take the initiative, had decided on a hard line. A strong statement against apartheid, Diefenbaker suggested to the Indians, would likely cause South Africa to withdraw from the Commonwealth and so avert the necessity for direct action by the other members.[58] Diefenbaker did not mention this reasoning when he reported to cabinet on the early discussion of the issue in London, and his ministers did not give him further guidance.[59] So, although unable to take the lead in formulating a declaration of principles, he remained free to support the efforts of the nonwhite leaders. This produced the result he had anticipated when he learned of the Indian position. Unable to persuade Verwoerd to compromise and concluding that the South African application for continued membership would be rejected by all but Britain, Australia and New Zealand, the British prime minister, Harold Macmillan, secured its withdrawal.[60]

Among Diefenbaker's strengths in dealing with South Africa were his access to well-balanced information and his ultimate control of the decision-making process. These were not always easy to achieve, even on matters involving his relationship with other heads of government. The question of British membership in the European Economic Community was of material interest not only to Diefenbaker but also to the economic ministers and the Secretary of State for External Affairs. Equally important, it was one in which George Drew took a major and sustained interest. During Drew's time at Canada House, subjects in this category were very much the province of the high commissioner, who generated a large volume of private telephone calls, telegrams and letters to Diefenbaker and the ministers concerned. In preparing these communications and in carrying out his own activities in Britain, Drew acted on his own, without seeking the advice of his staff or the views of his departmental headquarters. As a former premier of Canada's wealthiest province and a former leader of his party still respected by its establishment, Drew could speak with authority on an economic subject such as the Common Market. He therefore could expect both considerable latitude in the way he handled his office and a receptive audience where it counted most, in cabinet. In short, he was a source of highly potent opinion and advice on the Common Market, which reached ministers uninfluenced by and uncoordinated with that going forward through the bureaucracy.

Drew and the government began to give serious attention to the Common Market in 1960, in response to indications that Britain was planning to apply for membership. What they feared were the possible economic and political consequences if Britain sacrificed Commonwealth preferences in order to meet the requirements of the community: erosion of Canada's competitive position in the

British market, a weakening of Commonwealth ties based on shared economic interest, and the loss of a significant counterweight to United States economic and political influence on Canada. The Department of External Affairs, doubtful that the Canadian bargaining position was strong enough to do much about these problems, recommended that the government go to work on contingency plans.[61] Drew's position, founded on the belief that the community's conditions for membership were likely to be unpopular with a substantial element of British opinion, was very different. He favoured a vigorous campaign in Britain, reinforced as appropriate from home, to convince the public that the Canadian and Commonwealth markets were of continued and growing value, combined with a strong effort to get a commitment that British negotiators would protect the Commonwealth interest. The latter produced a public assurance in May of 1961 of "full consultation" with other Commonwealth governments,[62] a narrow interpretation of which formed the basis of Drew's subsequent action. This approach was more in line with ministerial attitudes in Ottawa than the cautious line favoured by External Affairs. "Too weak!" was Green's comment on guidance prepared in his department for the prime minister.[63]

Drew's view of the British undertaking about consultation was that it might offer a means of thwarting negotiations with the community if they seemed likely to produce a result unfavourable to the Commonwealth. He therefore set a very high standard of what constituted acceptable consultation and counselled his government against accepting anything less. He did not regard a trip to Ottawa in July of 1961 by the Commonwealth Secretary, Duncan Sandys, as meeting his requirements, and his negative comments helped to produce a cool reception for the visitor.[64] When Macmillan, on 31 July, announced his government's intention to open negotiations with the community, Diefenbaker reiterated his preference, already expressed in connection with Sandys's visit, for a Commonwealth heads of government meeting as a forum of consultation. This idea, which would have complicated matters for the British a good deal more than a series of bilateral talks, was not very welcome to them.[65] It was made even less so by a Commonwealth ministerial meeting in Accra in September. There, it was reported, the Canadian ministers of Finance and of Trade and Commerce, Donald Fleming and George Hees, took the lead in mobilising opposition to the British plans.[66]

The bad press which Fleming and Hees received led the cabinet in Ottawa to moderate its position. On the initiative of the minister of Justice, Davie Fulton, it agreed "that Canada should now accept as a fait accompli the United Kingdom decision to try to enter the European Economic Community."[67] This position was smartly communicated to the two ministers and was reflected in the reports which they made to Parliament on their return.[68] Diefenbaker was concerned as well about the reaction in Britain, a fact which led him to believe that Canadian hostility to the negotiations, if continued, might even have the undesired effect of helping Labour to bring down Macmillan's government at the next election.[69] This was not a worry to Drew, who suspected that the criticism of the Canadian ministers in the British press was at least partly inspired by promarket ministers and officials.[70] He therefore did not follow the line adopted in Ottawa but kept on the offensive, getting into a prolonged argument with the British over their refusal to provide Commonwealth representatives with the full text of their opening statement in negotiations with the community, on the ground that they had agreed with the other parties not to release it.[71] Diefenbaker himself had to instruct Drew to moderate his opposition when the high commissioner's conduct in the dispute received unfavourable public attention in Canada[72] and in the end the struggle proved to have been ill-advised. The text, when it became available as a result of a press leak, turned out to contain nothing of substance which the British had not already revealed in oral briefings and written summaries.[73]

Despite this chastening experience, Drew's name continued to appear in the papers, although with less frequency, as a source of criticism of the Common Market in Britain.[74] He also maintained the flow of negative comment to Ottawa, notwithstanding British efforts to promote a better relationship with Canada, a policy which included two visits to Ottawa by the minister responsible for negotiations with the community, Edward Heath, and agreement to convene a Commonwealth heads of government meeting.

On the eve of a visit to Ottawa by Macmillan at the end of April 1962, Drew commented alarmingly on the political implications of the British approach to the community. Its success, he warned, would weaken the Commonwealth link and make Canada more vulnerable to control by the United States, an objective he suggested the Americans had in mind in encouraging the British effort.[75] This was not an aspect of the problem that occurred spontaneously to External Affairs, nor was it informed of Drew's concern or asked to comment. But Drew's argument was one to which Diefenbaker was susceptible[76] and it affected his approach to the British, including his preparations for the heads of government meeting. Unlike other Commonwealth leaders, he was not interested in contingency plans against Britain's possible entry. Instead, encouraged by public opinion polls showing low support for the Common Market in Britain, he preferred to hope that the conference would help to change the mind of the government there. Having been warned by officials against placing himself in a position to be blamed if the British bid should fail, he told Green, who accompanied him to London and who also continued to hope Britain would stay out, that they must achieve their objective without "taking the part of the 'dog in the manger'."[77] This proved to be an impossible task, for Diefenbaker had no success with Drew's ideas about expanding Commonwealth trade and the political dangers if Britain joined the community. All he did was to alarm the British and arouse a hostile press in London, and he did not recoup his position by proposing that the Commonwealth take the lead in organising a broader international conference on the lowering of trade barriers. Hence the conference ended without forcing a change upon the British. While the subsequent failure of their application to the community could not be blamed on Canada or the Commonwealth, as officials in Ottawa and Diefenbaker himself had feared might happen, the conference nonetheless did the prime minister more harm than good, by exposing his conduct to savage criticism in the press. It also helped disappoint the Conservatives' hopes for a warm relationship with London, contributing instead to the feeling, noted by a British high commissioner in Ottawa during the period, that there was "something . . . awry" at the ministerial level.[78]

Diefenbaker might well have had better success in responding to the British negotiations with the European Economic Community had the advice from Drew been better integrated with that from public servants. Disparate advice, this time from different departments, was also a problem in dealing with the issue in external policy which was most troublesome for Diefenbaker's government, the crisis over nuclear weapons. Green's concern for Canada's credibility as an advocate of disarmament brought him into conflict with George Pearkes and his successor as minister of National Defence, Douglas Harkness, over their desire to reach agreement with the United States on the supply of nuclear equipment to the Canadian armed forces for their new weapons systems, and to American bases in Canada. This was an issue on which there had been differences between the departments of External Affairs and National Defence since Pearson's years as minister,[79] but they widened as a result of Green's personal interest in the subject and his approach to his work. Officials in External Affairs who dealt with the problem found that they could not count on Green to accept positions agreed to with their counterparts in National Defence. As a result, the matter became one for resolution between ministers or, if they could not find common ground themselves, by the prime minister. His convictions, as expressed privately at the time, seem to have inclined towards the nuclear side. Although he acknowledged the desirability of disarmament, he was not convinced that it was realisable, and both his view of the Soviet Union and his appreciation of the economic benefits of defence production sharing encouraged a favourable approach to agreement with the United States.[80] But of more pressing concern to him than the substance of the issue were its political implications. The emergence of an organised antinuclear movement in Canada, which could take encouragement from the positions of the three opposition parties, was a factor here, but the greatest cause of difficulty was the division in cabinet. If one or other of the lead ministers were so offended by Diefenbaker's position that he withdrew, possibly taking supporters with him, the government's position obviously could become precarious, especially after it was reduced to a minority in the election of 1962.

For a long time, Diefenbaker was able to control the issue by blurring it, keeping both protagonists somewhat off-base, but that strategy was put to an end by the Cuban missile crisis in October of 1962. By revealing the weakness of Canada's defences resulting from the failure to acquire the weapons required by the new delivery systems, the crisis placed the government under greater pressure to take a decision. It appears, especially from Harkness's account, that Diefenbaker responded first and foremost as a politician under siege, anticipating an early election and anxious to find an issue which might provide a basis for recovering his majority in Parliament. Keeping his cabinet together was an important concern in this endeavour, but it was not the only one.

Harkness took advantage of the situation created by the missile crisis to secure cabinet agreement to proceed with negotiations with the United States about acquiring nuclear equipment for use both in Canada and by Canadian forces in Europe. Green did not cause serious difficulties about the latter. Because of his attitude, however, the government took the position that weapons for use in Canada, or vital parts of them, should be stored in the United States and moved across the border in an emergency. When meetings with the Americans failed to produce a workable arrangement for doing so, Diefenbaker held off making changes for the forces in Europe alone, arguing that he wanted to announce a solution to the whole problem at once. The objective as he saw it was to find a formula that could be used to the government's advantage in an election. An idea that appealed to him was to reach a comprehensive agreement with the United States and make that the issue in going to the country to restore the government's majority. This course, however, was opposed not only by Green but even by pronuclear ministers, who did not want to fight on the single issue of acquiring the weapons although they were willing to make it one of the planks in a campaign platform.[81]

Having failed to carry the idea of a pronuclear campaign, Diefenbaker, encouraged by the antinuclear bias of his mail,[82] found renewed attraction in seeking votes from the other side. Pearson's announcement on 12 January 1963, that he had decided that Canada was obligated to accept nuclear weapons, provided Diefenbaker with an obvious opportunity to appeal to antinuclear sentiment, but to do so he had to resist strong pressure to accept the logic of Pearson's reasoning. One source was the statement of the retiring supreme commander of NATO forces in Europe, General Lauris Norstad, that Canada ought to provide the nuclear equipment required by its forces there; another and more urgent one was Harkness's threat on 20 January to resign from the cabinet if the issue were allowed to remain unresolved until after another election. Diefenbaker's response was to promise a discussion of defence policy in Parliament and to appoint a committee of cabinet to examine the nuclear question. After a close study of the relevant documentation, the other members of the committee persuaded Green to acknowledge, "reluctantly," that Canada had definite obligations to acquire nuclear weapons.[83] The committee then worked out an agreed position for presentation to the prime minister and cabinet. This provided for a request to NATO for clarification of Canada's nuclear role and, if that were reconfirmed, for acquisition of the appropriate weapons. With respect to NORAD, it was agreed that negotiations with the United States would "be continued with a view to reaching agreement to secure the highest degree of availability to Canada."[84]

If Green and Harkness were agreed on the report of the committee, it would seem that Diefenbaker need not have been concerned about an open split in cabinet if he accepted it. It is likely, therefore, that he was more influenced by doubts that a pronuclear position would be effective in an election and by the desire to be able to appear as a proponent of the other side if he considered it advantageous to do so. The outcome of the confused sequence of statement and counterstatement by himself and Harkness at the end of January reinforced these considerations. After the State Department in Washington released a note on 30 January taking issue with Diefenbaker's interpretation of Canada's obligations, he became if anything more resistant to Harkness's position, and informed his colleagues that he wanted to go to the country with an anti-American campaign.[85] Harkness, concluding that there was no hope of progress, carried out his threat to resign on 3 February and the government fell on an opposition vote of confidence two days later. Although he had not kept his cabinet together, Diefenbaker was able to go the people in what he considered the most viable position on the nuclear issue: uncommitted to the nuclear option and able to exploit Canadian resentment of criticism of his actions in the United States.

As events turned out, the election of 1963 was not a single-issue campaign, nor was foreign and defence policy its focal point. According to a Liberal strategist, domestic concerns were of more consistent interest to the voter, and the key to his party's success was [its] concentration [in] the final days of the campaign on the Diefenbaker government's reputation for indecisiveness, for which the Liberals offered an antidote in the form of "sixty days of decision."[86] But the outgoing government had to a considerable extent earned the reputation which helped defeat it in foreign policy, and hence the verdict of the electorate was in a sense a judgement on the way that activity had been conducted. The decision-making process under Diefenbaker enabled ministers to make good use of the bureaucratic resources available to them without giving up their autonomy. It did not guarantee, however, that they would always do so, or that they would keep out of trouble for other reasons. It may well be that the circumstances of Diefenbaker's fall deprived him and his government of credit for their achievements in foreign policy in a time of difficult transition in international affairs. Yet, as the handling of the Common Market and of defence policy shows, the problems were real, and they related as much to the way policy was made and implemented as to the principles on which it was based. It was reasonable, therefore, for the voters to be concerned about the progress of making foreign policy when they went to the polls in 1963.

Notes

1. My understanding of this subject has been much assisted by interviews with a number of participants in the policy-making process, to all of whom I am very grateful. I have also benefited from the comments of Basil Robinson. The views expressed are mine and not necessarily those of the Department of External Affairs.

2. Peter C. Newman, *Renegade in Power* (Carleton Library ed., Toronto, 1973), 252.

3. See, for example, Charles Ritchie, *Storm Signals* (Toronto, 1983), 158, and J.L. Granatstein, *A Man of Influence* (Ottawa, 1981), 324.

4. Peter Stursberg, *Diefenbaker: Leadership Gained* (Toronto, 1975), 147.

5. Public Archives of Canada (herafter PAC), Norman Robertson Papers, MG30 E163, Vol. 3A, J.W. Holmes to Robertson, 1 August 1957.

6. See, for example, Department of External Affairs (hereinafter DEA), File 11246–40, Holmes to W.D. Matthews, 27 June 1957.

7. Discussion of trade policy is recorded in DEA, File 50085-G-40, minutes of a meeting of the ministers of Finance and Trade and Commerce with officials. . . , 22 June 1957, and Privy Council Office (hereinafter PCO) Records, Cabinet Conclusions, 22 July 1957. I have not found confirmation in departmental sources that Diefenbaker consulted a senior member of External Affairs before agreeing to NORAD; cf. R.H. Roy, *For Most Conspicuous Bravery* (Vancouver, 1977), 209.

8. See, for example, PCO Records, Cabinet Conclusions, 11 April 1958.

9. DEA, File 11246–40, Holmes to Matthews, 27 June 1957.

10. Diefenbaker Centre, Saskatoon, Diefenbaker interview with John Munro, 4 December 1974.

11. See, e.g., PAC, Robertson Papers, MG30 E163, Vol. 3A, Holmes to Robertson, 1 August 1957.

12. Granatstein, *Man of Influence*, 325–6.
13. Diefenbaker Centre, Diefenbaker interview with John Munro, 14 December 1974.
14. DEA, File 12685–40, R.B. Bryce to Jules Léger, 16 September 1957; *ibid.*, Léger to Bryce, 15 October 1957.
15. Blair Fraser, "Backstage at Ottawa," *Maclean's*, 12 October 1957, 2; Telegram (Toronto), 16 September 1957.
16. Diefenbaker Centre, Diefenbaker interview with John Munro, 6 December 1974. See also Trevor Lloyd, *Canada in World Affairs, 1957–1959* (Toronto, 1968), 70, and Granatstein, *Man of Influence*, 326–7.
17. See Granatstein, *Man of Influence*, 316, 320–1 and 323–6.
18. Lloyd, *Canada in World Affairs*, 18 and 20.
19. DEA, File 50245–40, Léger to Prime Minister, 13 August 1958.
20. House of Commons, *Debates*, 20 February 1959, 1223.
21. Stursberg, *Diefenbaker: Leadership Gained*, 185; Blair Fraser, "The Lone Pine of Parliament Hill," *Maclean's*, 1 August 1959, 17 and 49–50.
22. CJOH television, Ottawa, "Insight", Peter Dobell interview with Douglas Fisher, 13 January 1980; Arnold Heeney, *The Things That Are Caesar's* (Toronto, 1972), 171.
23. Charles Ritchie, *Diplomatic Passport* (Toronto, 1981), 171.
24. See Granatstein, *Man of Influence*, 327–8.
25. *Ibid.*, 338–9.
26. Michael J. Tucker, "Canada's Roles in the Disarmament Negotiations 1957–1971," Ph.D. diss., University of Toronto, 1977, 81, 86 and n. 72.
27. Granatstein, *Man of Influence*, 339.
28. DEA, File 50210-F-40, Robertson to Léger, 10 August 1959.
29. DEA, Historical Division, Howard Green interview, Vancouver, 2 March 1980.
30. Granatstein, *Man of Influence*, 341.
31. DEA, File 11336-10-A-40, Ross Campbell to Under-Secretary, 3 May 1961.
32. Granatstein, *Man of Influence*, 343–9.
33. PAC, Marcel Cadieux Papers, MG31 E31, Vol. 2, Cadieux to Under-Secretary, 21 April 1959.
34. DEA, File 8260–15–40, Under-Secretary to Secretary of State for External Affairs (hereinafter SSEA), 7 November 1960.
35. PCO Records, Cabinet Conclusions, 10 April 1961.
36. DEA, File 11246–40. Far Eastern Division memorandum, 5 June 1959; File 10513–40, United Nations Division to Office of Under-Secretary, 9 March 1960.
37. DEA, File 5475-DW-74-40, United Nations Division to Under-Secretary, 15 September 1960, and enclosure. I have benefitted in preparing this account from a review of the files by Anne Hillmer.
38. Diefenbaker Centre, Diefenbaker Papers, Bryce to Prime Minister, 23 September 1960.
39. DEA, File 5475-DW-70-40, New York (UN) to External, 23 September 1960, telegram 1541.
40. Richard A. Preston, *Canada in World Affairs, 1959 to 1961* (Toronto, 1965), 270-1; DEA, Files 5475-DW-70-40 and 5475-DW-74-40.
41. DEA, File 26-BEU-40, Under-Secretary to SSEA, 8 May 1962; File 633–40, Under-Secretary to Prime Minister, 8 May 1962. I have been assisted in dealing with this question by an account by D.M. Page.
42. Diefenbaker Centre, Diefenbaker interview with John Munro, 4 December 1974; DEA, File 663–40, Under-Secretary to SSEA, 4 December 1957.
43. PAC, Robertson Papers, MG30 E163, Vol. 18, Office of SSEA to Under-Secretary, 3 July 1962.
44. PCO Records, Cabinet Conclusions, 6 September 1962.
45. DEA, File 11389-A-40, Prime Minister's Office to Under-Secretary, 16 November 1962.
46. *Ibid.*, New York (UN) to External, 24 November 1962, telegram 2370.
47. See, for example, DEA, File 6230–40, Basil Robinson to Commonwealth Division, 20 February 1959. I am grateful to F.J. McEvoy for a study which he has prepared on this subject.
48. DEA, File 11827–40, Robinson to Commonwealth Division, 8 April 1960.
49. DEA, File 50085-H-40, Bryce to Prime Minister, 18 April 1960.
50. See, for example, *ibid.*, External to London, 7 May 1960, telegram K-164.
51. John G. Diefenbaker, *One Canada: The Years of Achievement* (Toronto, 1976), 210-2.
52. PCO records, Cabinet Conclusions, 11 and 25 February and 9 March 1961.

53. DEA, File 50085-J-40, Drew to Prime Minister, 27 February 1961.

54. PCO Records, Cabinet Conclusions, 6 July 1957.

55. DEA, File 50085-J-40, SSEA to Prime Minister, 16 January 1961.

56. *Ibid.*; PCO Records, Cabinet Conclusions, 11 February 1961.

57. PCO Records, Cabinet Conclusions, 9 March 1961.

58. DEA, File 50085-J-40, Bryce, memorandum, 12 March 1961.

59. PCO Records, Cabinet Conclusions, 14 March 1961.

60. Harold Macmillan, *Pointing the Way* (London, 1972), 299.

61. DEA, File 12447-40, Under-Secretary to SSEA, 7 September 1960.

62. *Ibid.*, London to Prime Minister, 18 May 1961, telegram 1833. Like many of Drew's recommendations on this subject, this document was not added to the External Affairs file until some years later.

63. *Ibid.*, SSEA to Prime Minister, 2 March 1961 and minute, n.d.

64. *Ibid.*, London to Prime Minister, 2 June 1961, telegram 2005, and passim; also Peyton Lyon, *Canada in World Affairs, 1961-1963* (Toronto, 1968), 447.

65. DEA, File 12447-40, External to London, 1 August 1961, telegram E-1514, Lyon, *Canada in World Affairs*, 447-8.

66. *Ibid.*, 448-50.

67. PCO Records, Cabinet Conclusions, 14 September 1961.

68. DEA, File 12447-40, External to Accra, 14 September 1961, telegram M67; Lyon, *Canada in World Affairs*, 450-2.

69. PCO Records, Cabinet Conclusions, 26 September 1961.

70. DEA, File 12447-40, London to Minister of Trade and Commerce, 24 September 1961, telegram 3454.

71. *Ibid.*, London to Minister of Finance, 13 October 1961, telegram 3707.

72. See, for example, PCO Records, Cabinet Conclusions, 15 November 1961.

73. DEA, File 12447-40, SSEA to Prime Minister, 28 November 1961 and enclosure.

74. "Mr. Drew Writes a Letter," *Free Press* (Winnipeg), 7 May 1962.

75. DEA, File 12447-40, London to Prime Minister, 29 April 1962, telegram 1588.

76. See, for example, PCO Records, Cabinet Conclusions, 30 August 1962.

77. PAC, Howard Green Papers, MG32 B13, Vol. 9, Diefenbaker to Green, 31 August 1962, and passim; PCO Records, Cabinet Conclusions, 30 August 1962.

78. Lord Garner, "Britain and Canada in the 1940s and 1950s," in *Britain and Canada*, edited by Peter Lyon (London, 1976), 99-101; also Peyton Lyon, *Canada in World Affairs*, 463-76.

79. George Ignatieff, "Secrecy and Democratic Participation in the Formulation and Conduct of Canadian Foreign Policy," in *Secrecy and Foreign Policy*, edited by Thomas M. Franck and Edward Weisband (New York, 1974), 56.

80. See, for example, PCO Records, Cabinet Conclusions, 14 January 1960; Jocelyn Maynard Ghent, "Canadian-American Relations and the Nuclear Weapons Controversy, 1958-1963", Ph.D. diss., University of Illinois at Urbana-Champaign, 1976, 81-3 and 116-22.

81. PAC, Douglas Harkness Papers, MG36 B19, Vol. 84, "The Nuclear Arms Question and the Political Crisis Which Arose From It in January and February 1963."

82. Ghent, "Did He Fall or Was He Pushed?" *International History Review* I (1979), 258.

83. Harkness, "Nuclear Policy Muddied by Dief," *Citizen* (Ottawa), 24 October 1977.

84. PAC, Harkness Papers, MG36 B19, Vol. 84, "Nuclear Arms question."

85. Harkness, "A foolish move," *Citizen* (Ottawa), 25 October 1977.

86. Walter L. Gordon, *A Political Memoir* (Toronto, 1977), 115-6, 120-1 and 125-7.

CANADA AND THE VIETNAM WAR†

In February 1966, the Hon. Paul Martin said there were "fundamental differences" between Canadian and United States policy over Vietnam. These differences have not been obvious to critics. Fundamental differences do not mean, however, that policy is diametrically opposed. It can just be based on different premises. Mr. Martin in the mid-sixties came close on occasions to full support of the American premises, but he was defending them against the charge of evil intentions more than endorsing their basic approach. There were variations over the years in emphasis and attitudes by Canadian spokesmen during the Liberal and Conservative administrations, but one can detect a certain consensus.

The recurrent theme in official Canadian statements is that the issues in Indochina are complex and cannot be solved by military means — a theme which sounds sometimes profound and sometimes like a pious evasion of harsh reality. Canadians were not ingenuous about the difficulties involved in making the Geneva Agreements stick. They were aware of the attitude of communist countries and of Mr. Dulles to the concept of neutrality, but they thought there was a better chance of maintaining equilibrium in the area, the inviolability of the plate glass window, if outside powers recognized that it was safer to accept neutrality than to provoke interference. They deplored Mr. Dulles's denying moral support to the Geneva Agreements, his rounding up a paper alliance which alienated the more influential non-communist Asians and justified a cynical attitude to the Geneva bargain by the communists. They thought that forces loosed in Asia could not be traced solely to communist provocation. Canadians, by reason of the Commonwealth experience, had more sympathy for anti-imperalist forces than had the traditionally anti-imperialist Americans, no doubt because Canadians had less reason to feel betrayed by those whom they had helped.[1]

Differences over Vietnam have been concealed by the refusal of Canadian spokesmen to denounce United States policy. There were many reasons for this. The currency of international discourse is such that statesmen do not denounce each other with the freedom of private citizens. General de Gaulle expressed his disagreement indirectly and in terms which in the mouth of an editor would seem mild indeed. Whether or not one approves of this *politesse*, it is a convention and therefore official Canadian attitudes in Vietnam cannot be judged by the decibels of public statements. A diplomatic reason for tact was that public denunciation could undermine whatever influence Canada might have on United States policy. When Mr. Pearson gently suggested in Philadelphia in 1965 that the United States stop bombing the North, he drew the ire of President Johnson and forfeited the position of influence he had acquired. It is not only Canadians who resent criticism. The argument for loud diplomacy is that denunciation from Ottawa would have a shock effect on the United States government and public. It can be neither dismissed nor accepted without calculation. But one has to guard against inflation. Canadian advice has too often been written off in

†John Holmes, "Canada and the Vietnam War," in *War and Society in North America*, edited by J.L. Granatstein and R.D. Cuff (Toronto: Nelson, 1971): 184-199.

Washington because Ottawa was regarded as a tiresome and self-righteous nag. Canadian rhetoric on Indochina was also cautious (with certain notable exceptions) because of the requirements of impartiality of a Commission member. The United States was not denounced for its role in Vietnam, but neither was China. It would be silly to claim that public positions on Vietnam were determined entirely by Vietnamese issues. There have been practical economic reasons for treating both the United States and China with kid gloves, one case being, of course, stronger than the other.

It would be wrong to attribute the cautious Canadian attitudes on Vietnam to United States pressure. Naturally, the United States expressed its views in no uncertain terms. That is what diplomacy is all about. How much of a threat is involved thereby is for Canadian governments to calculate. There is no solid evidence of "blackmail." When Mr. Martin and others were defending United States motives they were expressing their own convictions, not acting as hired agents. In spite of doubts about the wisdom of United States policy Canadian spokesmen have been sympathetic to the United States reaction to communist provocation as they saw it. They recognize a dilemma for the Americans and one which involved the fate of an international security system in which Canada had a large stake. This attitude is largely shared by other allies of the United States, both in NATO and in SEATO. For Canadians, however, the attitude has been to a considerable extent the product of their unique experience in Indochina. To put it briefly, this has been an experience of the blundering, ineffectual and uncooperative government of South Vietnam, careless of the provisions of the Geneva agreement; the United States which grudgingly observed the terms of the Geneva armistices until they had become a farce; the North Vietnamese government which, from the beginning, thwarted and defied the efforts of the international control commissions in both Vietnam and Laos. When by the end of the 'fifties both sides were openly disregarding the truces, Ottawa had seen enough on the spot to regard the American intervention as a response to violation rather than as calculated imperialist expansion.

There has been, of course, an evolution over two decades in official Canadian attitudes. During the 'fifties the Americans did learn to see the value of the Geneva Agreements and the Commissions, and the differences between the two countries narrowed. Canadians had no reason to feel affection for the South Vietnamese government, which treated the Commission with scant respect, but by the late 'fifties there were increasing expectations that the Diem government would be able to make a go of it and create a state which, if hardly democratic in the Western sense, would, with massive American help, be the best hope of stability in a ravaged country. They saw with dismay the terrorist policies launched by the Viet Cong to upset the South Vietnamese experiment. It is clear from Canadian official statements, up until the mid-sixties at least, that this was seen as an operation directed from Hanoi and therefore an aggressive violation of the Geneva Agreements. That there were strong endemic revolutionary forces in the South was never denied. First-hand acquaintance with North Vietnam, however, discouraged regard for it as the democratic alternative.

The high tide of support of the United States — rhetorically at least — came in the early years of the new Liberal administration, 1963–1965, when the government looked upon the United States rush to the defence of the South Vietnamese government as being, on balance, justified. Then came a shift back towards the middle of the road. There were many reasons for this shift, including the intensification of articulate criticism of United States policy in Canada and the storm in the United States itself. Canadian leaders also wanted to make use of the Canadian access to Hanoi and Saigon to effect another armistice. The government knew that neither the United States nor the North Vietnam government would stop fighting because Ottawa told them to do so, and they concentrated on seeing if they alone or in collaboration with others might find some formula of agreement. Whether their chances of doing so had been spoiled, as has been charged, by the Minister's defence of American motives is a question hard to answer. When parties are angling for a truce, couriers are needed to convey to one side what the other is prepared to concede and they are likely to make use of the courier most convenient at the moment. Suspicion that the Canadian Commissioner was acting for the Americans could strengthen rather than weaken his credibility as a courier, although it might discredit his advice. It is possible that the messages which Canadian interlocutors carried back and forth during these years were, although not decisive, part of the process of reaching positions when both sides could go to Paris. The mediatory process is usually a maze.

By the late 'sixties it was hard for Ottawa to maintain positions which even United States Republicans were abandoning — although occasionally one wondered if hawks had flown north. Canadian spokesmen, however, had been defending United States ends, and the means now seemed to be fashioning different ends. The persistent Canadian belief that the issues could not be solved by military means was strengthened by the very escalation of the war. The bombing of the North was at first regarded as understandable, but the conviction grew that talks would never be possible unless it was stopped. This opinion crept more and more into public statements, and by 1968 the government seemed to have concluded that on this subject the time for unquiet diplomacy had come. So too had the other NATO allies, and the chorus was more effective than another yap from the tiresome neighbour.

The change in Canadian attitudes is most notable since the spring of 1968. Mr. Trudeau brought different preconceptions about Vietnam from those acquired in office by his predecessors. Neither he nor Mr. Sharp, however, has shifted to public criticism. On Vietnam they are cool, and largely silent.[2] The situation has, of course, changed. The bombing of the North has ceased, the United States has come to the conference table and the withdrawal of troops has started. Intermediaries are less obviously needed now that the two sides are in contact in Paris, and there has been a diminution of enthusiasm for the mediatory role in general on the part of the new government.

The International Control Commissions

Central to the Canadian experience of Vietnam is the part played in the International Control Commissions for Vietnam, Laos, and Cambodia. The obligation was to be judicious and impartial rather than neutral. This was not a UN super-visory body of the usual kind but a troika on which there was to be a representa-tive communist country, a representative Western country, with a neutral chairman. Canadians were prepared on many occasions to find the South Vietnamese guilty, but the Poles could not do likewise with respect to North Vietnam. Canadian impartiality was, of course, conditioned by Western per-spectives and prejudices, and the record was not impeccable. Nevertheless the single-minded advocacy of one party by the Poles pushed the Canadians into protecting the rights of the other. Since its first year, when it accomplished its most important mission by adjudicating many differences between the belliger-ents in the difficult post-hostilities period, the Commission in Vietnam has been humiliated and frustrated but maintained because no one wanted to destroy a last symbol of the Geneva Agreements. The Canadian Commissioner has not denied, as has been claimed, that the United States is acting contrary to the Geneva armistice. He has insisted, however, that this had to be seen in the con-text of violations by the other side. In 1962 a majority report of the Commis-sion, from which the Poles dissented, established this principle. However, Canada dissented a few years later from a report in which the Poles and the Indians criticized only the United States and South Vietnam for violation and refused to make public evidence in the Commission's hands concerning North Vietnamese actions in the South.

Over sixteen years a large number of Canadian Foreign Service and Army Officers have served in Indochina. They have had an enlightening experience of Asia at the grass roots, but it has been a particular kind of experience. The time has been largely spent combatting the knavish tricks of the North Vietnamese, not only in Vietnam but in Laos as well. Virtually all Canadian veterans of Indo-china have returned with more hawkish attitudes than prevail at home. One can agree or disagree with them or discount their special cause for prejudice, but it is not easy to write them off. It is hard for anyone who has honestly looked at the record to deny the consistent deceit and tendentiousness in Hanoi's attitude towards the Commissions and the terms of the agreement. The issues in Viet-nam are, however, broader and deeper than the truce and have to be judged in an historical framework longer than that during which Canada has been involved. Canadian officials may have seen Vietnam up too close and in a special context.

The Effect on Canadian Foreign Policy

Mackenzie King had argued, with considerable support, that Canada ought not to become involved in distant continents because it had no interests there. In 1954 Canada was obliged to accept a nasty obligation to help maintain the peace in Southeast Asia — an invitation issued precisely because Canada had no inter-ests in the area. The assumption had to be discarded that Canada led a sheltered existence and its youth and underdevelopment excused it from far-flung obliga-tions. Mr. King had been dead four years. Canadian zeal in NATO, in Korea, and in the United Nations had already set Canadian policy on a new course, but the Indochina requirement forced the country into a foreign policy involvement more exotic and less collective than had previously been contemplated. Canada found itself in an exposed position in the centre of world conflict. There were advantages for a country eager to make its mark in world politics. With responsibility came some degree of influence. Canada learned, for one thing, that to have influence in world politics it is an advantage to have special knowledge. Canadians scattered throughout these countries had access to areas denied to other peoples, Eastern or Western. Their deductions were listened to with respect in London, Paris, Delhi, even Washington. Canadian critics who have accused their government of "passing information" to the Americans ignore the function of political intelligence in persuasion. It is not easy to persuade Washington when it thinks it has a monopoly of the facts. Since the war began to rage throughout the area and the Commission lost its significance, this special advantage diminished — although the access to Hanoi and its leaders still gives Canadians special status.

Our role in Indochina was the classic case of middlepowermanship. There was not, before 1954, much theorizing about the role of a middle power. That came after the Suez crisis, when this phase of Canadian policy had reached its crest. The Indochina experience of the 'fifties confirmed the view of many Canadians and of our friends that this was our special destiny and our best contribution to international order. It satisfied our desire to do our own thing, complementary to that of the great powers but by no means that of a handmaiden. It enabled us to differ from the United States without opposing the interests of the United States as we saw them. It took some courage for the government in 1954 to accept an assignment in which we had no expectation of help or even moral support from our large ally, but of course it was not the audacity required to oppose the Americans directly. We had to suffer American scorn more than American hostility.

Then we had to pay for this heady experience. The role of the middleman is not simply that of the fairy godmother beloved by all. Powerful interests and passions were involved. Our role was useful but peripheral, and this was no peripheral quarrel. At times Canadian good judgment gained respect, at least in foreign offices, but we also gained enemies and disparagers. Relations with friends and allies may have suffered more than relations with antagonists. The Poles and the Russians had no reason to feel disappointed in our performance. This close association may not have been good for Canadian-Indian relations which by the mid-fifties had become close. Different perspectives encouraged mutual exasperation. At the same time personal associations developed between Indians and Canadians and with Poles as well which, because of the insights they provided and the lasting contacts they afforded, had their own reward. Our diplomacy was honed. But whatever was gained in the 'fifties may have been lost in the 'sixties when a confrontation became a war.

Among the casualties has been the Canadian belief in its role as a middle power. To this Vietnam has been only one contributing factor. The expulsion of UNEF [United Nations Emergency Force] was more important. The present scepticism is bred of disillusion bred of exaggeration. The function of the intermediary was mistaken for that of the international policeman and found wanting. As the war in Indochina has become more immoderate, there has been a revulsion in Canada against the approach to peace through moderate international action. On the one hand it is regarded as gratuitous do-goodism which interferes with our commerce. In the eyes of other critics this commitment to mediation has tied Canada to an ineffective policy of quiet diplomacy which has had no effect on the parties, in particular the United States, and been bad for our soul.

Has this thankless assignment in Asia turned Canada away from that continent? The recent White Paper with its Pacific orientation suggests not, but the emphasis in the White Paper is commercial and cultural, with little concern for security. Vietnam has certainly not encouraged us to seek a partnership with the Americans in Pacific security which we had never sought earlier. There is no clamouring for an extended "role" in Indochina. The government, it is implied, would not refuse useful service in a further commission but it wants to have a good look at the terms first. Over the years the Indochina assignment has kept the eyes of both our External Affairs and National Defence departments distracted from Europe to Asia, and made it harder for the government to slide back into the North Atlantic womb. It revealed to the government with a shock that so long as we assert our interest in world-wide "stability" and world-wide freedom of commerce, we are vulnerable to service farther away from home than Mr. King would have liked.

The Effect on Defence Policy

The ICC [International Control Commission] assignment was unwelcome to the defence authorities, although they did it well. There was at that time little disposition to regard peacekeeping as an acceptable or accepted role for armed forces. Vietnam had a hand in changing all that. Indochina was not an easy assignment, but it was often interesting and always challenging. In the first year there was a real sense of accomplishment. It was an exotic assignment for the permanent forces and a road to promotion. It was gradually built into the regular program of the services and helped prepare them, after UN assignments in the Middle East and Africa, to look upon peacekeeping as one of the continuing functions of the Canadian forces.

The most important impact of the Vietnam War on Canadian defence policy, however, may have been its effect on the alliance in general and in particular on our relations with the United States. Twenty years ago few Canadians doubted that when the United States was at war, Canada would be at war whether we liked it or not. Now we have got used to the idea that the United States is at war, as it has been in a *de facto* way for almost a decade, and Canada is not only not at war, it has never considered such a course. Our commitment to the ICCs has given us a valid excuse, but even without such a commitment it is doubtful that a majority of Canadians would have been disposed to join the Americans in battle. What is more, there has been no evidence of any undue pressure by the United States government to induce us to do so — although requests for support of South Vietnam have been made in general terms to the NATO allies. And we have suffered no sanctions. The consciousness of alliance obligations has been modified. The opposition to involvement has not been entirely idealistic. A "silent majority" of Canadians probably just think that Indochina is a good area for us to keep out of, especially as the United States has no pressing need of military assistance. Because of the Vietnam war, however, there is now an opposition to fighting as an ally of the United States sufficiently articulated to make the government sensitive. It has been a factor in the debate over a continuing commitment to NORAD and NATO, although not decisive. Before Vietnam, it was assumed that the United States would always be on the side of the angels and that, although we reserved our right to limit our contribution to the heavenly hosts, we would be on that side too. That the United States would be on the side of the angels, or at any rate on the side where our interests lie, is probably still the basic assumption of most Canadians, but it is not taken for granted as it one was.

This change is reflected in attitudes to the Defence Production Sharing Agreements. Up until the mid-sixties these were seen not as the harnessing by the United States of our resources to its war machine but rather as Canada demanding its rightful share in the alliance armaments business. Because of the circumstances of Vietnam and Canada's commitment to the Geneva agreements, Canadians have become aware of the ambiguity of their position consequent upon this pooling of continental resources. The assumption that the pooling of allied resources was inevitable because we were all involved in a common effort has been questioned because we are not all involved in the American effort in Vietnam. There has been no change of government policy but a change in the climate in which government policy is formulated. The case has at least been recognized for making ourselves less dependent in future on this profitable trade if we want to strengthen our independent hand in world politics.

This diminished sense of partnership may be the most important result of Vietnam on the relations between Canada and the United States. There is evidence that it is felt on both sides. Canadian defence officials have suspected an exclusion of Canadians from military intelligence they had previously shared.[3] On the Right Wing of American politics there is some husky criticism of Canada, but Canadian policy on Cuba, China, NATO, and sealhunting attract more comment than Vietnam — except that the latter is associated with the lively subject of deserters and draft-dodgers. On the whole Canada's non-belligerent position in Vietnam has created remarkably little antipathy in the United States, one of the blessings of being rarely noticed whatever we do. Americans do not seem to have changed their view of the principle of continental defence as inviolable and, what is more, sensible. It is hard for them to see that for Canadians the disconcerting realization that we could differ in our choice of enemies raises fundamental questions about joint defence. Who discerns — or provokes — the attacker? The implications for Canadians are unclear. For some, the obvious conclusion is disengagement from military association with an "imperialist power." For other Canadians the logic of joint defence, on the grounds both of efficacy and cheapness, remains so convincing that differences about policy in a distant part of the world can be disregarded. The climate of opinion has shifted to the extent that further commitments to continental defence on Canada's part, such as, for example, joining in an ABM or AWACS system, would be expected to rouse louder hostility than in the past. The Canadian hope seems to be that we can carry on avoiding new decisions until something has been resolved in Vietnam. Vietnam may simply have frozen joint defence. It is a question, however, whether a posture of not getting out of it and not getting on with it can be sustained in a decade when there is likely to be rapid technological and political change in the United States.

The horror of Vietnam has strengthened the desire of Canadians to search for non-military ways of making their contribution to international security — a disposition clearly evident in the underplaying of security issues in the recent White Paper on foreign policy. Such choices may not be open to great and super-powers — and it may only be an illusion that they are open to lesser powers. For the time being, however, Canadians have become less restless in their present status, less ambitious for a role in international security. Vietnam may have witnessed — and promoted — the rise and fall of Canada's affair with the middle power as a role, but it has also encouraged a sense of thanksgiving at not being a great power.

Social and Cultural Factors

Much of the impact on Canada of the Vietnam war is a spill-over or a mirror image of its impact on the United States. One must be careful in one's deductions because the Vietnam war is only one, although perhaps the major, element in the transformation of American society and attitudes in the past decade, and it is part of a world-wide movement, not just a North American phenomenon. It would be hard to say how much the increasing "anti-Americanism" in Canada is attributable to the Vietnam war and how much to the racial issue, United States policy in Latin America, or its heavy investment in Canada. It is the exercise of great military force in another continent, however, which especially seems to confirm the diagnosis of "imperialism."

The effect on Canadian attitudes to the United States has been ambivalent; the Vietnam war has stimulated in Canada both alienation and identification. In spite of the articulateness and the passion of the critics, probably just as many Canadians regard the US endeavour to "resist aggression" in other parts of the world as justified and worthy of moral support — even though they may increasingly consider it a losing cause.[4] Vietnam has raised the level of anti-American feeling in Canada and it has also tended to polarize attitudes towards the United States. For the majority, however, it may just have stimulated Canadianism, both of the affirmative and perverse varieties. It could once be assumed that all Canadians, with the exception of a few last-ditch Loyalists, regarded the United States as a frequently arrogant, not particularly lovable, but essentially benevolent power and, provided one was not expected to say so loudly, a good friend to have on our side. Few doubted that the United States was a good deed in a naughty world. For a large number of less articulate Canadians there was also a strong urge to share the higher standard of living in the United States or to make it in the big time. Now that the higher standard of living includes the possibility of compulsory military service in the Indochinese jungles and a much higher liability to municipal violence, calculations have shifted. Fewer Canadians are moving to the United States and more Americans are moving to Canada.[5] It is hard to say whether this trend will outlast the Vietnam war, because the motivation is ecological and romantic as well as political — or whether calculations will be altered by the threat of civil commotion in Canada.

Resistance to the United States, as a Canadian mood, has shifted leftwards. Canadian intellectuals are affected by the mood of American liberals, an apparent state of despair about American civilization. The Canadians do not know whether to respond by rejecting the United States and finding their own way or by wallowing in sin with the Americans. This dilemma is attributable to one virtue, fairmindedness — the realization that we share the horrid bourgeois civilization and the Cold War and it is not decent to attribute the wickedness to the United States and the virtue to Canada. It is attributable also to the hair-shirt hangup which makes it impossible for some Canadians to accept more fortunate circumstances when they have them. Out of a laudable effort to avoid hypocrisy, Canadian critics of United States policy in Vietnam have been anxious to blame their own government for complicity. They have got things out of proportion. They ignore the detachment from the war in Indochina which the Canadian government has maintained and the part it has tried to play in keeping peace in that area and they centre their attention on the less important fact that Canada has not denounced the United States or broken off its defence-production sharing agreements. The latter are legitimate criticisms but they are not central. Identification with the United States and its conflicts is found most notably on the extreme Left and the extreme Right — although it is probably the Lumpen Middle, brain-washed by television, that is least aware of the fact that Canada is not itself at war in Vietnam. Canadian radicals join anti-Vietnam parades in the streets of Washington and other Canadians assume an identity of interest with the United States government by calling for the exclusion of draft-dodgers and deserters. The Right and the Left do not worry about consistency. They both regard the United States and Canadian governments as linked inseparably in defence of the "capitalist system," and they must be destroyed together or preserved together in accordance with values more important than the preservation of national identity. The dilemma is for the pragmatic Canadian nationalist. The Vietnam war, which has given a strong stimulus to Canadian nationalism, could in the end contribute to the erosion of Canadian sovereignty or at least the idea of Canada, not by American intervention, but by the refusal of Canadians to accept their condition as non-Americans.

Finally, what impact has the Vietnam war had on Canada's view of itself, of its place in the world and on the view other people, including the Americans, have of Canada? How much of the increase in nationalism and self-confidence in Canada in the past sixteen years is attributable to the expansion of our economic growth to near great power figures and how much to our neighbour's misfortunes? Canadians have suffered in the past not from an inferiority complex *vis-à-vis* the United States but from a consciousness of smallness or perhaps of small-townness. Like small-towners they felt poorer and less sophisticated but had no doubt of their moral superiority. Those Canadians most convinced of the immorality of American policy are those most determined to associate Canada with the crime. Other Canadians think we are letting the Americans fight our crusade and they, therefore, feel morally inferior. What has shifted may be the Canadian view as to who has the luck — at least up until October, 1970. The comforts of a quieter life and in particular the freedom from the terrible obligations to keep the peace in all parts of the world have become more obvious. We seem to be in a period of retreat from the ambitions for world influence which characterized us at the time of the Geneva Conference of 1954. Whether this is a renunciation of world responsibility or a seeking after a different or more appropriate responsibility for a country economically rather than militarily strong remains to be seen. Strengthening of the yearning for independence or neutrality, for a non-military role, has certainly been encouraged by the Vietnam war, partly by the desire to keep out of something so messy and partly because of the apparent demonstration of the futility of military force.

The Vietnam war still rages and the results are uncertain. If it ended in a new Geneva agreement with a responsible part for Canada, an adjustment to reasonably independent régimes in Indochina, and an American withdrawal without too great a loss of face, we might all resume our active and constructive role in the building of a strong United Nations by experience. On the other hand an American withdrawal in disarray accompanied, or perhaps preceded, by upheavals in the United States would drive us into a frantic effort to isolate ourselves from contagion or, impelled by the death wish which plagues many Canadians, to jump into the flames in order not to be unlike the Americans. Whatever the shape of events, we are likely to feel a cold chill from a collapse of the *Pax Americana*. Whether we have liked it or not, and it is far from the ideal way to keep the peace, we have regarded it as a bulwark. *Sub specie aeternitatis* we may regard the disintegration of the American empire as a good thing, but at the moment it would leave Canada more exposed and vulnerable than it has ever been part of our philosophy to regard ourselves. The shock waves alone could be devastating. This is not an argument to join the Americans in the way they are going; it is simply to underline our vital interest in their fate. Canadian calculations about our own situation in the world, whether they are neutralist or alliance-minded, for the most part assume a strong and internationally active United States — as well as a strong Soviet Union in counterpoise. A shift in the capacity, stability, or disposition of either superpower would bring us hard up against the brute facts of survival as an over-resourced and underpopulated entity. Our present obsession with independence as the principal theme of foreign and defence policy may then seem to ourselves as heedless as it now does to most foreigners.

Preoccupation with Canada has never been an American obsession, but there is evidence of a changing attitude to us in the age of Vietnam. Persistent in American mythology, although never high in profile, has been the vision of Canada as the tranquil frontier and second childhood. It is a view which may be destroyed by recent events in Quebec, but Canada is a vast country. It is disconcerting to find Canada regarded as an oversized Walden Pond, a bucolic vision which Canadians have been anxious to cast off, but it is not unattractive to be a haven where brilliant and attractive Americans come to find rest and help fight our expressways. Most sober Canadians realize that we face many of the issues of American society and would like to avoid American mistakes. Many of the American immigrants, especially the intellectuals, see their mission in helping us do this. But we are not just the United States in the days of its innocence and we need different cures for different illnesses. Desegregation or school bussing is no panacea for our ethnic differences, and as for Vietnam, our national sin is under- rather than over-involvement in the affairs of other states. We must some time shake that paralyzing conviction that Canada's national purpose is catching up with the United States. Vietnam may have helped.

One is tempted to conclude, trying to avoid smugness, that the Vietnam war and all it has done to the United States, its soul and its image, has given Canadians more confidence in the quality of their own country or at least made them value more their habitat. But has it? Our liberation will not come through any form of obsession with the United States, even if it is hostile. Our artists and writers remain infatuated by the excitement and drama of Vietnam and the race riots — all of which they vividly deplore. The most successful English-Canadian play of the year is about the Chicago trials, a phenomenon which one critic described as "the ultimate US cultural invasion of our country." The expatriate actor, Donald Sutherland, whose views, if he were in Canada, would be called anti-American, says, "America is the most exciting country in the world because it is so volatile." Canadians have always been more attracted by its excitement than its republican virtue. The US has always been better theatre. The Vietnam war and the American tragedies it has provoked have fascinated Canadians and drawn their attention away from the incipient tragedy in their own country. And so the Canadian radicals — the Anglophones at least — have studied foreign remedies for domestic maladies which are unique. If it continues, that would be a sell-out by English-Canadian reformers with consequences as threatening to the Canadian survival as the sell-out of our physical resources with which they are preoccupied.

Notes

1. Official Canadians believed, of course, a lot of contradictory things about Indochina and United States policy. The attitude defined here is an over-simplification of the guiding assumptions.

2. In the *Monthly Report on Canadian External Relations* for 1967 there were 63 entries on Vietnam; in 1968, 15; and in 1969, 7.

3. See, for example, testimony of Dr. G.R. Lindsey at the Commons sub-committee on maritime forces, January 28th, 1970.

4. As late as 1966, according to polls of the Canadian Institute of Public Opinion (Gallup) only 31% of Canadians thought the United States should withdraw its troops from Vietnam whereas 18% favoured carrying on at the present level and 27% were for increasing the attacks. By 1967 these figures had shifted to 41%, 16% and 23%. In 1968, 35% of Canadians said they were grateful to the Americans for their efforts in Vietnam and 37% dissociated themselves from what the Americans were doing there. In May 1970, 36% said their opinion of the United States would go up if they withdrew all their troops from Vietnam and the same per cent said it would have no effect on their view of the great neighbour.

5. Since 1964 the annual immigration of Americans to Canada has doubled from 11,000 to 22,000 whereas the number of Canadians believed to have moved to the United States has declined from 50,000 to 30,000.

UNITED STATES-VIETNAM RELATIONS†

In 1964, Canadian diplomat Blair Seaborn was employed by the United States as an intermediary with the government of North Viet Nam. Seaborn, Canada's delegate on the International Control Commission, made six visits to Hanoi in 1964 and 1965. The purpose of these missions, the use to which the United States put Canada's good offices, and the sincerity of the peace bid, have become subjects of bitter controversy.

The Seaborn mission was documented and analyzed in the "Pentagon Papers", the top secret U.S. Defense Department documents leaked by Daniel Ellsberg. Seaborn's activities were covered in Volume VI. C.1. Previously unpublished, this volume formed the basis of a series of articles in the Toronto Globe and Mail *in July, 1973.*

Was Canada a genuine seeker after peace, or a cog in the American war machine? Did the United States use Canada to open negotiations, or to justify escalation of the war? All of these interpretations have been made in the press, on the strength of the fragments of the Pentagon Papers made available to this point.

The issues are important, too important to be decided on partial and partisan analyses. It is in this belief that the Forum *has decided to publish the Pentagon Papers on the Seaborn missions, and to publish them without commentary or analysis.*

We reproduce the full texts of the telegraphic despatches on the visits. The summaries, which precede the telegrams in Volume VI. C.1, have been omitted.

May 1, 1964

STATE 1821 (S/EXIDIS), PRIORITY, TO AMEMBASSY SAIGON, SENT 1 MAY, 1964. FOR THE AMBASSADOR FROM THE SECRETARY

I flew up to Ottawa yesterday to talk with Mike Pearson and Martin concerning the Canadian presence in Hanoi. . . .

They readily agreed that Seaborn should plan to spend much more time in Hanoi than have his predecessors in this assignment. They also accept as part of his mission an effort to establish ready access to and close contact with senior authorities in Hanoi, beginning with Ho Chi Minh. . . .

Following are some of the matters which we roughed out in Ottawa and which I will have further developed here. . . .

1. Seaborn should start out by checking as closely as he can what is on Ho Chi Minh's mind. We want to know whether he considers himself over-extended and exposed, or whether he feels confident that his Chinese allies will back him to the hilt. We want to know whether his current zeal is being forced upon him by pro-Chinese elements in his own camp, or whether he is impelled by his own ambitions.

2. Seaborn should get across to Ho and his colleagues the full measure of U.S. determination to see this thing through. He should draw upon examples in other

†"Canada and the Pentagon Papers," *Canadian Forum* (September 1973: 8-19).

parts of the world to convince them that if it becomes necessary to enlarge the military action, this is the most probable course that the U.S. would follow.

3. Seaborn should spread the word that he is puzzled by Hanoi's intentions. The North Vietnamese should understand that the U.S. wants no military bases or other footholds in South Viet Nam or Laos. If Hanoi would leave its neighbors alone, the U.S. presence in the area would diminish sharply.

4. The North Vietnamese should understand that there are many examples in which the Free World has demonstrated its willingness to live in peace with communist neighbors and to permit the establishment of normal economic relations between these two different systems. We recognize North Viet Nam's need for trade, and especially food, and consider that such needs could be fulfilled if peaceful condition were to prevail.

Pearson also agreed to instruct Seaborn and his people in general to work more actively on trying to break the Poles off from constant and active espousal of North Vietnamese aggression. He felt, however, that the Poles are playing something of a middle role in Sino-Soviet matters these days and doubted that there would be much profit in this.

SULLIVAN/RUSK

May 15, 1964

AMEMB SAIGON 2212 (S/NODIS), REC'D 15 MAY 64, 7:2 [*sic*] A.M.
FOR THE PRESIDENT FROM LODGE
    . . .

3. If prior to the Canadian's trip to Hanoi there has been a terroristic act of the proper magnitude, then I suggest that a specific target in North Viet Nam be considered as a prelude to his arrival. The Vietnamese Air Force must be made capable of doing this, and they should undertake this type of action.

4. I much prefer a selective use of Vietnamese Air power to an overt U.S. effort perhaps involving the total annihilation of all that has been built in North Viet Nam since 1954, because this would surely bring in the Chinese Communists, and might well bring in the Russians. Moreover, if you lay the whole country waste, it is quite likely that you will induce a mood of fatalism in the Viet Cong. Also, there will be nobody left in North Viet Nam on whom to put pressure. Furthermore, South Viet Nam's infrastructure might well be destroyed. What we are interested in here is not destroying Ho Chi Minh (as his successor would probably be worse than he is), but getting him to change his behavior. That is what President Kennedy was trying to do in October with Diem and with considerable success.
    . . .

6. This is a procedure the intensity of which we can constantly control and bring up to the point to which we think the Communist reaction would cease to be manageable. It should be covert and undertaken by the Vietnamese, but, of course, we must be clear in our own minds that we are ready and able to take care of whatever reaction there may be.

7. It is easy for us on the one hand to ignore our superiority as we did at the time of Berlin in 1948 (when we still had sole possession of the atomic bomb). It is also a relatively simple concept to go out and destroy North Viet Nam. What is complicated, but really effective, is to bring our power to bear in a precise way so as to get specific results.

8. Another advantage of this procedure is that when, as and if the time ever came that our military activities against the North became overt, we would be in a strong moral position both with regard to U.S. public opinion, the U.S. Congress, and the U.N. I say this because we would then have a record to show that we had given Ho Chi Minh fair warning to stop his murderous interference in the internal affairs of Viet Nam. Not only would we have given him fair warning, but we would have given him honest and valuable inducements in the way of some withdrawal of American personnel and in the way of economic aid, notably food . . . .

LODGE

May 22, 1964

STATE 2049 TO AMEMB SAIGON (TS/NODIS), PRIORITY, SENT 22 MAY 64, 7:40 P.M.
LITERALLY EYES ONLY FOR AMBASSADOR FROM SECRETARY
. . .

2. . . . in light of present Canadian attitudes we tend to see real difficulty in approaching the Canadians at this time with any message as specific as you suggest, i.e., that Hanoi be told by the Canadians "that they will be punished." But we are keeping this in mind and will see whether we can go further when we consult them next week than the more general type of message stated in my 1821. As you can see, the more specific message might lead us into a very difficult dialogue with the Canadians as to just what our plans really were.

3. On the other question, whether initial substantial attacks could be left without acknowledgement, it is our present view here that this would simply not be feasible . . . . Once such publicity occurred, I think you can see that the finger would point straight at us and that the President would then be put in perhaps a far more difficult position toward the American public and the Congress.

4. Thus, we are using GVN- or US-acknowledged enterprise as part of our main planning track at the present time, although we do recognize that something a little stronger than the present OPLAN 34-A might be carried on on the basis you propose.
. . .

BUNDY

May 25, 1964

AMEMBASSY SAIGON 2305 (TS/NODIS), REC'D 25 MAY 64, 5:22 A.M.
LITERALLY EYES ONLY FOR THE SECRETARY FROM LODGE

1. It is not rpt [repeat] not at all necessary that the Canadians either agree or disagree. What is important is that the Canadians transmit the message and be willing to do that and report back accurately what is said . . . .

2. The Communists have a great advantage over us in that they do things and never talk about them. We must not rpt not let them continue to have this advantage . . . .

LODGE

May 30, 1964

STATE 2133 TO AMEMBASSY SAIGON (TS/EXDIS), PRIORITY, SENT 30 MAY 1964, 10:40 A.M.

FOR THE AMBASSADOR FROM THE ACTING SECRETARY

President and Mac Bundy met May 28 in New York with Canadian Prime Minister Pearson. Simultaneously Sullivan met in Ottawa with Foreign Minister Martin, Deputy Under Secretary Smith, and ICC Commissioner-Designate Seaborn.

President told Pearson that he wishes Hanoi to know, that while he is a man of peace, he does not intend to permit the North Vietnamese to take over Southeast Asia. He needs a confidential and responsible interlocutor to carry the message of U.S. attitudes to Hanoi. In outlining the U.S. position there was some discussions of QTE [quote] carrots and sticks UNQUOTE.

Pearson, after expressing willingness to lend Canadian good offices to this endeavor, indicated some concern about this nature of QTE sticks UNQTE [unquote]. He stipulated that he would have great reservations about the use of nuclear weapons, but indicated that the punitive striking of discriminate targets by careful iron bomb attacks would be QTE a different thing UNQTE. He said he would personally understand our resort to much measures if the messages transmitted through the Canadian channel failed to produce any alleviation of North Vietnamese aggression, and that Canada would transmit messages around this framework.

In Ottawa Sullivan found much the same disposition among Canadian officials. While Foreign Minister Martin seemed a little nervous about the prospect of QTE expanding the war UNQTE, External Affairs officials readily assented to the use of Seaborn as an interlocutor . . . .

Seaborn, who struck Sullivan as an alert, intelligent and steady officer, readily agreed to these conditions and has made immediate plans for an accelerated departure . . . .
. . .

BALL

June 1, 1964

MEMO TO: G—MR. U. ALEXIS JOHNSON, FROM S/VN—JOSEPH A. MENDELHALL, DATED JUNE 1, 1964 (TS)

Subject: Instructions for Canadian Interlocutor with Hanoi.

I am enclosing a copy of the "Outline of Subjects for Mr. Seaborn" which Bill Sullivan prepared prior to departure for Honolulu. He gave a copy of this general paper of instructions to Mr. Robinson, Minister-Counsellor of the Canadian Embassy, on May 30.

At your request I have prepared and am enclosing a draft of a further outline in specific terms of the message which we would expect the Canadian interlocutor to get across in Hanoi. This further outline is based on the assumptions that (a) a U.S. decision has been taken to act against North Viet-Nam and (b) we plan to use "carrots" as well as a "stick" on Hanoi. I believe that we would probably not wish to hand this further outline to the Canadian Government pending the initial soundings of the Canadian interlocutor in Hanoi pursuant to Mr. Sullivan's original set of instructions.

Outline of Subjects for Mr. Seaborn

1. The President wishes Hanoi to understand that he is fundamentally a man of peace. However, he does not intend to let the North Vietnamese take over all of Southeast Asia. He wishes to have a highly confidential responsible interlocutor who will deliver this message to the authorities in Hanoi and report back their reaction.

2. The messages which may be transmitted through this channel would involve an indication of the limitations both upon U.S. ambitions in Southeast Asia and upon U.S. patience with Communist provocation. The interlocutor or his Government need not agree with nor associate themselves with the messages that are passed. The only requirement is that there be faithful transmittal of the messages in each direction.

3. Mr. Seaborn should arrive in Hanoi as soon as possible and establish his credentials as a political personality who can and will deal with senior representatives of the Hanoi regime.

4. Mr. Seaborn should also, by listening to the arguments and observing the attitudes of the North Vietnamese, form an evaluation of their mental outlook. He should be particularly alert to (a) differences with respect to the Sino-Soviet split, (b) frustration or war weariness, (c) indications of North Vietnamese desire for contacts with the West, (d) evidences of cliques or factions in the Party or Government, and (e) evidence of differences between the political and the military.

5. Mr. Seaborn should explore the nature and the prevalence of Chinese Communist influence in North Viet Nam; and perhaps through direct discussions with the Soviet representatives, evaluate the nature and influence of the Soviets.

6. Mr. Seaborn should stress to appropriate North Vietnamese officials that U.S. policy is to see to it that North Viet Nam contains itself and its ambitions within the territory allocated to its administration by the 1954 Geneva Agreements. He should stress that U.S. policy in South Viet Nam is to preserve the integrity of that state's territory against guerrilla subversion.

7. He should state that the U.S. does not seek military bases in the area and that the U.S. is not seeking to overthrow the Communist regime in Hanoi.

8. He should stipulate that the U.S. is fully aware of the degree to which Hanoi controls and directs the guerrilla action in South Viet Nam and that the U.S. holds Hanoi directly responsible for that action. He should similarly indicate U.S. awareness of North Vietnamese control over the Pathet Lao movement in Laos and the degree of North Viet Nam involvement in that country. He should specifically indicate U.S. awareness of North Vietnamese violations of Laotian territory along the infiltration route into South Viet Nam.

9. Mr. Seaborn should point out that the nature of U.S. commitment in South Viet Nam is not confined to the territorial issue in question. He should make it clear that the U.S. considers the confrontation with North Vietnamese subversive guerrilla action as part of the general Free World confrontation with this type of violent subversion in other lesser developed countries. Therefore, the U.S. stake in resisting a North Vietnamese victory in South Viet Nam has a significance of world-wide proportions.

10. Mr. Seaborn can point to the many examples of U.S. policy in tolerance of peaceful coexistence with Communist regimes, such as Yugoslavia, Poland, etc. He can hint at the economic and other benefits which have accrued to those countries because their policy of communism has confined itself to the development of their own national territories and has not sought to expand into other areas.

11. Mr. Seaborn can couple this statment with the frank acknowledgement that U.S. public and official patience with North Vietnamese aggression is growing extremely thin.

12. Insofar as Mr. Seaborn considers it might be educational he could review the relative military strengths of the U.S., North Viet Nam, and the available resources of Communist China in Southeast Asia.

13. In sum, the purpose of Mr. Seaborn's mission in North Viet Nam would be as an interlocutor with both active and passive functions. On the passive side, he should report either observations or direct communications concerning North Vietnamese attitude toward extrication from or escalation of military activities. On the active side, he should establish his credentials with the North Vietnamese as an authoritative channel of communications with the U.S. In each of these functions it would be hoped that Mr. Seaborn would assume the posture that the decision as to the future course of events in Southeast Asia rests squarely with Hanoi.

Further Outline for Mr. Seaborn

1. The U.S. objective is to maintain the independence and territorial integrity of South Viet-Nam. This means that the South Vietnamese Government in Saigon must be able to exercise its authority throughout the territory south of the 17th Parallel without encountering armed resistance directed and supported by Hanoi.

2. We know that Hanoi can stop the war in South Viet-Nam if it will do so. The virtually complete cease-fires which have obtained at Tet time for the past two years demonstrate the ability of Hanoi to control all Viet Cong operations in South Viet-Nam if it has the will to do so.

3. In order to stop the war in South Viet-Nam the United States is prepared to follow alternative courses of action with respect to North Viet-Nam.

(a) Unless Hanoi stops the war within a specified time period (i.e., ceases all attacks, acts of terror, sabotage or armed propaganda or other armed resistance to government authority by the VC), the United States will initiate action by air and naval means against North Viet-Nam until Hanoi does agree to stop the war.

(b) If Hanoi will agree to stop the war, the United States will take the following steps:

(1) Undertake to obtain the agreement of Saigon to a resumption of trade between North Viet-Nam and South Viet-Nam, which would be helpful to North Viet-Nam in view of the complementarity of the two zones of Viet-Nam and the food difficulties now suffered by North Viet-Nam.

(2) Initiate a program of foodstuffs assistance to North Viet-Nam either on a relief grant basis under Title II of Public Law 480 or on a sales for local currency basis under Title I PL-480 (as in Poland and Yugoslavia).

(3) Remove U.S. foreign assets controls from the assets of North Viet-Nam and reduce controls on U.S. trade with North Viet-Nam to the level now applicable to the USSR (i.e., strategic items only).

(4) Recognize North Viet-Nam diplomatically, and if Hanoi is interested, undertake an exchange of diplomatic representatives.

(5) Remove U.S. forces from South Viet-Nam on a phased basis, winding up with a reduction to the level of 350 military advisors or trainers as permitted under the Geneva Accords. (This was the number of U.S. military personnel in Viet-Nam when the Geneva Accords were signed in 1954.)

4. If Hanoi stops resistance in South Viet-Nam, the United States and South Vietnamese Governments will permit Hanoi to withdraw any Viet Cong personnel whom it may wish from South Viet-Nam. The Government of South Viet-Nam will also make a clear public announcement of full amnesty for all rebels who discontinue armed resistance to the authority of the Government.

5. If Hanoi agrees to cease resistance, the order from Hanoi to the Viet Cong units and personnel can be issued, if Hanoi prefers, either publicly or confidentially through the communications channels from Hanoi to the Viet Cong. The test the U.S. will apply will be whether or not all armed resistance to the authority of the Government at Saigon actually stops.

6. Timetable for these actions:

(a) All hostilities must cease within one week of the approach to the authorities at Hanoi. If they have not stopped within that time, the U.S. will immediately initiate air and naval action against North Viet-Nam.

(b) If agreement is reached between the U.S. and North Viet-Nam on the cessation of resistance in South Viet-Nam, the cessation of hostilities will be preceded by a general GVN amnesty announcement.

(c) If the DRV desires to repatriate Viet Cong from South Viet-Nam, this can be done over whatever period that DRV desires.

(d) If the DRV desires to announce an agreement publicly with the United States, the entire package of measures on both sides can be announced within three days of the complete cessation of hostilities. If the DRV does not desire a public announcement of its agreement to have the Viet Cong cease resistance, then the United States measures of concession to North Viet-Nam can be announced only over a phased period starting one week from the complete cessation of hostilities. Announcement of all steps taken by the U.S. as concessions to North Viet-Nam would be completed by three months from the cessation of hostilities.

(e) U.S. forces would be removed from South Viet Nam on a phased basis over a period of one year from the date of cessation of resistance to the Government of South Viet-Nam. At the end of one year U.S. military personnel would be down to the 350 permitted by the Geneva Accords.

June 18, 1964

STATE 115 TO AMEMBASSY (TS/EXDIS), SENT JULY 11, 1964, 5:19 P.M. EMBTEL 74.

As requested final paragraph reftel, texts first two Seaborn messages sent Ottawa follow:
1. June 20, 1964 message. QTE. Initial visit to Hanoi: Call on PM Pham Van Dong.

PM received me for hour and a half Thurs morning Jun 18 with only Lt Col Mai Lam, number two man of PAVN liaison mission, present. Conversation was entirely in French with no RPT no use of Vietnamese and interpretation which had been practice in earlier lower level calls on Vice Ministers of Defence and Foreign Affairs.

2. After very brief preliminaries, I told PM that I had on instructions specially requested interview with him and/or President Ho Chi Minh and I had oral message to convey from PM Pearson. Perhaps best explanation was to be found in my TSEC instructions from my PM which I was authorized to show him. Pham Van Dong read letter of May 30 from PM Pearson to myself carefully once and then quickly again. He said he greatly appreciated role Canada had undertaken to play, which he felt was important and desirable, and wished me also personal success in task. From tone of conversation thereafter, I believe Pham Van Dong has understood and accepted and perhaps welcomed my role as intermediary.

3. I said that I hoped he would let me elaborate on very general lines of my instructions from PM and in effect to convey to him first general msg from USA Govt. I prefaced msg by citing our close and friendly relationship with USA, our good understanding of American intentions and aspirations, and our constant detailed and intimate exchange of views and information with USA which gave us excellent insight into American thinking. On this basis, we were convinced that President Johnson was man of peace, that he would take pains to avoid and avert situations which could lead to confrontation between major powers, but that insofar as Southeast Asia was concerned he was determined that it would not RPT not fall under Communist control as result of subversion and guerrilla warfare. Intentions in Southeast Asia were essentially peaceful and USA ambitions were limited, but USA was also determined and its patience before provocation was not RPT not limitless.

4. This said, I went on to convey USA msg, following as closely as I could, though not RPT not necessarily in same order, points made in paras 6 through 11 of WASHDC tel 1951 May 30. In course of conversation, I made all these points explicitly and without circumlocution and in some cases with elaboration and repetition. I shall not RPT not therefore repeat them in this tel. I did not RPT not specifically make point in para 12 other than to say that if conflict in area should escalate, which I did not RPT not think was in anyone's interest, the greatest devastation would of course result for the DRVN itself.

5. I am convinced from later conversation that Pham Van Dong understood importance and context of msg I conveyed and seriousness with which USA views situation in Southeast Asia. To that extent, initial purpose of first contact has been successfully accomplished, he gave me careful hearing with no RPT no attempt to interrupt, disagree, contradict or even express displeasure even to

assertions which were clearly unpalatable or with which he would not RPT not agree, e.g. Viet Minh complicity in Pathet Lao activities and SVN insurgency and DRVN responsibility for future development of situation in area. This is not RPT not of course to say that I convinced him of correctness of USA interpretations (which obviously I did not RPT not) nor that he fully believes even yet firmness and durability of USA determination in area. He could not RPT not however claim that he has not RPT not had USA views and intentions conveyed to him most explicitly.

6. I concluded opening statement by saying I was at Prime Minister's disposal now or at any later stage to convey to USA via Ottawa any message he wished to give me orally or in writing. He said he had no RPT no immediate and specific message to send at this time, but that he would like to expound on DRVN point of view with particular reference to points I had raised in my comment. I shall be sending subsequently detailed report, based on notes made as he talked, of Prime Minister's remarks in his main statement and in course of subsequent discussion. In this initial tel however I shall summarize what appears to me to be his main point and give my first impressions.

7. Pham Van Dong opened remarks by saying we must learn to coexist and to find solution to problem which has wracked Indochina for 25 years. But just solution is only way to provide stability. What just solution means in DRVN is, as President Ho Chi Minh has explained (A) USA withdrawal (B) peace and neutrality for SVN in Cambodian pattern in accordance with programme of Liberation Front which must participate in determination of Vietnam as result of negotiation when SVN ready for negotiation.

8. PM said USA must demonstrate what he would consider good will but he realized it will not RPT not be easy for USA to do so. USA can increase aid to SVN in all fields, give greater material support to SVN army and increase its own army personnel also. If so, war will be prolonged and intensified, but QTE our people UNQTE will go on struggling and resisting. QTE It is impossible for westerners to understand strength of people's will to resist, to continue, to struggle. It has astonished us too UNQTE. Prospect for USA and friends is QTE sans issue UNQTE. SVN mercenaries and USA soldiers do not RPT not have heart in fighting whereas support for objective of Liberation Front is growing among Buddhists, students, intellectuals. Lippmann sees no RPT no light at end of tunnel and others speak of new Dien Bien Phu.

9. DRVN Govt, said PM, did not RPT not yet have concrete suggestions to put forward, but this was general line of their thinking.

10. In separate tel without "Bacon" restrictions I shall report in greater detail PM's comments on Laos situation. Essence of his remarks (A) only viable solution was return to status quo ante April coup d'etat and Govt. of National Coalition as per Geneva Accord of 1962 (B) necessity of convening 14 nation conference to achieve this result and (C) essentiality of no RPT no American interference in Laos. He said DRVN was very worried by step-up of USA military activities in Laos and complained of USA overflights of DRVN territory and of commando raids across border. He denied that PAVN had sent QTE units UNQTE across border to aid Pathet Lao but did not RPT not specifically deny my earlier state-

ment that USA was aware DRVN were helping Pathet Lao and Viet Cong with men, arms and material.

11. Returning to question of SVN, Pham Van Dong said situation could be summed up as choice between QTE guerre a outrance UNQTE which USA cannot RPT not win in any event in the long run or alternative neutrality for SVN.

12. I thanked PM for detailed exposé of DRVN views which I said I would transmit faithfully to my government. At this he said disarmingly that I might not RPT not believe all he had said but he wanted to assure me he has spoken in all sincerity and frankness. I shall not RPT not be so rash as to comment on this other than to say that he took pains throughout interview to give impression of quiet sincerity, of realization of seriousness of what we were discussing and of lack of truculence or belligerency. Certainly in presence and mental stature PM is head and shoulders above few other North Vietnamese whom I met and undoubtedly an impressive Communist personality by any standards.

13. At this stage I told PM I had no RPT no further formal message to convey but that I would like to put a few personal comments and questions.

14. I said I was interested to hear from him that as a condition for restoring peace SVN should become neutral as a first step prior to unification. He stopped me and said he had not RPT not referred to neutrality as a first step only. Whether SVN would continue neutral would depend upon people of SVN. He did not RPT not prejudge. As for Liberation Front I said I realized it represents a certain force in SVN, though not RPT not in my view all people as the propoganda asserted nor even majority. He did not RPT not demur at this downgrading. I said I appreciated that the Front would have to participate should a coalition ever emerge. My fear however was that coalition would soon be taken over by Front as had happened in other countries and that the rep elements would suffer or be ousted. PM merely said there was no RPT no reason to have such fears.

15. I then asked whether PM appreciated fully that USA's continued acceptance of obligations towards allies in SVN had implications which extended far beyond Southeast Asia and related to USA determination to resist guerrilla subversion in Asia, Africa and Latin-America? PM laughed and said he did indeed appreciate it. A USA defeat in SVN would in all probability start a chain reaction which would extend much farther, but USA should understand that principles and stakes involved were just as high for Liberation Front in SVN and its supporters and this helped to explain their determination to continue to struggle regardless of sacrifice.

16. PM said he was glad to hear that USA did not RPT not have aggressive intentions against DRVN and did not RPT not intend to attack it. I corrected him at this point and said USA did not RPT not want to carry war to north but might be obliged to do so if pushed too far by continuation of Viet Minh-assisted pressures in SVN. I repeated that USA patience was not RPT not limitless. PM said if war was pushed to north, QTE *nous sommes un pays socialists [sic], un des pays socialistes, vous savez, et le people [sic] se dressera* UNQTE. (This was the closest he came at any time to hinting that DRVN could or would count on outside assistance in event of attack). But, he said, we shall not RPT not provoke them.

17. Conversation had now continued for almost hour and a half and PM made move as if to terminate, so I did not RPT not put further questions. He asked me to send greetings to PM Pearson and to say that if my mission could contribute to this (grp missing) solution Canada would have done something very useful. I said I felt it was at minimum essential that no RPT no irrevocable steps be taken due to misunderstanding of intentions and objectives and that USA felt this strongly too. PM agreed, and said he looked forward to further conversation during my next (grp missing) when I would certainly meet Ho Chi Minh. President was on leave at present but had sent greetings. I closed by thanking him for time given me and repeating I was at his disposal anytime he wished to see me.

18. In separate msg I shall report first very tentative impressions on questions asked in paras four and five of WASHDC tel 1951 May 30.

19. I expect to be seeing Mr. Lodge shortly after my return to Saigon (this tel is being drafted in plane enroute from Hanoi) and will show him copy.

20. I would welcome comments from you and State Department and any suggestions for talking points for further conversations on next visit to Hanoi. END QUOTE.

2. June 22, 1964 message.

QUOTE. DRVN: ATTITUDES AND OUTLOOK.

To convey specific message and to report DRVN comment is relatively simple. To attempt evaluation suggested paras 4 and 5 WASHDC tel 1951 May 30 is extremely difficult on basis of 3 day visit and a few conversations especially for someone who has never had previous direct experience with Asia let alone Vietnam. Following comments, to be read in conjunction with my reftel, are therefore highly tentative and consist mainly of negative evidence.

Sino-Soviet split and prevalence of Chinese Communist influence:

2. No RPT no Vietnamese with whom I spoke made even reference by name to USSR or China. My enquiry of Vice-Foreign Minister Tien as to DRVN views on latest Soviet call for mtg on world CPS drew reply that question concerned party only and was not RPT not within competence of Foreign Ministry. To direct question he said DRVN had not RPT not commented on latest Moscow call but general views could be found in press. Eastern Europeans were closed mouthed on this issue. PM made only most oblique reference to DRVN's membership in group of socialist countries in context of possible results of USA taking war to north.

3. French Del Gen Debuzon asserts DRVN leaders are honestly concerned by bad effect of split on fortunes of World Communist Movement and have avoided polemics against USSR even when adopting Peking line. He thinks they fear definitive rupture which would (throw?) them full under Chinese control, a fate they hope to resist as long as possible. They are not RPT not however strong enough to play dispute for their own purposes as have Romanians.

4. In economic field, probes with Vietnamese and Eastern Europeans were little more rewarding. Strong Vietnamese emphasis at present in official propaganda and in private converstion is on lifting up by own boot-straps and near autarchy. During lengthy tour of exhibition of ten years of DRVN, guide RPT

guide managed to describe economic progress for at least half hour without once mentioning aid received from other socialist countries, (though?) when questioned Director admitted it had been great with lion's share by USSR and China. Reps of smaller Eastern European powers told me of their relatively modest aid and trade but would not RPT not be drawn on relative weight of Soviet and Chinese aid. Soviet Charge said that Soviet aid in form of technicians and training of students in USSR had diminished as DRVN capacity for training own cadres had grown. He admitted Chinese were still very active in aid field but would not RPT not be specific.

5. Foreign reps in Hanoi tell me Chinese technicians etc are not RPT not much in evidence but this proves little. Unskilled eye can easily fail to distinguish between North Vietnamese and Southern Chinese.

Cliques in factions in Party or Govt:

6. I can add nothing from observation or conversation in Hanoi to analysis of commonly accepted line-up of pro-Chinese extremists and pro-Soviet moderates other than to draw attention to moderateness of Pham Van Dong's tone during interview. Ho Chi Minh appears still to enjoy tremendous prestige and is venerated as demi-God, perhaps above any factional strife, non-Communist reps in Hanoi and Nationalist Chinese Ambassador here warn against over-emphasis on factionalism as (something?) from which West might derive benefit. National pride is apparent from Pham Van Dong's remarks and from call for economic self-help.

Differences between political and military:

7. I can adduce no RPT no evidence one way or the other.

Frustration or war weariness:

8. I can bring forward no RPT no evidence that such (exists?) and indeed all Vietnamese emphasized quiet determination to go on struggling as long as necessary to achieve in long run. While some discount should perhaps be made for fact they were speaking to me, these assertions carried a good deal of conviction as if really believed. This applies particularly strongly to Pham Van.

9. Hanoi itself though austere looked much less run down than I expected. Team site officers and others who have been north over course of year say supply of consumer goods while still pitifully small (has?) increased markedly. I saw some queues but no RPT no evidence of malnutrition nor RPT nor did I find people looking markedly sadder or more serious than those in the south. Team site officers have seen no RPT no evidence of overt discontent among people.

Desire for contacts with West:

10. Pham Van Dong seemed genuinely grateful for intermediary role Canada was trying to plan and also I think for USA desire to get msg through. It will take subsequent visits to decide whether this reflects interest in or desire to emerge from isolation, let alone interest in any accommodation or settlement of Laos and SVN problem.

Conclusions:

11. Tentative conclusion is that we would be unwise at this stage to count on war weariness or factionalism within leadership or possible material advantages to DRVN or kind of Asian Titoism as of such importance to cause DRVN to jump at chance of reaching accommodation with USA in this area. Certainly on

my brief visit I detected no RPT no evidence to suggest (as some columnists have been doing) that starvation, war weariness and political discontent are bringing regime close to collapse and that they would therefore grasp at any straw which might enable them to save something before country falls apart.

12. Prospect of war being carried to north may give greater pause for thought. But I would hesitate to say that DRVN are yet convinced, despite USA public statements and moves and private message I have conveyed, that USA would be prepared to take this step, ultimate consequences of which could be start of World War III. I am also inclined to think that DRVN leaders are completely convinced that military action at any level is not RPT not going to bring success for USA and Government forces in SVN. They are almost as completely convinced that Khanh Govt is losing ground on political front and are confident that in fullness of time success is assured for Liberation Front supported by DRVN.

13. I would however caution on the extreme difficulty of forming meaningful judgements on basis of brief or even longer period spent in North Vietnam, which is a singularly closed society even by Communist standards. Press is very uninformative and I suspect that most foreign reps including those of Eastern Europe know little of what is going on. Soviet and Chinese Ambassadors are probably only ones taken at all into DRVN confidence and councils and I am not RPT not sanguine about former, who was unfortunately absent during my visit, opening up to me at least on first mtg. I shall persevere of course with foreign representatives and North Vietnamese but the limitations should be fully understood.

END QUOTE

BALL

REMARKS OF PRIME MINISTER PHAM VAN DONG
TO J.B. SEABORN, HANOI, JUNE 18, 1964

President Ho Chi Minh has explained what we mean by a just solution. First it requires an American withdrawal from Indochina. Secondly it means that the affairs of the South must be arranged by the people of the South. It must provide for the participation of the Liberation Front. No other group represents the broad wishes of the people. The programme of the Front is the best one possible. There must be peace and neutrality for South Vietnam, neutrality in the Cambodian manner. Thirdly, a just solution means reunification of the country. This is a *drame, national, fondamental*. But we want peaceful reunification, without military pressure. We want negotiation 'round a table. There must be sincere satisfaction with the arrangement for it to be viable. We are in no hurry. We are willing to talk but we shall wait till SVN is ready. We are a divided people, without even personal links across the dividing line.

The United States must show good will, but it is not easy for the USA to do so. Meanwhile the war intensifies. USA aid may increase in all areas, not only for the SVN army but in terms of USA army personnel as well. I suffer to see the war go on, develop, intensify. Yet our people are determined to struggle. It is impossible, quite impossible (excuse me for saying this) for you Westerner's to understand the force of the people's will to resist and to continue. The struggle of the people exceeds the imagination. It has astonished us too.

Since the fall of the Ngo brothers, it has been a *cascade*. The prospect of the USA and its friends in SVN is *sans issue*. Reinforcing the Khanh army doesn't count. The people have had enough. The SVN mercenaries have sacrificed themselves without honour. The Americans are not loves, for they commit atrocities. How can the people suffer such exactions and terror?

. . .

Let me stress, insofar as the internal situation in SVN is concerned, the realistic nature of the Liberation Front's programme. It is impossible to have a representative government which excludes the Front. The idea of a government of national coalition *fait boule de niege* [sic] in the South. The Laos pattern of 1962 should serve as a guide for SVN.

As for Laos, we are not reassured by the USA role. We must return to the '62 Geneva Accord. The present government of Laos is *fantoche*. Souvanna Phouma, who is no better than a prisoner of the military, has acted like a coward. His present government provides no solution.

We do not send units to the Pathlet Lao. We do not demand more than a return to the situation which existed prior to the April coup. But there must be no American interference in Laos. There are daily incursions of air space across the Laotian border by overflights of military aircraft and by commando units bent on sabotage.

. . .

A new conference of the fourteen parties is necessary. Restoration of peace and neutrality for Laos are impossible otherwise. There is little utility in the Polish proposal. Only the 14-nation conference is competent to deal with the Laos situation.

To return to Viet Nam, it is a question of a *guerre a outrance*, which the USA won't win in any event, or neutrality. He had not (as I had suggested) referred to neutrality as a first step only. Whether SVN would continue neutral would depend upon the people of SVN. He did not prejudge the issue.

The DRVN realize that the "loss" of SVN for the Americans would set off (what was the atomic expression?) a chain reaction which would extend much further. The USA is in a difficult position, because Khanh's troops will no longer fight. If the war gets worse, we shall suffer greater [sic] but we shall win. If we win in the South, the people of the world will turn against the USA. Our people therefore accept the sacrifices, whatever they may be. But the DRVN will not enter the war.

If the war were pushed to the North *nous sommes un pays socialiste, vous savez, et le peuple se dressera*. But we shall not force the USA, we shall not provoke the USA.

As far as the ICC is concerned, we are very glad to have you here. But don't put too many items on the agenda, don't give yourself too much work to do.

August 8, 1964

STATE 169 TO AMEMBASSY, OTTAWA, STTE 383 TO AMEMBASSY SAIGON, IMME-
DIATE, (TS/EXDIS), SENT 8 AUG. 64, 4:41 P.M.

Following message was handed directly to Canadian Embassy here for transmittal to Seaborn by fastest channel. This is for your information only.

QUOTE Canadians are urgently asked to have Seaborn during August 10
visit make following points (as having been conveyed to him by U.S. Government since August 6):

A. Re Tonkin Gulf actions, which almost certainly will come up:

1. . . . Neither the MADDOX or any other destroyer was in any way associated with any attack on the DRV islands.

2. Regarding the August 4 attack by the DRV on the two U.S. destroyers,
the Americans were and are at a complete loss to understand the DRV motive
. . . . About the only reasonable hypothesis was that North Viet-Nam was intent
either upon making it appear that the United States was a INNER QUOTE
paper tiger END INNER QUOTE or upon provoking the United States.

3. The American response was directed solely to patrol aircraft and installa-
tions acting in direct support of them. As President Johnson stated: INNER
QUOTE Our response for the present will be limited and fitting. END INNER
QUOTE.

4. In view of uncertainty aroused by the deliberate and unprovoked DRV
attacks this character, U.S. has necessarily carried out precautionary deployments of
additional air power to SVN and Thailand.

B. Re basic American position:

. . .

9. Mr. Seaborn should conclude with the following new points:

a. That the events of the past few days should add credibility to the statement
made last time, that INNER QUOTE U.S. public and official patience with
North Vietnamese aggression is growing extremely thin. END INNER QUOTE.

b. That the U.S. Congressional Resolutions was [sic] passed with near unanimity,
strongly re-affirming the unity and determination of the U.S. Government and
people not only with respect to any further attacks on U.S. military forces but
more broadly to continue to oppose firmly, by all necessary means, DRV efforts
to subvert and conquer South Viet-Nam and Laos.

c. That the U.S. has come to the view that the DRV role in South Viet-Nam
and Laos is critical. If the DRV persists in its present course, it can expect to
continue to suffer the consequences.

d. That the DRV knows what it must do if the peace is to be restored.

e. That the U.S. has ways and means of measuring the DRV's participation
in, and direction and control of, the war on South Viet-Nam and in Laos and
will be carefully watching the DRV's response to what Mr. Seaborn is telling
them. UNQUOTE.

RUSK

August 9, 1964

STATE 389 TO AMEMBASSY SAIGON (TS/EXDIS)
FLASH, SENT 9 AUGUST 64, 6:42 A.M.
REF SAIGON 362, REPEATED INFO AS SAIGON 8 TO OTTAWA

. . . request you immediately contact Seaborn with view to deleting two words QUOTE to continue UNQUOTE from last sentence paragraph 9 c.

RUSK

August 18, 1964

SAIGON 467 TO SECSTATE (TS/EXDIS) PRIORITY, REC'D 18 AUGUST 64, 2:07 P.M.
DEPTEL 383

Seaborn called on Sullivan August 17 to show him copies his reports (which presumably Dept has seen) concerning his recent visit to Hanoi. As Dept probably aware, Seaborn was under instructions omit last two points reftel in his discussions with Pham Van Dong, but otherwise feels he made all points practically verbatim.

Principal observation which Seaborn expressed re his conversation was sense satisfaction that Pham Van Dong, despite his angry reaction to Seaborn presentation, was unhesitating in his statement that channel of communication to U.S. should stay open and that Seaborn should continue to bear U.S. messages, no RPT no matter how unpleasant they may be.
. . .

TAYLOR

August 17, 1964

REPORT OF CONVERSATION WITH PRIME MINISTER
PHAM VAN DONG–HANOI, AUGUST 13, 1964

(The following is close to a verbatim account of Prime Minister Pham Van Dong's remarks.)

2. We wish to have the best possible relations with the ICC . . . .

3. . . . The Government of the USA is obliged to carry out aggression against us. Official circles both political and military have decided that it is necessary to carry the war to the north in order to find a way out of the impasse in which they find themselves in the south. This is their goal and they have been pushed by it into attacking us. We see in this fact the essential cause of the act of aggression of August 5 . . . .

4. President Johnson worries also of course about the coming electoral battle in which it is necessary to outbid the Republican candidate. Hence the attempt to internationalize the war.

5. If we throw light in this way on the real reasons for the incidents in the Gulf of Tonkin, it enables us to make some evaluation of what the situation may be in the future. The essential causes, that is to say, remain and it is therefore possible that the Government of the USA will be led to new acts of aggression. They have said it themselves.

6. This is a very dangerous situation, I repeat a very dangerous situation. . . . There is no way out in the south and they are trying to carry the war to the north as a way out. That is the real miscalculation. Up to now we have tried to avoid serious trouble; but it becomes more difficult now because the war has been carried to our territory . . . .

7. . . . We are a socialist country and socialist countries will come to our aid . . .

8. If the USA is thinking of a new Korean war it should realize that conditions are not the same . . . . If the war comes to North Vietnam, it will come to the whole of Southeast Asia with unforseecable consequences . . . . We do not hide the fact that the people will have to make many sacrifices, but we are in a state of legitimate defence because the war is imposed upon us.

9. . . .

10. The solution lies in a return to the Geneva Agreement of 1954 . . . .

11. The ICC is called upon to play a more and more important role . . . .

12. . . .

August 19, 1964

MEMORANDUM FOR: THE SECRETARY
FROM: S/VN–MICHAEL V. FORRESTAL
THROUGH: S/S
Herewith the second installment of the Seaborn talks.

The verbatim account of the conversation still remains to come from Ottawa. Attachment

FM CANDEL SAIGON TSEC BACON (TS/EYES ONLY/NO DIS), IMMED., (FOR IMMEDIATE DELIVERY TO ARNOLD SMITH AND FAREAST DIV) REF OUR TEL 419, AUG15

Pham Van Dong's angry reaction to latest USA msg is not RPT not surprising . . . .

2. After visit to Hanoi and interview with PM I am still little wiser as to DRVN motivations in launching Aug 2 and Aug 4 attacks on USA vessels . . . . They may also believe, despite President Johnson's reassurances, that there is chance of new USA attack even if they do not RPT not provoke it. Again, they are at least acting as if this were their estimate and are taking various precautionary measures (air raid drills, slit trenches, brick bunkers, etc. and reportedly at least preparation for evacuation of women and children).

3. . . .

4. Pham Van Dong gave no RPT no indication of being worried by firmness of USA msg I delivered and in fact its immediate effect was to project anger rather than desire to discuss way out. But I find it mildly encouraging that he did calm down as he talked further and significant that (he?) should state unequivocally that he wanted to keep open DRVN-USA channel of communication. I do not RPT not however as result of this interview see likelihood of his using it for some time at least to put forward to USA side proposal or requests for discussion. I think he is genuinely convinced that things are bound to go his way in Indochina and that there is therefore no RPT no need to seek compromises. . . .

SEABORN

December 3, 1964

STATE 1210 TO AMEMBASSY SAIGON, STATE 645 TO
AMEMBASSY OTTAWA, IMMEDIATE, (TOP S/EXDIS),
SENT 3 DEC 64, 6:51 P.M.

The following message has been handed directly to Canadian Embassy here for transmittal to Seaborn through fastest channel. This is for your information only.

Quote: Canadians are asked to have Seaborn take following position during his next visit to Hanoi which, we understand, is currently scheduled for December 7th or 10th (Embtel 1618).

The United States has nothing to add to the points made by Seaborn on his last visit to Hanoi in August. All the recent indications from Washington, however, point to a continued and increasing determination on the part of the U.S. to assist the South Vietnamese in their struggle. Although he has no specific message on this trip, Seaborn has noted support of Viet Cong, and this together with reported high-level meetings Washington makes him feel that time is ripe for any new message Hanoi may wish to convey.

Seaborn should convey attitude of real personal concern over the growing possibility of direct confrontation between GVN and DRVN. End quote.

FYI: Purpose of this approach is to probe for any new DRV reactions.

HARRIMAN

CANDEL SAIGON 773 TO SEC BACON (TS/NODIS), IMMEDIATE, (FOR IMMEDIATE
DELIVERY TO ARNOLD SMITH AND FAREAST DIV)
REF: WASHDC TEL 4189 DEC 5 AND YOUR TEL 7833 DEC 4
. . .

2. In mtg with Ha Van Lau only Vietnamese personality with whom I talked, I developed theme in Washington DC Tel 4189 . . . . He did not RPT not pick up directly any of these ideas. Notes were taken throughout meeting and I assume higher authorities will be informed . . . .

3. . . . .

SEABORN

SAIGON 774 TO TT EXTERNAL (CONFIDENTIAL), IMMEDIATE DE DELHI TT LDN
EMBPARIS, NATO PARIS, GENEVA, WASH DC, PERMISNY CDS
. . .

3. Foreign Reps with whom I spoke all referred to DRVN concern over possibility of USA air strikes, though there was differing interpretations as to how likely DRVN thought this to be. None seemed to expect anything of a serious nature to be imminent. To those who tended to play down likelihood, I cautioned against complacency and said I did not RPT not rule out possibility of air strikes in retaliation of growing DRVN complicity in SVN insurgency. I detected during this visit to Hanoi none of tension (partly officially inspired, partly genuine) which was so evident in mid-August just after Gulf of Tonkin incident. Nor, as already reported, is there any sign of renewed digging of air-raid shelters or widespread drilling of militia.

4. . . .

8. There was general agreement as to DRVN concern lest UN became involved in Indochina. Some Reps apparently did not RPT not think this would be deplorable development but they all agreed that DRVN would refuse to allow UN intervention . . . .

9. By and large, impression gained . . . is no RPT no expectation of early and startling developments in Vietnam. To employ the DRVN jargon, the situation is not RPT not yet ripe for it.

SEABORN

January 29, 1965

AMEMBASSY PARIS 4295 TO SECSTATE (LIMDIS/NOFORN/S, REC'D 29 JANUARY 65, 2 P.M.

EmbOff has been shown in strictest secrecy large portions of record conversations on Viet Nam held here between ranking officials of Quai on one hand and separately with Chinese Charge Sung and North Vietnamese delegate Mai Van Bo on other. Conversation with Bo took place December 22 and was renewed again last week . . . .

In addition to discussion of international conference along Geneva lines, conversation with North Vietnamese XHIKXQK,* essentially to three questions put by French (1) Would Hanoi accept and join in guarantees for neutral and completely independent South Vietnam? (2) Would Hanoi agree to knock off political and military subversion in SVN? (3) Would Hanoi accept some control mechanism more serious and with wider powers than present ICC? Total ineffectiveness of latter and paralysis through veto demonstrated, especially in Laos.

Mai Van Bo showed considerable interest in (1) and (3) and spoke of settling on basis 1954 Geneva Accords but was obviously embarrassed and evasive on (2), since affirmative response would have constituted confession. French told Bo frankly they could not accept Vietnamese protestations that there was only American intervention and that French were convinced of Hanoi subversive role. If Hanoi did not wish to own up, would they at least undertake guarantee not to engage in such activities in future?

At second meeting in January above questions explored further and French said that in order to discuss meaningfully, Bo should obtain precise answers from Hanoi on above three points. No answer yet received.

. . .
*As received, will service upon request.

February 27, 1965

STATE 942 TO AMEMBASSY OTTAWA (S/EXDIS) IMMEDIATE, SENT 27 FEB 65, 4:11
We have passed to Canadian Embassy here text of that portion of Ambassador Cabot's presentation at latest Warsaw talks dealing with Viet-Nam situation. Text follows: QUOTE. I have been instructed to restate United States policy in South Viet-Nam. Our constant policy has been to assist South Viet-Nam in its

efforts to maintain its freedom and independence in the face of Communist aggression directed and supported by Hanoi. So long as the Viet Cong, directed and supported by North Viet-Nam and encouraged by your side, continues its attacks in South Viet-Nam, the United States will find it necessary to afford the Government of Viet-Nam such help as it desires and needs to restore peace. The pressures being mounted by the North Vietnamese across the frontiers of South Viet-Nam are intolerable. We must and will take action to stop them.
. . .

. . . It was our hope that the 1954 Geneva arrangements would allow the Governments in Indochina to exist in peace.
. . .

We would be satisfied if the Geneva agreements of 1954 were observed by all parties . . . . Any evidence of willingness on the part of the DRV to return to these accords would be noted and welcomed by our side.
. . . If there is any doubt in Hanoi as to this U.S. position, I hope that you will convey it to them. UNQUOTE.

We have asked Canadian Embassy here to seek Ottawa's approval for having Blair Seaborn convey above quoted passage to appropriate Hanoi authorities in course of next visit Hanoi . . . .
. . .

RUSK

March 5, 1965

CANDEL SAIGON 203 (TOPSEC BACON/NO DISRIB),
IMMED., FOR ARNOLD SMITH AND FAR EAST DIV

. . .

2. On afternoon Mar 4 I paid second call on Ha Van Lau in lieu of call on PM. Incidentally Stawicki managed without difficulty to see PM for farewell call. I explained nature of message and then read him slowly French translation of full text of Cabot's statement in Wsaw as given in Wash, DC Tel 642 Feb 27.

3. Interpreter took full notes. Ha Van Lau said he would pass msg on to PM though his personal opinion was that it contained nothing new. They had already had report of latest WSAW mtg from Chinese.

4. Ha Van Lau then made personal comment on msg and general situation. It contained no RPT no new elements and is of so little interest that I am sending close to verbatim account only by Bag.

5. . . .

6. My personal opinion is that in present circumstances DRVN have very little interest in CDN channel of communication with USA. They have never taken initiative to use it and this time were not RPT not even sufficiently interested to arrange for me to see PM.

7. . . .

SEABORN

March 7, 1965

AMEMBASSY SAIGON 2880 TO SECSTATE WASH DC (S/EXDIS),
REC'D 7 MAR 65, 2 P.M.

Seaborn also discussed his general impression on which he is drafting separate report. Because of his inability to see any senior official or have any substantive discussion with any Vietnamese, and discussions with Eastern Bloc diplomats primary impression is that Hanoi thus far not seriously concerned by strikes, it being Hanoi's interpretation of events that strikes arc only a limited attempt by US to improve its bargaining position for conference which USG is strenuously seeking in order to extricate itself from war in SVN which USG now recognizes is lost. Thus Hanoi not very concerned by strikes which have not seriously hurt it and as USG is one urgently seeking conference it is to Hanoi's advantage to continue to hold back on agreeing to any conference which at this time could only, as in 1954, result in depriving DRV of that full victory which it sees in sight as turmoil in SVN continues and pressures on U.S. for withdrawal continue to mount.

TAYLOR

March 27, 1965

STATE 2718 TO AMEMBASSY SAIGON (TS/EXDIS),IMMEDIATE, SENT 27
MAR 65, 3:48 P.M.

We are considering asking Canadians to instruct Seaborn to bear message to Hanoi, when he leaves May 31, for delivery to senior DRV official if and only if his first contacts with his normal liaison contact, in which he would inquire about availability senior officials, meet with forthcoming response and DRV intitiative for appointment . . . .

Proposed presentation Seaborn would make to senior official would be as follows:

1. In my last visit, I conveyed a statement of U.S. views concerning South Viet-Nam, which followed the lines of what the USG had stated to Peiping representatives at Warsaw . . . .

2. Since my last visit, the USG has of course further publicly stated its position in President Johnson's speech of April 7 and in the U.S. reply to the note of the 17 non-aligned nations, in which the USG further defined its readiness for unconditional discussions, its objectives, and the sequence of actions that might lead to a peaceful solution of the problem.

3. The USG has been disappointed to note that actions in the South supported and directed by Hanoi appear to continue without change, and even to be currently intensified . . . .

4. In addition, the USG informed Hanoi on May 12 that it was undertaking a temporary suspension of bombing attacks for a period of several days. The USG regrets that this action met with no response from Hanoi neither [sic] directly nor in the form of any significant reductions of armed action in South

Viet-Nam by forces whose actions, in the view of the USG, can be decisively affected from North Viet-Nam. Accordingly, the USG, in coordination with the Republic of Viet-Nam, was obliged to resume bombing attacks. Nonetheless, the USG continues to consider the possibility of working toward a solution by mutual example.

5. In making these points, the USG again must make it clear that in the absence of action or discussions leading to a political solution it must and will take whatever actions may be necessary to meet and to counter the offensive actions being carried out by North Viet-Nam against South Viet-Nam and against American forces acting to assist the Republic of Viet-Nam.

6. If but only if senior DRV representative gets on to Pham Van Dong four points of April 8, Seaborn would reply that he has no message from USG on this subject. However, his study of four points would indicate that some might be acceptable to USG but that others would clearly be unacceptable. It has also not been clear whether DRV statements should be taken to mean that the recognition of these points was required as, in effect, a condition for any discussions. He would say that the USG appears to have made its position clear, that it would accept unconditional discussions in the full sense, with either side free to bring up any matter, and that he would be personally interested in whether the DRV representative wished to clarify the question of whether their recognition is regarded by the DRV as a condition to any discussions. End proposed text.

. . .

Rusk

May 28, 1965

REC'D 28 MAY 1965, 4:10 A.M. (PASSED WHITE HOUSE, DOD, CIA, 5/28/65, 4:55) REF DEPTEL 2718

We see no objection to Seaborn seeking in manner set forth first paragraph RefTel to make approach.

With respect to substance, we offer following comments:

Last part third sentence of numbered para one appears to be worded in somewhat more astringent terms than useful or desirable in such private approach, although it is important point be made.

We are concerned by degree to which numbered para four continues to lead us towards commitment to cease bombing simply in return for cessation or even reduction of VC armed actions in SVN. Without laboring point, believe it is important not at this time at least to give away our position on withdrawal of VC . . . .

. . .

Taylor

June 6, 1965

AMEMBASSY SAIGON 4033 TO SECSTATE (CONFID/LIMDIS),
REC'D JUNE 7, 1965, 2:06 A.M.

Canadian ICC Commissioner Blair Seaborn told EmbOff this morning results of
his latest week-long visit to Hanoi, from which he had returned yesterday.

Seaborn said that he is persuaded from his conversations with diplomats and
DRV officials that DRV is not now interested in any negotiations. He said that
he was able to see new Foreign Minister Trinh but that discussion had revealed
nothing new.

Trinh followed standard line that U.S. offer of unconditional discussion was
"deceitful" since U.S. continued build-up in South Vietnam and bombing of
North. Seaborn pressed Trinh to elaborate on "Four Points," asking whether
points intended to be seen as preconditions to talks or as ultimate goals. Trinh
remained deliberately vague and gave no clear answers . . . .

. . .

TAYLOR

CANADA AND PEACEKEEPING:
IMAGE AND REALITY†

"The art and science" of peacekeeping, John Holmes of the Canadian Institute of International Affairs wrote in 1967, is of special interest to Canadians "because we have been involved in it more than almost any other country, and it has, in fact, been incorporated into our image of our role in the world."[1] So it was just a few years ago. The proudest boast of Canadian foreign policy was that Canada's servicemen had done duty in each of the United Nations peacekeeping operations and in Indochina on the International Control Commissions. The acronyms of peacekeeping — UNTSO, UNMOGIP, UNEF, ONUC, UNOGIL, UNFICYP, UNTEA, UNYOM, UNIPOM and ICC — were never part of the public's everyday vocabulary, but the record was popularly considered to be an excellent one, an unselfish one, a record worthy of a nation committed to peace.

Peacekeeping seemed to be the perfect middle-sized responsibility for a middle power in the late 1950's and early 1960's. Canada was tied to the American chariot wheels in the North American Air Defence Command and in the North Atlantic Treaty Organization, to be sure, but peacekeeping at the same time somehow smacked of independence from the United States, of a more-Canadian Canadian foreign policy. Peacekeeping was useful, too, something that seemed increasingly difficult to say about NORAD and NATO service. Equally important, peacekeeping did not require nuclear weapons or expensive equipment, nor did it demand large military forces. It was the ideal role for Canada: responsible, useful, inexpensive and satisfying.

The satisfaction, in particular, was intensive. As John Holmes noted, peacekeeping was part of Canada's world image. All too often Canadians had found themselves regarded as Americans when they travelled abroad, but peacekeeping helped to differentiate them. The Americans, after all, with their wild west, shoot first image, their huge military forces and their world-wide net of bases, advisors, and arms sales had a very different style from peaceful Canadians. Canadians were middlemen, honest brokers, helpful fixers in a world where these qualities were rare. Peacekeeping made us different and somehow better.

Colonel Charles Stacey has argued very convincingly that war shaped the nationalism of Canadians.[2] In the postwar period, peacekeeping bolstered and refined that nationalism. The image of the peacekeeper dominated the Canadian mind from the formation of the United Nations Emergency Force and Lester Pearson's subsequent Nobel Peace Prize in 1956 and 1957 until the expulsion of UNEF from Egypt by President Nasser just before the Six Day War in 1967. Today, notwithstanding new forces in Vietnam and in Egypt, the image appears much dimmer if not totally faded.

Was it ever substance? This paper is an attempt to examine the peacekeeping image from emergence to decline. Where did it come from? Who fostered it and accepted it? Why did it dissolve into nothing?

†J.L. Granatstein, "Canada and Peacekeeping: Image and Reality," *Canadian Forum* (August 1974): 14–19.

Canada emerged from the Second World War in 1945 as something close to a great power. We had the fourth largest air force, the fifth largest navy, and a well-trained, splendidly-equipped army of almost half a million men and women. We had demonstrated our capacity to produce the material of war and to grow food in abundance. We had shown that our society could be mobilized from being a nation of unemployed in 1939 to a society with full employment in 1945, a society that could produce the goods not only for its own people and armies, but also for those of its allies.

The triumph of Canadian achievement in the war effectively squelched the "little Canadianism" of non-internationalism and isolationism that seemingly had dominated Canadian policy in the interwar years. "Parliament will decide" had been the watchword for this era of supposed non-policy, but Parliament never did. The postwar Canada demanded something different and better, and the new men who were responsible for the making of policy were determined to give it to them. The change in attitude was highlighted by the emergence of Louis St. Laurent as Prime Minister in 1948 and of Lester Pearson as his Secretary of State for External Affairs in the same year. These two men were the architects of policy for the postwar era, and the policy would be that of involvement and responsibility.

As an idea, involvement was not new in Canada; as policy it was a radical departure. At the turn of the century, imperialists in Canada had demanded that Canada do its bit in helping to maintain the Empire. If Canadians could assume some responsibility in the world, then their nationalism would grow strong. Only by participation could Canadians demonstrate that they were prepared for ever greater responsibilities, and if all proceeded according to plan eventually a truly strong Canada would be ready to inherit Britain's world-wide role.

By the time that Canadian nationalism had developed, however, there was no longer any Empire worth inheriting. But the idea of fostering nationalism through service was still alive. Canadians could show the world that they were prepared to do their part. As Lester Pearson said, "we must convince the United States, by action rather than merely by words, that we are, in fact, pulling our weight in this international team."[3] Out of this responsible internationalism would grow a greater pride in Canada and in its place in the world. This attitude seems to have been at the root of the eagerness with which Canadians seized on responsibility after the war. Canadian diplomats had pressed for a strong United Nations, and when the world body by 1948 seemed to be a weak reed, they pressed with equal vigour for the formation of NATO. We met our commitments; we accepted our responsibilities. Canadians did not want power without responsibility — Rudyard Kipling had called that the privilege of the harlot through the ages. They wanted power and responsibility and for a time they had both.

In practice, this internationalism was sometimes little more than co-operation with the United States clothed in multilateral garb. But so long as the threat of Communist aggression seemed real, there was public support for this role. Canada's airmen and soldiers served in Europe and in North America while the navy patrolled the North Atlantic and the Pacific Oceans. Lester Pearson was our spokesman in New York, in Washington, in London, and in Moscow, everywhere the manifold interests of Canadian diplomacy took him. And in the respect and attention accorded Pearson wherever he went, Canadians took pride.

But throughout Canada during the early 1950's there was an undercurrent of grumbling at Canada's apparent willingness to hew to the American line. Already there were signs of concern at the huge amount of American capital invested in Canada, and on the political left the view was taking form that perhaps the simplistic Cold War tale of right and wrong was not the entire story. In this area, as in social policy, the Co-operative Commonwealth Federation was the forerunner. The public was being prepared to accept new initiatives.

The opportunity came with the Suez Crisis in 1956. The crisis marked the high water line of Canadian influence in the world, the last time that Canada could use the accrued prestige and influence with which she had emerged from the Second World War in 1945. Suez sundered the Western alliance, and Britain and France pursued a course diametrically opposite to that advocated by the United States — and Canada. For a few critical weeks, discourse between London-Paris and Washington ceased, and Canada seized the opportunity to become the channel of communication between the old world and the new. The linch-pin, the bridge, the interpreter — all the hoary clichés suddenly came true. It would never happen again.

Under Pearson's leadership Canada suddenly found itself promising to serve on a major United Nations force in the Middle East, a force that Pearson himself suggested and in a few days of inspired work with Dag Hammarskjold, the UN Secretary-General, largely created. It was a triumph on two fronts at once, and the Canadian reputation was high indeed. And when Pearson was awarded the Nobel Prize for Peace in 1957 this put the cap on Canada's newly minted image of itself.

Suddenly the locus of action for Canada had shifted back to the United Nations. Canada had been involved in sending peacekeepers to Palestine after 1948, to the India-Pakistan borders, and to Indochina in 1954, but there had been no public or official enthusiasm for these chores. After Suez, however, the enthusiasm was very strong, even among the Tory press and public that had felt qualms at Ottawa's reaction to the Anglo-French invasion of Egypt.

Surprisingly, the public satisfaction at Canada's new found role survived Egypt's reluctance to accept Canadian troops as part of the United Nations Emergency Force. The uniforms worn by the Canadians were too similar to those of the invaders, the Egyptian spokesmen argued, and the unfortunate name of the regiment chosen for Sinai Service — the Queen's Own Rifles of Canada —added to the potential confusion. Moreover, Canada was a Commonwealth partner of Britain, a NATO ally of Britain and France, and Canadian Jews were strong in their support of Israel. Those were all valid complaints, and the Egyptians were by no means wrong to object.

The upshot was that Canadian infantry did not go to Suez after all. What Canada did supply to UNEF was service and transport troops, aircraft and pilots, and an armoured reconnaissance squadron. Canada had the technical expertise and equipment of a nation with overseas defence commitments, and there were no other states acceptable to the Egyptians that did. Egypt did not want Canadians, but if UNEF was to function it had to accept them.

These vicissitudes notwithstanding, UNEF was still a Canadian triumph. And so strong was the reaction in Canada to this success that even when the government changed in 1957 there was no apparent alteration in Canada's newfound delight with peacekeeping. John Diefenbaker and many of his colleagues in the Conservative front bench had criticized the Liberals for letting down Britain in 1956, but few had criticized peacekeeping itself. When in 1958 another crisis erupted in the Middle East, therefore, the Conservatives were quick off the mark in sending a large contingent of observers to serve with the United Nations Observer Group in Lebanon. The public response was again strong and even newspapers that had bitterly criticized Canada's part in 1956 demonstrated a changed attitude.

The public's desire that Canada should serve the United Nations was so strong indeed that it could force the government's hand. This became clear in 1960 when the Congo won its independence and almost immediately sank into chaos. The UN decided to intervene with a new peacekeeping force to preserve order, and Canada was invited to contribute signallers and pilots. For the Diefenbaker government, well launched into its own time of troubles, the Congo was the wrong crisis at the wrong time. The country was hard hit by unemployment and budgetary problems, and there were in addition very few signalmen free in the army. The government stalled. But the press soon began to ask "Why is Canada not represented?" The *Ottawa Journal*, a good Tory newspaper, demanded a "most imaginative and wide-visioned and generous consideration" of UN requests. And even after the government caved in and agreed to send the men in a month, the Vancouver *Province* pointed out sharply that Ireland and Sweden had had their men underway in 48 hours.[4]

The response of press and Parliament had been quite extraordinary. The Congo was certainly not an area to which Canada had historic ties; there was no aggression involved; and until a few months after the UN decision there were not even any Communists suspected of trying to usurp the government. None of the usual triggers for public response were there. Except that Canadians clearly expected that their government would be eager and willing to assist the United Nations with any new peacekeeping forces. Peacekeeping was the Canadian role, and the Canadian people demanded the right to play it. The national self-image required it.

Small numbers of servicemen went abroad again in 1962 to West Irian and in 1963 to the Yemen. Both of these operations were small, but relatively successful, and neither did anything to harm the growing conviction that peacekeeping was the proper policy. Nor did the Cyprus operation of 1964. The UN Force in Cyprus was largely the creation of Paul Martin, Secretary of State for External Affairs in the Pearson government that had taken office in 1963. Martin had wheeled and dealed and successfully interposed a UN presence, for a time largely Canadian, between Greek-and Turkish-Cypriots. In the process he headed off a threatening war between Greece and Turkey and earned substantial American gratitude.

Cyprus was the last peacekeeping victory. In May, 1967 President Nasser expelled UNEF from Egypt and set in train the events that precipitated Israel's blitzkrieg invasion and conquest of the Sinai. Most important for Canadian opinion, Nasser singled out the Canadian component of UNEF and demanded immediate departure. Public reaction was stunned. "Peacekeeping has become the foundation on which much of Canada's foreign and defence policy is built," the Montreal *Gazette* said. "If the foundation is undermined . . . the superstructure built on that foundation will not last very long." The *Toronto Star* wondered: "Can UN peacekeeping survive the Sinai Crisis?" And as the *Canadian Annual Review* for 1967 noted, "It is not an exaggeration to say that the Canadian press was as concerned, if not more so, with the effect the UNEF withdrawal would have on one of the main 'cornerstones' of Canadian foreign policy than it was with the possible catastrophes that might befall both Jew and Arab in the region."[5]

The cornerstone had crumbled, and the Canadian government was forced to recognize this. Peacekeeping had held a very high priority through the 1960's and had been cited as one of the justifications for imposing unification on the armed forces after 1964. But after the Six Day War, peacekeeping was relegated further down the list of priorities. The new stress for the military would be to defend Canadian sovereignty and to maintain order in the streets of the big cities. The internationalism of 1948 and the idealism of 1956 had been superseded by the neo-isolationism of 1968. The concept of nationalism through international responsibility that had motivated the foreign policy of St. Laurent and Pearson had been replaced by a foreign and defence policy of unabashed self-interest.

Peacekeeping at no time was a very important military role for the country. At most perhaps 2200 servicemen were employed at any one time on UN operations, and while this was not an inconsiderable number or a minor expense, the commitment probably did not warrant the barrage of publicity or the weight of prestige that became attached to it. More men supported NORAD in Canada and the United States. More troops were stationed in Europe with NATO. More were on anti-submarine patrols off the coasts. Peacekeeping was only a minor role performed by the military forces of a minor power.

Of course it did not seem so from 1956 to 1967. Peacekeeping fostered the Canadian sense of self-importance. What could be more important than to be the mediator between Britain and the United States in 1956? What could be more important than to restore order in the Congo in 1960? What could be more vital to the West than to help prevent war between Greece and Turkey, ostensible NATO allies, in 1956? What could be more important than to keep the peace?

The questions were the right ones, but the answers did not demand Canadian participation. Few Canadians ever realized that peacekeeping, in most instances, would have been impossible without the direct logistical support of the United States. American aircraft, for example, had to be used to fly the Canadians' signal equipment to the Congo in 1960. American supplies were needed to get UNEF started in 1956. And Britain, though no longer a great power, provided most of the back-up support for the Cyprus force in 1964. Peacekeeping was not as independent as it seemed.

Moreover, on at least one occasion Canada was put onto an observer force precisely because she was attached to the Western alliance. In 1954 when the International Control Commissions were established in Indochina, Canada was the Western delegate, India the neutral, and Poland the Communist nominee. The same kind of reasoning held true in 1973 when new international commissions were established in Viet Nam.

Canadians similarly failed to grasp the fact that peacekeeping was fundamentally a political act that would have been impossible without support in the UN Security Council or in the General Assembly. Political consensus, not Canada participation, was the *sine qua non* of peacekeeping. The great powers had to agree to establish a force, or at the least not to oppose it, before peacekeeping could start. The nations in the area of the proposed intervention had to be receptive. The politics of the situation had to be right. In other words, Canada's role, however creditable, was usually a minor one and one that was mainly confined to the military side of the operation. Suez 1956 is the exception that proves the rule.

This should not be surprising because after 1956 Canada's power relative to the rest of the world was in decline. Europe had re-built itself and Japan was becoming a giant industrial power. The United Nations was in the process of tripling in size. Power had returned where it belonged, and Canada once again was simply a country with large territory and few people. The world had changed and Canada could not keep up. There was no way in which it could have been different.

Pearson's triumph in 1956 then has to be seen as the last hurrah of the golden age of Canadian diplomacy rather than as the beginning of a new era of influence. As such, it acquired a mythology of its own, and the accession of Pearson to the leadership of the Liberal Party in 1958 ensured that this would be so. The managers of Canadian Liberalism traded on Pearson's world repute as a marketable asset that could be used to restore the fortunes of the party. For a time in fact Pearson's reputation seemed to be the only asset on which the party could draw. To his great credit Pearson tried very hard to live up to the things that were said about him. After he became Prime Minister in 1963, he supported peacekeeping as much as possible. His speech in Philadelphia denouncing the United States for its bombing in Viet Nam was a courageous act, and one that fit well within the image of Pearson as peacekeeper pre-eminent. Peacekeeping was a satisfactory role for Pearson, one can surmise, because it was inherently useful, because it had good public relations value in Canada and abroad, and because it struck a responsive chord in Pearson's and the national soul.

Peacekeeping indeed should be viewed as analogous to the missionary impulse that was so much a part of Canada before the 1939 war. Almost every church in both English and French Canada helped to support a missionary family or an order of nuns somewhere in Latin America, Asia or Africa. Regularly the letters home would tell of the joys and hardships of bringing Christianity and God's peace to the unenlightened. The missionary impulse to service abroad was enormously strong and genuine, and nowhere did it live on in deeper form than among the officers in the Department of External Affairs. Sometimes it seemed as if every post had at least one or two sons of missionaries on staff. The Department sprang full blown from the church and its outposts.

While Pearson was not the son of missionaries, he was the child of the manse. As a boy he travelled around Ontario with his parents, moving from parish to parish, and exposed to the nascent social gospel idealism that characterized Canadian Methodism at the time. Who can doubt the strength of this upbringing in shaping the statesman? in shaping the course and character of Canadian policy?

So much of it bears this stamp. One can readily argue that Canadian foreign policy has been characterized by a mixture of idealism and realism. It was idealistic to want to bring peace to a divided world, but eminently realistic to offer to serve in the troubled parts of the globe. This is uplift, of course, but committed uplift. It resembles nothing so much as J.S. Woodsworth establishing his All Peoples' Mission among the immigrant poor of North Winnipeg. It smacks not at all of the antiseptic and businesslike Christianity of Toronto's Timothy Eaton Memorial church.

If uplift had its roots in the Canadian past, so too did a passion for order. Canada was a land of peace, order and good government. There was change, but always conservative and orderly change. There was no political violence, no real radicalism. This was never true, of course, but it was what Canadians were taught and what they seemed to believe. And peacekeeping fit right into this image. Had Sir John A. Macdonald not despatched a few red-coated Mounties to the untamed West? And had those strong men not imposed order on the land? Law and order was the Canadian way. If Canadians could help the United Nations in transferring this image to the world outside our borders, that would be a worthy goal. Peacekeeping was Canada's attempt to do this, but it failed.

The failure was not Canada's. The United Nations failed in its task of bringing the powers together. Peacekeeping was something that almost every nation could accept because it bought time, because it froze situations, and because it created a breathing space for negotiation. Unfortunately, all too often the negotiations never took place or got nowhere. Peacemaking almost never followed peacekeeping. The result was a decay in world morale, a lessening of faith in the UN. The disillusion was felt in Canada, too. Suez 1956 had stirred hope but Suez 1967 destroyed it. Suddenly Canadians began to question why peace had not followed peacekeeping. Suddenly they began to wonder why their troops should ever have been exposed to difficulty, hardship and danger in a thankless desert. The sense of futility was very sharp.

Nowhere was this more pronounced than among the Canadian military, for the very instruments of Canadian peacekeeping had never been sympathetic to the idea. The generals had never liked UN service and the political emphasis it received in Canada. To train for the UN's duties was to take time away from the important task of preparing to fight the Russians. For the rank and file, peacekeeping was simply boring, a dull duty away from home among people whose culture was too different to enjoy. The job was done and done well, but it was never liked. And the dislike increased among all ranks when Paul Hellyer, the Minister of National Defence in the Pearson administration, imposed unification on the reluctant three services, in part because it facilitated peacekeeping. If peacekeeping implied unification then the military wanted none of it.

The military's reaction was not entirely unfounded. Peacekeeping probably should have been recognized for what it was, a temporary expedient that met the needs of a certain period, not as a long term reality upon which equipment and force structure could be based. Possibly the instinctive military response was more correct than the politicians', although for the wrong reasons. To be luke-warm about peacekeeping because it clashed with the military's idea of Cold War imperatives was wrong; to oppose peacekeeping as an international fad might not have been.

Significantly, perhaps, the fad of peacekeeping had caught on least among French Canadians, traditionally the segment of the population most suspicious of foreign commitments. Part of the problem for Quebec was that it could not identify with the armed forces, for like other elements of Canadian society before 1968 they were grotesquely imbalanced in linguistic composition. Few officers at any level were French-speaking, and only among the most junior ranks was there any thing approaching the national percentages of English- and French-speaking citizens. There was little in the armed forces to which *Québécois* could identify, for the military, like Confederation itself, was flawed.

This does not mean that Quebec was opposed to peacekeeping for the United Nations. It was not. But although the evidence of opinion sampling is perhaps questionable, there seems to be enough evidence to support the generalization that French Canadians were markedly less enthusiastic than their English-speaking compatriots in supporting the sending of troops abroad for any pur-pose. Significantly, only the Suez Crisis, 1956, stirred any genuine enthusiasm in Quebec. At best, the national consensus for peacekeeping was a fragile one; at worst, it was only an English-Canadian consensus.

Another final factor needs to be mentioned. By the time Pierre Trudeau arrived on the stage as Prime Minister in 1968, domestic peace and order had begun to break down. Bombings had first occurred in Quebec early in the 1960's, and the sense of impending violence had developed ever since. The riot in Montreal just before the 1968 general election was a sign, as was the interven-tion of troops to maintain order in Montreal when the police went on strike in 1969. The significant shock, of course, was the kidnapping of James Cross, the British Trade Commissioner, and Pierre Laporte, the Quebec Minister of Labour, in the fall of 1970. The federal government's imposition of the War Measures Act just before Laporte's corpse was discovered resulted in the despatch of 10,000 troops to Montreal and Ottawa. The idea of Canada as an ordered, conservative society had been severely shaken.

For the government, the lesson of October, 1970 seemed to be that the barrel of available, reliable military force had been scraped. Just enough troops for the task had been available. If more had been necessary, Ottawa might have been forced to bring the boys home from NATO duty or from Cyprus peacekeeping. The lesson was clear enough, and already discredited peacekeeping abroad was replaced by the necessity for peacekeeping at home. At National Defence Head-quarters, aid to the civil power was priority number one.

So pronounced was this shift that when in 1972 it first seemed likely that Canadians would be be called on to serve in a new International Control Commission in Viet Nam, there was a marked disinclination in Ottawa, in the press, and so far as one can tell among the public, to take on any such task. American pressure presumably became intense, and the government apparently felt itself obliged to yield. A wide-ranging series of conditions was laid down, however, and the public response, while somewhat mollified, still seemed to be that no conditions went far enough if they permitted any Canadians to go to Viet Nam. Certainly when the Canadians withdrew from the ICCS at the end of July, 1973, 84 per cent of those questioned by the Canadian Institute of Public Opinion approved. The times had changed. In 1960 the public had forced the government to send troops to the Congo. In 1972–1973, if the public had had its way no troops would have gone to Viet Nam. Nor after the fourth Arab-Israeli War was there any evident public support for Canadian participation in a new UN force. Mitchell Sharp was initially wary in his comments in mid-October, but within a week or less he and his officials in New York and Washington were preaching for a call yet again. Just why is still inclear, but as the *Globe and Mail* noted,

> The desultory applause and comments in the House of Commons when External Affairs Minister Sharp made the announcement that Canadians would return to Suez are indicative enough that Canadians are skeptical about the whole idea of international peacekeeping. . . .[6]

Presumably Canadians now recognized that peacekeeping was just a dirty thankless job.

As an exportable and Canadian-designed commodity, then, peacekeeping had gone off the market almost completely, barely fifteen years after its introduction. But the concept had been useful to the United Nations and the world, if only because a frozen crisis was less dangerous than an uncontrolled one. For Canadians, too, peacekeeping had served a purpose, even if that was only to provide symbols and images for a nation that needed them.

Notes

1. Preface to Alistair Taylor, et al., *Peacekeeping: International Challenge and Canadian Response* (Toronto, 1968).

2. C. P. Stacey, "Nationality: The Experience of Canada," *Canadian Historical Association Papers 1967.*

3. See Lester B. Pearson, *Words and Occasions* (Cambridge, Mass., 1970), 106.

4. Toronto *Globe and Mail*, 20 July 1960.

5. Montreal *Gazette*, 19 May 1967; *Toronto Star*, 24 May 1967; John Saywell, ed., *The Canadian Annual Review for 1967* (Toronto, 1968), 230–231.

6. *Globe and Mail*, 31 October 1973.

FEDERALIST STYLE IN INTERNATIONAL POLITICS†

Most Canadians would agree that Canada does not pursue one of the world's most exciting foreign policies. Is our lack of concern caused by our awareness that we are not a major power and by our vision of the compelling, at times tyrannical, pressures of the international system which leave Canada little elbow room for imaginative, constructive action? Time after time we hear our opinion-leaders justify our monotonous and incoherent foreign policy by pointing to our status as a middle power.

I would argue however, that our infirmity in international affairs comes not from our limited power compared with other nations, but because of our *domestic* habits of mind, our Canadian political style. We tend to project into the international arena techniques and ideas that make sense domestically but which are useless internationally. The policy pronouncements of our politicians and the actions of diplomats who represent us abroad reflect the influence of national behaviour patterns.

The most familiar ingredient in the Canadian political tradition practised by almost all Canadian political leaders from Macdonald through King to Pearson is our preoccupation with federalism. To be sure, most Canadians could not cite a clear definition of federalism, but the diversity of the federal system's components may impel its political leaders to avoid ultimate questions of purpose in order to maintain a minimal common denominator of consensus. This demands only a basic agreement on the rules of the power game. A procedural consensus may be necessary but a substantive one is not. The international situation is hardly similar. There is as yet no consensus on the fundamental questions. The Canadian genius for compromise and temporary solutions bears little fruit in the international arena where the more basic conflicts have yet to be solved.

Organization Before Purposes

When our "federalist" impulse is appropriate, Canadians have not pursued its implications very far. We rely too much on the compromising tactics and thought-saving clichés of this approach rather than force ourselves to generate the deeper reforms that may be needed. Our preoccupation with holding the nation together has made the organization itself, not its purposes, our fundamental concern. We tinker so often with our own political system, continually adjusting the mechanism of Federal-Provincial relations, that mere survival after each shock seems a cause for relief and celebration. As John Robarts exulted after the 1964 Premiers' Conference "tough old Canada still hangs together." Royal Commissions, parliamentary committees and Federal-Provincial conferences have frequently produced positive results by giving a crisis time to cool down. To de-fuse political timebombs by calling another meeting is a device that has often worked inside Canada. It is not surprising then that we believe that these techniques will work in the world arena.

†Thomas Hockin, "Federalist Style in International Politics" in *An Independent Foreign Policy for Canada?* edited by Stephen Clarkson (Toronto: McClelland and Stewart, 1968): 119–130.

It is this century-old preoccupation with keeping Canada together that we transpose to international affairs. We hear far more Canadian speeches about the need to maintain the Commonwealth, Nato, Norad and the UN — to keep the grand old organization going — than we do about where these organizations should be going or what they should be accomplishing. It is often urged, for example, that if Canada can help hold Nato or Norad or the Commonwealth or the UN together she therefore keeps a forum for exercising her diplomatic influence and that this somehow enhances our independence. Perhaps it is time to inquire if, in fact, the organization itself may divert our energies from more independent action. There is no obviously direct correlation between independence or influence and membership in bickering, sometimes purposeless organizations. The Americans in Seato and, of course, the French in Nato did not hesitate to jettison or to ignore an organization once they felt it had outlived its usefulness. The classic Canadian position was Mr. Pearson's on the first day of the Lagos Conference over Rhodesia: "I have come to listen . . . and help if I can."[1] Canada's External Affairs Minister verbalized the Canadian style when he praised Prime Minister Pearson's participation in this meeting called to decide what to do about Rhodesia's Unilateral Declaration of Independence.

> Canada took an important part in the Conference as you know. At
> the suggestion of our Prime Minister, consultations will continue in
> two committees. . . . These committees provide an interesting
> example of new Commonwealth machinery devised to help deal with
> a particularly awkward problem. . . . No country has left the
> Commonwealth on this issue.

"Committees," "new machinery," no one "has left" the association — all these phrases are eerily reminiscent of Federal-Provincial relations. How useful was this transposition? The commonwealth committees did not prevent Rhodesia from surviving the sanctions. The "new machinery" did not prevent several African nations from refusing to participate in the ensuing Commonwealth deliberations. And finally the irrelevance and failure of the "new machinery" impulse became obvious when the Rhodesian issue was turned over to the UN at the end of the year.[2]

The answer to "awkward problems" is not always "new machinery" but more likely a new policy or decision. We Canadians too often assume that the mere readiness of antagonists to meet, to talk or to reconstitute themselves in a new forum is in itself a major step forward. In fact, it is frequently a postponement, or worse, a device to divert our attention from the root of the problem at hand. More importantly, our willingness to expend tireless efforts in getting organizations to meet again and to talk can deflect us from working out a concrete programme which alone would make the new meetings and new committees meaningful. Countries with a reputation for constructive ideas rarely need to clamour for new or renewed machinery for the right to be consulted, or to make an impact with a new policy.

This point should not be misunderstood. There is nothing intrinsically wrong in Canada's effort to keep multi-national organizations together or to formulate new machinery for consultation and decision. These steps, however, should not be substitutes for thought about what these groupings are supposed to do once they meet. Mr. Martin has spoken with pride of the "10,000 votes" Canada cast in "international conferences in 1963."[3] He might better have spoken of the ten relevant ones.

Our Defence Ministers talk the same way. Paul Hellyer admitted March 1, 1966 to the Canadian Club of Ottawa that Nato needs to be revised

> What is needed is a look at the real strategic situation in the world today. A look at the change in the balance of power since the treaty was signed. A look at the restored and increasingly powerful Europe and the part it should play in relation to its North American partners.

His suggestions for revision however, soon degenerated into the familiar plea for better organization and administration: ". . . the organization is becoming top-heavy with headquarters and their bureaucratic machinery."

To call for better machinery is not irrelevant. Nato seriously needs it, but there are compelling reasons for basic and fundamental changes also. Defence Minister Hellyer's *White Paper on Defence* provides further evidence: "flexibility is the key to our new defence policy." We should not forget that "flexibility" can be another word for "indecision" or even worse, for leaving all decisions to others. An independent foreign policy is not always a mediatory and flexible policy; it must also be a declaratory one.

The propensity to substitute pleas for the establishment, continuance or reconstitution of multi-national conclaves, in place of discovering a new policy or consensus for these conclaves can be seen throughout our international activity. Expending great diplomatic effort as international organization man seriously diminishes our ability to act and sound independent. Our position is seldom heard. Our style can also lead to a kind of intellectual inertia, because we tend to regard our success in setting up a new forum or reactivating an old one, as if this were almost a solution in itself. (How often, for example, does our Federal Government praise the establishment of a Royal Commission as if this were almost a solution in itself?) We often project this domestic style into the world scene when we grope for "détentes," "relaxations of tensions" or "new hopes." The complexities of international politics unfortunately are not amenable to this type of solution.

Patience and compromise have sometimes worked in Canada. This trait is interesting because it is so distinct from American attitudes. Public opinion in the US has shown, and continues to show (especially during the Vietnam conflict in 1966) alarming signs of impatience and omnipotence. Here Canada is quite different. Canadians are quite familiar with apparently insoluble problems. Our English-French split makes us so. Nor have we ever been accused of harbouring visions of omnipotence. Our patience and sensitivity to obstacles is an important diplomatic resource.[4] For example we do enjoy the goodwill and even the ear of Americans. However our patience and sense of obstacles will not, of themselves, impress Americans. We must combine these Canadian traits with positions that clearly point to the contours of a positive new solution.

If we do not exhibit the more heady enthusiasms and feverish impatience so evident in the United States, and so dangerous for the world, our patience has its disadvantages as well. Aside from Howard Green's more optimistic and moralistic speeches ("This is no day for a pessimist in world affairs"),[5] we are so deeply impressed with the complications in international society that we seldom propose any independent or clear policy positions for the multitude of organizations of which we are members. We are afraid to lest we look ridiculous not only to others, but more importantly to ourselves. We retreat into banal generalities. Witness Mr. Green in the House of Commons:

> What is Canada's role in this world? As a people we have traditions of courage, of commonsense and of religious faith . . . we must then take our full part in world affairs and do it with a spirit of optimism.[6]

Compare Mr. Martin's reply to this homily accusing the then Minister of External Affairs of vagueness and calling for his own brand of clarity instead:

> We urge him now to appreciate . . . the urgency that attends us and to indicate in bold and clear terms something that represents the character and wishes of our people along the lines spoken by people like C. P. Snow, Barbara Ward, and other strong protagonists of the Western position. This is the kind of leadership we need at this time, not only here at home but throughout the West and throughout the world.[7]

This reluctance to formulate clear policy positions produces two consequences: first, our disinclination to be frank; secondly, our almost Pavlovian peace-keeping response to international conflagrations. We seem to insist on speaking ambiguously and on carrying a peace-keeping baton.

We prevent ourselves from raising issues of possible embarrassment to the Soviet Union or the United States, for example, because (we tell ourselves) we must not destroy the climate of confidence by making "unacceptable" proposals. We are careful not to confront various absurdities of the Soviet or Chinese positions, because we don't want to "poison the air". We believe that the mere readiness of our adversaries to talk is considered encouraging. An aura of unintended cynicism then surrounds our policies with Communist countries. It could well be that the Soviet Union, or Poland (in its role on the ICC) would prefer us to be frank. As Henry Kissinger has explained, evidence of goodwill or reliance on friendly personalities is a frivolous, ultimately irrelevant, way to negotiate with any nation that understands negotiations to be tests of power.[8] It may be true that federal-provincial relations are as much a test of goodwill as of power. For Ottawa to be brutally frank publicly about a Provincial Premier's ideas might break up the federation. It is by no means evident that the same kind of public ambiguity ought to surround our relations with Communist countries. They would probably prefer us to be frank so they could know our attitude before bothering to meet with us.

Mr. Martin's circumlocutions in attempting to explain how Canada and Poland had "moved closer together" on Vietnam left his Polish audience "visibly amused" according to the *Toronto Star* reporter, November 10, 1966. The major loser, however, is the Canadian public. We are told that we are flexible, mediatory and of good will so are disconcerted to hear our action in Vietnam denounced as being solidly pro-American.

The organizational imperative of Canadian domestic politics has led to the tendency to see in peace-keeping, not so much the need for basic social reform, but the necessity to prevent or at least postpone violence. In the post-Suez litany of objectives for Canadian foreign and defence policy, peace-keeping has almost unreserved approval. We are careful not to be clear about the various kinds of peace-keeping we engage in because the very word has emotive, moralistic appeal. We assume so readily that peace-keeping is positive that we fail to address ourselves to the original conflict. In our naïveté, we were willing to believe that the UNEF had solved the Egypt-Israel war not just postponed its next battle. And again we fool ourselves thinking that by peace-keeping we are being the neutral, international Good Guy. We fail to see that the intervention of UN Emergency Forces in the Congo, Cyprus or (if necessary in the future) Kashmir is not neutral in its effect. There is always a bias. To prevent violence in Cyrpus or Kashmir has meant the entrenchment of the status quo, the artificial freezing of a naturally untenable social and political situation. It is not necessarily "just" and "right" to race into these conflagrations without first demanding that a "just" and "right" political solution follow these interventions.

This is inordinately difficult for Canadians to grasp. We are proud of our non-violent history. Whatever may be questionable about W. L. Morton's thesis on the stability and conservatism of the Canadian identity, we do have something of a consensus on the proposition that "peace and order" are as vital as "good government."

This Canadian insistence on "law and order" and therefore peacekeeping forces should not be disparaged in an age when small violences could erupt into nuclear ones. But our unthinking belief in peace-keeping as an end in itself, the romance of being a sort of "international RCMP," blots out thought of how to achieve lasting solutions. The mere stationing of interpositioning, de-fusing or disarming forces in an untenable political status quo is neither glorious nor despicable. It is merely a postponement of the major task. We should not think our duty is done when we go only this far.

The Limitations of Pragmatism

Another ingredient in the Canadian political style is faith in pragmatism. It is related to (in fact may underpin) all the rest. The Aberharts, Bucks and a few other ideologues may rant at the extreme Right and Left of national policies but the huge middle ground is pragmatic. The pragmatists, not the ideologues, take the credit for holding Canada together, for preventing internal explosions. Our federal-provincial relations are conducted by pragmatists confronting each other over basically commercial problems. We know that the instrument for settling disputes in international politics during periods of peace is piece-meal diplomacy. But we too easily conceive this as being analogous to commercial negotiations and this attaches disproportionate emphasis on bargaining technique and sometimes on personalities. This makes Canadian tactics almost continually inappropriate when we try to negotiate with an ideologically inclined government.

Communists, for instance, look for what they call "objective" factors. Objective reality here consists not in what a country's diplomats or statesmen say, but in its social and economic structure.

A good example of our failure to recognize objective factors is this statement on Vietnam by Mr. Martin:

> We did not think it profitable at this stage to enter a controversy with President Ho Chi Minh over the interpretation of events in Vietnam. . . . Rather [in our reply to him] we availed ourselves of this opportunity to re-state the Canadian view that there could be no lasting solution of the present conflict other than through negotiations.[9]

To say this is to put faith in technique over objectives: that the momentum of negotiation will somehow overcome all brutal realities.

Our position on disarmament is based on the same mistake. Howard Green, in explaining why the 1960 autumn session of the UN failed to produce results on disarmament (and why the spring 1961 session might succeed), never once mentioned structural, political, or military factors. The key, he argued, was the atmosphere of the UN:

> The atmosphere at the United Nations last fall was very tense. . . . It was very difficult to have agreement reached on many questions, let alone . . . disarmament. . . . Fortunately, during the session which ended last Saturday morning, there was far less tension. I cannot say whether this was because there had been a change of administration in the United States, or because everyone was tired of that quarrelsome attitude just as we in the House get tired of such an atmosphere after a few hours and decide it might be better to be less pugnacious.[10]

The UN debate on the Arab-Israel conflict should surely have shown that the mere process of negotiation does not generate solutions on its own. We ought to be less reluctant to face the structural cases of "ill will," "bad atmosphere" or "hard line" positions. Our pragmatic dependence on personalities is understandable domestically. The personalities of provincial premiers explain a good deal of the positions their governments take vis-à-vis Ottawa. But in our efforts to defrost the cold war we must not rely on this alone. If we do so we run the risk, not of being dishonest, but of being irrelevant. A nation that bases its policies and attitudes on what it sees as the "objective forces" in international society cannot concede to another nation or personality but only to the reality of these forces.

This point is especially difficult for Canadians to grasp, for Canadian public policy and constitutional evolution have not been based on a clear recognition of, let alone agreement on, a systematic set of ideas. Our federal politicians have survived by acting as brokers and pragmatists. They have proof in the Canadian setting at least, that negotiations often generate enough momentum in themselves to permit solutions to be found. But we cannot assume the same about relations between armed and ideologically inclined sovereign states. Canadian pragmatism, compromise and our concomitant faith in negotiations have their place in international politics when sovereign states are not arguing ideology or are agreed on interpretations of events and potentialities. Otherwise our pragmatism can be irrelevant, escapist and therefore a liability. It was useful to be pragmatic and to act as a broker during the 1956 Suez Crisis. All the antagonists were agreed that their interests would not be gravely undermined if there was a compromise. But now in the Middle East or in Vietnam pragmatic negotiations are impossible while both sides believe that their objective must be almost total victory. Negotiations will succeed once the objectives change. And to say that negotiations or the conference table *alone* will somehow miraculously change objectives is a faith with little confirmation in history. Canadian diplomacy must work on changing the objectives of antagonists, not simply on urging negotiations. An independent foreign policy position must be based upon assessments of the causes of conflicts not simply on the forums where they might be resolved. The latter question is for nations with no opinions to concentrate on. The former is for nations which honestly want to help resolve the world's basic conflicts.

Canadian foreign policy since the Second World War has shown a remarkable capacity to escape into tactical postures so that our strategic positions become clouded or forgotten. It is true, that we are participating in the world in ways remarkably varied and demanding compared to three decades ago. Mr. Martin speaks with pride of the 118 International Conferences we participated in in 1965. This does point out the extent of our international responsibilities but we must not forget that the huge effort that these conferences imply for Canada can sometimes dilute our capacity to make bold and useful contributions.[11] We have not marshalled enough independent thought to make all this business as useful as it could be. Immersion in detail can be a substitute for thought.

It would be unfair to say that our foreign policy-makers have been wilfully trying to escape from reality. What is closer to the truth, and very debilitating for an independent foreign policy, is that these policy-makers are not aware of the extent to which they are escaping.

But the proof of this flight from reality is becoming all too clear. Our tendency to put organizational viability before purposes of organizations, our penchant to put ambiguity and peacekeeping in the place of clear declaratory policy, our naïve faith in the magic of negotiations: all these behaviour patterns flow genuinely from our domestic experience. When Howard Green claimed that the great Canadian virtue of common sense will work internationally because it has worked domestically, we are hearing honest but irrelevant attempts to articulate a view of Canada's international role.

Perhaps these tendencies are the best our domestic attitudes can produce for international attention. In some cases they are salutory. But we must recognize that they do not add up to a vivid picture of an independent power. They do not prompt other nations to say, "Here is a nation that knows what is to be accomplished through international organizations, through negotiations or after the peace-keeping forces have pacified the populace."

This identification has been difficult to make because we have prided ourselves on not taking public positions. We seem to believe that ambivalence, far from being a vice, is a virtue. We are saved from pursuing a more declaratory policy in Vietnam because we are on the International Control Commission. We have been saved from declaring how the Congo, or Cyprus or Kashmir should be ruled lest we not be invited to take part in peace-keeping forces in these areas. We have discovered a dozen ways to avoid speaking firmly and creatively. In short, we have found dozens of ways to avoid controversy.

However, the measure of a nation's independence is not found in its ability to avoid controversy. The price of progress internationally is often argument. If Canada is to remain independent with a voice in world affairs that emphasizes it, it is inevitable that we will create some controversy.

We have, nonetheless, through our federalist view of world affairs an outlook that could generate ideas of real relevance for the international system. We have relied too much on the expedient tactics this outlook sometimes implies instead of pressing the strategies and structural reforms that outlook could produce. By concentrating on finding solutions to particular conflicts lies both the hope for a useful independent foreign policy and one of the justifications for our independence in the first place.

Notes

1. *Globe and Mail*, 10 Jan. 1986, 1.
2. See Cranford Pratt and Clyde Sanger, "Towards Justice in Rhodesia" in *An Independent Foreign Policy for Canada?* edited by S. Clarkson (Toronto, 1968), 212 ff.
3. Speech to I. R. Club of University of Montreal, 12 March 1966.
4. This is precisely what Wolfers calls for in his *Anglo-American Tradition in Foreign Affairs* (New Haven: Yale University Press, 1956).
5. Canada, House of Commons, *Debates*, 26 April 1961, 4020.
6. *Ibid.*, 4022.
7. *Ibid.*, 4037.
8. H.A. Kissinger, *The Necessity for Choice* (New York: Harper, 1961), 180–91.
9. Canada, House of Commons, *Debates*, 4 April 1966.
10. *Ibid.*, 26 April 1961, 4021
11. See the *Toronto Star*'s Centenary Special, 13 Feb. 1967, 7.

THE IMPACT OF TRUDEAU ON FOREIGN POLICY†

When assessing the impact of Prime Minister Trudeau on Canadian foreign policy, we must remind ourselves that the subject of international relations has been something of a sideline to both his intellectual and his political activities. His earlier student travels, which took him off the ordinary academic cavalier's tour path of that period, certainly attest to an unorthodox disposition and an intellectual curiosity, but his interests were cultural and anthropological rather than political in nature. Nor was international relations the focus of analysis in his writings as a political theorist. Trudeau's output as a journalist for *Cité Libre* was directed toward other subjects, although occasionally he took issue with current Canadian foreign policy, notably with respect to the recognition of the People's Republic of China and the acquisition of nuclear weapons for Canada's forces. In both of these cases his stand was strongly critical of the policies of the Pearson government. His brief political career as parliamentary secretary to Prime Minister Pearson and as justice minister engaged him in his own area of specialization and offered a minimum of direct exposure to foreign policy. Because his tenure of office as prime minister coincides with the most serious challenge that has ever confronted the Canadian federal system, his domestic preoccupations tend to be reinforced, whatever his personal predilection. In assessing Trudeau's impact on Canadian foreign policy, we are therefore dealing with a residual function of his over-all political activity and hardly the one which will ultimately determine his place in Canadian history.

Given Trudeau's desire to provide an intellectual rationale for Canadian foreign policy, it might be useful to examine briefly his own intellectual roots by concentrating on those concepts in his political writings which may have a bearing on his foreign policy views. On the broader intellectual map, Trudeau's work fits comfortably into the classical tradition of nineteenth-century liberalism exemplified by John Stuart Mill. The central focus is on the individual, on the relationship of individuals within society, and, finally, on the role of the state in providing an environment conducive to the optimum fulfilment of individual needs and aspirations. The central focus on the individual is preserved even as the analysis shifts from domestic to international politics. Trudeau's reasoning is therefore most firmly linked to the global society paradigm and has less of the traditional state-centric orientation. At the same time, those foci of analysis which are of primary interest to the student of international relations, namely the state in relation to other international actors and to the international system, are less well developed in his political writings and can often be established only by inference. There is no evidence, however, that the concepts of rationality and equilibrium — the former relating to the decision-making process and the latter to political structure — which occupy a central place in Trudeau's thinking on national politics are treated any differently, or assume less significance, when applied to international relations. In fact, the isomorphism in Trudeau's political

†Harald von Riekhoff, "The Impact of Prime Minister Trudeau on Foreign Policy" *International Journal* XXXIII (Spring 1978): 267–286.

analysis has been so complete as to equate domestic with foreign policy. *Foreign Policy for Canadians* reflects this fusion in its definition of foreign poilcy as "the extension abroad of national policies" (p. 9). What is meant, presumably, is that foreign policy should serve national rather than purely global objectives, but, as defined, the erroneous assumption is made that international relations operate in the same milieu of centralized authority and high consensus that characterizes domestic politics.

The idea of balance or equilibrium is perhaps better represented in French culture than in any other contemporary society. Trudeau's ethnic background and classical French education may thus have contributed to his abiding interest in the concept as it relates to the realm of politics rather than to art or architecture. In the context of Canadian domestic politics, equilibrium means primarily the creation and maintenance of a viable federal system based on ethnic pluralism. In Trudeau's view, the creation of a solid federal system is not only Canada's most important political task but also its most significant contribution to international peace, for such a system becomes a condition for Canada's active international participation, removes the country as a potential source of international conflict, provides its policy-makers with skills in political accommodation that can be applied internationally, and, moreover, allows Canada to serve as a mentor for other states.[1] In a similar vein the Prime Minister stated, in his address to the United States Congress on 22 February 1977, that he was immodest enough to suggest that a break-up of Canada "would create shock waves of disbelief among those all over the world who are committed to the proposition that among man's noblest endeavours are those communities in which persons of diverse origins live, love, work and find mutual benefit."[2]

The emphasis on the concept of balance in Trudeau's political thought provides for an easy linkage with international relations theory which has long focussed on the balance of power. The Prime Minister's occasional references to the need to create counterweights to offset at least some of the effects of Canada's concentration of linkages with the United States is in line with this traditional balance-of-power thinking. Usually, however, the concept is treated differently and is defined as harmony of man with himself, with his fellow men, and with nature. And in his career as prime minister, Trudeau has been most vocal and most actively engaged in precisely those three issue-areas — international economic disparity, environmental deterioration, and nuclear proliferation — which most seriously threaten to destroy one or all of these essential balances. The social injustice of profound economic disparities within and between nations threatens the harmony of relations among men and nations. Further environmental degradation will endanger the delicate balance of the biosphere, while nuclear proliferation poses the ultimate threat to both international relations and the natural environment. In his much-cited Mansion House speech of 13 March 1975, the Prime Minister noted that having succeeded in creating the classical positive freedoms of speech, conscience, association, and assembly, the task facing today's decision-makers was "to establish with equal sanctity the negative freedoms — the freedoms 'from': from want, from hunger, from disease, from nuclear holocaust, from environmental degradation." This task was in many ways a more complex undertaking than establishing the earlier freedoms because it was not directed against a single target; nor could it be resolved on the battlefield or in the House of Commons. Instead, it would require "institutions and regimes of immense dimensions and novel attributes," and, in the last analysis, worldwide co-operation.[3]

Perhaps it is not without a sense of irony that one observes the reactive component of Canada's previous foreign policy being criticized in the foreign policy review papers, for much of Trudeau's own thinking on foreign policy evolved in reaction to what he observed at the beginning of his political career rather than by deduction from any *a priori* theoretical scheme. His principal objections to Canada's foreign policy in the late 1960s, as he interpreted it, centred on three arguments: that Canadian foreign policy inadequately served domestic political needs, that it was too slow in coming to terms with changed international circumstances, and that it lacked a proper rational foundation which could be used to reconcile the diverse policy components.

During his first years in politics, Trudeau gained the impression that Canada's foreign policy was motivated in part by altruistic principles of internationalism which did not adequately reflect Canadian domestic requirements, particularly the need to cement the Canadian federal structure. In part, this apparent failure was attributed to a fault in the existing decision-making process which saw little cabinet deliberation on foreign policy issues. These tended to be handled directly by Prime Minister Pearson and his Secretary of State for External Affairs, Paul Martin, both professionals in the field, rather than being referred to cabinet as a whole. What was lacking therefore was the proper nexus which would bring together domestic and foreign policy considerations at the highest level where an over-all evaluation could be undertaken and trade-offs could be arranged.

Secondly, Trudeau became convinced that Canadian foreign policy was not sufficiently attuned to changed international circumstances, notably the waning of the Cold War and Canada's decline, as he perceived it, in global status following the reconstruction of Europe and Japan and the entry of significant new actors into the international system. The failure to take account of the former explained Canada's continued reluctance to recognize the People's Republic of China and what Trudeau viewed as an illogical relationship between defence and foreign policy, where foreign policy too often operated as a function of defence policy rather than the reverse.[4] The failure to recognize the relative decline in status left Canadians with an inflated sense of global significance and thereby promoted a fruitless search for an international role and a degree of international posturing which Trudeau regarded as both unrealistic and unbecoming. It might be that on this count he was reacting more to the style of Paul Martin's brand of foreign policy than to its content, even confusing style with content. In his public statements and in discussions with other world leaders, Trudeau has repeatedly struck a note of modesty in cautioning his audience against exaggerating Canada's power or influence.[5] During the foreign policy review process, the contemplated withdrawal or reduction of the European component of Canada's forces contribution to the North Atlantic Treaty Organization (NATO) was justified on the grounds that it was out of keeping for a country of Canada's stature to maintain a forward defence position and that this move, moreover, would help rectify the apparent imbalance between defence policy and foreign policy considerations.

Thirdly, Trudeau found existing foreign policy devoid of a proper intellectual foundation with whose aid one might adequately rationalize ongoing behaviour, in ways other than merely seeking legitimacy through an appeal to the status quo, and create a logical relationship among its various component parts. To Trudeau this was a shortcoming in conceptualization which impaired the quality of decision-making.

It is safe to conclude that Trudeau's impact on Canadian foreign policy has been entirely confined to his tenure of office as prime minister. During this period, we should distinguish between the impact which he has had on reshaping the processes by which foreign policy decisions are made and his more direct contribution to specific issues.

When asked to identify Trudeau's single most important contribution to Canadian foreign policy, most analysts would probably cite the foreign policy review itself, although in making this judgment they might well be influenced more by the uniqueness of the highly visible review process than by a rational calculation of its long-range influence. The foreign policy review, which was launched on Trudeau's orders shortly after he became prime minister and which may be regarded as having been terminated with the publication of the options paper on Canada-United States relations in September 1972, was a novel experience for Canadians and may well be unique in the annals of long-time international actors. What distinguished it from other periodic stocktaking exercises was its scope and its critical re-examination of the underlying assumptions of Canadian foreign policy.[6]

The Prime Minister's own impact on the review process was substantial, not merely initially but also during its evolution. It is therefore not surprising that the ensuing policy papers incorporate much of his thought and even imitate his language. The review offered the Prime Minister maximum scope for a preceptorial role, which he exercised by raising a whole series of questions and by suggesting diverse, and sometimes competing, solutions. With varying nuances, this role was played at all levels: within cabinet and caucus, vis-à-vis the bureaucracy, and before the public at large. The whole enterprise provided a learning experience of heroic dimensions for the federal bureaucracy, for the attentive public, and, as became evident, for the Prime Minister himself. There are several positive results which can be credited to the review process. In the first place, it did create greater awareness of and concern for the inter-relationship between foreign policy and national interests. Concomitant with this it marked the end of the fruitless endeavour to invent a suitable foreign policy role for Canada which had occupied analysts during the mid-'sixties. Secondly, it conditioned policy-makers to be more precise in outlining foreign policy objectives and in monitoring policy performance in accordance with the fit between objective and behaviour. The effect has been one of creating a more favourable environment for policy planning and control. Thirdly, having been conditioned to examine the underlying assumptions of Canadian foreign policy, the Ottawa bureaucratic establishment was better equipped to respond to the dramatic changes which occurred after 1973 on the international scene.

Education, however, has its price. Holding a nation's foreign policy in a state of suspended animation for four years placed great stress on the operational side, resulting in considerable delays and confusion in making routine policy decisions. With few exceptions, Canada's European allies reacted negatively to this experiment which both mystified and worried them and thereby complicated subsequent negotiations for a contractual link with the European Communities (EC). The contractual link, incidentally, was a direct result of the options paper and was thus a product of the review process itself. One thus had the extraordinary case in which conceptualization and realization were in competition. Finally, the frank discussions which accompanied the review process and the opportunity for participation by academics and journalists raised considerable expectations of greater access to official information and of a general opening up of the foreign policy decision-making process. On the whole, these expectations have not been fulfilled, and this may explain some of the disillusionment of the press and the academic community with the Trudeau government. It remains a moot question why a government that is so firmly committed to the idea of raising the intellectual quality of policy-making has not been more successful in establishing a meaningful dialogue with relevant academic and research groups or in stimulating external research in order to make it more responsive to specific government needs.

In retrospect, the over-all results of the foreign policy review process seem disappointing and out of proportion to the energy invested. The most concrete and also the most controversial decision stemming from the review — the reduction of Canadian forces in Europe — bears the strong imprint of a hastily improvised political compromise which could have been arranged equally well without the intellectual guidance of a fundamental review.[7] The six foreign policy goals articulated in *Foreign Policy for Canadians*, particularly social justice, an enhanced quality of life, and a harmonious natural environment, appear somewhat unorthodox in comparison with more traditional foreign policy objectives and are deeply rooted in Trudeau's over-all political credo. As the Prime Minister explained to a Toronto audience: "the pursuit of these objectives, and not the search for any specific role, governs the conduct of Canada's foreign policy. . . . In their totality . . . they represent, in conceptual form, Canada's national policy."[8] The vagueness of some of the terms, the overly general nature of the goals, and the lack of specificity concerning the relative priorities under varying conditions make these objectives inadequate tools for policy planning and prediction. On occasion they might even be counterproductive in the pursuit of improved planning and more regional decision-making, for the liberal incantation of these six goals in the presentation of a specific proposal may lend it an aura of legitimacy despite faulty logic or poor reasoning.

The Prime Minister's impact on foreign policy planning and the nature of decision-making has been far greater as a result of imaginative innovations which he has introduced into cabinet proceedings and staff operations within the Prime Minister's Office and the Privy Council Office than through the foreign policy review process, even though his role in the latter has been publicly more visible. Trudeau's interest in the mechanism of planning and rational decision-making stems from his total commitment to the principle of rationality in all forms of human behaviour. He thus approaches cybernetics more from the perspective of a rational humanist than from the professional orientation of the technocrat. This, it seems, allows him to avoid the narrowness and professional obduracy which frequently characterize the latter. When the creation of a superministry of foreign affairs composed of all principal government departments with external activities and programmes proved unfeasible, the experiment was quietly shelved. Unlike Paul Hellyer's approach to unification of the armed forces, there was no attempt to force through a formal model regardless of adverse consequences simply because it had the appeal of technical neatness.

The structural and procedural reforms of cabinet which have been instigated by Trudeau involve two essential components, both of which are relevant to foreign policy decision-making.[9] The first is an upgrading of the practice of cabinet collegiality. A more structured system of cabinet committees, together with more detailed documentation, tighter agendas, and improved staff work, have created the basis for a more meaningful input by individual ministers into the deliberative process. The second is a greater effort to define policy objectives, to determine priorities among them, and to ensure correspondence between government programmes and policy objectives. The Cabinet Committee on Priorities and Planning, which is chaired by the prime minister himself, plays a pivotal role in this effort to give policy a firmer sense of direction.

The first innovation has produced a much more thorough discussion of foreign policy issues at the cabinet level and has drawn in more ministers than have customarily participated in this sphere in preceding governments. This "collectivization" trend has been further cemented by the Prime Minister's disinclination to follow his predecessors' practice of conferring special status on the secretary of state for external affairs and of forging an intimate partnership with him. The fact that Trudeau is the only prime minister, with the exception of Diefenbaker, who has not served as foreign minister or carried that portfolio as part of his broader prime ministerial functions may explain his reluctance to create a special relationship with his external affairs minister which would tend to reduce the foreign policy role of cabinet as a whole. It may be further explained by the degree of personal aloofness which Trudeau has displayed towards his cabinet colleagues. This is not merely a function of his personality but also a reflection of his desire not to undermine the system of cabinet collegiality through the creation of underlying axes. Trudeau's intent has been to bring diverse domestic considerations to bear more directly on foreign policy decisions and thus to make foreign policy more responsive to domestic needs. This tendency has been particularly noticeable in the energy and environmental fields and in Law of the Sea (LOS) issues.

The Trudeau government has been distinctly less successful in applying the second innovation to the foreign policy sphere. As was noted, the foreign policy review process failed to come up with a workable formula that would allow the specification of objectives and their translation into concrete policy instructions. The sheer complexity of the subject, the inability of competing government departments to agree on a generally accepted order of priority among objectives, and the essentially reactive nature of foreign policy, all have frustrated the attempt to make greater use of objectives as a policy steering device.

Moving from Trudeau's broad conceptualization of foreign policy and his efforts to modify the process of foreign policy decision-making to the actual substance of foreign relations, one can locate at least three areas which have been of marked concern to the Prime Minister. These are safeguards against nuclear proliferation, protection of the environment, and aid to developing countries.

Canada's strong engagement in the problem of nuclear safeguards can be explained by the seriousness of the threat which proliferation poses for international security and environmental safety as well as by Canada's direct involvement as a principal global exporter of nuclear material, equipment, and technology. Trudeau had criticized the Pearson government's reluctant decision to accept nuclear warheads for its forces as part of Canada's earlier commitments to NATO and North American Air Defence (NORAD). The reduction and redeployment of Canadian troops in Europe in 1969, together with the phasing out of the Bomarc missile, allowed Canada to divest itself of all aspects of its nuclear role with the exception of some 60 Voodoo aircraft which were retained on their North American continental air defence mission. Trudeau has noted with satisfaction that Canada was the first, and for some time the only, country in the world which possessed both the technology and the economic capacity to produce nuclear weapons but purposely rejected this option. Moreover, Canada was the first country which chose to "divest itself of the nuclear weaponry which it had acquired under defensive alliances. When this task has been completed in the near future we will be the only country in the world to have taken this important step toward nuclear sanity."[10]

In virtually all of his private discussions with Commonwealth heads of governments and other world leaders, Prime Minister Trudeau has pressed for the adoption of more stringent international safeguards and has tried to explain Canada's policy on this question. Canadian efforts in this direction, which were notably accelerated by the shock of India's nuclear explosion in 1974, have been undertaken in multilateral and bilateral relations and in the domestic context. Canada has exerted itself within the London group of nuclear exporters to obtain international consensus on strengthening safeguards. In addition, a number of domestic decisions taken in 1974 and 1976 — with the intention of eventually raising international safeguards at large — have made Canada's regulations the most stringent of any nuclear exporter in the world. Under existing regulations, Canada demands a renunciation of so-called peaceful nuclear explosions by the prospective recipient and retains a veto over reprocessing and retransfer to third countries of any nuclear material which it has provided. In addition, a non-signatory of the Non-Proliferation Treaty is required to submit its entire nuclear programme to international inspection and not merely the component which is of Canadian origin. As was recently noted by a United States analyst, in the international sphere of nuclear energy and safeguards Canada is what some nationalists have declared its over-all international status to be, namely "a foremost nation."[11] In tightening its safeguard standards, Canada has terminated existing co-operative nuclear programmes with India and Pakistan and temporarily suspended uranium sales to Euratom members. These actions have imposed strains on otherwise friendly and important ties precisely at a time when Canada's official policy was to seek diversification in its foreign relations in order to give substance to the

Third Option. The safeguards policy thus ran into opposition even in foreign policy circles at home. In addition, powerful domestic interests were quick to point out that these stringent safeguard requirements would jeopardize foreign sales of Candu reactors and related equipment and technology in a highly competitive world market and thus undermine Canada's own industrial development strategy. In the face of these objections from diverse domestic quarters, a considerable degree of assertion and involvement by the Prime Minister was essential to bring about an intensified safeguards policy.

A second area of particular concern to and commitment by the Prime Minister has been that of environmental protection. The preservation of a harmonious natural environment, an unlikely preoccupation under traditional diplomacy, figured as one of the six goals in *Foreign Policy for Canadians*. This is an issue where domestic and international activities overlap and thus it corresponds to Trudeau's predilection for a close integration of these two policy spheres. A healthy natural environment, as he has repeatedly pointed out, is a biological and economic necessity for all people. The principle should therefore become firmly established as an essential human right in international law and practice. For Canadians, with more wilderness per capita than any other nation and a history of struggle in settling in an inhospitable environment, the concept of uncontaminated nature transcends the purely physical implications and acquires a deep symbolic meaning which promotes a sense of national identity and purpose. The wilderness, Trudeau once told a group of reporters, "encourages a reluctance to selfishness, a stimulus to self-confidence, and a reticence to find fault in others. Here, there is no inhibition about destiny or purpose, no assumption that good fortune is either preordained or inaccessible."[12]

As with nuclear safeguards, the Prime Minister's strategy has been to create maximum momentum by moving simultaneously on the home and international fronts. His behind-the-scenes efforts were instrumental in bringing about the Stockholm Conference on the Human Environment and have helped keep alive the principles adopted by that conference. The most important domestic move has been the passing of the Arctic Waters Pollution Prevention Act in 1970 which established nationally enforced marine pollution control standards over a 100-mile zone north of the 60th parallel. The legislation, which, as Trudeau admitted, was "at the outer limits of international law,"[13] ostensibly broke with the Canadian tradition of internationalism by removing the issue from the jurisdiction of the International Court of Justice (ICJ). In justification of this decision, the Prime Minister cited the urgency of the threat to the environment and the lack of existing international law and practice to provide the protection required. In its absence the ICJ might be prompted to decide negatively, thereby providing a serious setback rather than a stimulus to the creation of international law for this critical issue. In contrast, individual state practice, if properly conceived and matched by an assertive diplomacy, could give the necessary impetus to the development of international law. In retrospect, Trudeau's finesse appears to have succeeded. Rather than aborting the emergence of international rules, Canada's pollution control measures have had a catalytic effect in promoting international consensus within the context of LOS negotiations. The right of coastal states to take steps to control marine pollution in accordance with accepted international norms is now widely recognized, as is the need for special provisions to govern Arctic waters.

The third area of special involvement by the Prime Minister relates to Third World development and those relations between industrial states and developing countries which affect it. Trudeau's concern reflects an ethical commitment to social justice, both within Canada and in the broader global context, together with the realization that industrial states will have to rely increasingly on the expansion of markets in developing countries to compensate for the declining economic momentum within their own ranks. Recently he reminded his political colleagues that the greatest potential for trade increase was to be found amongst less developed countries (LDCs) rather than with Canada's traditional trading partners.[14]

The Prime Minister's rhetoric on the subject of development has been persuasive and no doubt reflects a high degree of personal commitment. In a speech to the Canadian Jewish Congress he declared that "Canada's foreign policy would be meaningless if it were not caring, for it would not reflect the character of Canadians," nor would such a narrow foreign policy serve Canada's national interests.[15] In his Mansion House speech, Trudeau called for a new global ethic which would favour "an equitable distribution, world-wide, of resources and opportunities." One could cite numerous activities designed to give support to this rhetoric. Under the government's austerity budget of 1969, foreign aid remained a priority item and was allowed to increase despite spirited opposition within cabinet. In the general atmosphere of bitterness and confrontation which prevailed after the sixth special session of the United Nations General Assembly in 1974, the Prime Minister played a particularly active role in maintaining contact with leaders of the Third World in order to avoid a rupture in the global dialogue. After the critical developments of 1973 and 1974, the Canadian government established the Interdepartmental Committee on Economic Relations with Developing Countries which was designed to produce a high-level government review of Canada's policies toward developing countries under the new circumstances and to assess the level of consistency between Canada's over-all economic policies and its development strategy. In an unprecedented move, Ivan Head, the Prime Minister's special adviser on foreign policy, initially chaired the meetings of this committee in order to instil the necessary momentum and direction.

Despite these high-level exertions, Canada's development record during the years of the Trudeau government is at best a mixed one. Its most satisfactory component remains the official foreign aid programme which even critics of the government's development policy have called "reasonably respectable."[16] There has been a five-fold increase in the amount of official development assistance since Trudeau took office. There has also been a move to increase the proportion of aid handled by multilateral agencies and an attempt — not very successful so far — to reduce the proportion of tied aid. In 1976 Canada ranked fifth among Western donors in the total amount of official development aid and seventh when aid is calculated on a per-capita basis.[17] But when it comes to other aspects of a full-fledged international development strategy, notably the reduction of tariff and non-tariff barriers against manufactured and processed goods from LDCs, the creation of international buffer stocks, participation in raw material producers' associations, and the conclusion of specific commodity agreements, to name only a few of the proposed methods for the achievement of a new international economic order, the Canadian government response has been either distinctly negative or at least extremely cautious. The prominence of the Departments of Finance and of Industry, Trade and Commerce in international development negotiations provides a partial explanation of this discrepancy between declared intention and performance, for these departments have been least effective in adopting the global ethic for which Trudeau has called. Another factor has been the government's inability to devise a comprehensive and organic approach to international development co-operation. In a recent evaluation of development performance by the North-South Institute this failure was singled out for particular criticism.[18] These factors are essentially manifestations of the more basic failure of the government to devise socially acceptable means of restructuring, or eliminating, chronically weak sectors of Canadian industry. This lack makes the government a perpetual hostage to powerful interest groups and their claims for special protection which arise from their precarious position. It is this situation more than any other that impedes the adoption of a more effective international development strategy.

In conclusion one is inclined to ask how successful Canadian foreign policy has been over the last decade, in terms of the criteria which Trudeau set himself. Whatever unforeseen events and vicissitudes may have occurred to frustrate the realization of the goals set, at least it cannot be argued in this case that premature loss of office prevented the incumbent from carrying through a well thought-out foreign policy design.

One criterion of success which would rank high in Trudeau's value system is the learning experience itself. There is no doubt that a decade in office has provided such an experience for the Prime Minister and this explains certain shifts in his foreign policy orientation. Initial statements by Trudeau indicated a tendency to downgrade the importance of Western Europe as a focus for Canadian foreign relations. In part, this may have reflected his personal curiosity and interests which drew him toward less familiar cultures and regions. Most important perhaps was his perception that European ties in general, and affiliation with NATO in particular, reinforced the status quo in Canadian foreign policy and would therefore have to be de-emphasized if there was to be a change of direction. It did not take long, however, for Europe to reassert its natural attraction for Canadian foreign relations. Trudeau himself has played an active role in forging the contractual link with the EC and in trying to influence the outcome of the Conference on Security and Co-operation in Europe, particularly with regard to human rights.

Similarly, the visible caution and aloofness that marked his attitude towards the Commonwealth on the eve of his first Commonwealth Conference has, on closer experience, given way to an enthusiastic endorsement of that institution. Even more important than the mediatory role which he played during the 1971

Singapore conference has been his input into devising new operating rules to govern the meetings of Commonwealth heads of government. This has created a tighter but more imaginatively structured agenda, freer-flowing dialogue rather than sterile formal speeches, and a restoration of intimacy in place of the crisis atmosphere, reminiscent of the United Nations General Assembly, that had come to dominate Commonwealth meetings. Trudeau has come to place great weight on the cultivation of direct ties with Commonwealth and other world leaders and views this as a valuable method of cutting through the complexity of international issues. In his opinion heads of government need to perfect the techniques of learning about governing while in office, and the Commonwealth is seen as an ideal instrument for this purpose. In his closing address to the 1973 Commonwealth Conference in Ottawa, Trudeau dwelt on the business of governing and reminded his colleagues that there was "no graduate school to prepare heads of government for their tasks, no sabbatical refresher courses, no evening seminars or summer schools." Unless heads of government could freely discuss their experiences and techniques of governing, they would not broaden their horizons.[19]

The foreign policy learning experience has been far less successful when applied to a broader sector of the Canadian populace. The review process did go some way in offering an over-all rationale and stimulated both discussion and analysis. But the government has not been able to sustain the same level of public involvement, and the dialogue between officials and outside foreign policy experts has fallen far short of maximizing the learning potential on either side.

Applying the criterion of realism in foreign policy, the Trudeau government scores quite well. The tone of public statements is more modest, and there is less tendency to make exaggerated claims about Canada's international influence. Moreover, there seems to be a better public understanding that foreign policy is not a matter of inventing a role which Canada, as a disinterested sponsor, can offer to a grateful world, but that it is an attempt to affect the international environment in a manner which best suits Canada's national interests.

A third criterion which initially received considerable emphasis in Trudeau's foreign policy was the ability to reduce the reactive component in Canada's foreign policy in favour of innovative practices. In actual performance this has met with little success. Virtually all of the Trudeau government's key foreign policy decisions have been essentially reactive in nature: the Arctic waters pollution legislation of 1970 was triggered by the exploratory Arctic voyage of the United States oil tanker, *Manhattan*; the Third Option paper was drafted in shocked reaction to the 1971 economic measures of the Nixon administration; the tightening of nuclear export standards in 1974 and 1976 was directly related to the explosion of a nuclear device by India. This is not to deny that these and other reactive measures entailed concepts that were original and innovative. But the prevailing orientation of Canadian foreign policy tends to confirm that Trudeau's initial formulation rested on false premises. Foreign policy is by its very nature reactive because it deals with the international environment which is marked by an absence of central authority and control. Moreover, one notes a certain discrepancy between Trudeau's repeated cautioning that Canada was not a major power and his insistence on non-reactive policies. Whatever scope for innovative international behaviour the world's key actors possess, it must be considerably less for other powers.

Fourthly, if we apply the criterion of achieving greater complementarity between domestic and foreign policy, the foreign policy of the Trudeau government appears reasonably successful. The degree of domestic input into foreign policy deliberations has been increased at the cabinet level. With respect to environmental protection and nuclear safeguards, the Trudeau government has been less inclined than its predecessors to await international developments. Instead, it has taken important domestic decisions and tried to use these to provide both direction and impetus for international developments. Closer integration between domestic and foreign policy activities is, of course, not merely a response to the Prime Minister's own preference but also a reflection of the change in focus of the international agenda during the past five years.

Unlike Mr. Pearson and the Suez crisis, there has been no dramatic episode in Trudeau's political career which irreversibly links his name with a specific international doctrine, crisis, or settlement. The terms isolationism, when referring to Mackenzie King's inter-war foreign policy, or internationalism, when describing Pearson's approach to international relations during the postwar period, capture the essence of their respective foreign policy orientations. No single label can encapsulate Trudeau's more amorphous foreign policy. His leadership role in foreign policy has been principally that of providing the intellectual input on which to base the underlying rationale for a certain course of action. This has made for greater speed and consistency of response than would otherwise have been the case. It has also helped prepare Canadians for a changed global environment in which there is relatively less emphasis on issues of military security and deterrence and relatively more concern for problems of international economic disparities, resource scarcity, human rights, and environmental deterioration.

Notes

1. Pierre E. Trudeau, *Federalism and the French Canadians* (Toronto, 1968), 31.

2. Office of the Prime Minister (PMO), Remarks by the Prime Minister to a Joint Session of the United States Congress, Washington, 22 February 1977.

3. *Ibid.*, Remarks by the Prime Minister at the Mansion House, London, 13 March 1975.

4. Transcript of a Press Conference, National Press Building, Ottawa, 7 April 1968, 18–19. The claim that Canadian foreign policy was subordinate to defence policy does not seem convincing, particularly when one considers the modest decision-making input coming from the Canadian military. Even with respect to NATO there were significant foreign political and not merely strategic considerations which determined Canada's contribution to the alliance.

5. Policy-makers generally tend to err on the side of exaggerating the power position of their own country. Here Trudeau seems to deviate in the other direction, for virtually all composite indicators of national capability place Canada somewhere in fifth or sixth place in the international system without much change over time.

6. For a discussion of the foreign policy review, see Bruce Thordarson, *Trudeau and Foreign Policy: A Study in Decision-Making* (Toronto, 1972), 105–214. For the papers themselves, see *Foreign Policy for Canadians* (Ottawa, 1970) and "Canada-U.S. Relations: Options for the Future," *International Perspectives* (Autumn 1972).

7. A very thorough analysis of this particular decision is found in Thordarson, *Trudeau and Foreign Policy*, 105–65.

8. PMO, Speech to the Canadian Jewish Congress, Toronto, 16 June 1974.

9. Mitchell Sharp and Michael Pitfield offer a useful account of these reforms from an insider's perspective. See Thomas Hockin, ed., *Apex of Power: The Prime Minister and Political Leadership in Canada* 2nd ed. (Toronto, 1977), 54–68.

10. PMO, Circular letter to Liberal MPs, 16 February 1978.

11. Edward Wonder, "On Comparing Nuclear Export Policies," paper delivered at the 1977 annual meeting of the Amerian Political Science Association, 13.

12. PMO, Address to the Annual Meeting of the Canadian Press, Toronto, 15 April 1970.

13. *Ibid.*

14. PMO, Circular letter to Liberal MPs, 15 April 1975.

15. Speech to the Canadian Jewish Congress, 16 June 1974.

16. G.K. Helleiner, "Canada and the New International Economic Order," *Canadian Public Policy* II (Summer 1976), 456.

17. OECD, *Development Cooperation*, (Paris 1976), 207.

18. North-South Institute, *North-South Encounter: The Third World and Canadian Performance* (Ottawa, 1977), 6–7.

19. PMO, Remarks to the closing plenary sessions, Commonwealth Heads of Government Meeting, Ottawa, 10 August 1973.

FURTHER READING

The best guide to the literature on the history of Canadian foreign policy is to be found in J.L. Granatstein and P. Stevens, eds., *A Reader's Guide to Canadian History*, Vol. 2: *Confederation to the Present*. This brief section, by contrast, must omit much.

The only good history of Canadian foreign policy is C.P. Stacey's *Canada and the Age of Conflict*, which treats the subject from Confederation through to 1948. John Holmes' *The Shaping of Peace* carries the story from 1943 to 1957. Both are well written accounts that miss none of the essentials.

For the early period, the best sources are biographies of Prime Ministers. On Laurier, Skelton's work remains unequalled; on Borden, the authorized biography by R. Craig Brown is judicious and thorough; on Mackenzie King, the official biography by R.M. Dawson and H.B. Neatby, is calm and detailed. King's diary for 1939 to 1948 has been published as *The Mackenzie King Record* in four volumes, and the entire huge and invaluable diary is readily available on microfiche. Biographies and memoirs of other practitioners of foreign policy abound: Sir Joseph Pope, Arthur Meighen, Newton Rowell, Vincent Massey, Lester Pearson, Charles Ritchie, Arnold Heeney, George Ignatieff, Hugh Keenleyside, Chester Ronning, Norman Robertson, John Diefenbaker, Paul Martin, and others. One collective biography is J.L. Granatstein's *The Ottawa Men*, a study of the mandarins from 1935 to 1957.

Studies of special aspects of policy are fewer. Philip Wigley's book on Canada and Britain in the years when Canada began to break away from the mother country has been mentioned earlier. James Eayrs' five volume *In Defence of Canada* looks at defence policy from the interwar years to Vietnam, while Ian Drummond's *Imperial Economic Policy 1917–39* sets Canada neatly into the imperial context. Richard Veatch looked at Canada and the League of Nations and Richard Kottman at the impact of Canadian-American-British trade negotiations in the 1930s on the state of the North Atlantic triangle. On the Second World War, one old but still useful study is R.W. James' *Wartime Economic Cooperation*, which examined Canada and the U.S. Another such study is Robert Cuff and J.L. Granatstein's *Ties that Bind* and their study of postwar economic relations, *American Dollars/Canadian Prosperity*. The best study of the formation of NATO is Escott Reid's *Time of Fear and Hope*. Studies of more recent events tend either to be more ephemeral and based on scanty documentation or to be books of essays emerging from conferences. One notable exception is Stephen Clarkson's *Canada and the Reagan Challenge*.

The volumes in the "Canada and World Affairs" series offer extremely useful data to the late 1960s, and the *Canadian Annual Review*, which ran from the turn of the century to the beginning of the 1939 war, and which began again in

1960, is simply invaluable. The major journals publishing on the history of Canadian foreign policy — and it is in the article literature that most of the best material exists — are *International Journal, International History Review, Journal of Imperial and Commonwealth History*, and the *Canadian Historical Review*. The *Documents on Canadian External Relations* series, published by External Affairs, runs from the formation of the Department to the end of World War II and will eventually go further. It is very useful, as are other publications of the Department, the House of Commons Hansard, and the publications of the Senate foreign affairs committee, National Defence publications, and a variety of government white papers.

1 2 3 4 5 135521 90 89 88 87 86